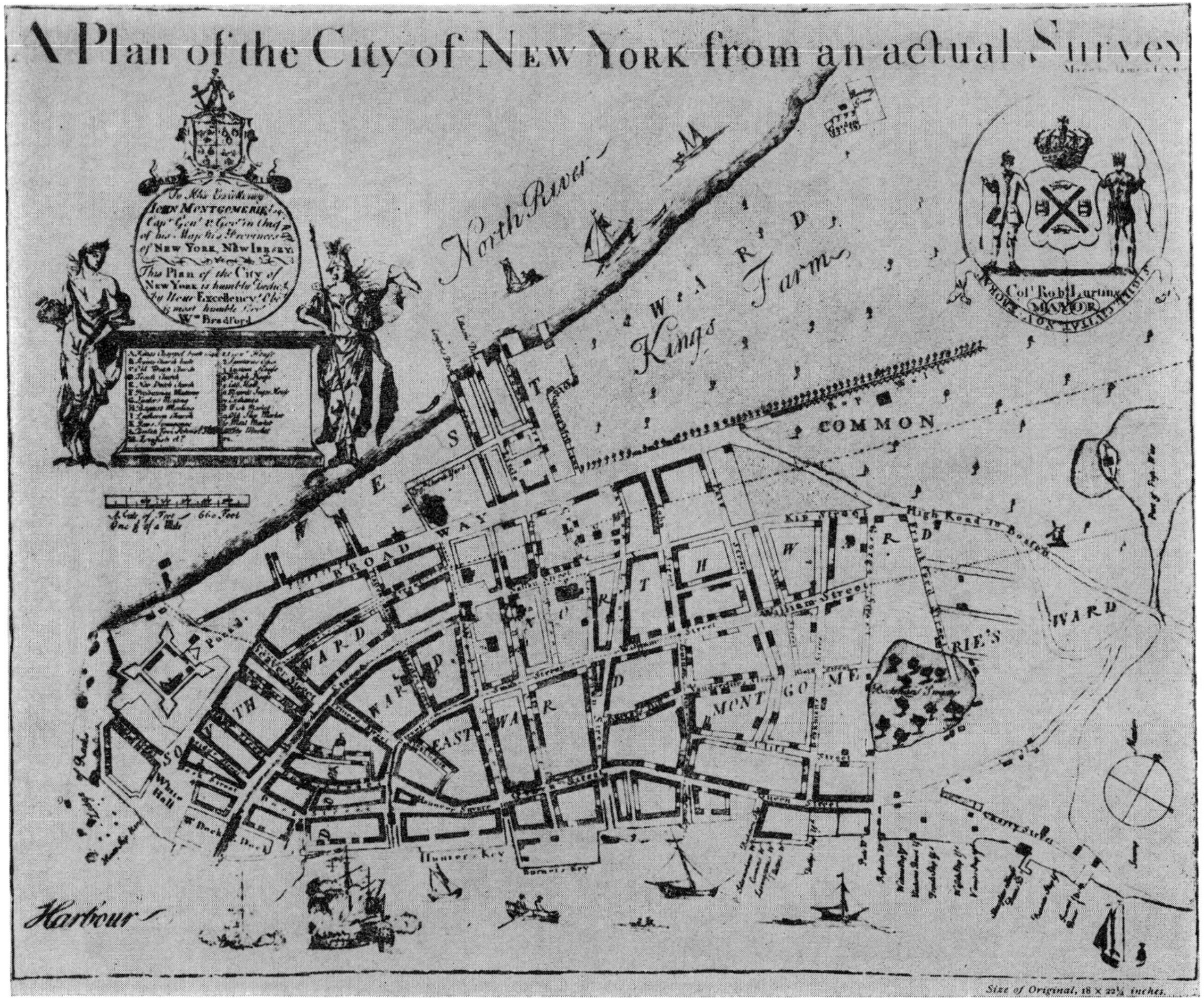

Courtesy of the Rare Book Division of The New York Public Library

JAMES LYNE MAP OF NEW YORK CITY (1731)

(Published by William Bradford)

STUDIES IN AMERICAN JEWISH HISTORY

Number 4

WILLS OF EARLY NEW YORK JEWS

(1704–1799)

BY

LEO HERSHKOWITZ

Associate Professor, Queens College
of the
City University of New York

WITH A FOREWORD BY

ISIDORE S. MEYER

Editor, American Jewish Historical Society

AMERICAN JEWISH HISTORICAL SOCIETY
150 FIFTH AVENUE
NEW YORK, N. Y. 10011
1967

PRINTED IN THE UNITED STATES OF AMERICA
PRESS OF Maurice Jacobs, INC.
1010 ARCH STREET, PHILADELPHIA, PA. 19107

IN MEMORY

OF THE

ISAAC AND CLARA ENGEL FAMILY

OF BOSTON

CONTENTS

* An asterisk indicates that the will is reproduced herein in facsimile. For reproductions of signatures, marks and seals of twenty-two signatories, see pp. 107–112.

FOREWORD

The location, registration and preservation of, and the historical research into written and nuncupative wills, letters of administration and inventories of the founders of the American Jewish community during the colonial and early Federal period of its history is a desideratum. It is a challenge to historians, devoted to early American Jewish historiography. The forty-one wills of eighteenth-century Jews proved in New York that have been ingathered by Dr. Leo Hershkowitz* and so expertly presented in this volume,[1] together with the facsimiles of more than half of the original wills reproduced therein, may serve as a guide and model for further research in this neglected area of American Jewish historical investigation. Gradually a corpus of such records, that normally constitute the documentary sources required in the probating of wills, might be built up. If such endeavors of ingathering and scholarly investigation were undertaken in such early budding Jewish communities of Baltimore, Charleston (S. C.), Newport, Philadelphia, Richmond and Savannah during their formative years, our knowledge of them would be greatly enriched.

There is a dearth of such material and related documents that serve not merely the whim of the antiquarian but are of great value to the historian of a community during its formative years and of the individual pioneers who aided in its establishment. They are essential as basic auxiliaries when applied to historical discipline.

Wills are not only fruitful sources for genealogical studies or as legal records related to the conveyance of real and movable property. They reflect not only familial relationships but are also the signs of the times. These early wills are a source of information of

* Dr. Hershkowitz is Assistant Professor in the Department of History at Queens College of the City University of New York, Associate Director of the Institute for Early New York History whose member historians and others are dedicated to the preservation of New York City archives. As Research Director of the Mayor's Committee, he directs a project commenced during the summer of 1966 to inventory those archives. The Historical Documents Collection at Queens College was in part instituted by him. This Collection houses archival records of the city and state, where they are indexed, catalogued, microfilmed, and preserved. These records from the New York County Surrogate's Court, the Court of Appeals (Albany), the New York City Comptroller's Office and elsewhere might very well have otherwise been destroyed.

[1] The forty-one wills included herein were first published in three installments in the *American Jewish Historical Quarterly*, vol. LV, no. 3 (March, 1966), pp. 319–363; vol. LVI, no. 1 (Sept., 1966), pp. 62–122, and no. 2 (Dec., 1966), pp. 163–207. The facsimiles are published in this volume for the first time.

the economic activities and occupation of their respective authors.[2] They also shed light on the ties of the testators with their fellow Jews in their own respective communities as well as their relations with those dwelling in distant places abroad. From them we learn of their religio-cultural traditions and of their concerns towards the end of their earthly life, or before they set sail for far-off shores when they are compelled to consider "the hazards of a voyage" and "the dangers of the sea and the uncertainties of this mortal life," — of strife and storm, of pirates and privateers in traversing land and ocean. We learn also of their contacts with relatives not only in other parts of this country, outside of New York, in Connecticut, New Jersey, Rhode Island and South Carolina, but also with their co-religionists and communities in other parts of the Diaspora, in Jamaica, Nevis and Curaçao in the Caribbean area, and with those residing in Europe — in London, Amsterdam, Fürth and Bohemia — and in Asia — in faraway Calcutta, India.

We learn of their concern for the maintenance not only of their own schools and synagogues but also with those in distant places. These are reflected in their charitable bequests for the support of the congregational school "to teach poor children the Hebrew tongue," and of "the Jews college [ישיבה] in Jerusalem." The "fidelity and faithfull" services of a slave are remembered with the provision made for the manumission of that slave.

As for other religio-cultural traditions as revealed in these wills, one notes immediately the formula with which they begin: "In the Name of God Amen," which follows the general custom of colonial wills in English America. Provision is made for burial according to the traditional Jewish rites and ceremony; a Jewish burying ground [בית חיים] is requested; mourning rings and mourning suits are bequeathed. Where the testator possesses a scroll of the Five Books of Moses [ספר תורה], its vestments and silver bells [rimonim: רמונים], provision is made for its retention in the possession of the family by the eldest son, or it may be presented to the local congre-

[2] On the significance of wills for historical research, see, for example, Donald Dean Parker, *Local History: How to Gather It, Write It and Publish It* (New York, 1944), p. 60; Kenn Stryker-Rodda, "Our Willing Ancestors," *National Genealogical Quarterly*, vol. LII, no. 1 (March, 1964), pp. 3–13; Anthony Richard Wayne, *English Genealogy* (Oxford, 1960), pp. 238, 282, 354–358 and 359–371; and for legal and historical background of colonial American English wills, the introductory section of *Documents relating to the Colonial History of the State of New Jersey Wills, Volume I, 1670–1730*, edited with an Introductory Note on the Early Testamentary Laws and Customs of New Jersey, by William Nelson (Paterson, N. J., 1901). For methods of research in wills, see *Genealogical Research: Methods and Sources*, by the American Society of Genealogists, edited by Milton Rubincam and Jean Stephenson (Washington, D. C., 1960), pp. 55–64 and 81–83. We wish to thank Kenn Stryker-Rodda, editor, and Harold Hazelton, librarian, of the New York Genealogical and Biographical Society for their assistance during our visit to their headquarters and library.

gation. In other instances, a bequest is made for the purchase and presentation of a Torah Scroll to the Kahal Kadosh Shearith Israel, the Spanish-Portuguese Synagogue of New York. Arrangements are also made for the recital of the traditional Sephardic memorial prayer on *Rosh Hodesh* [the beginning of each month] and on *Yom Kippur* [the Day of Atonement].[3] In connection with the proving of the will of Hayman Levy, we learn from the deposition of the Reverend Gershom Mendes Seixas of his "saying the prayers of a dying person" at the time of Levy's death. Aaron Hart of London arranges to have a hearse, four mourning coaches and six others, a marble tombstone, and that "ten persons may come to read every morning and evening for one month" after his decease and for this service the executors of the estate should "give them twenty shillings each."

* * *

One final word — we have been extremely fortunate that Dr. Hershkowitz, author of this book, was able to locate and retrieve the forty-one wills that make up the volume. From his wide experience and profound knowledge of early New York history, he drew upon all available sources in the fashioning of it and was thereby enabled to identify the persons mentioned therein and to place them appropriately in their proper setting and context. He has set the standards for the editing of early American Jewish wills. May this volume be a harbinger for further studies in these hitherto neglected sources. We are indebted to him for making this auspicious beginning — a volume made possible as a memorial to the family of Isaac and Clara Engel through a generous bequest of the late Sylvia Engel of blessed memory.

ISIDORE S. MEYER

[3] Dr. Louis Gerstein, Minister of Congregation Shearith Israel informs us that the *Hashcaboth* [השכבות: memorial prayers] are recited in perpetuity, preceding the morning Shaḥarith service every month on *Rosh Ḥodesh* and on *Yom Kippur*. In the Congregation's manuscript "Roll of Perpetual Hashcaboth from the Year 5478–1718," the Hebrew and English names and respective *Jahrzeit* dates are recorded of those for whom the prayer is offered to this very day. Thirteen of these are: Moses Michaels, Mordecai Gomez, David Gomez, Isaac Gomez, Benjamin Gomez, Samson Simson, Isaac Adolphus, Joseph Simson, Moses Daniel Gomez, Hayman Levy, Manuel Myers, Rachel Luis (Lewis, Louisa) and Simcha de Torres, whose wills are published in this volume.

Wills of Early New York Jews (1704–1799)

INTRODUCTION

Writing early New York Jewish history has always been especially formidable. Jews were a small, highly mobile minority in an essentially heterogeneous population. Assimilation was fairly common and communal identification less than intense. As an important segment of the mercantile population, few of their extant letters and accounts are concerned with other than business matters. Comparatively little is known with regard to their every day affairs or their relationships among themselves and with others. Since the ordinary materials of history, diaries, journals, and letters are scarce, it is essential that a major area of study, official archives containing legal and financial records, be carefully scrutinized. Yet this research has rarely been attempted, perhaps because such materials are difficult to locate and even more difficult to use once located. There are only very few archival inventories extant and seldom are the records catalogued or indexed properly to make them useful for the scholar.

Yet taking all of this into consideration, the public archives of New York remain rewarding and invaluable for the study of American Jewish history. As an example, are the almost forgotten original wills and will libers which had been filed in the Surrogate's Court of New York County. The wills in this volume are taken in large part from these records.

Abstracts of wills published by the New-York Historical Society, although very useful, contain many errors. The will of Michael Michaels (who signed his name Mickalls) mentions "Rachel Levy, spinster," and is witnessed by Samuel Myers Cohen. The abstract omits "spinster" and the Samuel of Myers Cohen. One Rachel Luis made a will, not Rachel Lewis. In it she lists her pewter, bed and bedding, pots, pans and cupboard spoons to be sold for the benefit of the *Kall Kados* [Kahal Kadosh] (=Holy Congregation) of Shearith Israel, details again omitted. Among the witnesses who saw her sign was Abraham De Rivera who is not mentioned in the abstract. Lewis Gomez left bequests to "my five living sons" Mordecai, Daniel, David, Isaac, and Benjamin. In the abstract Mordecai's name is omitted. Uriah Hyam left "my Negro boy named Cavandro" to his youngest son Andrew Israel, not as the abstract states to the "youngest son of my son." Also excluded is a bequest of £6 to the Congregation of the Children of Israel to be "imployed in the Lining of the place wherein the five books of Moses is kept." The Hayman Levy will proved in 1789 is a six-page document which was never signed, thus requiring the affidavits of witnesses to attest to Levy's intention to sign and his demise before this was possible. All of this material is so condensed as to give but little meaning to this very human document.

Will libers containing the official copies of wills are likewise replete with error, especially in the spelling of names, and what is even more important, some wills admitted to probate have been entirely omitted, for example, Moses Levy. Moreover, the extant wills contain touches of personality missing from the copies. Thus, we find both Isaac Levy's and Rachel Luis' scrawls, obviously signed just prior to their demise. These rare touches make the sense of history more intimate. The seals reproduced here present still another aspect of history which has seldom been touched upon.

Apart from purely genealogical and sentimental value these published documents provide valuable and historical source material. Based on the number of original wills found among the four thousand extant eighteenth century wills in the Surrogate's Court, New York County the Jewish population of New York and adjacent counties was approximately one-half of one per cent of the total population. However, it is possible that Jews may have constituted a larger segment of the population since many of them were transients, equally at home in London, Amsterdam, Jamaica, Curaçao, and other places in the Caribbean area — a factor which could have reduced the number of wills drawn in the New York area. However, accurate or inaccurate such estimates may be, the wills do provide some basis for demographic study.

Of the forty-one wills, four are made by women. Eleven make no mention of spouse or children. As to congregational interest, sixteen bequeathed sums to a religious organization. The largest bequest was that of Joshua Isaacs in the amount of £50, and £5, the smallest sum, was that given by Moses Gomez. Even though less than half bequeathed sums for religious purposes, this is seemingly no different than bequests made by Gentiles — although it is perhaps less than what might have been expected. Interestingly, twenty-three wills were not witnessed by Jews at all and only six were witnessed only by Jewish co-religionists. The remaining twelve were witnessed together by Jews and non-Jews. This seems to reflect a close social relationship of Jews with their Christian neighbors. It should also be noted that only one will has a Hebrew signature and that only a few depart from the official terminology and procedure in the formulation and probating of wills. Few make mention or use phrases such as the "God of Israel" or similar language or use the Jewish calendar in dating. For whatever reason, the names of many eighteenth century New York Jews tend to disappear with the influx of newer immigrants. Gone to a great extent are such names of Jews as Fonseca, Nunez, De Lucena and others. Perhaps, this underlines the transiency of the community. Few of the wills mention real property and fewer define that property. Colonial Jewry did not seem to speculate in real estate. Few, if any, joined in the vast eighteenth century land schemes which attracted so many of the great of New York society, maybe because of a socio-economic barrier which Jews could not surmount. Jews, however, like other New Yorkers owned other kinds of property, including slaves. Nine of the forty-one testators were slave owners; three, Manuel Myers, Benjamin Gomez and Moses Michal manumitted their slaves.

The wills themselves are, of course, highly personal documents. They represent a kind of sum total of private existence. Meant for the use of the immediate family, they have become public domain and a part of history. Hopefully, those involved would approve.

Provisions for the probate and filing of wills in colonial New York were made as early as the Dukes Laws of 1665. Wills were to be proved by the Court of Assizes or Court of Sessions and returned to the Office of Records at New York for filing. The "Clarke" of the Court of Sessions was given the responsibility for entering them for a prescribed fee. The Dongan Charter of 1683 provided that written wills attested to by "two Credible Witnesses" would be effective as conveyances for the transfer of title to land. In 1691, three witnesses were required. A year later, authority to probate was granted to the "Governor or such Persons as he shall Delegate," except that in those counties remote from New York the Court of Common Pleas was empowered to take the examination of witnesses to the will and to certify the same to the Secretary in New York so that probate could be granted. Most often the Secretary of the Province was delegated to probate and under an enactment of 1709 was given fees for ingrossing, probating, and recording wills. He was paid by the line which probably affected the writing of documents most of which are redundant.[1] The Governor, however, on occasion delegated someone other than the Secretary to probate and also on occasion did so himself, thus retaining the fees. There is some evidence that a regular office of Surrogate existed in colonial New York, but if it did it was on an *ad hoc* basis.[2]

[1] *Colonial Laws of New York* (Albany, 1896), vol. I, pp. 34, 75, 114, 247, 302 and 639.

[2] The Joseph Bueno will is an example of the Governor acting as surrogate, as was his prerogative. Thomas Wenham, former Collector and Receiver General of the Province, signs as surrogate in the probate of the Esther Brown will, but no such office is mentioned in the Colonial Laws or in the Civil List. Some references to a surrogate, however, do exist. In 1769, Sir Henry Moore appointed Philip Livingston, Jr. as Surrogate and Registrar of the Prerogative Court. E. B. O'Callaghan and Berthold Fernow, eds., *Documents Relative to the Colonial History of the State of New York* (Albany, 1856–1887), [=*DCNY*], vol. VIII, p. 187. In a very interesting letter written by Governor William

After 1777, a number of radical changes were adopted with respect to the probate and filing of wills. As a consequence of the Revolution, the power of the governor was greatly curtailed. He was divested of his authority in testamentary matters, the Prerogative Court was abolished, and this power transferred to a single Judge of the Court of Probates. The earliest officials appointed were Thomas Tredwell on March 13, 1778, Peter Ogilvie on April 6, 1787, and Leonard Gansevoort on April 5, 1799. The Court sat in different parts of the state until 1783 when it came to New York; in 1787 it removed to Albany.

On May 1st of that year, a law took effect providing for the appointment by the Governor, with the advice and consent of the Council of Appointment, of Surrogates for each county who were given authority to prove wills and grant letters of administration. The Court of Probates continued to have jurisdiction in cases where residents died out of the state and of non-residents who died within the state. Although in the colonial period, most wills were filed in New York City, after 1787 they were filed in the Surrogates Courts of the various counties within the state.[3]

Since the early colonial laws provided for the filing of all wills in New York City, the original wills of the city, parts of Orange, Westchester, Richmond, Kings, Queens, and present day Nassau and Suffolk are presently under the jurisdiction of the Surrogate of New York County. The oldest extant wills dating from 1664 to 1736 are presently located in Room 303 of the Surrogate's Court at 31 Chambers Street, New York City. Recently the Surrogate permitted the transfer of a large body of wills dating from 1736 to 1820 to the Historical Documents Collection of the Paul Klapper Library, Queens College where they are being preserved and indexed. Others were found in the Clerk's Office of the Court of Appeals, Albany, and in the case of the Joshua Isaacs' Will the original is in the Museum of the City of New York. A photograph of Joseph Brown's Will, the original of which is lost, is found in the Samuel Oppenheim Collection of the American Jewish Historical Society.

Tryon in 1772 to the Board of Trade, the right of the Secretary to probate was questioned. Tryon cited the 1692 and 1709 laws as evidence of the Governor's right to probate. While not denying that the Secretary had proved wills from 1692 to "as low down as to the year 1766," he pointed out that the Governor had also constituted a Surrogate or Deputy in "constant succession" for the "business of the Prerogative Court." Tryon attacked the Secretary's Office claiming that one man filled too many jobs. He felt that in the growing community a division of office was necessary. *Ibid.*, pp. 322–327.

[3] *Civil List*, pp. 223–225; Rayden Woodward Vosburgh, "Surrogates Courts and Records in the Colony and State of New York 1664–1847," *The Quarterly Journal of the New York State Historical Association*, vol. III (1922), pp. 105–117; Charles P. Daly, *The Nature and Extent and History of the Jurisdiction of the Surrogates' Courts of the State of New York* (New York, 1863), pp. 21–22.

Copies of wills, known as will libers are in Room 402 of the Surrogate's Court. These libers while containing a record of most Jewish wills omit some which exist in the original, e.g. Moses Levy, and also contain numerous errors made by the copyists of the nineteenth century. The wills in the libers have been abstracted by the New-York Historical Society and published as part of their collections. While useful, these abstracts contain errors of omission and commission.[4]

Few records such as those of birth, marriage, and death relating to Jews have survived from the Colonial and Federal periods. Perhaps they were destroyed, but more likely the smallness of their population and the close community spirit did not make such documents particularly necessary. Whatever the reason, those papers that do exist are all the more unique and important. Wills are for Jewish history a vital source of knowledge of economic and social life and are invaluable for genealogical reference. A study of the witnesses reveals that in many cases Jews had relationships with the leading members of the non-Jewish community, e. g. Jacobus Van Cortlandt and Phillip French, both former mayors, witnessed the execution of Abraham De Lucena's will and William Peartree and Ebenezer Willson, also mayors of New York, and Rip Van Dam, later President of the Governor's Council, as well as Governor Cornbury served in the execution of the will of Isaac Roderecus [Rodriquez] Marques, who was incidentally the wealthiest Jewish New York merchant of his day.

The wills presented here comprise the body of such material known to the editor. It is possible that there may be others in scattered libraries, archives, or private collections, but a thorough search of such depositories, as far as practicable, has not revealed any. The Eardley Collection of the Long Island Historical Society containing abstracts of wills found outside of New York City has been searched with little result. There also remains the problem of names, a confusing item in Jewish history. Isaac Rodrigues who died in 1781 was probably not a Jew, neither was Monmouth Hart (d. 1761) nor Isaac Hays (d. 1774), but Aaron Hart and Judah Hayes were Jewish. The editor must rely on his own knowledge and experience to serve as a guide. Finally, those New York Jews who died out of the province or state and whose wills were not recorded in New York are not included, nor are those of Jews who converted to Christianity.

[4] Lee M. Friedman edited a few of the abstracts in an article entitled "Wills of Early Jewish Settlers in New York," *Publications of the American Jewish Historical Society* [=*PAJHS*], vol. XXIII (1915), pp. 147–161. An index to the early original wills in the Surrogate's Court has been compiled by Kenneth Scott, "Early Original New York Wills," *New York Genealogical and Biographical Record*, vol. LI (1963), pp. 98–99 and 174–178.

All extant wills found in New York, made by Jews up to 1800, are here edited and published so that for the first time this body of records will be available as a convenient reference. The editor has kept to the literal text and spelling except that for purposes of clarity, punctuation has been added in a few cases and diacritical marks (wriggle) and abbreviations expanded except in signatures. Empty brackets have been used where a word or words is missing or unintelligible and not conjecturable. Where the missing word is conjecturable it has been inserted in a bracket. The salutations and names of individuals appearing in the wills have been capitalized whether or not this is so in the original. It should also be noted that we have only reproduced facsimiles of the original wills in this volume and have omitted secondary statements which appear on the reverse side of the wills and are not part of the text of the respective wills.

The editor gratefully acknowledges the help, advice, and encouragement of many people, without whom this work could not have been published. Chiefly among these was Dr. Isidore S. Meyer, Editor of the *American Jewish Historical Quarterly* and of the publications of the American Jewish Historical Society who has given the needed interest, attention, time, and most importantly impetus and understanding in seeing this volume through the printing in the Quarterly and through this edition. His help has been of the greatest value and is sincerely appreciated. Mention should be made of Professor Kenneth Scott and Julius M. Bloch of the Department of History, Queens College of the City University of New York, who with the editor have collected for preservation archival material now in the Historical Documents Collection where many of the wills are now housed. Their help is most thankfully noted. In addition, appreciation is extended to Dr. Malcolm H. Stern for his expert genealogical counsel, and to Mr. Alfred Baragwaneth, Curator of the Museum of the City of New York, Messrs. Arthur J. Lennon, Samuel Meyerowitz and Oscar Rubin of the Surrogate's Court, New York County, all of whom provided necessary co-operation, and finally to my wife Marcia whose labor and astute criticism made much of this volume possible. A word of thanks also to Palma Barbaro who assisted in the typing. For all errors and shortcomings the editor is fully responsible.

LEO HERSHKOWITZ

Wills of Early New York Jews
(1704–1799)

I

JOSEPH NUNEZ[1]

[1704]

In the name of God Amen

Bee it known & manyfest unto all people that I JOSEPH NUNEZ of this City of new York Merchant considering my present Sickness the Shortness of this present life the certainty of Death & the uncertain time & hour thereof have thought fit to make & ordein these Presents to be my last Will & Testament in manner Following revoaking & hereby annulling all former Wills & testaments by mee made requiring these Presents to be only of Force after my Decease.

Imprimis

I do recommend my Soule to God that gave it me & my body to the Earth there to be decently buried in hopes of a glorious resurrecion at the last day And as for what Temporall Estate God of his mercy has been pleased to bestow upon mee my Debts being first paid is to be disposed of as Follows: I give and bequeath unto my brother SAMUEL NUNEZ[2] all my Estates whatsoever I have in this World without any reservacion whatsoever to be unto him his heires Executors & Administrators for Ever.

I do hereby nominate & apoint my true & Well beloved Friends PAUL DROILLET[3] & LEWIS GOMEZ[4] of this City Merchants to be Executors of

[1] Original Will no. 251, Clerk's Office of the Surrogate's Court, New York County, 31 Chambers Street, New York City; Will Liber 7, p. 624, also in the Clerk's Office; *Collections of the New-York Historical Society, Abstract of Wills* (New York, 1894) [=NYHSC], vol. II, p. 58. This Joseph Tores Nunez testament is the earliest extant probated Jewish will in the city archives. The will of Joseph Brown is written earlier, but can not be found except in copy (see following will). Nunez was an early merchant who died in New York City on October 2, 1704. He was very much interested in Jewish affairs and was one of the successful petitioners for a Jewish burial ground. David De Sola Pool, *Portraits Etched in Stone* (New York, 1953) [=*Portraits*], pp. 188–189; Elvira N. Solis, "Note on Isaac Gomez and Lewis Moses Gomez from an Old Family Record," *PAJHS*, vol. XI (1903), p. 142; *Minutes of the Common Council* (New York, 1905) [=*Minutes*], vol. III, pp. 447–448. An Inventory of Estate valued at £695.18.11½ was filed by the executors of the estate. Will Liber 5–6, p. 414; *NYHSC*, vol. I (1893), p. 322. Original at the Historical Documents Collection, Paul Klapper Library, Queens College [=HDC], where this class of material is presently being indexed and preserved.

[2] Little is known of Samuel Nunez. He is probably not the Dr. Samuel Nunez who settled in Georgia in 1732. Abram Kanof, "Uriah Phillips Levy," *PAJHS*, vol. XXXIX (1949), p. 3.

[3] Paul Droillet was made freeman of New York on May 3, 1692 and held numerous civic positions including collector of the Dock Ward and assistant alderman of this ward. *Collections of the New-York Historical Society, Burghers and Freemen of New York* (New York, 1886) [=*Burghers*], p. 5; *Minutes*, vol. II, pp. 308, 311 and 329.

[4] See Will of Lewis Gomez, *infra*, pp. 62–63.

this my last Will & Testament & in the absence or death of the One the other to have the whole power to Act & do as all Executors may by the Law.

In Witness whereof I have hereunto Set my hand & Seale in New York this Twenty Second day of September in the third year of her Majesties Reign 1704

s/ JOSEPH NUNEZ [seal]

Signed Sealed and Published
as the last Will & Testament
of Joseph Nunez in the presence of

s/ JOHAN: HARDENBROOK[5]
s/ P. CHAIGNEAU[6]

New York November 10th 1704

There appeared before me SAMSON SHELTON BROUGHTON Esq. thereunto authorized by his Excellency EDWARD VISCOUNT CORNBURY Captain-General & Governor in chief of the Province of New York New Jersey etc. JOHANNES HARDENBROOK and PETER CHIGNEAU the witnesses to ye within written will and proved ye same in ye usuall forme.

Jurat coram me s/ SA:SH:BROUGHTON[7]

New York November 10th 1704

PAUL DROILETT & LEWIS GOMEZ Ye Executors within named were duly sworn to ye Execution of ye within written will

Coram me[8] s/ SA: SH: BROUGHTON

[5] Hardenbrook, a cordwainer, was made a freeman in 1698 and was an alderman in 1732. *Burghers*, pp. 70–71 and 487.

[6] Peter Chigneau, a cooper, was made freeman in 1691. *Ibid.*, pp. 55 and 596.

[7] Sampson S. Broughton was Attorney General of the Province during 1701–1705. Stephen C. Hutchins, *Civil List of New York* (Albany, 1880) [=*Civil List*], p. 161.

[8] *Coram* in Latin means "before."

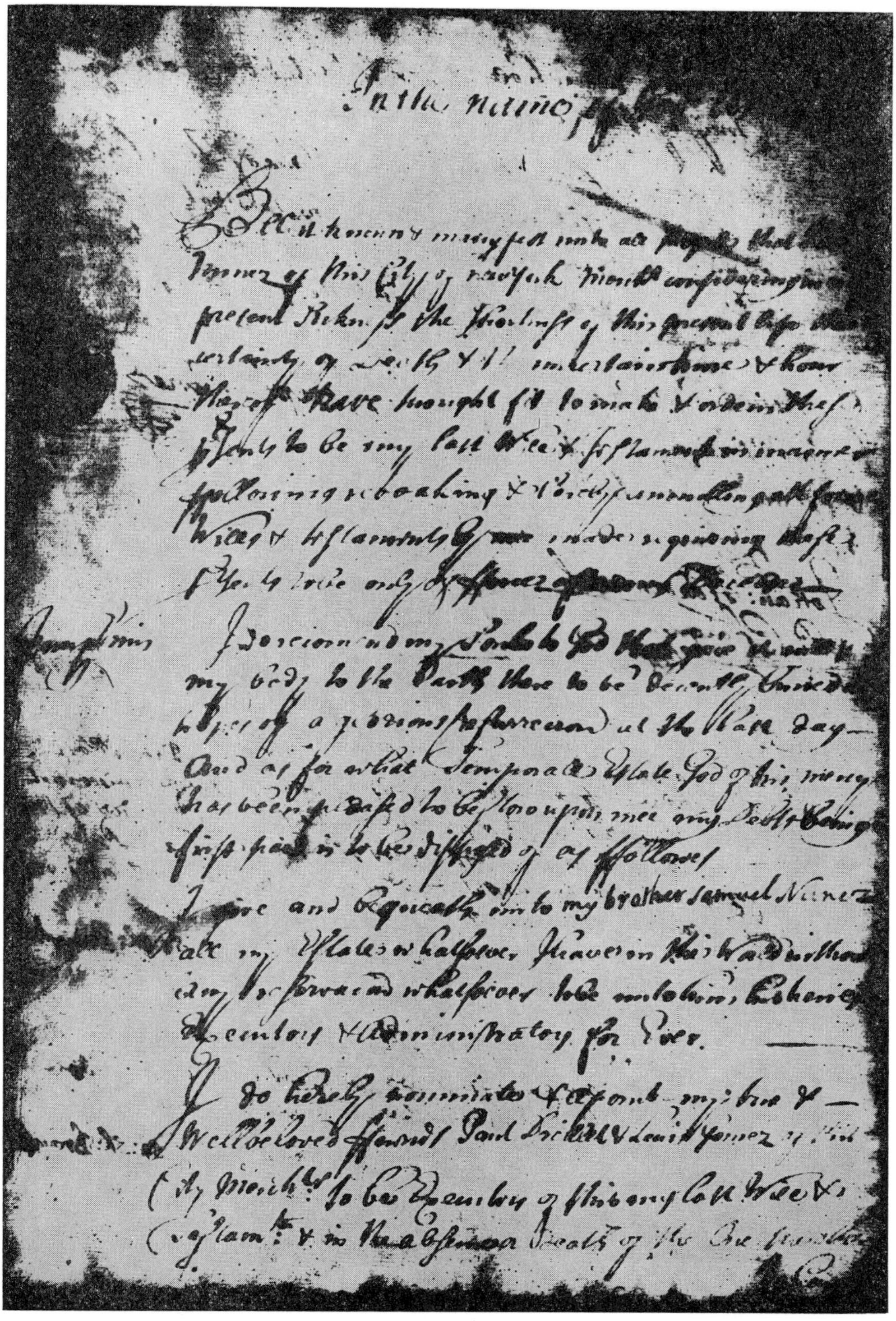
In the name [illegible]

Be it known & manifest unto all people that [illegible]
Nunez of this City of New York Merch.t considering the
present sickness & the frailty of this present life the
certainty of death & the uncertain time & hour
thereof have thought fit to make & ordain these
presents to be my last will & testament in manner
following revoking & making void all former
wills & testaments by me made requiring these
presents to be my only [illegible]

I do recommend my soul to God [illegible]
my body to the earth there to be decently buried
in hopes of a joyful resurrection at the last day
And as for what temporal estate God of his mercy
has been pleased to bestow upon me my debts being
first paid is to be disposed of as followeth

I give and bequeath unto my brother Samuel Nunez
all my estate whatsoever I have in this world without
any reservation whatsoever to be unto him his heirs
executors & administrators for ever.

I do hereby nominate & appoint my true &
well beloved friends Paul [illegible] & Lewis Gomez of this
City Merch.ts to be executors of this my last will &
testam.t & in the [illegible]

I. JOSEPH NUNEZ [1704]

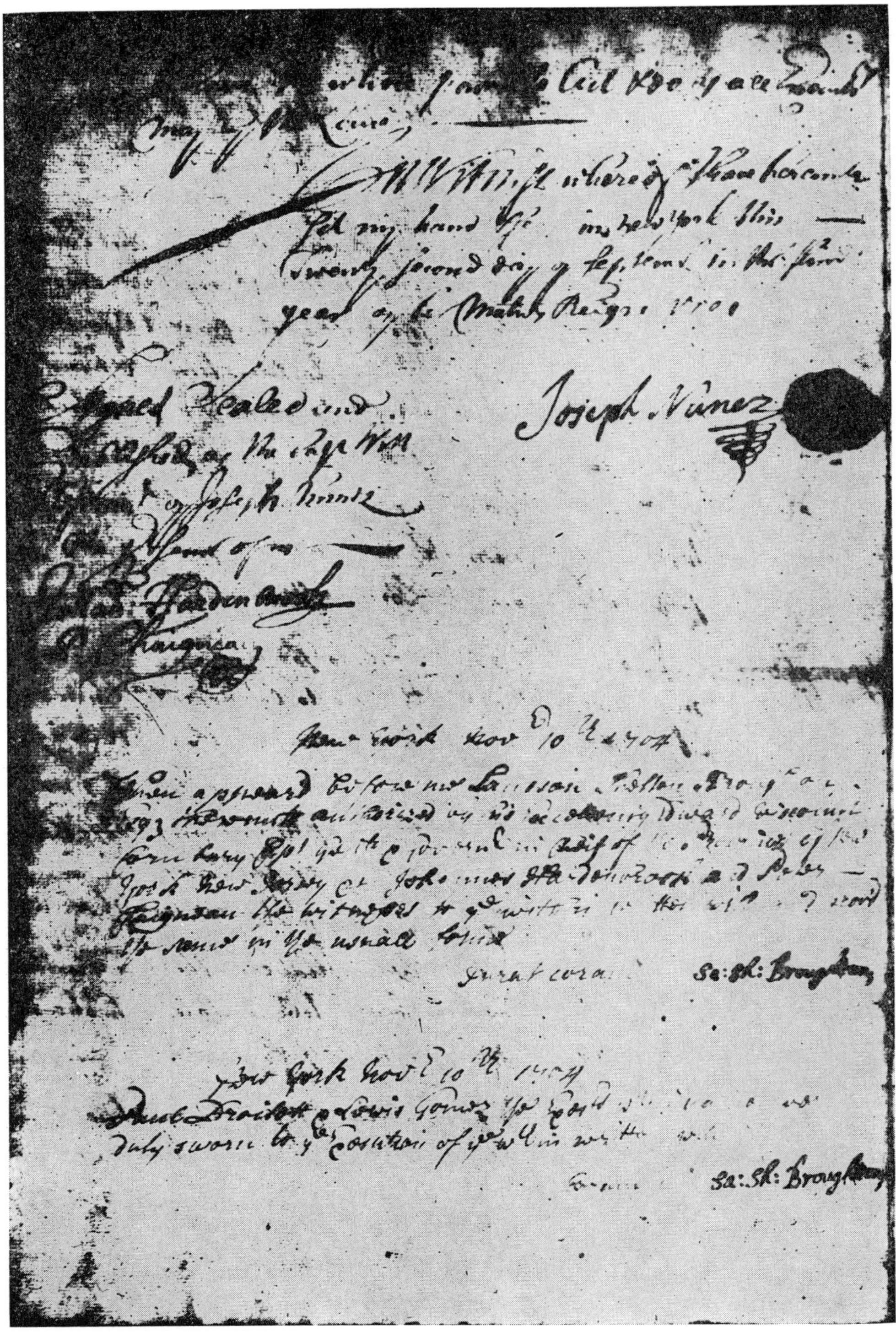
Signed Sealed and

Joseph Nunez

New York Nov 10 1704

Sa: Sh: Broughton

Sa: Sh: Broughton

I. JOSEPH NUNEZ [1704]

II

JOSEPH BROWN[1]

[1704]

Know All Men by these Presents, That I JOSEPH BROWN, inhabitant in this City of New York Have by these Presents made, ordained, constituted, and in my place and stead put and deputed my trusty and loving Friends, JOSEPH BUENO,[2] and the widdow ESTER BROWN,[3] both Residents in this City of New York, my true and lawful Attorneys for me, and in my Name, and for my Use, to ask, demand, sue for, levy, recover and receive all such Sum and Sums of Money, Debts, Goods, Wares, Dues, Accounts, & other Demands whatsoever, which are or shall be due, owing, payable and belonging to me, or detained from me any manner of ways or means whatsoever, by any person or persons Whatsoever, or Wheresoever, Giving and granting unto my said Attorneys by these Presents, my full and whole Power, Strength and Authority, in and about the Premises, to have, use and take all lawful ways and means, in my Name, for the Recovery thereof. And upon the Receipt of any such Debts, Dues, or Sums or Money aforesaid, Acquittances, or other sufficient Discharges, or me, and in my Name to make, seal and deliver, And generally, all and every other act and acts, thing and things, device and devices in the Law whatsoever needful and necessary to be done in and about the Premises, for the Recovery of all or any such Debts or Sums of Money aforesaid, for me, and in my Name, to do, execute and perform, as fully, largely and amply, to all intents and purposes, as I my self might or could do, if I was personally present, or as if the matter required more special Authority than is herein required. And Attorneys, one or more under them for the purposes aforesaid, to make and constitute, and again at pleasure to Revoke, Ratifying, allowing and holding for firm and effectual all and whatsoever my said Attorneys shall lawfully do in and about the premises by virtue hereof have Signed these in My perfect Understanding In N. York And the said, JOSEPH BROWN in My intire Will, considering the incertainty of this transitory Life, do make & declare these Presents to

[1] Will Liber 7, p. 214; *NYHSC*, vol. I (1893), p. 399. This earliest known written will exists only in a photographic copy in the Oppenheim Collection, American Jewish Historical Society Library — the whereabouts of the original is unknown. Interestingly this is in printed form — a rare example of the use of such forms. Joseph Brown, a merchant and nephew of Saul and Esther [Pardo] Brown, received a license to trade in Ulster County and was granted letters of denization in 1686. The family name Pardo was translated to Brown, although literally meaning grey. See also Will of Esther Brown. Max J. Kohler, "Civil Status of Jews in Colonial New York." *PAJHS*, vol. VI (1897), p. 194; *Portraits*, pp. 443–446.

[2] See will of Joseph Bueno de Mesquita, *infra*, pp. 15–17.

[3] See will of Esther Brown, *infra*, pp. 11–12.

contain my Last Will and Testament, That is to Say, I give and bequeath unto My Loving Brother DAVID BROWNE,[4] and My Cousin JOSIAS BROWNE,[5] Son of the Widdow ESTER BROWNE, And Also to my Niece RACHEL SARPHATIN,[6] all My Estate Real or personall, to be divided in Thirds, Equally, Provided My Lawfull and Just Debts, be payd First, with My Funerall Expenses, and all the rest of my Estate be it Lands, Tenements, Goods, Chattles, Debts, Dues or other Demands whatsoever wherewith at the time of my Decease, I shall be possessed or invested, or which shall then belong or of Right appertain unto me, I do give, devise, and bequeath, unto the Above Named DAVID BROWN, JOSIAS BROWN, And RACHELL SARPHATIN, in the Manner Aforesaid, And I do hereby nominate and appoint Executors for this My Last Will and Testament My good Friends JOSEPH BUENO & ESTER BROWN aforesaid. And I do hereby Revoke, [disannul] and make void all former Wills & Testaments by me heretofore made, and do hereby declare this to be my last Will & Testament. In Witness whereof I have hereunto set my Hand and Seal this — Day of August 1704.

Signed Sealed and D.D. [Declared] s/ JOSSEPH BROWN [seal]
in the Presence of us, as
the Last Will and Testament

s/ ISAAC GRANADA[7]
s/ SAMUEL LEVY[8]
שמואל לוי

New York November 21st 1704

Then came and personally appeared before me SAMPSON SHELTON BROUGHTON (being thereto authorized and appointed by his Excellency EDWARD VISCOUNT CORNBURY[9]) the within named ISAAC GRANADA and

[4] David Brown was probably the Jew granted the right to settle in Rhode Island in 1684 who later in the year received a license to trade in New York. He may have been the David Pardo who in June, 1701 purchased five slaves at public auction in Curaçao. A David Brown died in Surinam in 1716/17. Max J. Kohler, "The Jews in Newport," *PAJHS*, vol. VI (1897), p. 66; *Portraits*, pp. 446–447; Isaac S. Emmanuel, *Precious Stones of the Jews of Curaçao (1656–1957)* (New York, 1957), p. 199.

[5] Josias, the son of Saul Brown, was born on September 22, 1694. *Portraits*, p. 443. Possibly named after Saul Pardo's father. Emmanuel, *op. cit.*, p. 199.

[6] Possibly a member of the Sarfati family in Amsterdam. Mayer Kayserling, "The Earliest Rabbis and Jewish Writers of America," *PAJHS*, vol. III (1895), p. 17; David de Sola Pool, "Notes on American Jewish History," *PAJHS*, vol. XXII (1914), p. 170.

[7] Isaac Henriques Granada admitted as freeman of New York in January 1688 and mentioned as a butcher in 1703 was buried in the New Bowery Cemetery in 1717. *Portraits*, p. 453; Rosalie S. Philips, "A Burial Place for the Jewish Nation Forever," *PAJHS*, vol. XVIII (1909), p. 120; *Burghers*, p. 54.

[8] Samuel Levy (d. 1719), brother of Moses Levy, a merchant of New York. See his will, *infra*, pp. 27–29. He signed this document in both English and Hebrew.

[9] Edward Hyde, Lord Cornbury, was Governor of New York, 1702–1708. He is usually credited or discredited with being the worst or next to worst administrator of the province.

SAMUELL LEVY Witnesses to the within written will and declared upon their Oath that they Saw the within named JOSEPH BROWNE being in good & perfect mind and memory Signe Seal publish and declare this within written will to be his Last Will and Testament and that also they did att the same time subscribe the Same as wittnesses in the presence of the Testator.

Coram me s/ SA. SH. BROUGHTON

Then also at the Same time personally appeared before me SAMPSON SHELTON BROUGHTON, JOSEPH BUENO and HESTER BROWNE the Executor & Executrix within named and were duly Sworne to the Execution of the within written Will.

Coram me s/ SA. SH. BROUGHTON

III

ISAAC RODRIQUEZ MARQUES[1]

[1707]

In the Name of God Amen the seaventeenth day of October in the Fifth year of his Majesties Reigne Anno Domino one Thousand seven hundred and Six I ISAAC RODERECUS MARQUES of the Citty of New Yorke merchant Being of perfect Remembrance and bound on a Voyage to Jaimca in the west Indies and Considering the certainty of death and the uncertaine Time of the Coming of the same Do make this my last Will and Testament in manner and forme following (that is to say) First I doe bequeath my Soul to God Almighty and my Body to the Earth to be decently Buryed and as for the Disposall of my worldly Estate It is as followeth (that is to say) First I do desire that all such Just Debts, as I doe owe shall be honestly paid In convenient time after my Decease Item it is my Will and minde that my Deare mother RACHELL MARQUES[2] be maintained out of my Estate and live with my Wife or my Daughter dureing her naturall life But if she cannot agree with them or like to live by her Self that then she shall Receive out of my Estate before division be made the Sume of fifty Pounds Current money of New Yorke and a God Serviceable Negro woman shall alsoe be Purchased for her out of my sd Estate to attend her during her naturall life which at her decease shall fall to my son and daughter the Vallue thereof to be Equally divided Betwixt them, and I doe give hereby a Strict charge to my wife and children be Dutifull to my said Deare Mother Item I give and Bequeath to my Daughter EASTER[3] Fifty pounds to Buy her a Jewell at her age of Eighteen yeares or marrage with her mothers consent the rest of my Estate Reall and Personall I give devise and Bequeath as followeth (that is to say) one third parte thereof to my deare and loving wife RACHELL MARQUES to have and to same hold the same to her, her heires and assignes for Ever

[1] Will Liber 7, p. 296; *NYHSC*, vol. I (1892), pp. 439–440. Isaac Rodriquez Marques appears to have been a resident of New York as early as 1695 when he was made denizen of the province. A merchant, he lived in the city at Pearl Street and at Queen Street. *Portraits*, pp. 460–461; *PAJHS*, vol. VI (1897), p. 101. Isaac Gabay indentured his sixteen year old son, Solomon to Rodriques on December 1, 1704. *Burghers*, pp. 610–611. The Marques inventory filed on April 8, 1708 showed the gross value of his estate at £3580.8.¼, HDC.

[2] Rachel's second marriage was to Moses Peixotto of Barbados. Conveyance Liber 28, cf. 497–498, Register's Office, 31 Chambers Street, New York, N. Y. Unless otherwise indicated, all Conveyance Libers, referred to in footnotes, are located at the aforementioned address.

[3] Esther purportedly married Lewis Gomez. *Portraits*, p. 462. It is doubtful, however, that she is the Esther Marchaze who married Gomez. Her age and the age of Gomez's children would almost rule out any such possibility.

one other Third part thereof to my Son JACOB MARQUES[4] to him his heires and assignes for ever the Remainding third part thereof to my loving Daughter EASTER MARQUES her heires and assignes for ever Further it is my Will, that the Two Thirds of my estate Bequeathed as aforesaid to my Children shall Imediately after my decease be deposseted in the hand of Mr. AARON LA MEGOA Merchant in Jaimaica who I hereby constitute to be supervisor over my Children and it is my Will that my sd Childrens Portions shall be put out at intrest for the maintainace of my sd Children during theire minority which Intrest shall be yearly Paid to my sd Wife towards theire maintainace as aforesd And I doe desire Mr. LEWIS GOMAS[5] and Mr. ABRAHAM LUCENA[6] to assist my wife in the management of all her affaires when and as often as she shall make application to them Sole Executrix of this my Last Will I make my deare and Loveing Wife RACHELL MARQUES and Revoaking all other and former wills at any time heretofore by me made Either in word or writeing I Declare this to be my Last Will and Testament In Testimony whereof I have hereunto Set my hand and seale the day and yeare first above written ISAAC R^{CS} MARQUIZ [L. S.] Signed sealed Published and declared by the above mentioned ISAAC RODERECUS MARQUES as his Last Will and Testament In the presence of us W^{M} PEARTREE[7] EBENEZER WILLSON,[8] RIP VAN DAM,[9] EDWARD VISCOUNT CORNBURY Captain Generall and Governor in Chiefe of the Provinces of New Yorke New Jersey and Territorries pending thereon in America and Vice Admirall of the same & To all to whome these presents Shall come or may concerne Greeting Know Yee that att New Yorke the Twenty fourth day of March the Last Will and Testament of ISAAC RODERICUS MARQUES was proved approved and allowed of by me having while he lived and att the time of his death Goods Chattles and Creditts in diverse places within this Province by means whereof the full disposition of all and singular the sd Goods Chattles and Creditts and the the Granting the administracon of them also the hearing of accounts Calculation or Reckoning and the finall Discharge and Dismission from the same unto me solely and not

[4] Jacob born in 1699 in New York City died in the Barbadoes in 1725. Joseph R. Rosenbloom, *A Biographical Dictionary of Early American Jews* (Lexington, 1960) [=*Dictionary*], p. 109.

[5] See Will of Lewis Gomez, *infra*, pp. 62–63.

[6] See Will of Abraham De Lucena, *infra*, pp. 33–34.

[7] William Peartree, a noted New Yorker, was Mayor of New York City beginning October 14, 1703 to October, 1707, so that he witnessed this document while Mayor. Edmund B. O'Callaghan, ed., *Calendar of New York Colonial Commissions, 1680–1770* (New York, 1929) [=*Calendar*], pp. 10–13.

[8] Ebenezer Wilson was Sheriff of New York from June, 1702–March, 1707. He succeeded Peartree as Mayor on October 14, 1707 for a two year term. *Ibid.*, pp. 7–8 and 10–14.

[9] Rip Van Dam's (c. 1660–1749) career as merchant and politician was long and argumentative. He is most well known for his dispute with Governor William Cosby during the early 1730's. In 1705, he held the office of Justice of Peace. *Burghers*, p. 612.

unto any other Inferior Judge are manifestly knowne to belong and the Administration of all and singular the said Goods Chattles & Creditts of the said deceased and his said last Will and Testament in any manner of ways concerning was granted unto RACHELL MARQUES Executrix in the said Last Will and Testament named Chiefly of well and truely administering the same and of makeing a true and perfect Inventory of all and singular the Goods Chattles and Creditts of the said deceased and Exhibiting the same into the Registry of the Prerogative Court in the Secretarys Office, att or Before the Twenty fourth day of September, Next Ensueing and of Rendering & Just and true account calculation or Reckoning when thereunto Required In Testimony whereof I have Caused the Prerogative Seale to be hereunto affixt att New Yorke the Twenty Fourth day of March 1706.

GEO. CLARKE[10]

[10] George Clarke (1676–1760) was appointed Clerk of the Governor's Council on February, 1705 and Secretary of the Province in March, 1703. *Calendar*, pp. 12 and 32.

IV

ESTHER BROWN[1]

[1708]

In The Name of Almighty God Amen,

The Twentieth day of may in the yeare one Thousand and Seven hundred & Eight I ESTHER BROWNE of New York widdow Being Sick in Body, Butt of good and Perfect Memory, Thancks be to almighty god and Calling to Remembrance the uncertaine Estate of this Transitory Life, and that all Flesh must yield unto Death when it Shall please god to Call do make, Constitute, ordaine, and Declare this my Last Will and Testament in Manner and form following Revokeing and adnulling by these Pressents all and Every Testament and Testaments will and wills heretofore by me made and Declared Either by word, or writting, and this is to be taken for my Last will and Testament and None other; and first Being Penitent and Sorry from the Bottom of my heart for my Sins Past, most humbly Desireing forgiveness for the Same I give and Committ my Soul unto almighty god in whouse trust and Believe assuredly to be Saved and to have full Remission and forgiveness of all my Sins and that my Soul with my body at the general day of Resurection Shall Rise againe with Joy through the mercy of Almighty god. I Desire my body to be Decently buried and now for the Setling of my Temporall Estate and such goods, Chatles and Debts as it hath pleased god to bestow upon me; I doe order, give & Disposs the Same in Manner & forme following (That is to say) first I will that all Those Debts and Duttys as I owe in Right or Concience to any Manner of Person or Persons whatsoever; shall be well and truly Contented & paid, or ordained to be paid within Convinient time after my Decease by my Executrixe my Deare & Loveing Daughter ABIGAIL BROWNE. Item, I give & Bequeath the Remainder found Bellonging to me to be equally Divided Between my foure Children viz. JOSIAH BROWNE, ABIGALL, SARAH & SIMHA BROWNE[2] alloweing over and above Their Equall Porcions the Sume of Three pounds to my Deare and Beloved Sonn JOSIAH BROWNE together with my Blessings In witness whereof I have Sett hereunto my hand & Sale in Presence of JOSEPH

[1] Original Will no. 194, Will Liber 7, p. 494; *NYHSC*, vol. II (1894), pp. 3–4. Esther Brown was the widow of Saul Pardo Brown, minister of Shearith Israel in 1695. John Miller, *New York Considered and Improved* (Cleveland, 1903), p. 54; *Portraits*, pp. 443–444; Emmanuel, *op. cit.*, p. 199. The inventory of the estate made at the request of Abigail Brown on July 1, 1708 was valued at £60 and is recorded in Will Liber 5–6, p. 481. The original inventory is located in the Historical Documents Collection.

[2] The testatrix's children all died in Curaçao. Simha died January 5, 1768; Josiah, May 22, 1755; Abigail, November 20, 1742; and Sarah, July 27, 1723; Emmanuel, *op. cit.*, pp. 239, 327, 338 and 358.

BUENO and ABRAHAM DE LUCENA of this Citty Merchants the date and year above mentioned By me

Signed Sealed & Delivered in presence

s/ ESTER BROWN [seal]

s/ JOSEPH BUENO[3]
s/ ABRAHAM DE LUCENA[4]
s/ NATHAN SIMSON[5]
s/ MORDEJAY GOMEZ[6]

New Yorke May the 28th 1708

Their appeared before me THOMAS WENHAM[7] Esq. Surrogate ABRAHAM DE LUCINA & JOS. BUENO Two of the wittnesses to the within written will & made oath on the ~~holy evangelists~~ five books of Moses that they Saw the Testatrix (who was then of Sound mind & memory) Signe Seale & publish the within written Instruement as her Last will & Testament & that NATHAN SIMSON & MORDEGAY GOMEZ the other wittnesses to the Sd will Subscribed their names as witnesses thereto in the presence of the Testatrix.

s/ THOS. WENHAM
New Yorke May 28th 1708

ABAGAIL BROWNE the Executrix within named was duly Sworne to the Execution of the within written will

coram me s/ THOS. WENHAM

[3] See Will of Joseph Bueno, *infra*, pp. 15–17.

[4] See Will of Abraham De Lucena, *infra*, pp. 33–34.

[5] Nathan Simson, a wealthy English merchant, made various trips to New York. Jacob R. Marcus, *Early American Jewry, 1649–1794*, vol. I (Philadelphia, 1951), pp. 64 and 163. His Letter Books, important accounts of his and other merchants' business, are located in the Public Record Office, C104/13, London, England. A copy is in the American Jewish Archives in Cincinnati, Ohio.

[6] See Will of Mordecai Gomez, pp. 84–91.

[7] Thomas Wenham was appointed Receiver General of New York in 1702 and third Justice of the Supreme Court in April, 1703. He was also a member of the Council and held this post as well as Justice until his death in September, 1709. He also served on the bench of the Court of Chancery and acted as Surrogate, as in this instance. *Civil List*, p. 164; *Calendar*, p. 10; Paul M. Hamlin and Charles E. Baker, eds., *Supreme Court of Judicature of the Province of New York 1691–1705* (New York, 1959), pp. 111 and 214–220.

IV. ESTHER BROWN [1708]

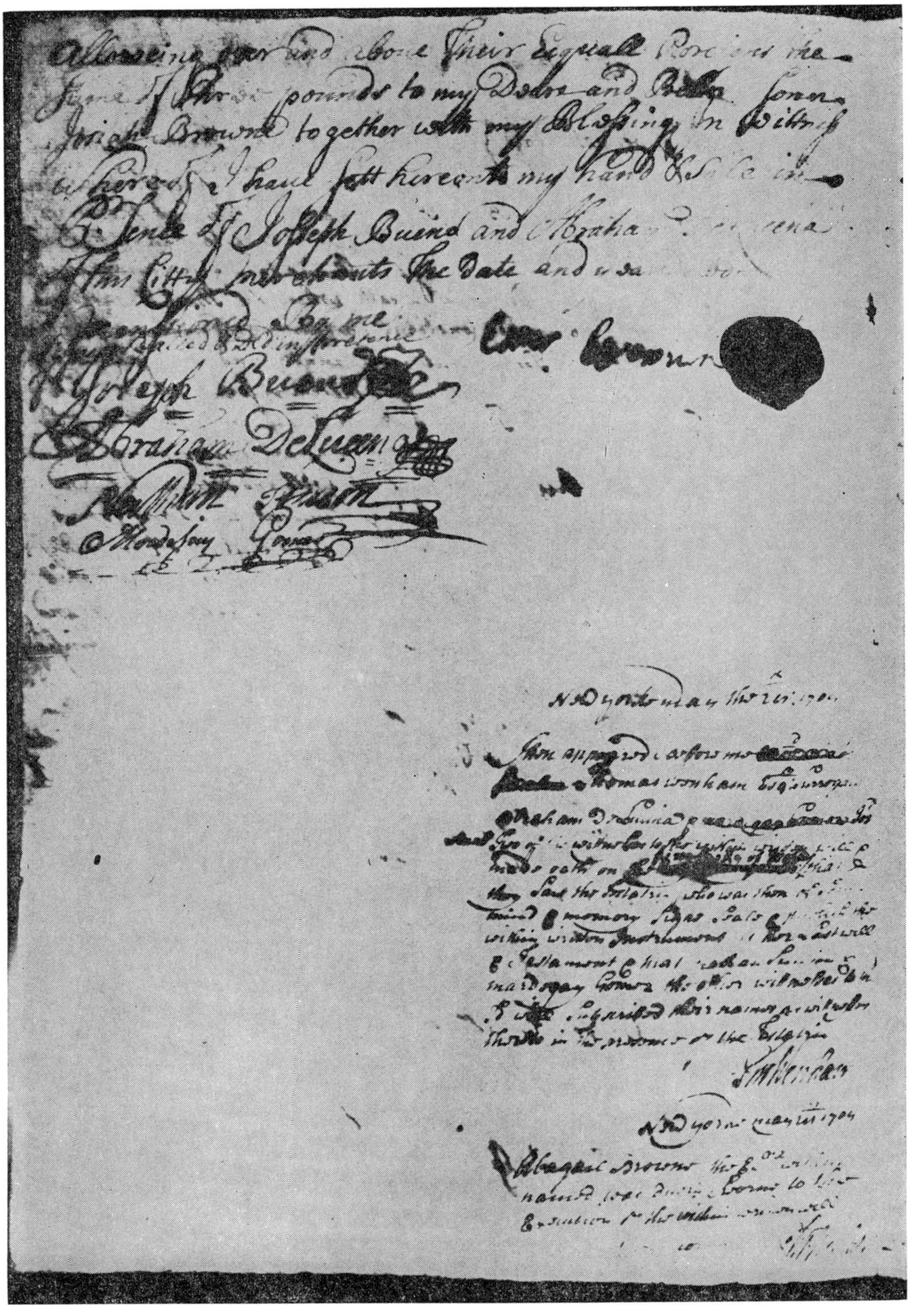

Allowing over and above Their Equall Porcions the
Sume of Three pounds to my Deare and ... Sonn
Joseph Browne together with my Blessing In Witness
whereof I have sett hereunto my hand & Seale in
Presence of Joseph Bueno and Abraham De Lucena
of this Citty merchants the Date and year above

Esther Browne

Joseph Bueno
Abraham DeLucena
Mordecay Gomez

IV. ESTHER BROWN [1708]

V

JOSEPH BUENO DE MESQUITA[1]

[1708]

In the Name of God Amen I JOSEPH BUENO DE MESQUITA of the City of New York Merchant, being at this Present Sick in bedd yet of Sound memory & understanding & knowing the Certainty of death & the uncertain time and hour thereof have thought fit to make this my last Will & Testament hereby revoking and annulling all former Wills and Testaments by me heretofore made willing that these presents shall only be of force after my Decease First I recomend my Soule to God & my body to the Earth in hopes of a glorious Resurrection at the last Day.

Item

I will and desire that my Debts & funerall charges be paid and Satisfyd.

Item

I do give and bequeath unto my Loving wife RACHELL the daughter of RACHELL DOVALE[2] & to her heires forever the Sum of Six hundred pounds Current money of New York to be paid unto her by my Executor within Six months after my decease and I do further give unto her all my plate household stuff & furniture of what kind soever as Linnen woollen bedding Tables Chairs looking glasses brass Pewter yron etc All her waring apparell rings Jewells necklaces whatsoever which is or hath been Esteemed hers or in her Possession (my Sloop[3] goods & merchandises only excepted and reserved) as allso all the Slaves now belonging to mee And that in full Satisfaction of her Dower claim of lands & all other demands whatsoever.

[1] Original Will no. 181; Will Liber 7, p. 512; *NYHSC*, vol. II (1893), p. 13. Bueno was one of the earliest Jewish merchants of the City. He is credited with having purchased the first Jewish burial ground in 1682. There is an extensive record of Bueno's activities. David and Tamar de Sola Pool, *An Old Faith in the New World* (New York, 1955), pp. 280, 468 and 469; Lee M. Friedman, "Early Jewish Residents in Massachusetts," *PAJHS*, vol. XXIII (1915), p. 83. Mesquita's inventory filed February 9, 1710 shows a total value of £912.13.5 in which was included Mesquita's *Five Books of Moses* with Silver Bells and ornaments "belonging to the altar" which were sold to Isaac Pinheiro for £25.6 even though the will seems to direct that it be delivered to his brother Abraham. At Pinheiro's death his *Five Books of Moses* with bells and vestments were valued at £150. Inventories of Joseph Bueno Mesquita and Isaac Pinheiro, HDC. For legal action, see e. g. *Bueno v. Lockhart* (1685?), Mayor's Court Papers, file 1684–1686, Nov. 7, 1685, New York County Clerk's Office, 31 Chambers Street, New York City [=MCP]. These papers have been microfilmed by the American Jewish Historical Society and the microfilms are available in its Library.

[2] A Rachel Doval who was the aunt of Saul Brown died February 26, 1678. Emmanuel, *op. cit.*, pp. 148–149.

[3] The sloop mentioned was the "Mary." See *DCNY*, vol. IV, pp. 1142–1144; Inventory of Joseph Bueno Mesquita, HDC.

Item

I give unto my beloved Brother ABRAHAM BUENO DE MESQUITA of the Island of Nevis the West Indies and his heirs for ever my five bookes of the Law of Moses in Parchment together with the two Ornaments of plate thereto beloning in full of all his pretensions & demands of my Estate whatsoever, & I do further give & bequeath unto my Said brother ABRAHAM the Sume of One hundred Sixty one Pounds two shillings and three Pence which he now oweth unto me upon ballance of Amount be it more or less over and above the Said books.

Item

I do give and bequeath unto my mother in Law RACHELL DOVALE the Sume of fivety Pounds of Currant money of New York to be paid unto her within Six months after my decease.

Item

I do give & bequeath unto my brother in Law SAUL DOVALE the Sume of fivety Pounds like money to be paid him as he comes of Age with the improvements thereof frome time of my death untill he come of the Age of Twenty One years.

Item

I do give & bequeath unto my God Child ASHER CAMPANELL[4] Twenty Pounds like money to be paid to him together with the interest arising by the Said sume from the time of my death for his own use, when he comes to the Age of Twenty One Yeares And if my God Child should dy before that time then it is my Will that his Sisters and brothers shall have that Legacy amongst them in equall shares and Proportions.

Item

I do give and bequeath unto the Poor of the Jewish nation in New York Twenty Pounds like money to be distributed by my Executors at their disercion according to my true Intent and meaning.

Item

I do dispose of all the Rest of my Estate whatsoever in manner following that is to say it is my will and desire all be converted as soon as Possible into money and put out to interest in the Province of New York by My Executors hereafter named & the interest as it comes to be in like manner improved untill the time of Payment herein & hereby directed to be made And I do give and bequeath the Same as follows One half thereof unto the Child or Children of my Said Brother ABRAHAM to be paid to them in even & Equall Shares and proportions with the improvement thereof when they severally come to the age of Twenty One yeares, And the other half

[4] Asher Campanell, who died in 1753, was a *shamash* [sexton] for Shearith Israel. He was also a butcher. *Dictionary*, p. 10; *Marks v. Campanell* (1752), MCP, file 1750–1752, Sept. 22, 1752.

thereof I do give and bequeath unto the Children of ISAAC GABAY[5] & my Sister ESTHER deceased to be paid to them in even & Equall Shares & proportions with the improvement thereof when they severally come to the age of Twenty One yeares — And Lastly I do nominate Constitute and appoint my good friends Messrs LOUIS GOMEZ,[6] ABRAHAM DE LUCENA[7] of this City of New York Merchants & my Dear Wife RACHELL aforesaid to be the Executors of this my last Will and Testament And In Testimony thereof I do Sign Seal & publish this to be my last Will & Testament at New York this Twentyeth day of October in the Seaventh year of her Majesties reign 1708

the marke of

X [seal]

JOSEPH BUENO

Signed Sealed & Published as the last Will
& Testament of JOSEPH BUENO DE MESQUITA
he being Sick on bedd yet in his Right
Senses to our understanding in the presence of us
s/ ABRAH KETELTAS
s/ HENRICK KERMER
s/ JOHANNES BANT[8]

New York 1st November 1708

LEWIS GOMEZ, ABRAHAM DE LUCENA and RACHELL BUENO the Executors the within written will were duly sworn to the Execution thereof coram me

s/ CORNBURY

New York 1st November 1708

ABRAHAM KETTLETAS, HENDRICK KERMER and JOHANNES BANT the witnesses to the within written will appeared before me and made oath on the holy Evangelists that they saw the Testator JOSEPH BUENO DE MESQUITA sign Seal and publish the within written Instrument as his last will and Testament and that at the time of the Publication thereof he was of Sound and perfect mind and memory to the best of their Judgemts and understanding

s/ CORNBURY

[5] Isaac Gabay lived in the Dock Ward. Entry of January 20, 1708, Dock Ward, New York Assessment List, vol. 1702–1709, New York City Comptroller's Office, Rhinelander Building, 238 William Street, New York City [=NYAL]. Microfilm copies are located in the HDC. Gabay, along with the testator, De Lucena, Samuel Levy, and Isaac Rodrigues Marques, signed a petition dated February 19, 1705, asking for the regulation of the currency. *DCNY*, vol. IV, p. 1135.

[6] See Will of Lewis Gomez *infra*, pp. 62–63.

[7] See Will of Abraham De Lucena *infra*, pp. 33–34.

[8] Abraham Keteltas, blacksmith, Henrick Kermer, and Johannes Bant, cooper, were all residents of New York City. *Burghers*, pp. 65 and 67. Kermer and Bueno were next door neighbors for a number of years when Bueno lived in Robert Sinclair's house. NYAL, vol. 1699–1702, East Ward, Jan. 28 and Dec. 28, 1702.

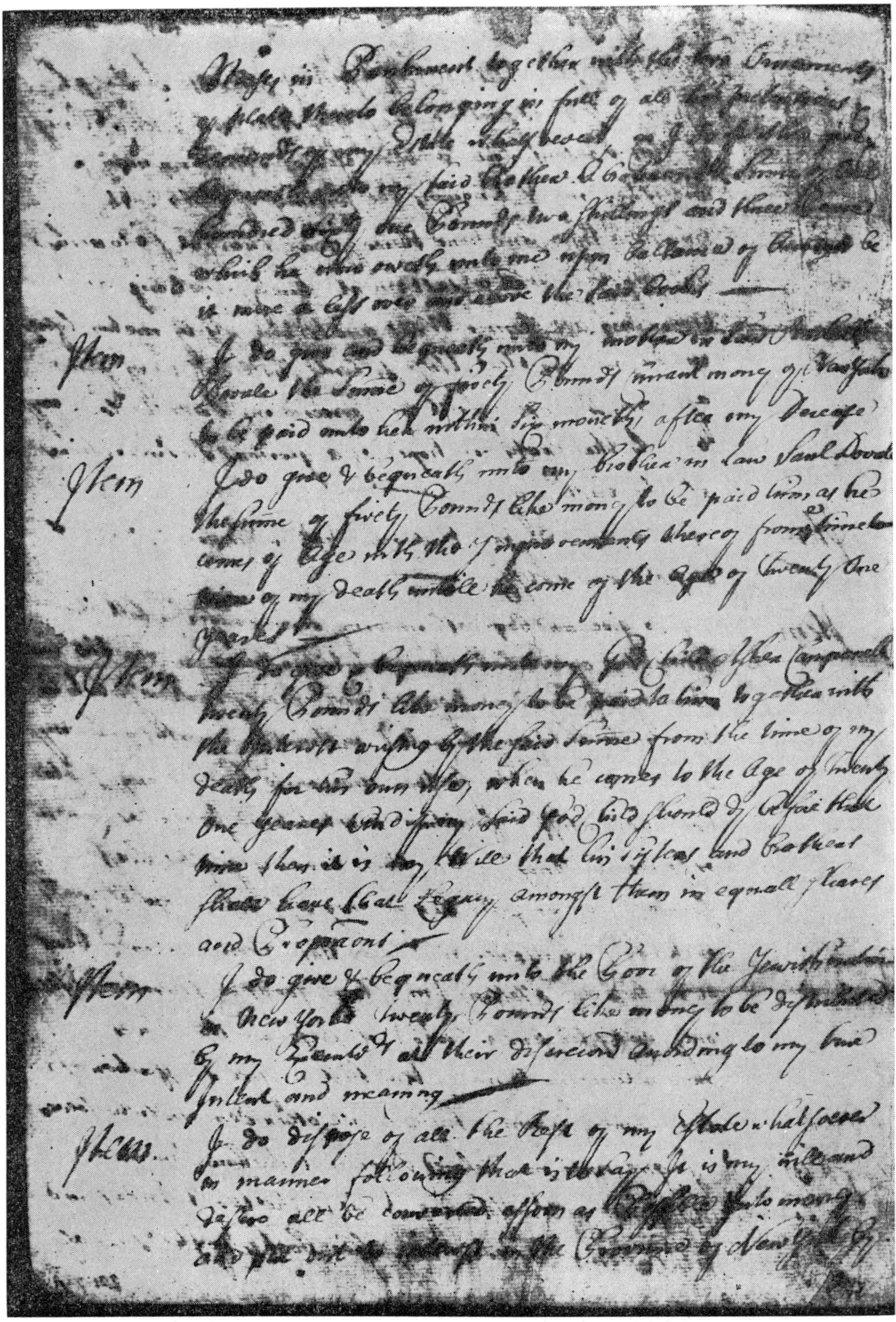
[illegible] in Parchment together with the two Ornaments
of plate thereto belonging in full of all [illegible]
[illegible] my [illegible]
[illegible] my said brother [illegible] the sum of [illegible]
hundred [illegible] one pounds two shillings and three pence
which he now owes unto me upon ballance of [illegible] be
it more or less over and above the said [illegible]
Item I do give and bequeath unto my mother in law [illegible]
[illegible] the sume of forty pounds current mony of [illegible]
to be paid unto her within six months after my decease
Item I do give & bequeath unto my brother in law Saul [illegible]
the sume of forty pounds like mony to be paid him as he
comes of age with the improvements thereof from time
of my death untill he come of the age of twenty one
years
Item I do give & bequeath unto my [illegible]
twenty pounds like mony to be paid to him together with
the interest arising of the said sume from the time of my
death for his own use, when he comes to the age of twenty
one yeares and if my said god child should dy before that
time then it is my will that his sisters and brothers
shall have that legacy amongst them in equall shares
and proportion
Item I do give & bequeath unto the poor of the Jewish nation
in New York twenty pounds like mony to be distributed
by my Executors at their discretion according to my true
intent and meaning
Item I do dispose of all the rest of my estate whatsoever
in manner following that is to say it is my will and
desire all be converted as soon as possible into mony
and [illegible] in the Province of New York by

V. JOSEPH BUENO DE MESQUITA [1708]

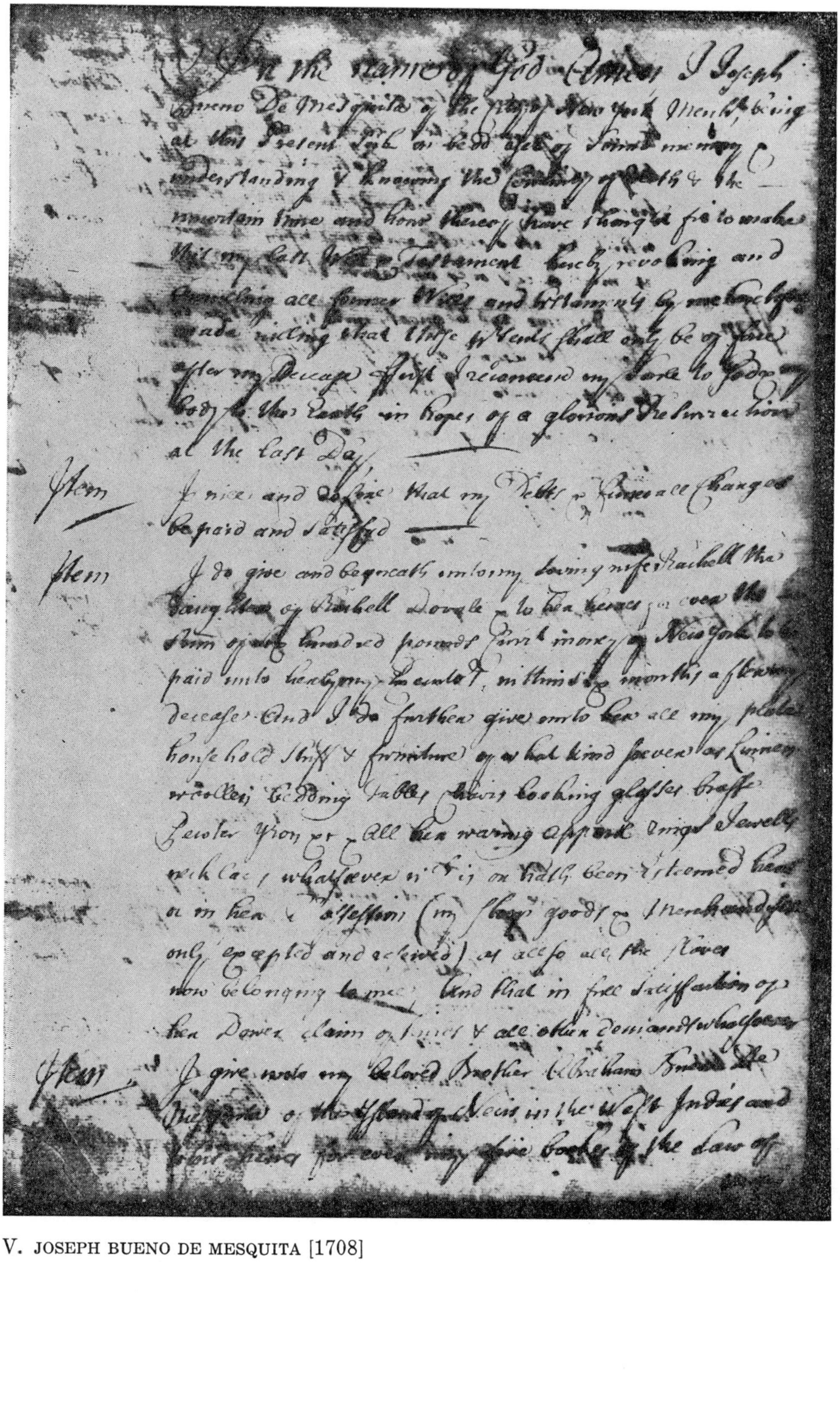
In the name of God Amen I Joseph
Bueno De Mesquita of the City of New York Merch^t being
at this present sick in bedd of sound memory
understanding & knowing the certainty of death & the
uncertain time and hour thereof have thought fit to make
this my last Will & Testament hereby revoking and
annulling all former Wills and testaments by me heretofore
made willing that these presents shall only be of force
after my decease First I recomend my soule to God my
body to the earth in hopes of a glorious Resurrection
at the last Day
Item I will and desire that my Debts & funerall Charges
be paid and satisfied
Item I do give and bequeath unto my loving wife Rachell the
daughter of Rachell [illegible] to her heires for ever the
sum of [illegible] hundred pounds curr^t money of New York to be
paid unto her [illegible] within six months after my
decease And I do further give unto her all my plate
household stuff & furniture of what kind soever as Linnen
woollen bedding tables chairs looking glasses brass
pewter Iron &c All her wearing apparell rings Jewells
necklaces whatsoever which is or hath been esteemed hers
or in her possession (my shop goods & Merchandizes
only excepted and reserved) as also all the slaves
now belonging to me And that in full satisfaction of
her Dower claim of thirds & all other demands whatsoever
Item I give unto my beloved Brother Abraham Bueno De
Mesquita of the Island of Nevis in the West Indies and
to his heirs for ever my five bookes of the law of

V. JOSEPH BUENO DE MESQUITA [1708]

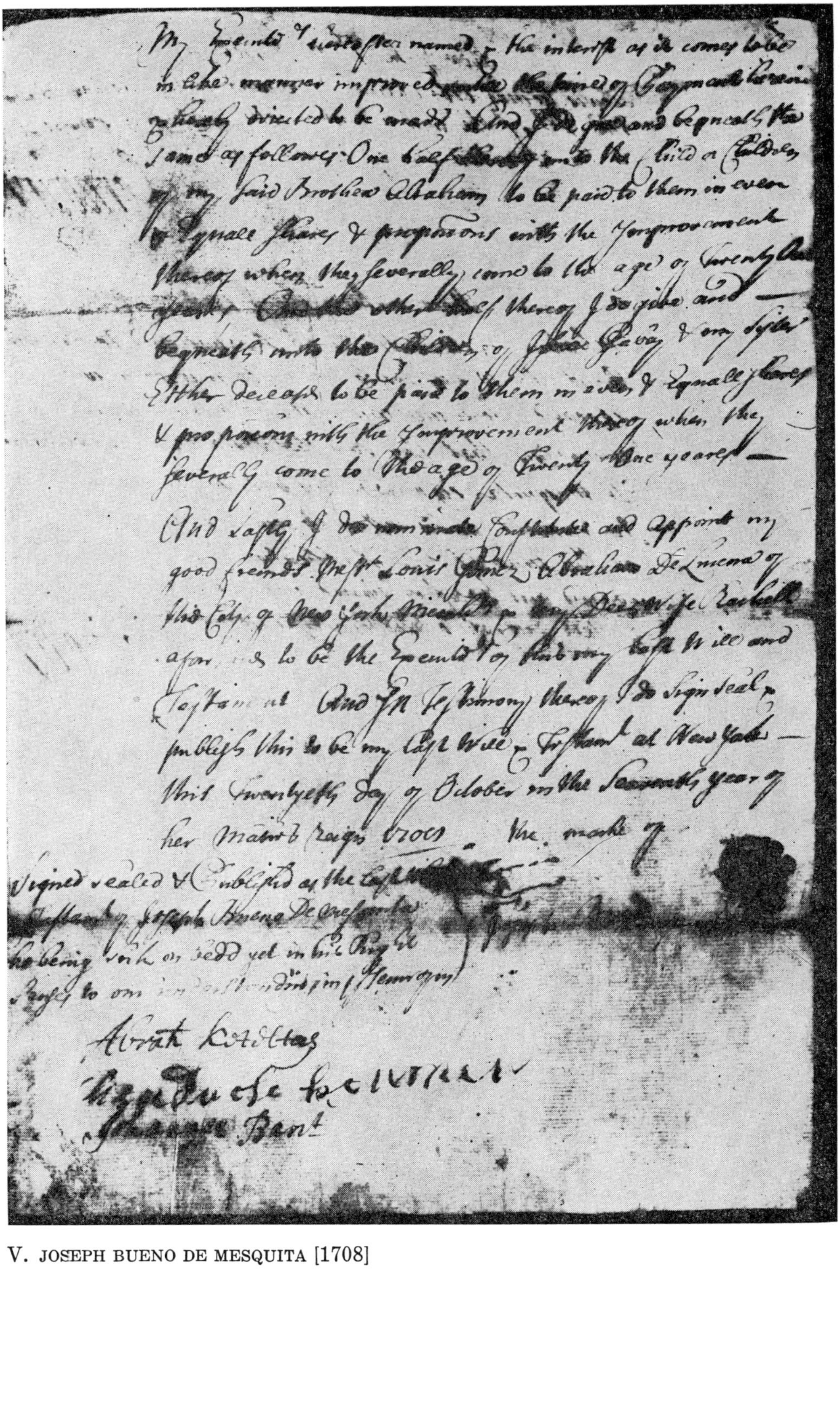

my Executors hereafter named & the interest as it comes to be
in like manner improved under the kind of Payment herein
particularly directed to be made And I do give and bequeath the
same as followes One half thereof unto the Child or Children
of my said Brother Abraham to be paid to them in even
& Equall shares & proportions with the Improvement
thereof when they severally come to the age of twenty one
years, And the other half thereof I do give and
bequeath unto the Children of Isaac Pavia & my Sister
Esther deceased to be paid to them in even & Equall shares
& proportions with the Improvement thereof when they
severally come to the age of Twenty one years —
And Lastly I do nominate Constitute and appoint my
good friends Messrs Louis Gomez Abraham De Lucena of
this City of New York Merchants & my Dear Wife Rachell
aforesd to be the Executors of this my Last Will and
Testament And In Testimony thereof I do Sign seal &
publish this to be my Last Will & Testament at New York —
this twentyeth day of October in the Seaventh year of
her Majties Reign 1708 the marke of [illegible]

Signed sealed & Published as the Last Will &
Testament of Joseph Bueno De Mesquita
he being sick in bedd yet in his Right
Senses to our understanding in [illegible]

Abrah Keteltas
[illegible] De Kermer?
Johannes Bant

V. JOSEPH BUENO DE MESQUITA [1708]

VI

ISAAC PINHEIRO[1]

[1710]

In The Name Of God Amen

[Probated in] Nevis

I ISAAC PINHEIRO of ye Nation of Jews Merchant being Sick & Weak of Body, but of Sound, & perfect Memory, prayse be therefore given to Allmighty God, Doe make, & Ordaine, this my Last Will and Testament first & principally, I Commend my Soul to Allmighty God my Creatour & Redeamer, hoping through his Aboundant Mercyes to Obtain pardon & forgiveness of all my Sins, my Body I Comitt to the Earth, to be Interred in the Buriall place belonging to the Jewish Nation, of ye Island of Nevis aforesaid, after their rites & Ceremonies, & for what Temporall Estate, God of his goodness hath bestowed on me (my Funerall Expenses, & Debts being first payd, & Discharged) I Give Devise & Bequeath ye same as followeth:

Imprimis

I Give & Bequeath unto my Son JACOB PINHEIRO, the Sume of two hundred & fifty pounds Currant money of this Island to be paid unto him when he shall arive, to ye age of Twenty One years.

Item

I Give & Bequeath unto my Said Son, JACOB PINHEIRO, A Negro Boy Named ANDOVER, to be Delivered unto him when he shall arrive to the Age aforesaid.

Item

I Give & Bequeath unto my said son JACOB PINHEIRO, one Sorral horse (on which he Commonly rides) with one paire of pistolls, with a Saddle, holsters & other furniture, to the same belonging, to be delivered unto him Immediately after my Decease.

Item

I Give & Bequeath unto my Son MOSES PINHEIRO, one hundred pounds Currant Money of this Island — together wth. one Negro boy, named

[1] Original Will no. 500; *NYHSC*, vol. XI (1902), pp. 1–3. Isaac Pinheiro, a prominent merchant died in New York on February 17, 1710. He had been made freeman of New York on February 2, 1695. *Portraits*, pp. 453–454. This will proved in Nevis was also probated in New York, probably because he had property and assets here. Letters of Administration were granted to Lancaster Symes, John Cholwell, and Isaac Gabay in February, 1710. Pinheiro, was mistakenly mentioned as having died intestate. *Portraits*, p. 454; *NYHSC*, vol. II (1894), p. 38. Symes and Cholwell filed the Inventory of Pinheiro's estate showing a value of £596.04.7½, HDC.

SHARLOW to be delivered unto him, when he Shall Arrive to the Age of Eighteen Years.

Item

I Give & Bequeath unto my Daughter SARAH PINHEIRO, Five hundred pounds Sterling Money to be paid unto her, at the Day of her Marriage.

Item

I Give & Bequeath unto my daughter REBEKAH PINHEIRO, the Sume of Five hundred Pounds Sterling Money to paid unto her, at the Day of her Marriage.

Item

I Give & Bequeath unto my Daughter JUDITH PINHEIRO, the Sume of Five hundred pounds Sterling money to be paid unto her, at her Day of Marriage.

Item

I Give & Bequeath, unto my Dear & Honoured Father ABRAHAM PINHEIRO of the Citty of Amsterdam the Sume of Thirty pounds Sterling Money to be paid unto him Annually Dureing his naturall Life, AND after the Decease of my said Father, I Give & Bequeath, unto my Dear Mother in law RACHEL PINHEIRO, the Sume of Thirty pounds Sterling to be paid unto her Annually During her Naturall Life,

Item

I Give & Bequeath unto my Loving Sister SARAH DAGAMA wife of DAGAMA of Corasoe, One hundred Pieces of Eight to be paid unto her in three Moneths after my Decease.

Item

I Give & Bequeath, unto my Loving Sister RACHEL PINHEIRO, now living in the Citty of Amsterdam the Sume of thirty pounds Sterling Money to be paid unto her in twelve Moneth, after my Decease.

Item

I Give Devise & Bequeath unto my aforesaid sons, JACOB PINHEIRO & MOSES PINHEIRO & to their heirs, for ever share & share alike, when my Said Son Moses, shall arrive by ye Age of Eighteen years, a Certain plantation or parcell of Land by Me lately bought & purchased of GEORGE BROWNE and FRANCES BROWNE his Wife & SARAH MADRIN, being part of the plantation formerly THOMAS MADRINE.

Item

I Give & Bequeath unto my said sons JACOB PINHEIRO & MOSES PINHEIRO & to their heirs for Ever share & share alike when my Said son MOSES shall arrive by ye age of Eighteen years one Case Mill which is now standing & being on ye plantation by me Leased of WILLIAM & RICHARD BOWRY together with ye following Negros (viz.) TOM, MINGO,

PIERO, VENTURA, TOBY, PETER, MANUEL, BASTIANO,[2] WILL, JACK, CATTOC, LEWISA, BLACK SARAH & MARIA together wth. one stile & Worm.[3]

Item

It is my Express Will that if JACOB LATTUR & MARY LATTUR his wife now Living in South Carolina doe Sell & Dispose of her the said MARY, her plantation or parsell of Land, in this Island that my Executrix hereafter Named Doe purchase the same for & to the only use and behoofe of my Said Sons, JACOB PINHEIRO & MOSES PINHEIRO & their heirs Share & Share alike To be delivered unto them when the Said MOSES shall Arrive to ye Age of Eighteen years, It is also my Express Will that if any of the land which is near or joyning with the aforesaid plantation be Exposed to Sale, that my Said Executrix doe purchase the same for the only use & behoofe of my aforesaid Sons in Manner as aforesaid, *And* whereas by a Certain Deed of Gift (Some years past) I have & bestowed to my sons ABRAHAM PINHEIRO (who is Since Deceased) and the aforesaid JACOB PINHEIRO Seven Negros three whereof are Dead & Lost by the late French Invasion on this Island & the other four Namely WILL, SHARLOW, DOGGU & FANSHOW, are now in my possession, It is my Express Will, that if my said Son JACOB or any other person, by or under him, shall at any time hereafter, Claim, Demand or any wise Disturbe my Executrix hereafter Named, her heirs etc. from the Quiet peaceable possession & enjoyment of the Said Negros, WILL, SHARLOW, DOGGU, and FANSHOW, then in Such Case the Two hundred & Fifty pounds Currant Money, by me hereby Given & Bequeathed unto him my Said Son JACOB, I Give & Bequeath unto Dear and Loving Wife ESTHER PINHEIRO my Executrix hereafter Named to be at her Disposall & he my Said Son to be ever barrd of the same

Item

It is also my Express Will that my Dear & Loving Wife ESTHER PINHEIRO shall possess & enjoy the before mentioned plantation or parcell of Land, Negros, Mill Stile & Worm, by me Given Devised & Bequeathed to my said Sons JACOB PINHEIRO & MOSES PINHEIRO, & that the Issues & profits thereby arising or accruing to be at her own Disposall & not to be anywise accomptable for the same to any person or persons whatsoever, untill my said son MOSES shall arrive to the age of Eighteen years.

Item

I Give Devise & Bequeath unto my said Dear & Loving Wife ESTHER PINHEIRO & to her heirs forever all the Houses and Land that I am now possessed of & of right belongs unto me in Charles Towne in this Island or Else where (allwayse Excepting the Land by me hereof Devised to my said Sons) *Item* I Give & Bequeath unto my said Dear & Loving Wife

[2] In 1707, Esther, Isaac's wife, purchased a Negro woman named Bastiana. *Portraits*, p. 454.

[3] A still and worm are parts of a distillery.

ESTHER PINHEIRO all the Rest & Residue of my Estate be the Same of what Nature or Quality foever in this Island or Elsewhere.

Item

It is my Express Will that if my Said Dear & Loving Wife Should Die Intestate or before she hath Disposed or Sold what I have hereby given Devised & Bequeathed unto her, then & in such Case the same shall redound & properly belong unto my aforesaid Sons & Daughters to be Divided among them share & sharle a Like, It is my Will & Desire that if my said Daughters should happen to be unmarried at the Decease of my said Wife that then & in Such Case they be Imediately sent to Corasoe to my aforesaid Sister SARAH DAGAMA to live with her, & what part of my Estate shall fall or redound to them to be Sent with them, & then my aforesaid Brother in Law ISAAC DAGAMA to take upon him the Guardianships over my said Daughters.

Lastly I doe hereby Nominate & appoint my said Dear & Loving Wife ESTHER PINHEIRO, my whole & sole Executrix of this my Last Will & Testament, Requesting & Impowering my Loving Friends Capt. SAMUEL CLARKE FIGTREE, Gent. and SOLOMON ISRAEL, Merchant to be Trustees and Overseers of this my Will, to Each of them I Give & Bequeath, Tenn pounds Currant Money of this Island to be paid to them Immediately after my Decease to buy them a Mourning Sute hereby revokeing making. Null & Voyd all Wills by me heretofore made & this to be my Last Will & Testament *In Witness* whereof I the said ISAAC PINHEIRO, have hereunto set my hand & Seal this Twelfth day of November in the Seventh year of our Sovereign Lady Anne by the Grace of God of Great Britain France & Ireland etc. one thousand Seven hundred & Eight.

Signed Sealed Published & Declared
to be his Last Will & Testament, in
the presence of us whose Names are
hereunder written

ISAAC PINHEIRO

EVAN DAVIS
JOHN HILTON
JOHN CARPINTER
GIDEON DEVREDE

Nevis *By the Honourable* WALTER HAMILTON ESQ.
Lieutenant Governour, Etc.

Personally Appeared before my Messrs. EVAN DAVIS & JOHN HILTON (both of full age) who made oath upon the Holy Evangelists of Allmighty God that they did see the within named ISAAC PINHEIRO Signe Seal Publish & Declear the within Instrument of Writing to be his Last Will & Testament, and that he was at the Same time in perfect sence & Memory to the best of their knowledges & Judgments, And those Deponants further Declears that they see Mssrs. JOHN CARPENTER & GIDEON DEVREDE Signe to the same as Witnesses, and Further Saith not.

Sworne before me the 12th Day
of April 1710

s/ WALTER HAMILTON

Nevis Copia Vera Recorded
1710
13th Day of April
s/ MICHAEL NOWELL Secry.

Nevis

To All to Whome These presents shall come, I WALTER HAMILTON Esq. Lieut. Governeur etc. of the Island aforesaid Send Greeting *Know* yee that on the day of the Date hereof personally appeared before me MICHAEL NOWELL of this Island Secretary and Did by solemn oath which he took on the Holy Evangelists of Allmighty God, solemnly Declare, Testife, Depose that the foregoing will (& Probate) of ISAAC PINHEIRO is a true & exact Coppy taken from the books of records of the said Island for Inhabitants etc. *No. B.* Pages One hundred Eighty Eight to one Hundred Ninety three. In Testimony whereof I have hereunto Sett my hand Affixed my Seal te Eighteenth Daye of April in the year of our Lord one thousand Seven Hundred & Tenn & in the ninth year of her Majesties Reigne.

s/ W. HAMILTON

To All to whome these presents Shall Come I ESTER PINHEIRO of the Island of Nevis doe Send Greeting that whereas my Late Husband ISAAC PINHEIRO Merchant Deceased Did make his Last will and Testament in writeing bearing Date the Twelfth Day of November in the yeare of our Lord one Thousand Seaven hundred and Eight and therefore did make and Constitute me whole and sole Executrix as by a true Coppy of the Said Will attested by the Honourable WALTER HAMILTON Esq. Lieut. Governour of the said Island and hereunto annexed if doth and may more fully and at Large appeare, And whereas my Said late husband after the makeing of his Said last will and Testament (to witt) the Seaventeenth Day of February now last past att the Citty of New York departed this Life leaving behind him Divers goods, Merchandizes, wares, ready monies Debts due by bond, Note under hand or Simple Contract and Divers other Goods and Chattles as well in the hands possession and Keeping of as alsoe owing unto him the said ISAAC PINHEIRO by and from severall persons in the said Citty of New York and places thereunto adjacent *Now Know Ye* That I the said ESTER PINHEIRO in my Capacity aforesaid have Constituted, Nominated appointed made and putt and by these presents Doe Constitute Nominate appoint and in my place and stead putt my Trusty friends RIP VAN DAM, and LUIS GOMEZ of the said Citty of New York, Merchants. They and every of them Jointly and severally to be my true and Lawfull attorneys and attorney for me and in my name and to my proper use and behoofe to ask, demand, sue for Levy,

Recover, Receive and Take all Such Sume or Sumes of moneys goods, wares, merchandizes, Debts, dues accounts and other demands whatsoever which my Said late husband ISAAC PINHEIRO was possessed of Interested in and intitled unto [ ] in the hands of or due and owing unto him at the time of his Decease from any person or persons whatsoever in the Said Citty of New York or any other parts thereunto adjacent giving and alsoe granting by these presents unto my Said Attornies Jointly or to any one of them by himself my Full and obsolute power and authority in and about the premises to have use and take all Lawfull wayes and Means in my name for the Recovery thereof and of every part and parcell thereof and upon Receipt of any such Sume or Sumes of money Debts Dues wares or other goods and Chattles as aforesaid acquittances or Sufficient Discharges for me and in my name to make Seale Subscribe and Deliver and Generally all and every other act and acts, thing and things Device and Devices in the Law whatsoever Need full and Necessary to be done in the premises for the Recovery of all or any Such Sume or Sumes of money, Debts, Dues, wares, and other goods as aforesaid for me and in my name to Doe, execute, and performe as fully largely and amply to all Intents and purposes as I my Selfe might or Could Doe if there personally present or as if the matter Required more Speciall Authority then is hereby given and Attorneys one or more under them to make and Constitute and againe at pleasure to Revoke Ratifying Allowing and holding firme and Effectual all and whatsoever my said Attorneys or any of them Shall lawfully doe or Cause or procure to be done in and about the premises by Virtue of these presents *In Witnesses* whereof I have hereunto sett my hand seale this *Nineteenth* Day of Aprill in the Ninth yeare of the Reign of her Majesties ANNE by the grace of God of great Brittaine France and Ireland Queen Defender of the Faith etc. and in the yeare of our Lord according to the Computation of the Church of England 1710

s/ ESTER PINHEIRO [seal]

Signed Sealed and Delivered
in the presence of us

Boston in New England
5th June 1710

s/ JOHN WOODLEY
s/ JNO. THATCHER

JOHN WOODLEY and JOHN THATCHER whose names are subscribed as Witnesses to this Instrument or power of Attorney personally appearing before me One of Her Majesty's Justices of the Peace Made Oath that they Saw the within named ESTHER PINHEIRO Signe Seal and deliver the same as her Act and Deed to the use therein mentioned and that they the Deponents Set to their Names as Witnesses of the Execution thereof.

Jurat cor. s/ JS ADDINGTON J. Pac.

VII

SAMUEL LEVY[1]

[1719]

In The Name of God Amen, I SAMUELL LEVY of the City of New York Merchant being Sick and weake in body but of Sound mind memory and under standing (by Gods blessing) Doe make this my Last will and Testament (hereby Revokeing all former Wills by me heretofore made) in manner following *Imprimis* I recommend my Soul to God Almighty my Great Creator and my body to the Earth to be Buryed in Such Decent manner as my Executors hereafter named Shall think fitt, And as to what temporall Estate it hath pleased God to Bless me with I Give and Bequeath the Same as followeth, In the First place, I will and Desire that all Such Debts as I Shall owe in right or Conscience to any person or persons whatsoever either in New York London or Elsewhere be fully Satisfyed Contented and paid by my Executors hereinafter named as Soon as possibly they Can after my Decease. *Item* I Give and Bequeath unto my Dearly beloved wife RACHELL LEVY[2] all my house hold Goods and Furniture belonging to my house and all my Linnen and plate, Excepting my Silver Tea Pott and One of my Silver Tankards which I give and bequeath to my beloved Daughter ABIGAL LEVY,[3] *Item* I Give and Bequeath unto MERIAM HART, my Brothers Daughter the now wife of MOSES HART of the City of New York, the Sume of Ten pounds to Buy a peice of plate in remembrance of me *Item* I Give and Bequeath unto my Mother in Law REBECCA ASHER One annuity or Yearely Sume of Ten pounds to be paid to her Yearely Dureing her natural Life out of my

[1] Original Will no. 588; Will Liber 9, p. 53; *NYHSC*, vol. II (1894), p. 189. Samuel Levy (d. May 5, 1719), brother of Moses Levy, was a New York merchant. At the time of Samuel's death, neither brother had much to do with each other. Financial difficulties and charges of fraud and deceit between the two led to years of court litigation and engendered bitter feelings. See *Moses Levy v. Isaac Levy, Nathan Simson, and Jacob Franks, as executors of the estate of Samuel Levy* (1722), Minutes of Chancery, vol. 1720–1748, p. 8, New York County Clerk's Office, 31 Chambers Street, New York City, as well as pp. 10–11, 21, 24, 25, 34, 37 and 41–43 of this volume. For legal involvement of Samuel Levy, see *Levy v. MacDonall* (1715), Mayor's Court Minutes, vol. 1715–1718, p. 28, New York County Clerk's Office, 31 Chambers Street, New York City [=MCM]. James Alexander who represented the Executors of Samuel Levy wrote of him as the "honestest jew that has been in this place and a man of the most Easy temper." James Alexander Papers, Box # 10, New-York Historical Society Library. See also *Portraits*, p. 193. The testator was constable of the North and Dock Wards. Minutes vol. III, pp. 186 and 204; vol. IV, pp. 346 and 351. An inventory of Samuel Levy's household goods divided by rooms is in the Nathan Simson Letter Books.

[2] Rachel Levy (d. October 22, 1732), *née* Rachel Asher, married Samuel Myers Cohen. Book of Deeds, no. 12, p. 356, Cohen to Franks, Oct. 17, 1732, Office of the Secretary of State, Albany, New York.

[3] Abigail (Bilah) Levy, aged 14 in 1732, was sent to her uncle Michael Asher of Boston who acted as her guardian. MCM, vol. 1731–1736, p. 188.

Estate by my Executors hereinafter named. It is my Will and Desire and I Doe Order and Direct my said Executors hereinafter named as Soon as conveniently may be after my all Debts are fully paid and Satisfyed to Remitt and pay out of my Estate to my Brother JOSEPH LEVY and his Son ISAAC LEVY of London Merchants or the Survivors of them the Sume of Two Hundred pounds current money of New York to be Disposed of and Distributed by my Said Brother and his Said Son or the Survivour of them unto and amongst Such of my own poor relations Liveing in Germany as they in their Discretion shall thinke fitt, And after payment of all my Just Debts Legacies and Funerall Charges I Give and Bequeath all the rest residue and remainder of all my Goods Chattells rights Creditts and Estates whatsoever unto my said wife RACHELL and Daughter ABIGALL to be Equally Divided betweene them Share and Share alike The Share of my Said Daughter to be paid to her when She Shall attaine the Age of Twenty One Years or be marryed which, Shall first happen And that in the meane time and untill She Shall Attaine the Said Age or be Marryed as aforesaid my Will is that my Said Child Shall be brought up Educated and maintained by my Said wife out of the Income profitt and benifitt of my whole Estate And to that End it is my further will and Desire that the Share of my Said Estate Soe Bequeathed to my Said Daughter as aforesaid — Imediately after my Death or as Soon after as Conveniently may be, Shall be putt out to Interest by my Executors hereinafter named or be by them otherwise Disposed of to the best benifitt and advantage of my Said Daughter as my Said Executors in their Discretion Shall think fitt And my further Will and meaneing is that in Case my Said Daughter shall happen to Dye before she shall attaine the age of One and Twenty Yeares or be Marryed as aforesaid That then I Doe here by give and bequeath One Equal halfe of the Said Share of my Estate Soe given and bequeathed to my Said Daughter as aforesaid unto my Said wife RACHELL her Executors Administrators and Assignes and the other halfe thereof I Doe hereby Desire and Direct may be likewise remitted and paid by my said Exectors to my Said Brother JOSEPH LEVY and ISAAC LEVY or the Survivour of them or to the the Executors of the Survivour of them to be by them Disposed of and Distributed to and amongst Such of my own poore relations Liveing in Germany as aforesaid as they in their Discretion Shall think fitt and it is my will and Desire that my Share and interest in the pinck Charlott[4] and Sloop Abigall[5] of New York be imediately after my Decease Sold and Disposed of to the best Advantage by my Said Executors or Such of them as live in New York the better to Enable them to perform this my will And Doe hereby Nominate and appoint my Said

[4] The forty ton *Charlotte* was owned also by Henry Cuyler, Moses Levy, Jacob Franks, and Nathan Simson. See Entry of June 23, 1720, Naval Office Lists, CO 5/1222, Public Records Office, London [=NOL].

[5] The twenty ton *Abigail* was also owned by Moses Levy and Jacob Franks, as well as Jacobus Van Cortlandt and Adolph Philipse. As an example of this vessel's activities, see NOL, CO 5/1222, April 14, 1720.

Loveing kinsman ISAAC LEVY Son of my Said Brother JOSEPH LEVY and my Loveing Kinsmen NATHAN SIMPSON and JACOB FRANCKS[6] of the City of New York Merchants Executors of this my Last Will and Testament Desireing that the said NATHAN SIMPSON and JACOB FRANCKS Imediately after my Decease in the presence of my Said wife Doe Seale up all my Letters and Copy Book of Letters without Inspecting into the Same and forthwith Send and Transmitt them to my Said kinsman ISAAC LEVY at London *In Witness* whereof I have hereunto Sett my hand and Seale this Twenty Eighth Day of Aprill in the Fifth Yeare of the reigne of our Soveraigne Lord GEORGE by the grace of God of Great Brittaine France and Ireland King Defender of the Faith, etc. Anno Dom 1719.

s/ SAMUELL LEVY [seal]

Signed Sealed published and
Declared in the presence of us
who Subscribed our names in
the presence of the said
SAMUELL LEVY
s/ JOSEPH ISAAC[7]
s/ MORD. GOMES
s/ H. WILEMAN[8]

Memorandum that on the twenty first day of May 1719 JOSEPH ISAAC and MORDECAI GOMEZ two of the Subscribing witnesses to the within will appeared before me who being Jews were duly Sworn upon the five books of Moses & upon their oath did Declare that they saw SAMUEL LEVY deceased publish and Declare the within to be his Last will and Testament and that at the time thereof he was of Sound and Disposing mind & memory to the best of their knowledge and that they saw HENRY WILEMAN with them & each other Subscribe as witnesses to the Same in presence of the Testator.

s/ RO. HUNTER[9]

Memorandum that on the twenty first day of May 1719 the within NATHAN SIMPSON and JACOB FRANCKS took the oath of Executors of the within will & did Declare that the other Executor within named was beyond Seas to the best of their knowledge.

s/ RO. HUNTER

[6] Jacob Franks (1688–1769) had an extensive career as a merchant and was made freeman of New York on August 21, 1711. He was interested in communal affairs serving in many offices of the Congregation Shearith Israel. He was the synagogue's president in 1729. Highly respected by the community, he was often a witness or named executor. *Burghers*, p. 90; *Portraits*, 14–15, 17, 23 and 26, *passim*.

[7] Possibly the Joseph Isaacs identified as a butcher and made freeman of New York City on August 23, 1698. *Burghers*, p. 65.

[8] Henry Wileman was granted a license as an attorney at law on November 15, 1709 and was named coroner in 1721. *Calendar*, pp. 15 and 19.

[9] Robert Hunter, Governor of New York, 1710 to 1719.

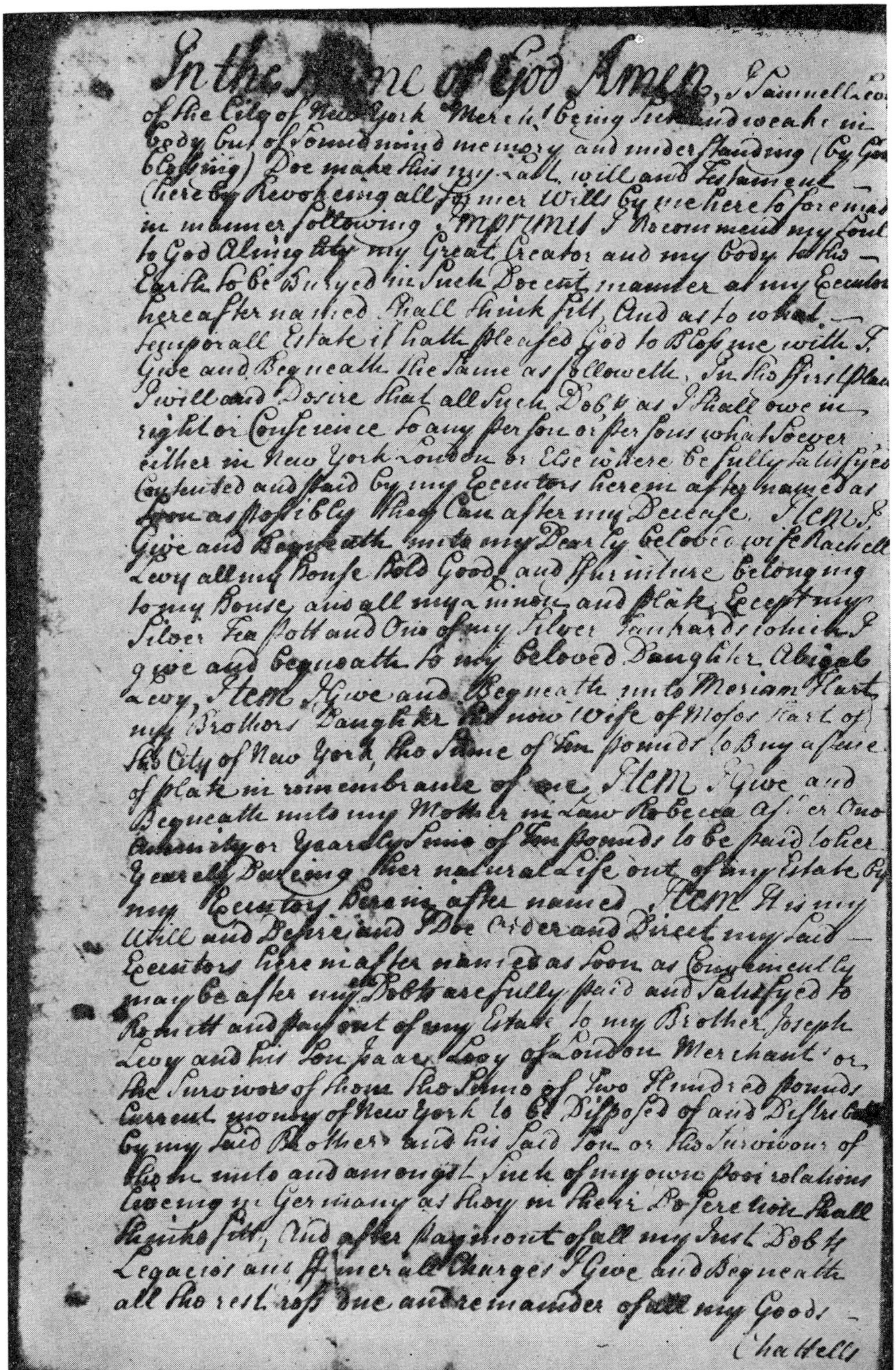
In the Name of God Amen, I Samuell Le[illegible]
of the City of New York Merch[t] being Sick and weake in
body but of Sound mind memory and understanding (by Gods
blessing) Doe make this my Last will and Testament
(hereby Revokeing all former Wills by me here to fore made)
in manner following Imprimis I Recommend my Soul
to God Almighty my Great Creator and my body to the
Earth to be Buryed in Such Decent manner as my Executors
hereafter named Shall think fitt, And as to what
temporall Estate it hath pleased God to Bless me with I
Give and Bequeath the Same as followeth, In the ffirst Place
I will and Desire that all Such Debts as I Shall owe in
right or Conscience to any person or persons whatsoever
either in New York London or Else where be fully satisfyed
Contented and paid by my Executors herein after named as
soon as possibly they Can after my Decease. Item I
Give and Bequeath unto my Dearly beloved wife Rachell
Levy all my House hold Goods and ffurniture belonging
to my House and all my [illegible] and plate Except my
Silver Tea pott and One of my Silver Tankards which I
give and bequeath to my beloved Daughter Abigail
Levy, Item I Give and Bequeath unto Meriam Hart
my Brothers Daughter [illegible] now Wife of Moses Hart of
the City of New York, the Sume of Ten pounds to Buy a peice
of plate in remembrance of me, Item I Give and
Bequeath unto my Mother in Law Rebecca After One
Annuity or Yearly Sume of Ten pounds to be paid to her
Yearly Dureing her natural Life out of my Estate by
my Executors herein after named Item It is my
Will and Desire and I Doe Order and Direct my said
Executors here in after named as soon as Conveniently
may be after my Debts are fully paid and Satisfyed to
Remitt and pay out of my Estate to my Brother Joseph
Levy and his Son Isaac Levy of London Merchants or
the Survivors of them the Sume of Two Hundred pounds
Current money of New York to be Disposed of and Distributed
by my said Brother and his said Son or the Survivour of
them unto and amongst Such of my owne poor relations
liveing in Germany as they in their Discretion shall
thinke fitt, And after payment of all my Just Debts
Legacies and ffunerall Charges I Give and Bequeath
all the rest residue and remainder of all my Goods
Chattells

VII. SAMUEL LEVY [1719]

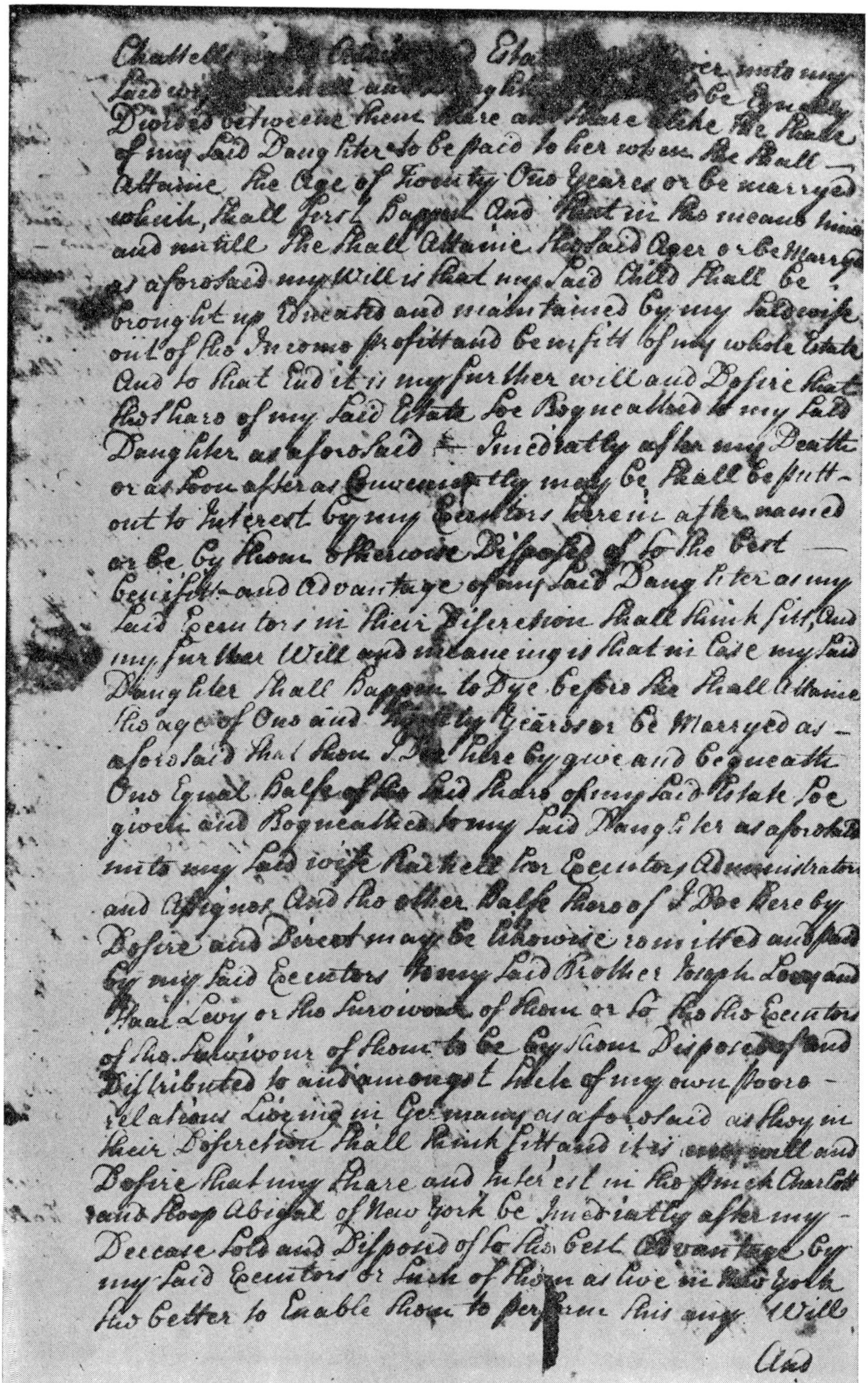

Chattells [illegible] Estate [illegible] unto my
Said wife [illegible] to be Equally
Divided betweene them share and share alike the Share
of my Said Daughter to be paid to her when she Shall
attaine the Age of Twenty One Yeares or be marryed
which Shall first happen And that in the meane time
and untill She Shall attaine the Said Age or be Marryed
as aforesaid my Will is that my Said Child Shall be
brought up Educated and maintained by my Said wife
out of the Income profitt and benefitt of my whole Estate
And to that End it is my further will and Desire that
the Share of my Said Estate bequeathed to my Said
Daughter as aforesaid Imediatly after my Death
or as soon after as Conveniently may be shall be putt
out to Interest by my Executors herein after named
or be by them otherwise Disposed of to the best
benefitt and Advantage of my Said Daughter as my
Said Executors in their Discretion Shall think fitt, And
my further Will and meaneing is that in Case my Said
Daughter Shall happen to Dye before she Shall Attaine
the age of One and Twenty Yeares or be Marryed as
aforesaid that then I Doe hereby give and bequeath
One Equal halfe of the Said Share of my Said Estate Soe
given and bequeathed to my Said Daughter as aforesaid
unto my Said wife Rachell her Executors Administrators
and Assignes And the other halfe thereof I Doe hereby
Desire and Direct may be likewise remitted and paid
by my Said Executors to my Said Brother Joseph Levy and
[illegible] Levy or the Survivour of them or to the Executors
of the Survivour of them to be by them Disposed of and
Distributed to and amongst Such of my own poore
relations Living in Germany as aforesaid as they in
their Discretion Shall think fitt and it is my will and
Desire that my Share and Interest in the Sloop Charlott
and Sloop Abigail of New York be Imediatly after my
Decease Sold and Disposed of to the best Advantage by
my Said Executors or Such of them as live in New York
the better to Enable them to perform this my Will
And

VII. SAMUEL LEVY [1719]

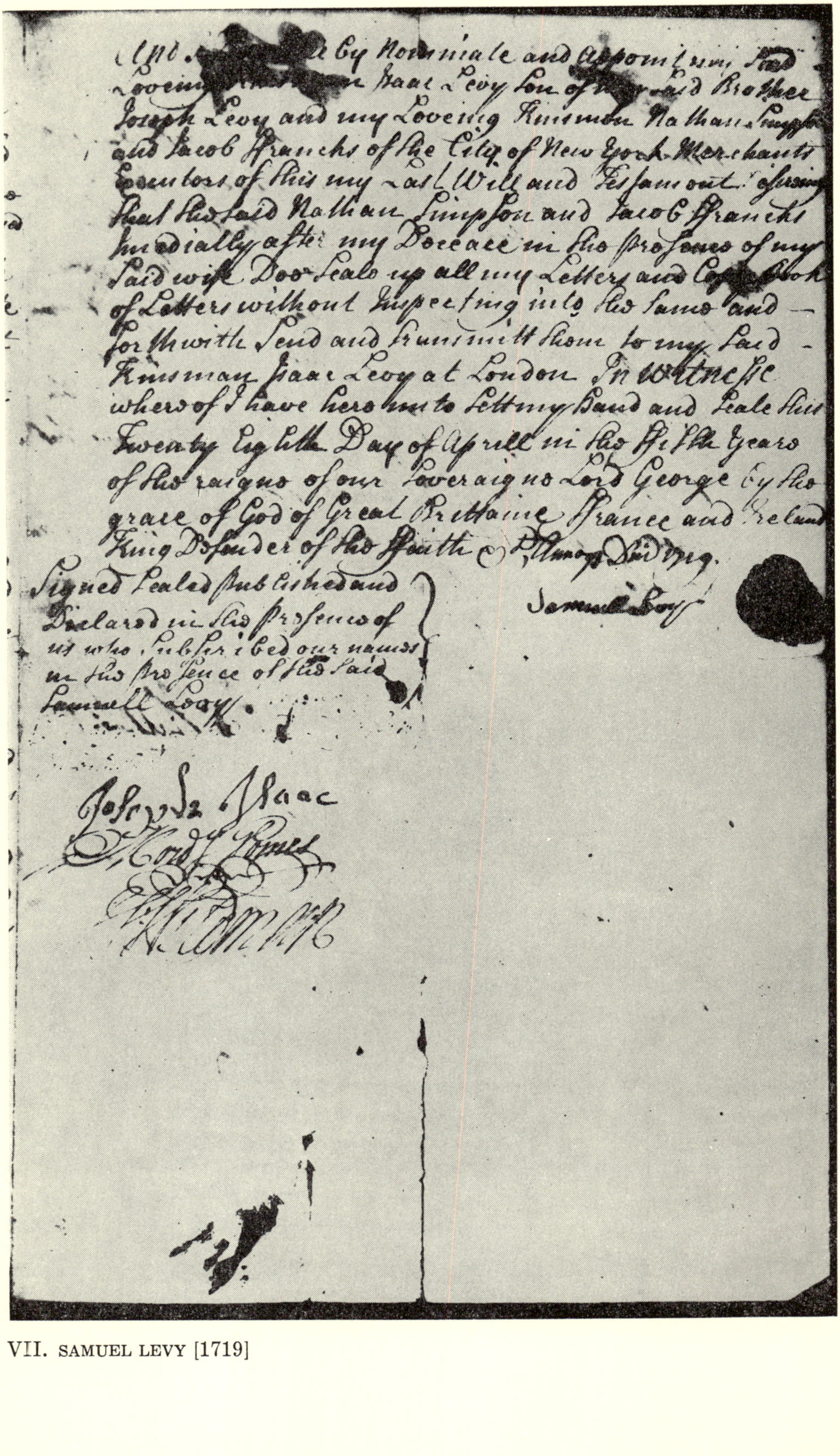
[illegible] by Nominate and Appoint my Said
Loving [illegible] Isaac Levy Son of my Said Brother
Joseph Levy and my Loving Kinsman Nathan Simpson
and Jacob Franks of the City of New York Merchants
Executors of this my Last Will and Testament desiring
that the Said Nathan Simpson and Jacob Franks
Imediately after my Decease in the presence of my
Said wife Doe Seale up all my Letters and Copy Book
of Letters without Inspecting into the Same and —
forthwith Send and transmitt them to my Said —
Kinsman Isaac Levy at London In Witness
whereof I have hereunto Sett my hand and Seale this
Twenty Eighth Day of Aprill in the ffifth yeare
of the raigne of our Soveraigne Lord George by the
grace of God of Great Brittaine France and Ireland
King Defender of the ffaith &c Annoq Dom 1719.

Samuel Levy

Signed Sealed Published and
Declared in the presence of
us who Subscribed our names
in the presence of the Said
Samuell Levy

Joseph Isaac
Mord Gomes
[illegible]

VII. SAMUEL LEVY [1719]

VIII

Abraham De Lucena[1]

[1725]

In the Name of God Amen

I Abraham De Lucena of New York Merchant (by Gods Grace) proceeding upon A Voyage to Jamaica Considering the Dangers of the Sea And the Uncertainty of this Mortal Life Do my Last Will and Testament as followeth Vizt.

Imprimis

I bequeath my Immortal Soul into the hands of the Almighty God of Israel My Creator Trusting in his Mercy for pardon of All my Sins and hoping for A Joyful resurr[ection] to Life Eternal *And* as touching my Worldy Estate I Give Bequeath Devise Dispose of the Same in manner and form following That is to Say After all my [lawful] and just debts be paid And Satisfied my Will and Desire is That all my Estate Real and personal be Divided into Six Equal parts Shares or proportions; One Sixth part or Share whereof I Give and Bequeath unto my Loving Wife Rachel De Lucena for and During the Term of her Natural Life and at her Decease to be Equally Divided Amongst All or those of my Children that Shall be then Living *Item* I Give and Bequeath unto my Son Moses De Lucena[2] his heirs and assigns for Ever one other Sixth part or share thereof *Item* I Give and Bequeath unto my son Samuel De Lucena[3] his heirs and assigns for Ever one other Equal Sixth part or Share thereof *Item* I give unto my Daughter Hester her heirs and assigns for Ever one other other Sixth part or share thereof *Item* I give and Bequeath unto my Daughter Judith her heirs and assigns for Ever One other equal Sixth part or Share thereof *Item* I give and Bequeath unto my Daughter

[1] Original Will no. 725; Will Liber 10, p. 73; *NYHSC*, vol. II (1894), p. 319. Abraham De Lucena was made freeman of New York on July 6, 1708. *Burghers*, p. 88. A prominent merchant of the city, he was also minister of Shearith Israel. *PAJHS*, vol. VI (1897), p. 126. De Lucena frequently appeared in court, generally as plaintiff in cases of debt. For example, see *De Lucena v. Boston* (1699), MCM, vol. 1695–1704, pp. 115–116, 125, 127 and 130; *De Lucena v. Smit* (1704), MCM, vol. 1704–1710, pp. 20–21 and 31–33. In this latter case De Lucena won a suit for payment of six half barrels of Jewish beef. *De Lucena v. Abigail Brown, executor of the estate of Esther Brown* (1708), MCM, vol. 1704–1710, pp. 346, 350 and 355–356; *De Lucena v. Noble* (1716), MCP, file 1676–1710, July 20, 1716. Lucena died August 4, 1725. For general background, see *Portraits*, pp. 456–459. At the time of his death he resided in the South Ward. NYAL, March 2, 1725. His wife continued to reside there after his death. *Ibid.*, March 1, 1726.

[2] Moses De Lucena was born October 30, 1723. *Portraits*, p. 458.

[3] Possibly the Samuel De Lucena made freeman of New York on July 3, 1759. *Burghers*, p. 193.

REBECCA[4] one other Equal Sixth part or share thereof to her, her heirs & assigns for Ever *And Lastly* my Will and Desire is that in Case any or either of my Said Children Shall happen to Die before his, her or their age of one and twenty years, or before Receiving their said Sixth part That then the said part or parts of him her or thems so Dying shall be Equally Divided amongst the Survivors of them And I do hereby Nominate and Appoint my said Loving wife RACHEL DE LUCENA Executrix of my Last Will and testament and [ ] revoke all former Wills by me at any time heretofore made and declare this to be my Last Will and Testament *In Testimony* Whereof I have hereunto Set my hand and Seal at New York this twelfth day of February the third year of the Reign of King GEORGE of Great Britain anno domino 1716.

s/ ABRAHAM DE LUCENA

Signed Sealed published and
Delivered in the presence
s/ J. V. CORTLANDT[5]
s/ PHILLIP FRENCH[6]
s/ FREDERICK VAN CORTLANDT[7]

[seal]

New York September 2 1725

There personally appeared before me WILLIAM BURNET Esqure[8] Captain General and Governour in Chief of the Province of New York etc. JACOBUS VAN CORTLANDT and FREDERICK VAN CORTLANDT two of the subscribing Witnesses to the [ ] will of ABRAHAM DE LUCENA and made Oath on the Holy Evangelists of Almighty God that they Saw the said ABRAHAM DE LUCENA Sign Seal Publish and Declare the same to be his Last Will and Testament and that at the time thereof he was of sound disposing mind and memory to the best of their knowledge And that they likewise Saw PHILIP FRENCH sign as witness to the same in the presence of the testator.

s/ W. BURNET

Be it remembered at the same time RACHEL DE LUCENA the Executrix in the within written Will named took an Oath upon the five books of Moses for the execution and performance of the said Will.

s/ W. BURNET

[4] Rebecca became the second wife of Mordecai Gomez in 1741. See his Will, pp. 84–91.

[5] Jacobus Van Cortlandt, Mayor of New York during 1710–1711 and 1719–1720 and Alderman on numerous occasions, was a well known merchant. *Burgher*, pp. 90, 99 and 578–583.

[6] Philip French was a merchant and Mayor of New York in 1702. *Calendar*, p. 8.

[7] Frederick Van Cortlandt, son of Jacobus, is chiefly remembered for building his manor house in Van Cortlandt Park, Bronx, New York. Martha J. Lamb and Mrs. Burton Harrison, *History of the City of New York* (New York, 1896), vol. III, p. 807.

[8] William Burnet was appointed Governor of New York on June 24, 1720, and died in office September 7, 1729. *Ibid.*, vol. II, p. 525.

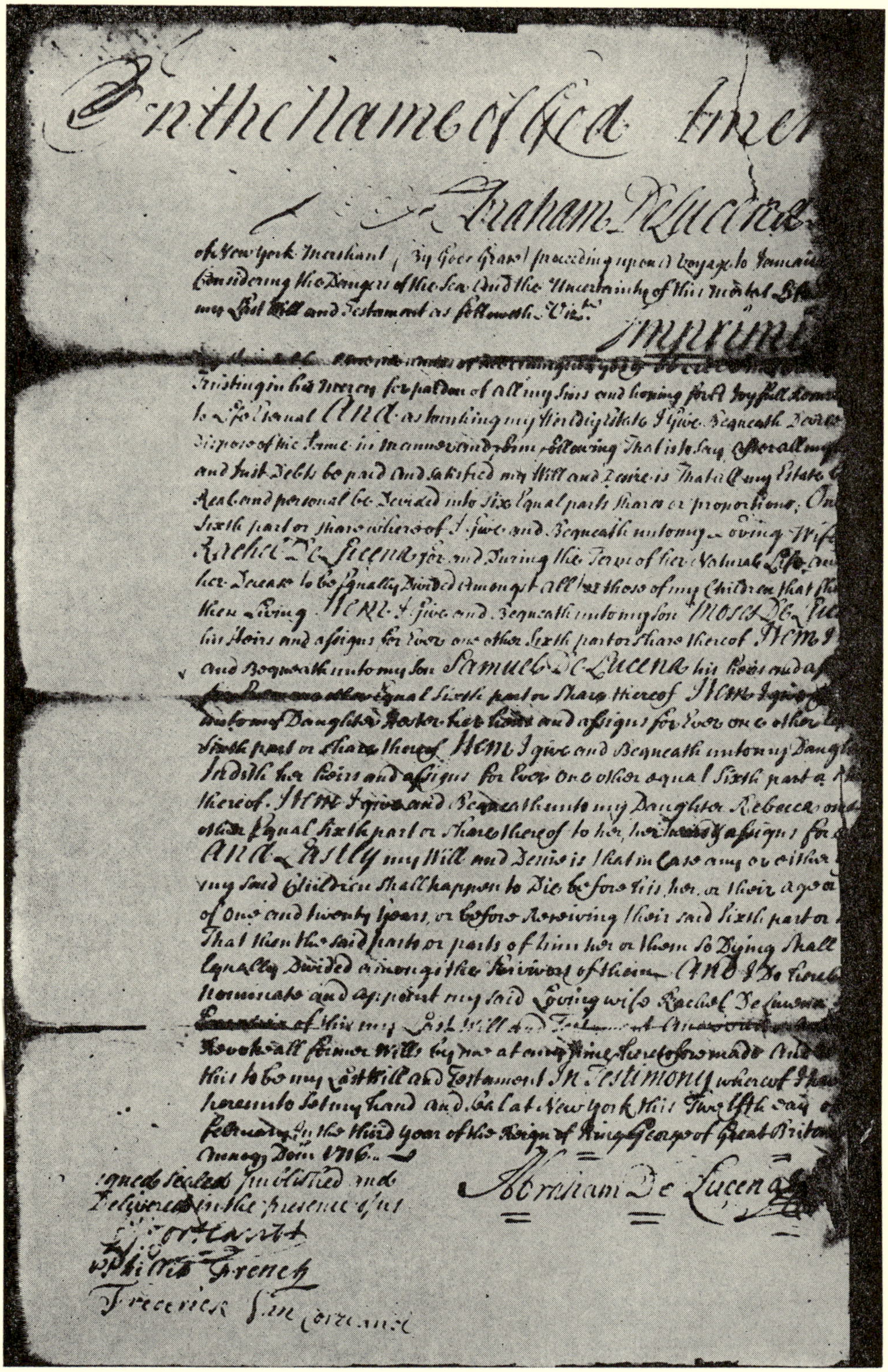

In the Name of God Amen

I Abraham De Lucena

of New York Merchant, By Gods Grace proceeding upon a Voyage to Jamaica [illegible] Considering the Danger of the Sea And the Uncertainty of this Mortal Life [illegible] my Last Will and Testament as followeth Viz:

Imprimis

[illegible] Trusting in his Mercy for pardon of all my Sins and hoping for a Joyfull [illegible] to Life Eternal And as touching my Worldly Estate I give Bequeath [illegible] dispose of the same in manner and form following That is to say after all my [illegible] and Just Debts be paid and satisfied my Will and Desire is That all my Estate [illegible] Real and personal be Devided into Six Equal parts Shares or proportions; One Sixth part or Share whereof I give and Bequeath unto my Loving Wife Rachel De Lucena for and During the Term of her Natural Life and [illegible] her Decease to be Equally Divided Amongst all or those of my Children that [illegible] then be Living Item I give and Bequeath unto my Son Moses De Lucena his Heirs and assigns for Ever one other Sixth part or Share thereof Item I [illegible] and Bequeath unto my Son Samuel De Lucena his Heirs and a[illegible] one other Equal Sixth part or Share thereof Item I give [illegible] unto my Daughter Hester her heirs and assigns for Ever one other [illegible] Sixth part or Share thereof Item I give and Bequeath unto my Daughter Judith her heirs and assigns for Ever one other equal Sixth part or Share thereof. Item I give and Bequeath unto my Daughter Rebecca one other Equal Sixth part or Share thereof to her, her heirs & assigns for [illegible] And Lastly my Will and Desire is That in Case any or either [illegible] my said Children shall happen to Die before his, her, or their age of One and twenty years, or before Receiving their said Sixth part or [illegible] That then the said part or parts of him her or them so Dying shall [illegible] Equally Divided amongst the Survivors of them And I Do hereby Nominate and appoint my said Loving wife Rachel De Lucena Executrix of this my Last Will and Testament [illegible] Revoke all former Wills by me at any time heretofore made And [illegible] this to be my Last Will and Testament In Testimony whereof I have hereunto set my hand and Seal at New York this Twelfth day of February in the Third year of the Reign of King George of Great Britain Annoq Dom 1716.

Abraham De Lucena

Signed Sealed Published and Delivered in the presence of us

[illegible]

Philip French

Frederick Van Cortlandt

VIII. ABRAHAM DE LUCENA [1725]

IX

MOSES LEVY[1]

[1728]

In the Name of God Amen I Moses Levy of the City of New York Merchant being Sick & weak in body but of Sound perfect & Disposeing mind Memory and understanding Praised be Almighty God for the Same &

[1] Original Will no. 859; *NYHSC*, vol. XI (1902), p. 72. Moses Levy (c. 1665–1728), one of the wealthiest and best known of New York Jews, had one of the most interesting and involved careers. Levy was made freeman of New York on June 5, 1695 and in 1719 was elected constable of the South Ward, but refused to serve. Levy married twice, first to Rycha Asher (d. Sept. 29, 1716), who bore him four sons, Nathan, Asher, Isaac, and Michael and a daughter Abigail. He then married Grace Mears in 1717 and had eight children, one of whom died in infancy. Chancery Decrees before 1800, File H, No. 19, Clerk's Office of the Court of Appeals. *Burghers*, p. 57; *Minutes*, vol. III, pp. 210 and 214; Max J. Kohler, "Phases of Jewish Life in New York Before 1800, Part 1" *PAJHS*, vol. II (1894), p. 82; *Ibid.*, part 2, *PAJHS*, vol. III (1895), p. 85; N. Taylor Phillips, "The Levy and Seixas Families of Newport and New York," *PAJHS*, vol. IV (1896), pp. 189–191 and 196; *Portraits*, pp. 198–201. Levy was involved in many law suits, including *Levy v. Jewell* (1703), MCM, vol. 1695–1704, pp. 344 and 371 where the court directed him to pay a fine for raising a "false clamor" when he charged that Jewell had been paid to serve in his place as a soldier at Albany when he had not in fact done so. Levy also lost the case in the action of *Evans v. Levy* (1722), MCP, file 1711–1724, Oct. 6, 1722, MCM, vol. 1720–1723, pp. 434–435, 438, 459, 493. For references to Levy's commercial career, see NOL CO5/1222, *passim*; Entry and Manifest Books, 1726–1764, New York State Library, Albany, *passim*; Nathan Simson Letter Books. These Letter Books also contain a copy of an earlier will, dated July 30, 1717, in which Samuel Levy, Moses' brother is mentioned. At the time of his death Levy lived in the South Ward which had the greatest number of resident Jews and where his assessment of £100 was one of the highest. NYAL, Feb. 24, 1727. Only Frederick Philipse was assessed at a higher total, that being £120. Augustus Jay received the same valuation as Levy, while Daniel Jamison and Stephen Richards were rated at £100.

Of his sixteen Jewish neighbors, residing in the South Ward, the assessments were as follows:

Pacheco, Rodrigo, house and est.	£95
Levy, Nathan, house and est.	50
Lopes, Moses, house and est.	35
Judah, Baruch, house and est.	30
Jacobs, Benjamin, house and est.	25
Jacobs, Abraham, est.	20
De Costa, Daniel Nunes, est.	15
DeLucena, Rachel, widow, house	15
Lewis, Rachel, house and est.	15
Medina, Isaac, est.	15
D'Auguilar, J[oseph?], est.	10
Hart, Moses, est.	10
Hyams, Uriah, est.	10
Isaacs, Philip, est.	10
Perero, Moses, est.	10
Louzada, Jacob	5

well Considering the Certainty of Death & the Uncertain time thereof do hereby make Publish & Declare this my last Will and Testament hereby Revoaking & Disannulling all other Wills heretofore by me made Either in word or writing and this only to be Derived & taken for my last Will & Testament in manner & form following That is to Say First & Principally I Give & bequeath my Soul to God that gave it & my Body to the Earth to be Decently buryed at the Discretion of my Executors hereafter named *Item* my Will is That all my Just Debts which I Owe to any manner of Person or Persons be duely & Justly paid & Satisfied in Some Short time after my Decease by my said Executors *Item* my Will is and I do hereby give Devise & bequeath unto my Son ASHER LEVY[2] One Silver Mugg of the Weight of Twenty Ounces *Item* I give & bequeath unto my Daughter MIRIAM LEVY[3] One hundred pounds Current Money of New York to be paid her by my Executors when She Shall Come of Age or be Married & above her part and Share herein after bequeath unto her. *Item* I Give and Bequeath unto my Grandson NAPHTALI FRANKS[4] one piece of Silver Plate of the Value of Twelve pounds *And* all the Rest Residue and Remainder of my Estate both real & personall whatsoever & wheresoever (after the Same is Sold & Disposed of by my Executors hereafter Named which I do Direct & Empower them to do as Soon as Conveniently may be) I DO give Devise and bequeath unto and Among my loving wife GRACE LEVY my Sons NATHAN LEVY,[5] ISAAC LEVY,[6] MICHAEL LEVY,[7] SAMSON LEVY,[8] BENJAMIN

[2] Asher Levy was in New York in 1718. Some time after that he went to London where he met with financial reverses and was declared bankrupt in 1732. He returned to the colonies in 1740 and died in Philadelphia in 1742. Conveyance Liber 28, cp. 513–514; *New-York Gazette*, June 3, June 17, June 24, 1728; *Gentleman's Magazine* (London), vol. II (1732), p. 1032; Abigail Franks to Naphtali Franks, July 6, 1740 and Aug. 29, 1742 (Abigail Franks letters, Friedman Collection, American Jewish Historical Society).

[3] Miriam Levy (1720–1748). See *PAJHS*, vol. XXXIII (1934), p. 210.

[4] Naphtali Franks (1715–1796), eldest son of Jacob Franks and Abigail, daughter of Moses Levy, was an important merchant who spent most of his life in England. Samuel Oppenheim, "Genealogical Notes on Jacob Franks from Official Records," *PAJHS*, vol. XXV (1917), p. 77. See Abigail Franks letters, Friedman Collection, American Jewish Historical Society, *passim*.

[5] Nathan Levy (1704–1753), was a Philadelphia merchant interested in the communal affairs of New York and Philadelphia. *PAJHS*, vol. IV (1896), pp. 193 and 195; Elvira, N. Solis, "Some References to Early Jewish Cemeteries in New York City," *PAJHS*, vol. VIII (1900), pp. 139–140; Sabato Morais, "Mickve Israel Congregation of Philadelphia," *PAJHS*, vol. I (1905), p. 20.

[6] Isaac Levy (1706–1777) was a New York, Philadelphia, and Boston merchant. Lee M. Friedman, "Early Jewish Residents in Massachusetts," *PAJHS*, vol. XXIII (1915), p. 85.

[7] Michael Levy (b. 1709), a New York merchant was part owner of the brig *Prince Frederick*, Entry of Sept. 26, 1722 (NOL Co 5/1225). In 1739, he was indicted for assaulting Henry Breasted, High Constable of New York (Minutes, Court of General Sessions, vol. 1722–1743, p. 276, New York County Clerk's Office, 31 Chambers Street, New York City). In 1742, he was in Jamaica (Abigail Franks to Naphtali Franks, Aug. 29, 1742 [Friedman Collection, American Jewish Historical Society]).

[8] Samson Levy (1722–1781) went to Philadelphia with his sister, Hetty, and his

LEVY,[9] & JOSEPH LEVY[10] & my Daughters RACHELL LEVY,[11] MIRIAM LEVY, HESTER LEVY,[12] & HANNAH LEVY[13] Share & Shares alike to be paid them by my Executors in the Manner following That is to Say The Severall parts Shares & portions of my Said wife GRACE LEVY[14] & of my Sons NATHAN LEVY ISAAC LEVY & MICHAEL LEVY to be paid them by my Executors within five Years after my Decease And the Severall Parts Shares or portions of my sons SAMSON LEVY, BENJAMIN LEVY, & JOSEPH LEVY & of my Daughters RACHEL LEVY, MIRIAM LEVY, HESTER LEVY, & HANNAH LEVY to be paid them when they Shall respectively come of Age or be Married And that in the meantime the Same to Remaine in the hands of my Executors hereafter Named to be by them Employed in Trade or put to Interest as they shall think most Convenient, And the Profitts of Such Trade, or the Interest to be by them Employed for & Towards the Support and Maintenance of my Said wife & Children untill they Shall respectively receive their Shares hereby bequeathed unto them. And if any or Either of my Said Children Shall happen to dye before they Shall Come of age or be Married That then the Share or portion of Such child or Children Shall be & remaine to and Among the Surviving Child or Children Share & Share alike as aforesaid But if it Shall So happen that my Said wife GRACE LEVY shall not be Satisfied and Contented with the part or portion Allotted her by this my Will but Shall Insist upon the performance of Certain Articles of Agreement made between & my Said wife GRACE LEVY

---

brother, Joseph, in 1740, after the death of their mother, Grace (Abigail Franks to Naphtali Franks, Nov. 9, 1740 [Friedman Collection, American Jewish Historical Society]).

[9] Benjamin Levy (1726–1822) became a settler of Newport. *PAJHS*, vol. IV (1896), pp. 190, 203 and 213.

[10] Joseph Levy (1728–1772) became a freeman of New York on November 7, 1752. *Burghers*, p. 177; *Dictionary*, p. 92.

[11] Rachel Levy married Isaac M. Seixas about 1740. *Portraits*, p. 470; *Dictionary*, p. 95. See Will of Michael Michaels in which she is left a legacy of £300. *Infra*, pp. 47–48.

[12] Hester is depicted in a contemporary account by William Black, Secretary of Commissioners appointed by Gov. William Gooch of Virginia to deal with the Indians. He records:

> . . . . I went to Mr. Levy's a Jew and very Considerable Merch't, he was a Widdower And his Sister Miss Hettie Levy kept his House. We Staid Tea and was very agreeably Entertain'd by the Young Lady; She was of the middle Stature, and very well Made her Complection Black but very Comely she had two Charming Eyes and well turn'd, with a Beautiful head of Hair, Coal Black . . . She was a Lady of a Great Deal of Wit, Join'd to a Good Understanding, full of Spirits, and a Humour Exeeding Jocose and Agreeable.

R. Alonzo Brock, "Journal of William Black, 1744," *Pennsylvania Magazine of History and Biography*, vol. I (1877), pp. 415–416. The editor of the Journal identifies the Mr. Levy as Samson Levy, a subscriber to the dancing assembly of 1748. The account is dated Philadelphia, Tuesday, June 5, 1744.

[13] Hannah Levy (1723–1751) later married Joshua Isaacs. Iyda R. Hirsh, "Mears Family and Their Connections, 1696–1824," *PAJHS*, vol. XXXIII (1934), p. 210.

[14] Grace Levy, *née* Grace Mears (1694–1740), daughter of Sampson Mears, married David Hays in April 1735. *Portraits*, pp. 225–226.

(then GRACE MEARS) & JACOB MEARS[15] before our Marriage That then my Will is And I hereby Order & Direct That my Said Executors Shall and do within five Years after my Decease pay to my Said wife GRACE LEVY Such sum & Sums of Money Plate and other things whatsoever as I by the Said Articles have Covenanted & agreed to leave her by my Will which payment Shall be in Lieu & Stead of her Part Share & Portion herein before by me bequeathed unto her and the Same Shall be a Barr to her from any further Claime or Demand whatsoever by Vertue hereof or any other whatsoever. *And Lastly* my Will is and I Do hereby Nominate and Appoint my loving wife GRACE LEVY my sons NATHAN LEVY & ISAAC LEVY, my son in law JACOB FRANKS[16] & my brother in law JUDAH MEARS[17] Executors of this my last will and Testament And do Desire them to See the same duely & truly performed According to the true Intent and meaning of these Presents *In Testimony* whereof I Do hereby Publish & Declare this to be my last will and Testament and have hereunto in the presence of the Witnesses Subscribed Set my hand & Seal in New York the Thirteenth day of June in the Second Year of the Reign of our Sovereign Lord GEORGE THE SECOND by the Grace of God King of Great Brittain France & Ireland Defender of the faith etc. In the Year One Thousand Seven Hundred & Twenty Eight.

s/ MOSES LEVY [seal]

Signed Sealed Published & Declared by
the Said MOSES LEVY as his last Will &
Testament in the presence of us who have
Subscribed our Names as Witnesses hereunto
in the presence of the Testator /
s/ MATTHEW CLARKSON[18]
s/ MOSSES LOPEZ DE FONSECA[19]
s/ RICH. NICHOLS[20]

[15] Jacob Mears, seemingly brother of Sampson Mears and Grace's uncle, was a merchant of St. James, Westminster, England. Chancery Decrees before 1800, File M, No. 19, Clerk's Office of the Court of Appeals, Albany.

[16] See *supra*, Will of Samuel Levy, p. 29, note 6.

[17] Judah Mears (d. 1762), brother of Grace Mears, was a merchant of New York and Princeton, New Jersey, as well as president of Shearith Israel in 1741–1742. "Minutes of Shearith Israel," *PAJHS*, vol. XXI (1913), p. 211; vol. XXXIII (1934), p. 201; *Portraits*, pp. 14, 15, 201, 229 and 240. For business dealings see Elizabeth Schuyler Account Book, p. 79, New-York Historical Society Library. He was very litigious and often appeared in court. He was also involved in an action when he was assaulted by Stephen and Oliver Delancey. See *King v. Delancey and Montagne* (1742), Minutes of the Court of General Sessions, vol. 1722–1743, pp. 320–321, New York County Clerk's Office, 31 Chambers Street, New York City.

[18] Matthew Clarkson, merchant of New York, was made freeman on January 9, 1728. *Burghers*, p. 110.

[19] See *infra*, Will of Jacob Fonseca, p. 46, note 13.

[20] See *infra*, Will of Michael Michaels, p. 48, note 7.

New York December 18, 1728

Be it known to all persons whom it may Concern *That* I JACOB FRANKS of the City of New York aforesaid Merchant for Diverse good Causes & Considerations have Relinquished my right and title as Executor to the Last will and Testament of MOSES LEVY Late of the Said City Merchant and *In Witness* whereof I have hereunto Set my hand & Seal the day & Year above written.

s/ JACOB FRANKS [seal]

Testis
s/ J. HUGHES

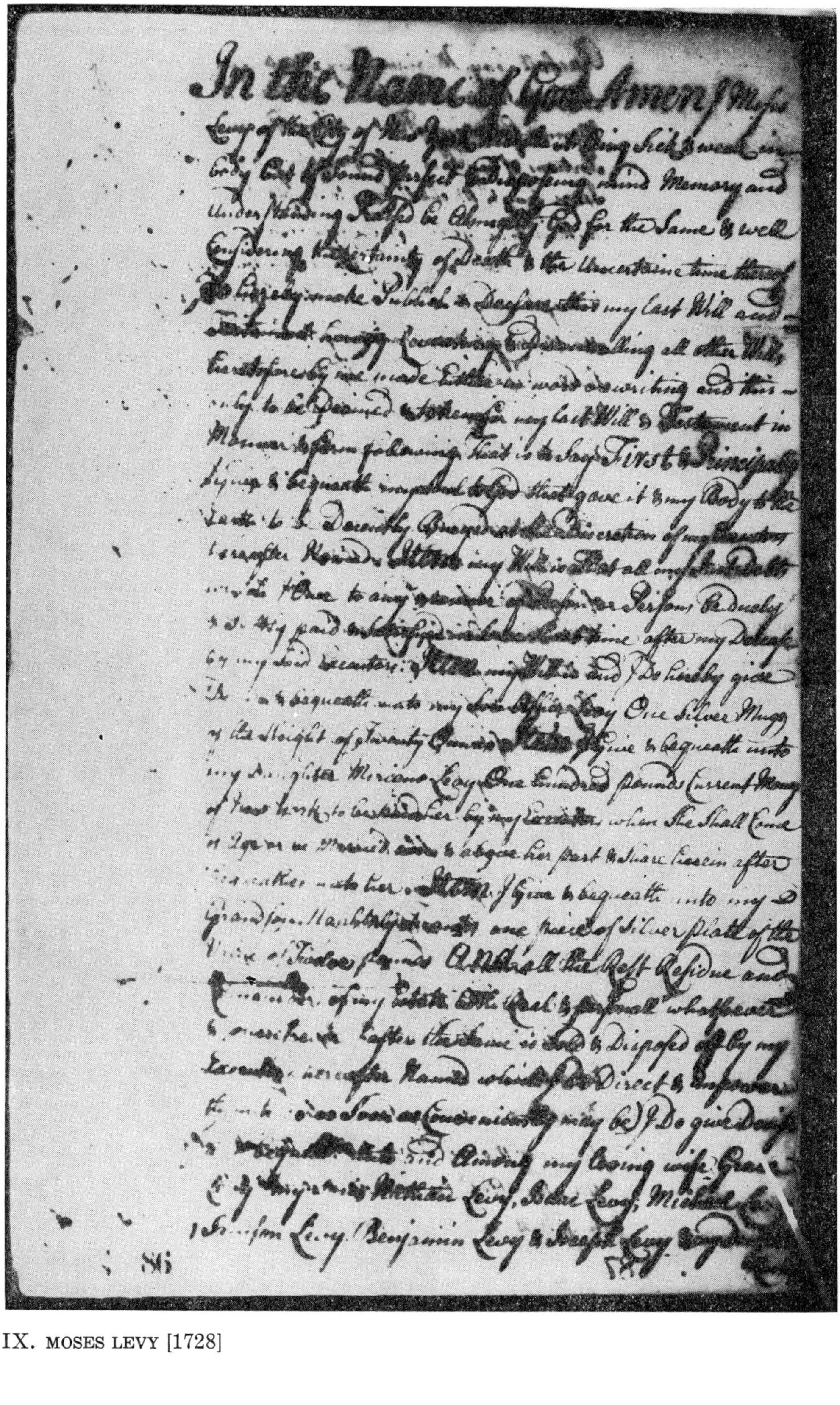

In the Name of God Amen I Moses
Levy of the City of New York Merchant being Sick & weak in
body but of Sound & perfect disposing mind Memory and
understanding Praised be Almighty God for the Same & well
Considering the Certainty of Death & the Uncertaine time thereof
Do hereby make Publish & Declare this my last Will and
Testament hereby Revoking & [illegible] all other Wills
heretofore by me made either in word or writing and this
only to be Deemed & taken for my last Will & Testament in
Manner & form following That is to say First & Principally
I give & bequeath my soul to God that gave it & my Body to the
Earth to be Decently Buryed at the discretion of my Executors
hereafter Named. Item my Will is that all my just Debts
[illegible] Owe to any [illegible] Person or Persons be duely
[illegible] paid [illegible] time after my Decease
by my said Executors. Item my Will is and I Do hereby give
[illegible] & bequeath unto my [illegible] Levy One Silver Mugg
of the Weight of Twenty Ounces. Item I give & bequeath unto
my Daughter Miriam Levy One hundred pounds Current Money
of New York to be [illegible] her by my Executors when She Shall Come
of Age or be Married [illegible] her part & Share herein after
[illegible] unto her. Item I give & bequeath unto my
Grandson [illegible] one piece of Silver plate of the
Value of Twelve pounds And all the Rest Residue and
Remainder of my Estate both Real & personall whatsoever
& wheresoever after the Same is Sold & Disposed of by my
Executors hereafter Named which I Direct & Impower
them to [illegible] as Conveniently may be) I Do give Devise
& bequeath [illegible] and Amongst my loving wife Grace
[illegible] Nathan Levy, [illegible] Levy, Michael Levy
[illegible] Levy, Benjamin Levy & [illegible] Levy [illegible]

86

IX. MOSES LEVY [1728]

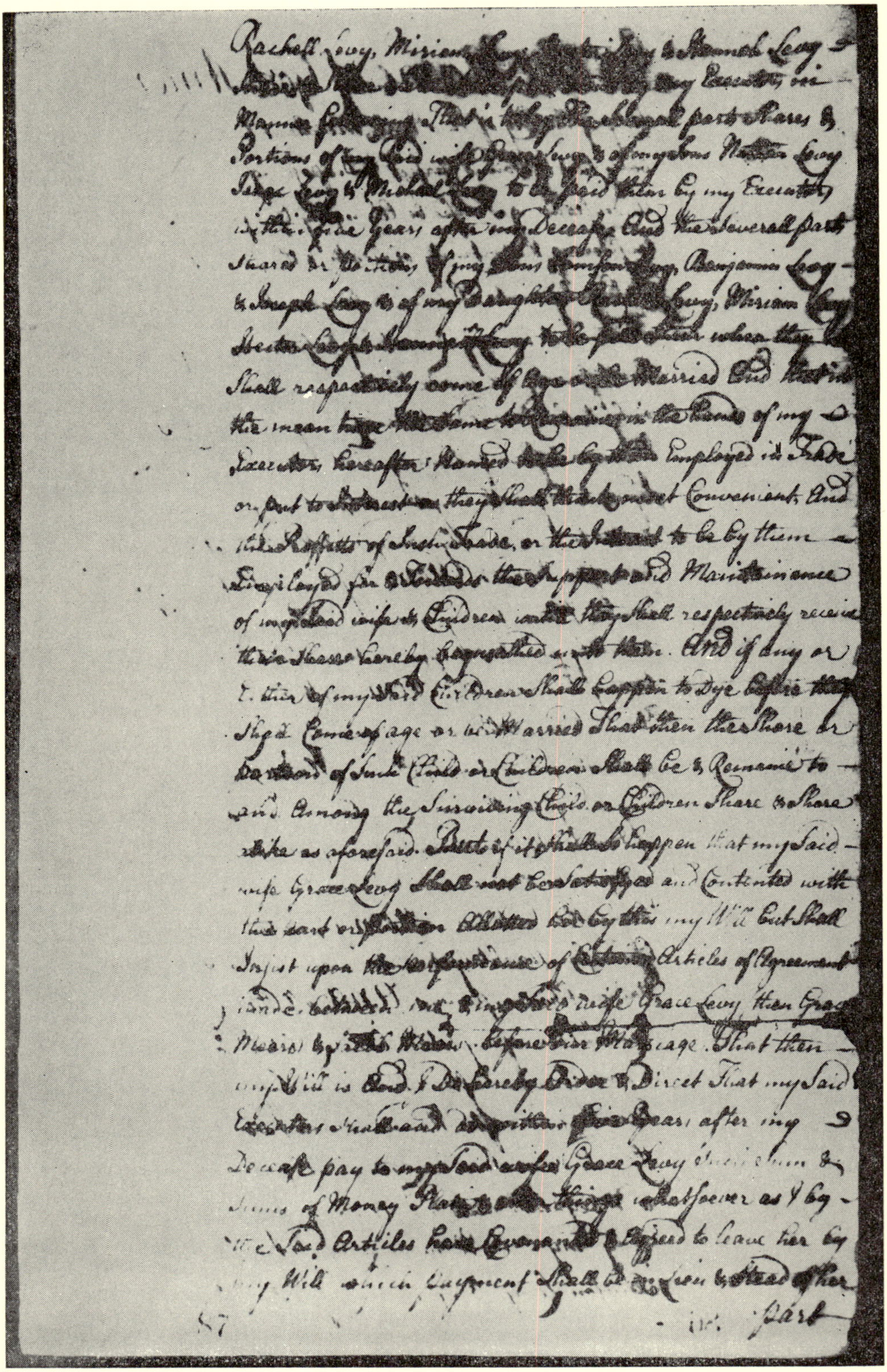

Rachell Levy, Miriam [illegible] & Hannah Levy -
[illegible] my Executors in
Manner following That is to say The Severall parts Shares &
Portions of my said wife Grace Levy & of my Sons Nathan Levy
Isaac Levy & Michael Levy to be paid them by my Executors
within five Years after my Decease And the Severall parts
Shares & Portions of my Sons Samson Levy, Benjamin Levy
& Joseph Levy & of my Daughters Rachell Levy, Miriam Levy
Hester Levy & Hannah Levy to be paid them when they
Shall respectively come of Age or be Married And that in
the mean time the Same to Remain in the hands of my
Executors hereafter Named to be by them Employed in Trade
or put to Interest as they Shall think most Convenient And
the Proffitts of Such Trade or the Interest to be by them
Employed for & towards the Support and Maintenance
of my Said infant Children untill they Shall respectively receive
their Shares hereby bequeathed unto them. And if any or
Either of my Said Children Shall happen to Dye before they
Shall Come of age or be Married That then the Share or
Portion of Such Child or Children Shall be & Remaine to
and Among the Surviving Child or Children Share & Share
alike as aforesaid. But if it Shall so happen that my Said
wife Grace Levy Shall not be Satisfyed and Contented with
the part or Portion allotted her by this my Will but Shall
Insist upon the performance of Certain Articles of Agreement
made between me & my present wife Grace Levy then Grace
Mears by [illegible] before our Marriage That then
my Will is And I Do hereby Order & Direct That my Said
Executors Shall and do within five Years after my
Decease pay to my Said wife Grace Levy Such Sum &
Sums of Money Plate & other things whatsoever as I by
the Said Articles have Covenanted & Agreed to leave her by
my Will which payment Shall be in Lieu & Stead of her
part

IX. MOSES LEVY [1728]

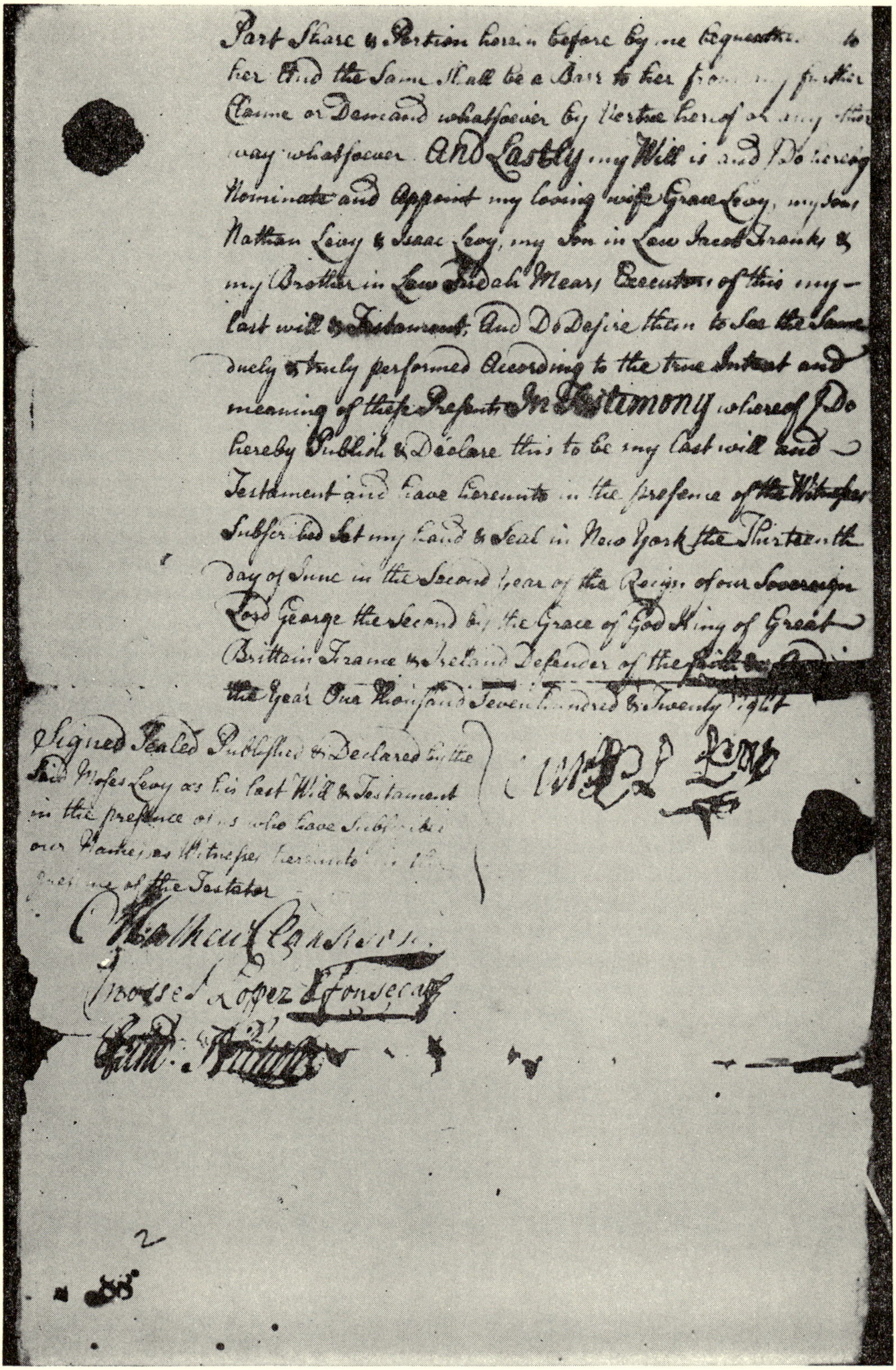

Part Share & Portion herein before by me bequeathed to
her And the Same shall be a Barr to her from any further
Claime or Demand whatsoever by Vertue hereof or any other
way whatsoever And Lastly my Will is and I Do hereby
Nominate and Appoint my loving wife Grace Levy, my sons
Nathan Levy & Isaac Levy, my son in Law Jacob Franks &
my Brother in Law Judah Mears Executors of this my
last will & Testament; And Do Desire them to See the Same
duely & truly performed According to the true Intent and
meaning of these Presents In Testimony whereof I Do
hereby Publish & Declare this to be my last will and
Testament and have hereunto in the presence of the Witnesses
Subscribed Set my hand & Seal in New York the Thirteenth
day of June in the Second Year of the Reign of our Sovereign
Lord George the Second by the Grace of God King of Great
Brittain France & Ireland Defender of the Faith &c
the Year One Thousand Seven hundred & Twenty Eight

Moses Levy

Signed Sealed Published & Declared by the
said Moses Levy as his last Will & Testament
in the presence of us who have Subscribed
our Names as Witnesses hereunto in the
presence of the Testator

Matthew Clarkson
Mosses Lopez Fonseca
Wm. [illegible]

2

IX. MOSES LEVY [1728]

X

Jacob Fonseca[1]

[1729]

In the Name Of God Amen I Jacob Fonseca of the City of New York merchant being in Good health of Body and of Sound & perfect mind and Memory and considering with my Self the Certainty of Death And the uncertainty of the time & hour thereof as also the danger & hazards unto which I am Likely to be Exposed during A voygage I intend Speedily (by Gods Grace) to take to the Island of Jamaica[2] do make ordain And declare this to be my Last will and Testament in Manner and form following And First and principally I Commend my Soul into the hands of Almighty God my Creator and my Body to be disposed of as providence Shall order it and Such Estate as the Lord hath graciously bestowed on me I give devise and bequeath unto the Several persons following, that is to Say, for all Such debts as I shall owe at the time of my Decease I desire that the Same may be paid by my Executrix herafter named *Item* I give devise and bequeath unto my Eldest Son Isaac Fonseca[3] The Sum of Five pounds of Currant money of This province of New York for his birthright moreover I Give devise and bequeath unto my said son Isaac the Sum of fifty pounds of Like money for his proper use and behoof for ever & to be debarred from all claims & pretentions either on my seal or personal Estate *Item* I give devise & bequeath unto my dear beloved wife Rebecca Fonseca[4] three Negro's Women named Betty Sarah & Faba with her child & a Negro man named Gnatto, *To Have and to Hold* unto my Said Rebecca the three said Negro Women Negro Man & Child[5] for proper use & behoof for & during her Life & after her decease to be divided amongst my Six Children hereafter named Share and Share Alike *Item* I give devise and bequeath all my Estate not hereinbefore mentioned as well real & personal either in possession or expectant in reversion whatsoever & wheresoever unto my Six Children Abraham Fonseca,[6] Joseph Fonseca,[7] Rachel Fonseca, Esther Fonseca,

[1] Albany Will no. F-5, Clerk of the Court of Appeals. Except for this will, there is very little to identify Fonseca.

[2] Jacob Fonseca possibly died in Jamaica.

[3] For reference to Isaac in the Minutes of Shearith Israel, see *PAJHS*, vol. XXI (1913), pp. 27–28.

[4] For similar references to Ribca De Fonseca, see *ibid.*, p. 16.

[5] The widow Fonseca was paid some £7 by the Congregation for the hire of two Negroes. *Ibid.*, pp. 18–19.

[6] Abraham Fonseca's account to Shearith Israel is listed as of 1729 in *ibid.*, p. 21.

[7] Perhaps this is the Joseph Fonseca who married Abigail Nunes. P. A. Hilfman, "Notes on the History of the Jews in Surinam," *PAJHS*, vol. XVIII (1909), pp. 189 and 207.

JUDITH FONSECA & SARAH FONSECA To Have & to hold Each of them one Equal Sixth part thereof to be divided & distributed to them when they from time to time Shall come to Age or as my daughters Shall marry for their respective use behoof & benefit unto them the said ABRAHAM, JOSEPH, RACHEL, ESTHER, JUDITH, & SARAH Their heirs (of their bodys, bodys, Lawfully begotten) and Assigns forever, And in case anyone or Some of my Aforesaid Six Children Should happen to dye Under Age then his her or their Share or Shares Shall come to the Survivor or be Equally divided Amongst the Survivors of them as aforesiad *Item* I do hereby constitute and appoint my Said Loving wife REBECCA FONSECA to be Sole Executrix of this my Last will and Testament and I do desire my Loving Friend Mr. DANL. NUNEZ DA COSTA[8] to help and Assist my aforesaid Wife and Executrix in the Managing of the Affairs (if by her required) *In Witness* whereof I the Said Testator JACOB FONSECA do hereunto Set my hand and Seal and published and declared this only to be my Last will and Testament this thirtieth day of November in the first Year of the reign of our Sovereign Lord GEORGE THE SECOND by the Grace of God of Great Brittain France & Ireland King Defender of the faith etc. or *Anno Domini* 1727. JACOB FONSECA LS. Signed Sealed published and Declared by the Said Testator JACOB FONSECA as and for his Last will and Testament in the presents of us WM. WALLING,[9] GABRIEL LA BOYTEAUX[10] DAVID LE TELLIER[11]

Know All Men That I the Said JACOB FONSECA have made & ordered this Codicil that is to Say that I do empower my Said Dear beloved wife REBECCA FONSECA to hire out or Sell [ ] & dispose of my House & Yard being in Spanishe Town in the Island of Jamaica, as Likewise one thousand acres of Sand Lying in the parish of Martha Bree in the Island of Jamaica aforesaid & that the moneys arising from such Sale Shall be divided into Seven Equal Shares one Share Thereof for the proper use & behoof of her the Said REBECCA FONSECA for Ever and unto ABRAHAM FONSECA, JOSEPH FONSECA, RACHEL FONSECA, ESTHER FONSECA, JUDITH FONSECA, & SARAH FONSECA *To Have* and to hold one Equal Sixth part thereof, as it is mentioned in The Testament, *Item* that all my plates, pearls, and Jewels shall also remain for the proper ownuse and behoof of my Said Loving wife for & during her Lifetime and After her decease to be Equally divided Amongst my Six Children as in the Testament before mentioned Moreover I confirm my said Loving wife to be Sole Executrix as aforesaid and I desire Mr. DAN. NUNEZ DA COSTA to help and assist my said Wife as aforesaid *In Witness* whereof I have hereunto Set my

[8] Daniel Nunes Da Costa (c. 1704-1789) possibly married Philah Nunes who died in 1818. *Portraits*, p. 383; *Dictionary*, p. 136.

[9] William Walling, a baker, was made freeman of New York on August 21, 1722. *Burghers*, p. 103.

[10] Laboyteaux was made freeman of New York on August 3, 1688. *Ibid.*, p. 54.

[11] Le Tellier also witnessed the will of Peter Alard dated August 12, 1730. *NYHSC*, vol. III (1895), p. 3.

hand and Seal in New York the 28th day of July 1728 JACOB FONSECA LS Signed Sealed & delivered in presents of us ABRAHAM RODRIQUES DE RIVERA[12] MOSES LOPEZ D FONSECA[13] DAVID LE TELLIER.

New York October 14th 1729

Reed from the Secretary's Office of this province The Original of this Will and Codicil of which the above is a true Copy.

s/ REBECCA FONSECA

Testis

s/J. B. HUGHES

[Frontispiece]

Copy of the Will & Codicil of JACOB FONSECA both proved before ISAAC BOBIN[14] Esq. Aug. 9th 1729 by DAVID LE TELLIER one of the Subscribing Witnesses to both: the Estate of the Testator Lying in Jamaica the Original Will delivered to the Executrix

[12] Abraham De Rivera (d. 1765) became a freeman of New York on July 19, 1726, was naturalized in 1740, and about 1748 moved to Newport, Rhode Island. He was an early officer of Shearith Israel. *Burghers*, p. 103; *Dictionary*, p. 149, *PAJHS*, vol. XXI (1913), pp. 5, 8, 10, 15–16 and 19–20.

[13] Moses Lopez de Fonseca (d. 1752), *ḥazzan* [reader] for Shearith Israel, 1728–1736, left for Curaçao sometime in late 1736. He seems to have returned to New York City in 1743 since his name is listed in an account book of that year. *PAJHS*, vol. XXI (1913), pp. 35–36; Peter Jay Day Book, September 19, 1743, New-York Historical Society Library.

[14] On July 3, 1721 Isaac Bobin was granted a commission to be registrar of the Court of Chancery and in the following month was permitted to administer the oath of Executors and Administrators of Wills. *Calendar*, p. 19.

XI

MICHAEL MICHAELS[1]

[1737]

In the Name of God Amen I MICHAEL MICHAELS of the City of New York Merchant being Weak of Body but of Sound and perfect mind Memory and Understanding Do make and Ordaine this my last Will and Testament in Manner and form following That is to Say *First* and Principally I Recommend my Soul to Almighty and my Body to the Earth to be Buryed at the Discretion of my Executors hereafter Named And as touching Such Worldly Estate as it has pleased God to bless me with I give and bequeath the Same as follows *First* my Will is that my Just Debts and Funeral Charges be paid and Satisfyed in Some Short time after my Decease *Item* I Give and bequeath unto RACHAEL LEVY[2] of the City of New York Spinster Daughter of MOSES LEVY late of the said City Merchant Deceased the Sum of Three Hundred Pounds Current Money of New York which I hereby Order my Executors hereafter Named to pay her out of the first Moneys which Shall come to their hands *And* all the Rest and Residue of my Estate of what kind or Nature Soever I Give and bequeath unto my Honoured Father MOSES MICHAELS[3] of the City aforesaid Merchant And I Do hereby Nominate Constitute and Appoint my Said Father MOSES MICHAELS, SAMUEL MYER COHEN[4] and DAVID HAYS[5] of the Said City of New York Merchants Executors of this my last Will and Testament and do Desire them to see the Same duly and truly performed According to the true Intent and meaning hereof And I Do hereby Revoke all other Wills by me heretofore made Either by word or writing and this only to be Deemed and taken for my last Will and Testament *In Testimony* whereof I the said MICHAEL MICHAELS have hereunto put my hand and Seal this Twelfth day of February in the Tenth Year of the Reign of our Soverign Lord GEORGE THE SECOND by the

[1] Original Will no. 60A, HDC; Will Liber 13, p. 74; *NYHSC*, vol. III (1895), p. 222. Michaels is mentioned in the Minutes of Shearith Israel as contributing three shillings toward the purchase of a burial ground in 1728 and as being an officer on March 3, 1737. *PAJHS*, vol. XXI (1913), pp. 8 and 36. He died shortly after that date and sometime before March 31, 1737 when his will was probated. The name Michaels appears also as Michael and as Michal, etc.

[2] See *supra*, Will of Moses Levy, p. 38, note 11.

[3] See Will of Moses Michal, *infra*, pp. 59–61.

[4] See Will of Samuel Myers Cohen, pp. 65–68.

[5] David Hays (d. 1778) was a merchant who was made freeman of New York on September 16, 1735, and who earlier in that year and on April 28th married Grace Mears. Chancery Decrees before 1800, File H, No. 19, Clerk's Office of the Court of Appeals, Albany. For business records of Hays, see Entries on pp. 130 and 173–174, Day Book of Peter Jay, New-York Historical Society Library. For his legal involvements, see *Hays v. Peek* (1735), MCM, vol. 1731–1736, pp. 466 and 472; and *Hays v. Bowman* (1747), MCM, vol. 1742–1748, p. 593.

Grace of God King of Great Britain France and Ireland Defender of the faith and So Forth And in the year One Thousand Seven hundred and Thirty Six.

Signed Sealed Published and *Declared* by the said MICHAEL MICHAELS as his last Will and Testament in the presence of us who have Subscribed our Names as Witnesses thereto in the presence of the Said Testator

s/ MICHL MICKALLS

[seal]

s/ ELISABETH CARTHEW
s/ ALEXANDER ALLAIRE[6]
s/ RICHD: NICHOLLS[7]

March 31 Jurat &
Saw ye other two wittnesses
Sworn tors
3 Executors Sworn on
ye old Testament

New York March 31–1737

Be it remembred that on the Day and year above written pesonally appeared before me FREDERICK MORRIS[8] being thereunto Delegated & appointed RICHARD NICOLLS & made oath on the holy evangelists of Almighty God that he Saw MICHAEL MICHAELS Sign Seal Publish and Declare the within Writen to be his Last will & Testament & that at the time thereof he was of Sound Disposing mind & Memory according to the best of his Judgment & Understanding & that he Signed his Name as Wittness thereto in his presence and that he Saw ELIZABETH CARTHEW & ALEXANDER ALLAIER Sign their Names as Wittnesses to Said Will in presence also of the Testator

Be it also Remembred that on the Day and year first above Written personally peared before me FREDERICK MORRIS authorized as aforesaid MOSES MICHAELS, SAMUEL MYER COHEN, DAVID HAYS and were on the old Testament to the Due Execution & performance thereof

Jurat
Coram

[6] Alexander Allaire, a cooper, was made freeman of New York on May 15, 1705. Possibly a son by the same name was made freeman twenty six years later. *Burghers*, pp. 86 and 116.

[7] Richard Nicholls was coroner of New York during 1732–33 and 1735, was appointed notary public in 1740 and registrar of the Court of Vice Admiralty in 1763. *Calendar*, pp. 22–23, 25 and 34.

[8] Frederick Morris was granted a license to practice law in December, 1728, and was made registrar of the Court of Chancery in November, 1730 and deputy secretary of the Province in March, 1738. *Ibid.*, pp. 21–22 and 33.

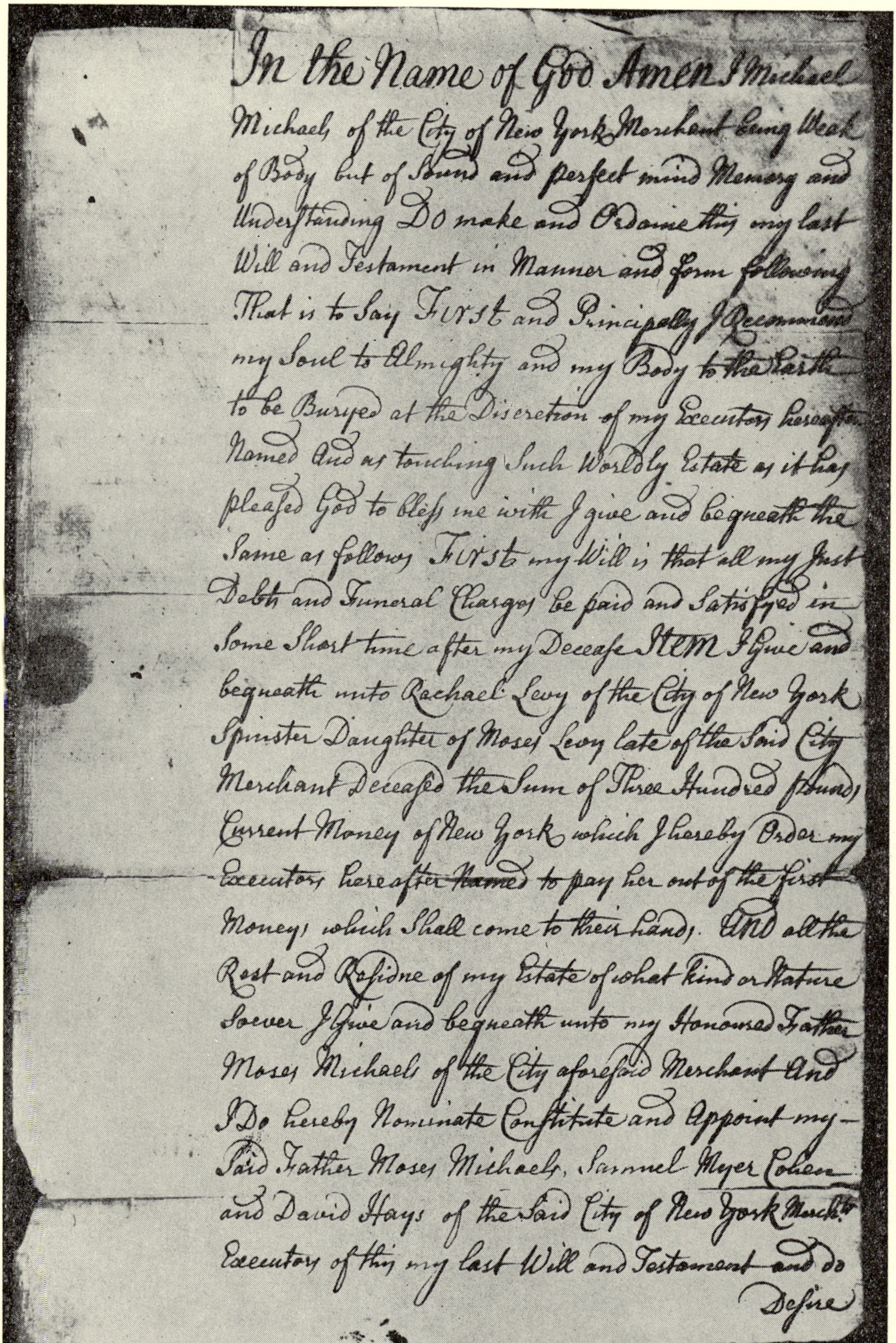

In the Name of God Amen I Michael
Michaels of the City of New York Merchant being Weak
of Body but of Sound and perfect mind Memory and
Understanding DO make and Ordaine this my last
Will and Testament in Manner and form following
That is to Say First and Principally I Recommend
my Soul to Almighty and my Body to the Earth
to be Buryed at the Discretion of my Executors hereafter
Named And as touching Such Worldly Estate as it has
pleased God to bless me with I give and bequeath the
Same as follows First my Will is that all my Just
Debts and Funeral Charges be paid and Satisfyed in
Some Short time after my Decease Item I Give and
bequeath unto Rachael Levy of the City of New York
Spinster Daughter of Moses Levy late of the Said City
Merchant Deceased the Sum of Three Hundred Pounds
Current Money of New York which I hereby Order my
Executors hereafter Named to pay her out of the first
Moneys which Shall come to their hands. AND all the
Rest and Residue of my Estate of what kind or Nature
Soever I Give and bequeath unto my Honoured Father
Moses Michaels of the City aforesaid Merchant And
I Do hereby Nominate Constitute and Appoint my
Said Father Moses Michaels, Samuel Meyer Cohen
and David Hays of the Said City of New York Merchts
Executors of this my last Will and Testament and do
Desire

XI. MICHAEL MICHAELS

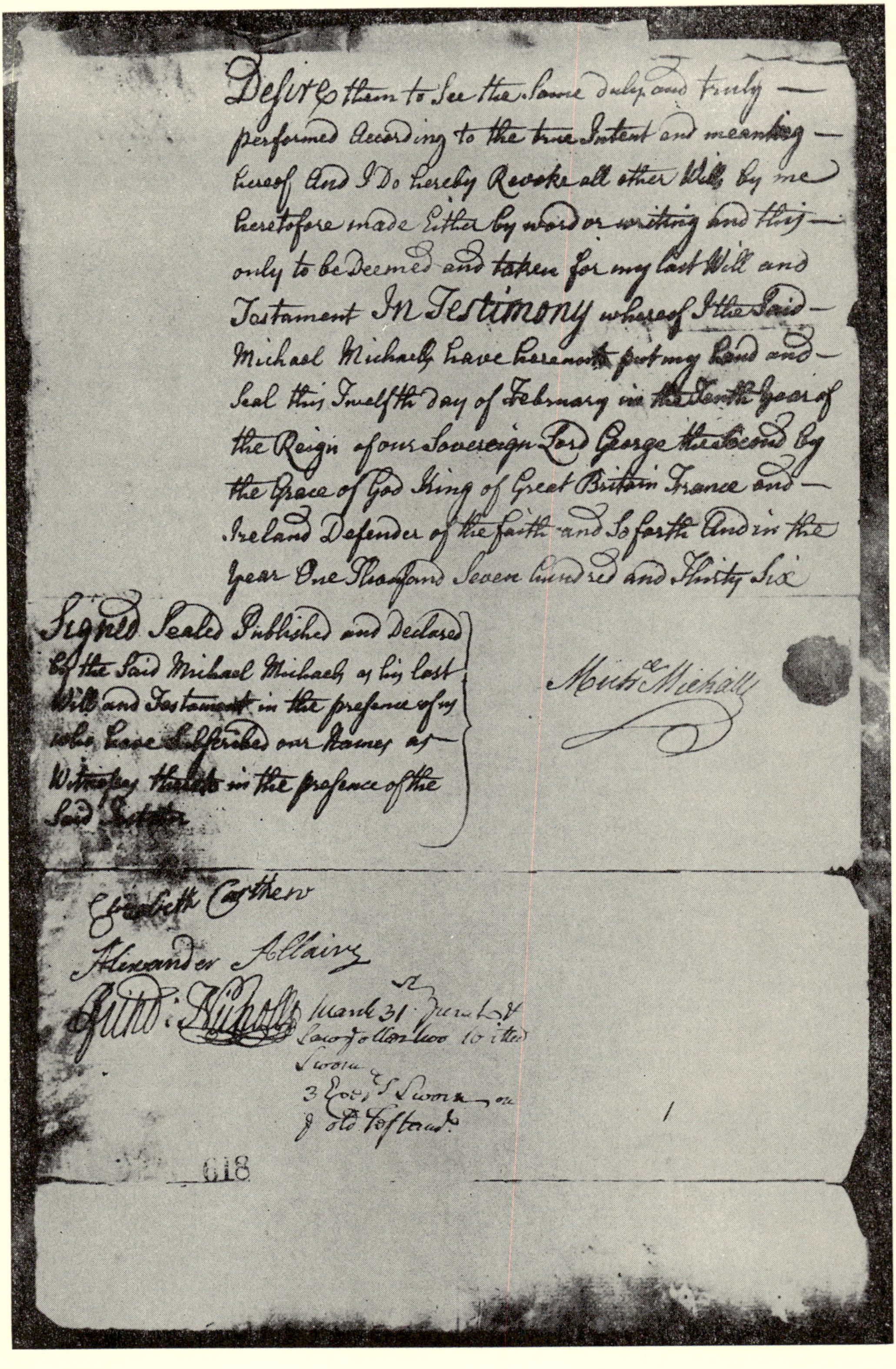

Desires them to See the Same duly and truly —
performed According to the true Intent and meaning —
hereof And I Do hereby Revoke all other Wills by me
heretofore made Either by word or writing and this —
only to be Deemed and taken for my last Will and
Testament In Testimony whereof I the Said —
Michael Michaels have hereunto put my hand and —
Seal this Twelfth day of February in the Tenth Year of
the Reign of our Sovereign Lord George the Second by
the Grace of God King of Great Britain France and —
Ireland Defender of the faith and So forth And in the
Year One Thousand Seven hundred and Thirty Six

Signed Sealed Published and Declared
by the Said Michael Michaels as his last
Will and Testament in the presence of us
who have Subscribed our Names as
Witnesses thereto in the presence of the
Said Testator

Mich^l Michaels

Elizabeth Carthew
Alexander Allaire
Richd: Nicholls

March 31 [illegible]
[illegible] to it
Sworn
3 Exrs Sworn on
y old Testamt

618

XI. MICHAEL MICHAELS

XII

RACHEL LUIS[1]

[1737]

In the name of God Amen I RACHEL LUIS being sick of body but of sound mind and Memory Do make this my last will and Testamit in manner and form following that is to say I wish and order that after my Decease my body be intered in a Decent manner after and according to the Ceremonies used among the Jewish nation Item after my Debts and funeral Charges being first paid I will give and bequeath and DAVID MACHADO[2] of this City of New York Merchant all and every my goods and Chattells and all my personall Estate whatsoever and wheresoever to him his Executors and Administrators forever Except only the houshold furnitur such as pewter bed and Bedding chairs tables potts and pans and Cubbard spoons which furnitur I order to be sold by my Executors and the money arising therefrom to be applyed to buy a Shefer Tora [Torah Scroll] for the use of the Kall Kados[3] of Sherith Ysraell in New York Lastly I do nominate and appoint my friend DAVID MACHADO above named to be my Executor of this my last will and Testemt in Witness whereof I have hereunto put my hand & Seal this Eighth Day of April in the Tenth year of the Reign of his present Majesty King GEORGE THE SECOND [of] great Britain etc.

s/ RACHL LUIS [seal]

Published and Declared signed & sealed to be the last will and testamit of RACHEL LUIS in the presence of the witnesses hereto Subscribing in her presence

s/ LUIS GOMEZ[4]
s/ RODRIGES DE RIBERA[5] s/ ABRAHAM DE RIVERA[6]
s/ WILLIAM JAMISON[7]

[1] Original Will no. 37, HDC; Will Liber 13, p. 75; *NYHSC*, vol. III (1895), p. 223. Little is known about Rachel Luis or Lewis. In the Minutes of Shearith Israel mention is made that she left ten pounds to purchase a Sepher Torah [parchment scroll of the Five Books of Moses]. Since this sum does not appear in the will, the value of her household goods which she directed to be sold for this purpose must have been of that amount. No mention is made in the will of an *Escaba* or *Hascaba* [memorial prayer for the dead], but this is ordered as part of her will directives by David Machado, her executor. *PAJHS*, vol. XXI (1913), p. 37. In 1730, she resided in the South Ward in the house of widow Symes, NYAL, Feb. 28, 1730.

[2] David Machado (d. 1747) was a merchant and minister of the Congregation Shearith Israel. *Ibid.*, pp. 11, 20, 23, 28, 30 and 35-38; *Portraits*, p. 409.

[3] Spelled also Kahal Kados, meaning Holy Congregation.

[4] See Will of Lewis Gomez, *infra*, pp. 62-63.

[5] Possibly Isaac Rodriques De Rivera or Daniel Rodriques De Rivera. Both were contemporaries who donated funds to Shearith Israel. *PAJHS*, vol. XXI (1913), pp. 44-45, 53 and 63.

[6] See *supra*, Will of Jacob Fonseca, p. 46, note 12.

[7] William Jamison, an attorney, was made freeman of the city on February 11, 1731. *Burghers*, pp. 116 and 483.

New York April the 13th 1737

Be it remembered that on the day & year above written personally appeared before me FREDERICK MORRIS being thereunto Delegated & appointed ABRAHAM RODRIGES DE RIBERA one of the Subscribing Witnesses to the within Will of RACHEL LUIS & made oath on the holy Evangelists of Almighty God that he saw the said RACHEL LUIS sign seal Publish & Declare same to be her last Will & Testament and that at the time thereof she was of Sound & Disposing Mind and Memory to the best of her understanding that he the Doponent Signed his Name as Wittness thereto in presence of the testatrix and at the same Time saw LEWIS GOMEZ and WILLIAM JAMESON, sign their Names as witnesses thereto in presence of the Testatrix also.

The last will of
RACHELL LUIS
13 April 1737

Be it remembred that on the day & year above written personally appeared before me FREDERICK MORRIS being thereunto Delegated & appointed DAVID MACHADO the Executor in the within Will Named & took the oaths of an Executor for the Due Execution & performance of the said Will

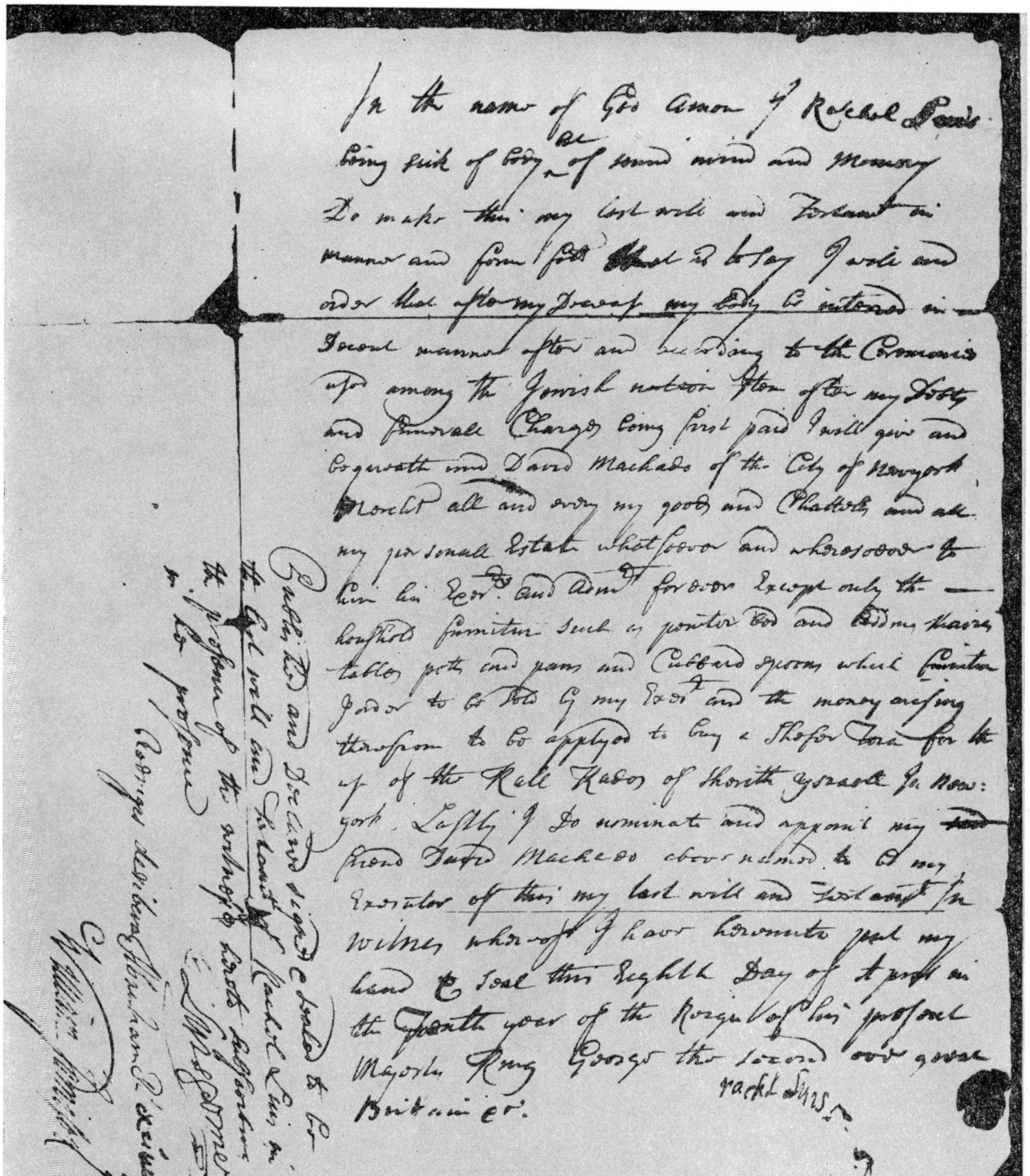

In the name of God Amen I Rachel Luis being sick of body but of sound mind and memory Do make this my last will and testament in manner and form following that is to say I will and order that after my decease my body be interred in decent manner after and according to the Ceremonies used among the Jewish nation Item after my debts and funerall charges being first paid I will give and bequeath unto David Machado of the City of New york Merchant all and every my goods and Chattells and all my personall Estate whatsoever and wheresoever to him his Exors and Admrs forever Except only the household furniture such as pewter bed and bedding chairs tables pots and pans and Cubbard spoons which furniture I order to be sold by my Exor and the money arising therefrom to be applyed to buy a Shefer Tora for the use of the Kall Kados of Shearith Ysrael in New: york. Lastly I do nominate and appoint my friend David Machado above named to be my Executor of this my last will and testament In witness whereof I have hereunto sett my hand & seal this Eighth Day of April in the tenth year of the Reign of his present Majesty King George the second over great Britain &c.

rachel Luis

Signed Sealed Published and Declared by the said Rachel Luis as her last will and testament in the presence of the witnesses ... in presence

[illegible]

XII. RACHEL LUIS [1737]

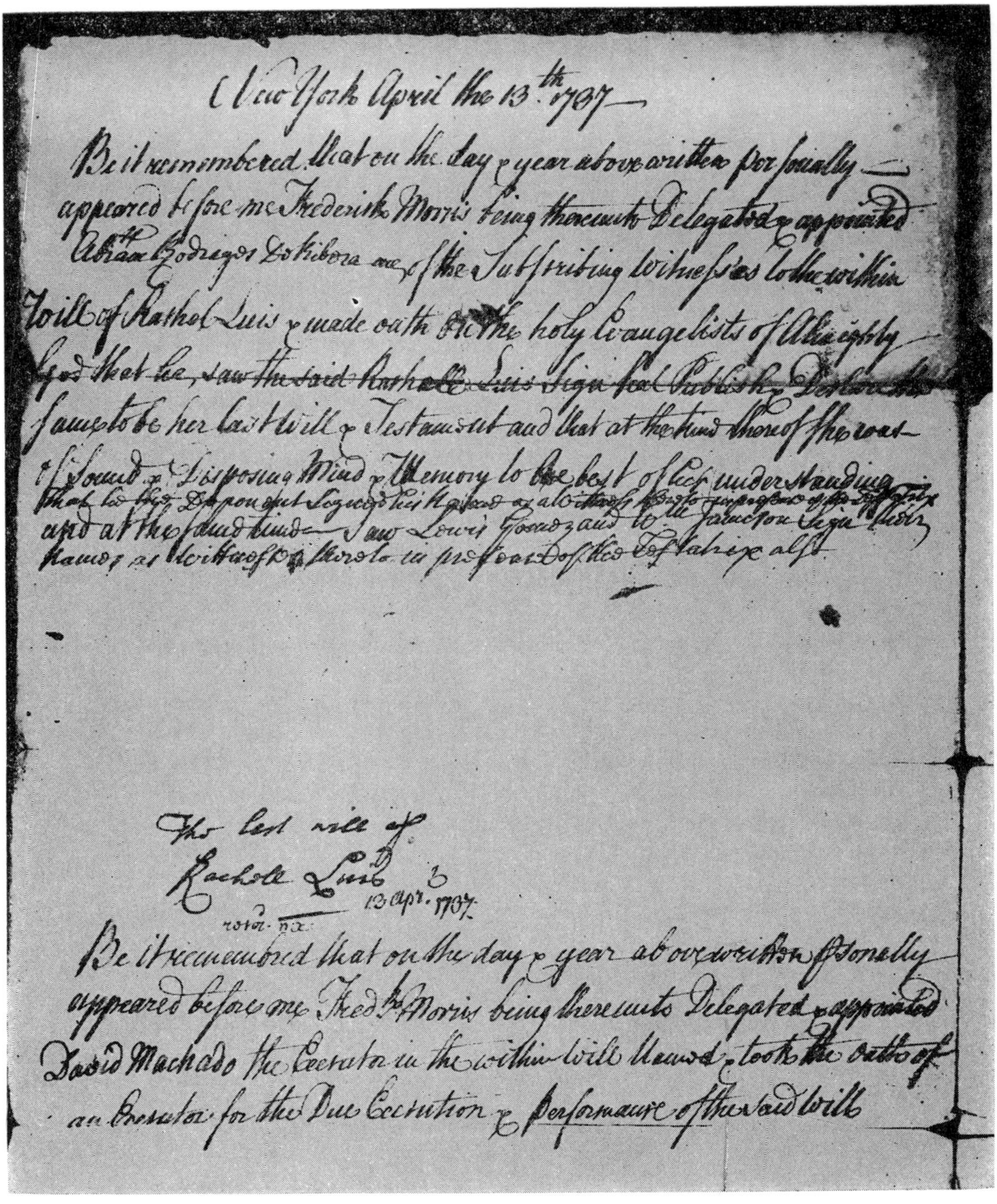
New York April the 13th 1737

Be it remembered that on the day & year above written personally appeared before me Frederick Morris being thereunto Delegated & appointed Abraham Rodrigues De Rivera one of the Subscribing witnesses to the within Will of Rachel Luis & made oath on the holy Evangelists of Almighty God that he saw the said Rachell Luis Sign Seal Publish & Declare the same to be her last Will & Testament and that at the time thereof she was of Sound & Disposing Mind & Memory to the best of his understanding [illegible] and at the same time saw Lewis Gomez and [illegible] Sign their names as witnesses thereto in presence of the Testatrix also

The last will of Rachell Luis 13 Apr. 1737

Be it remembered that on the day & year above written personally appeared before me Fredk Morris being thereunto Delegated & appointed David Machado the Executor in the within Will named & took the oath of an Executor for the Due Execution & Performance of the said Will

XII. RACHEL LUIS [1737]

XIII

URIAH HYAM[1]

[1740]

In the Name of God Amen this first Day of November 1740 I URIAH HYAM now resident of the City of New York Chandler, being very Sick & weak of Body but of perfect mind & memonory thanks be given unto God, Therefore calling unto mind the Mortallity of my body & knowing it is appointed for all men once to dye Do make & ordain this my last will & testament. That is to say, principally & first of all I recommend my Soul unto the hands of God that gave it & my body I recommend to the earth, to be buryed in a Decent Manner at the Discretion of my Executors not doubting but at the General Resurrection I shall receive the same again by the Mighty power of God, & as touching the worldly estate wherewith it hath pleased God go bless me in this Life, I give Demise & Dispose of the Same in manner & form following.

Imprimis, I give & bequeath unto my brother ENOCH, Living in Bohemia The Sum of Twenty pounds, current money of this province, to be raised & leavied out of my estate.

Item, I give & bequeath to the youngest Son, my Son ANDREW ISRAEL now has in the Island of Jamaica my Negro boy named CAVANDRO.

Item, I give & bequeath to the Congregation of the Children of Israel here in New York, the Sum of Six pounds currant money of the province to be raised & Levied out of my estate, to be imployed in the Lining of the place wherein the five books of Moses is kept. Lastly, I give & bequeath to my dear & well beloved son ANDREW ISRAEL of the Island of Jamaica whome I likewise, make ordain and constitute one of my Executors of this my Last will & testament All the residue & remainder of my Estate both real and personal (after my funeral charges & Just and Lawfull debts are paid out of the same) freely to be possessed and enjoyed by him his Heirs & assigns forever. I also constitute ordain & Apoint Mr. JACOB FRANKS[2] & Mr. MORDECAI GOMEZ[3] Merchants of the City of New York, Executors of this my Last will and testament.

And I do hereby utterly disallow revoke & disannul all and every other will & testament by me before this made, Rattifying & confirming this

[1] Original Will no. 110A, HDC; Will Liber 14, *NYHSC*, vol. III (1895), pp. 320–321. Outside of this will little is known of Hyam, although his name does appear occasionally in the Minutes of Shearith Israel. In 1738, he paid £3 to the Congregation. In 1740 he donated £2, but an account of £1.4 in his name is noted as "bad." Uriah appears to also have been known as Henry. *PAJHS*, vol. XXI (1913), pp. 39, 42–43, and 45. Unlike most Jewish testators, Hyam made his mark rather than writing his signature.

[2] See *supra*, Will of Samuel Levy, p. 29, note 6.

[3] See Will of Mordecai Gomez, pp. 84–91.

& no others to be my last will and Testament. In Witness whereof I have hereunto set my hand & seal the Day & year above written.

Signed, Sealed & Published
pronounced & Declared
by the Said URIAH HYAM as
his Last will & Testament
In the presence of all the
Subscribers,

URIAH HYAM his mark [seal]

s/ JOS SIMSON[4]
s/ DAVID MACHADO[5] 14 January 1740/1 sworn and saw the other two sign
s/ JOSHUA ISAACS[6]

Mr. FRANKS and Mr. GOMEZ Renounced and the other Executor living in Jamica administrator with the will annexed granted to ABRAHAM ISAACS[7] and JOSEPH SIMSON

[4] See Will of Joseph Simson, pp. 201–203.

[5] See Will of Rachel Luis, *supra*, p. 51.

[6] See Will of Joshua Isaacs, pp. 69–71.

[7] Abraham Isaacs (d. 1743), merchant, was made freeman of New York on August 6, 1723 and was elected Constable of the South Ward in 1725. He was prominent in Jewish affairs, being one of the petitioners to obtain a burial ground. *PAJHS*, vol. XXI (1913), pp. 7–8, 10, and 19–20; *Minutes*, vol. III (1905), p. 374.

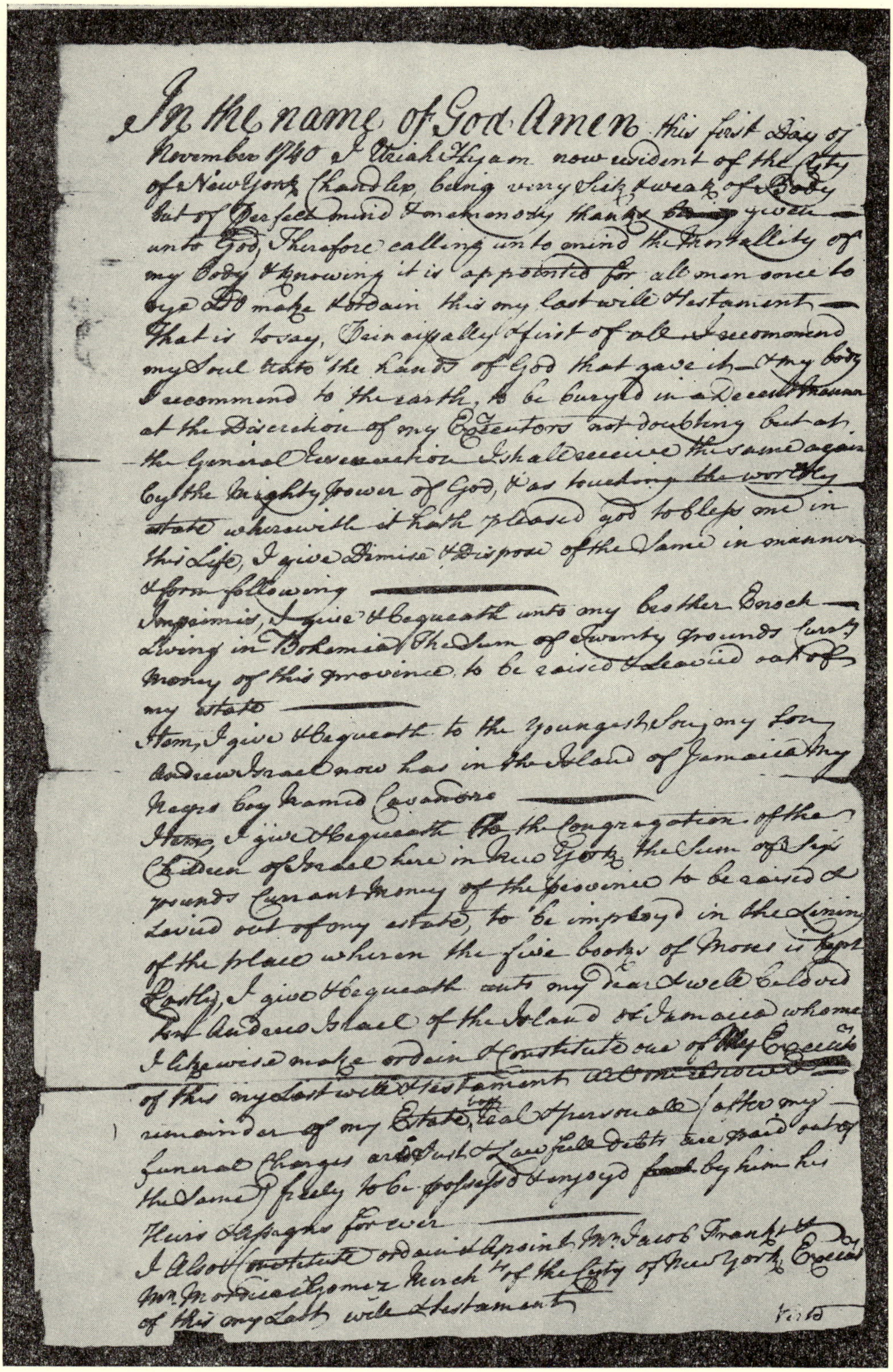
In the name of God Amen this first Day of
November 1740 I Uriah Hyam now resident of the City
of New York Chandler being very sick & weak of Body
but of perfect mind & memory thanks be given
unto God, Therefore calling unto mind the Mortallity of
my Body & knowing it is appointed for all men once to
dye Do make & ordain this my last will & testament
That is to say, Principally & first of all I recommend
my Soul unto the hands of God that gave it & my body
I recommend to the earth, to be buryed in a Decent manner
at the Discretion of my Executors not doubting but at
the General Resurrection I shall receive the same again
by the mighty power of God, & as touching the worldly
estate wherewith it hath pleased god to bless me in
this Life, I give Demise & Dispose of the Same in manner
& form following
Imprimis, I give & bequeath unto my brother Enoch
Living in Bohemia the Sum of Twenty pounds Curt
Money of this province to be raised & leavied out of
my estate
Item, I give & bequeath to the youngest Son my Son
Andrew Israel now has in the Island of Jamaica my
Negro boy named Cavandore
Item, I give & bequeath to the Congregation of the
Children of Israel here in New York the Sum of Six
pounds Currant Money of the province to be raised &
levied out of my estate, to be imployd in the Lining
of the place wherein the five books of Moses is kept
Lastly, I give & bequeath unto my dear & well beloved
Son Andrew Israel of the Island of Jamaica whome
I likewise make ordain & Constitute one of my Executors
of this my last will & testament all the rest &
remainder of my Estate both real & personal (after my
funeral Charges and Just & Lawfull debts are paid out of
the Same) freely to be possessed & enjoyed by him his
Heirs & Assigns forever
I Also Constitute ordain & appoint Mr. Jacob Franks &
Mr. Mordecai Gomez Merchts of the City of New York Executors
of this my Last will & testament
Vide

XIII. URIAH HYAM [1740]

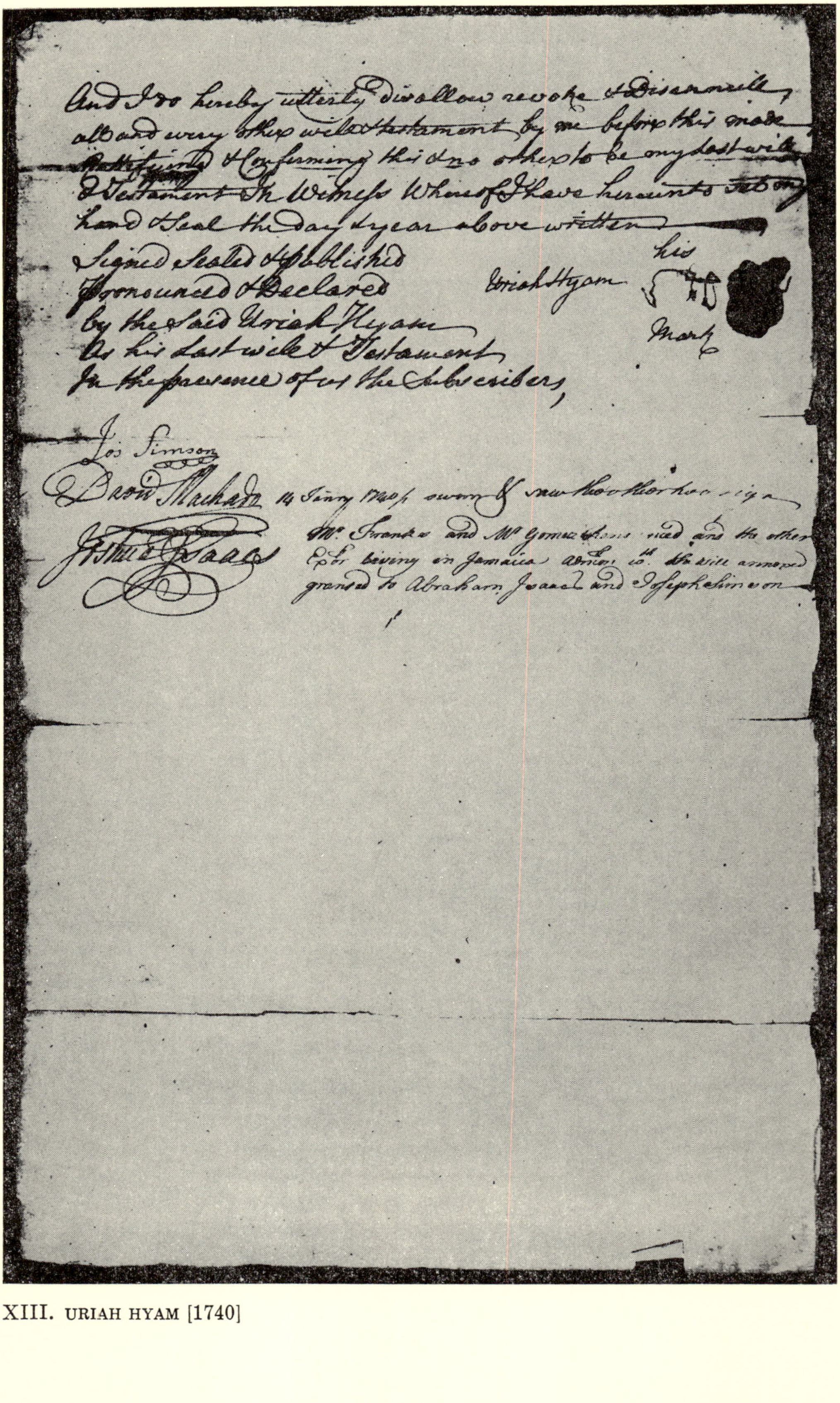
And I do hereby utterly disallow revoke & Disannull all and every other will & testament by me before this made Ratifying & Confirming this & no other to be my last will & Testament In Witness Whereof I have hereunto set my hand & Seal the day & year above written

Signed Sealed & Published
Pronounced & Declared
by the said Uriah Hyam
As his last will & Testament
In the presence of us the Subscribers,

Uriah Hyam his [mark] mark

Jos Simson
Dan'l Machado
Joshua Isaacs

14 Janry 1740/1 sworn & saw the other [illegible]
Mr. Franks and Mr Gomez renounced and the other
Ex'or living in Jamaica Admon. c.t. the will annexed
granted to Abraham Isaacs and Joseph Simson

XIII. URIAH HYAM [1740]

XIV

MOSES MICHAL[1]

[1740]

In the Name of God Amen

On this 22 January 1740 appeared before me ALDERT POTTEY[2] Secretary in the Service of the generall West India Company of the Netherlands Residing on the Island of Curaçao in the Presence of the witnesses hereinafter named Mr. MOSES MICHAL, widdower of late Mrs. CATHARINA HACHER of the Jewish nation now being on the said Island and known by mee the Secretary and witnesses being he the appearant Sickly but well having and using his understanding memory and Speech as unto us the Secretary and witnesses evidently appeared, who in Consideration of the Certainty of death and the uncertain time and hour thereof was designing to dispose of his Temporall estate given him by almighty God, which he the appearant declared to do by these presents and that out of his own and free will without Induction or Persuasion of any Person and before Proceeding therein, he the appearant has Recomended his Soul to the mercy of god and his dead body to the earth in the Jewish *Bethaim* [cemetery] with a decent funerall.

Further the Testator has Revoaked and annulled and by these presents Revoaking and annulling mortifying and made void all former Testaments and other Sort of Last wills by him the Testator before the date hereof made or Passed neither willing nor desiring that the same nor any of them shall have any the least effect or Force and Proceeding to his disposition, the Testator declared by these presents to bequeath to his grand daughter ELKALY MEYER COHEN the Sum of Two hundred Pounds New York money But in case she happens to dy underaged or unmarried then the said legacy shall devolve on her sister HAYA MEYER COHEN.[3]

[1] Albany Will no. M-10, Clerk's Office of the Court of Appeals, Albany; Will Liber 13, p. 378; *NYHSC*, vol. III (1895), pp. 294–295. This will written in Dutch, contains an official translation which is published here. Emmanuel in his book, *Precious Stones*, p. 264, was correct in assuming that since Michael's will was not in the State Archives in The Hague, it would be in New York. Moses Michal was the father of Michael Michaels and of four daughters, Jochebed, Rachel, Rebecca, and Bloeme. An early resident of New York, he appeared in the Mayor's Court in 1707. *Porto v. Michael et ux.* (1707), MCM, vol. 1704–1710, pp. 288, 301–302 and 304. For other litigation, see *Michael v. Nathan Simpson* (1713), MCM, vol. 1710–1715, pp. 354, 360, 363, 369–370 and 375. In 1730, he resided in the South Ward next to Rodrego Pacheco. NYAL, vol. 1721–1734, Feb. 5, 1730. He probably left for Curaçao shortly after this date, since he appears in a number of accounts of Shearith Israel in 1729 and 1730. *PAJHS*, vol. XXI (1913), pp. 19–25 and 38. His career in Curaçao is traced by Emmanuel, *op. cit.*, pp. 261–265.

[2] Aldert Pottey [Potteij] was Secretary of Curaçao from 1738 to 1754. Jacob A. Schiltkamp, *De Geschiedens Van Het Notariaat in Het Octrooigebied van de West Indische Compagnie* (s'Gravenhage, 1964), p. 314. See also pp. 96–97, 127, 129 and 143.

[3] Elkaleh Myers Cohen (1735–1765) and Haya Myers Cohen were daughters of Samuel

In like manner the Testator Bequeaths to his said [grand] daughter HAYA MEYER COHEN the sum of One hundred [pounds] new york money. It being the Testators will and desire that the Said bequeathed Sumes shall be put on Interest for the [use of] the said Legatees.

Further the Testator bequeaths unto his negro PIRO [his] freedom and discharge of all slavish Service whereof [the] hereafter named Executors the due Act may be Executed.

Further the Tystator desires that all his Clouthes [ ] gold and Silver as also his Two Negros Called THAM and PRINS as also a Pair of Rimonim or Silver Bells[4] by him sent out of holland after the Receipt thereof shall be Remitted to his Children and heires.

And further disposing the Testator declares to nominate and Institute for his only and universall [heirs] his four Children by name JOHEVIT MICHAL marryed [to] JUDAH MEARS,[5] RACHEL MICHAL marryed to SAMUEL MEYER COHEN,[6] REBECCA MICHAL marryed to JUDAH HAYS[7] and BLOEME MICHAL marryed to ARON LOUZADA[8] and that in all the goods and effects as well moveable as Immoveable none Excepted which the Testator in any ways shall leave by his death to Receive and possess the Same as their Inheritance.

The Testator allso declares to nominate and appoint for Executors of this his Testament, at New York his Said four Sons in Laws and here on this Island Mr. ISAAC LEVY MADURO and Mr. COHEN HENRIQUES JUNIOR[9] with Such ample Power and authority as the Executors by Law can Be given and granted.

Myers Cohen and Rachel, Michaels' daughter (1707–1749) who on May 26, 1748, petitioned for guardianship over her daughters both of whom were under fourteen at the time. Orders in Chancery, vol. 1740–1770, pp. 4–5, Clerk's Office of the Court of Appeals, Albany.

[4] These were used as ornaments on the Torah or Five Books of Moses.

[5] See *supra*, Will of Moses Levy, p. 39, note 17.

[6] See Will of Samuel Myers Cohen, pp. 65–68.

[7] Judah Hays (1703–1764) became a freeman of New York on December 2, 1735, and was elected constable of Montgomerie Ward in 1746. *Burghers*, p. 129; *Minutes*, vol. IV, p. 346. His career is marked by a great deal of litigation, see e. g. *Hays v. Brendege* (1734), MCM, vol. 1731–1736, pp. 434 and 440; *Hays v. Nox* (1738), MCM, vol. 1736–1742, p. 221. For business accounts, see Harold Korn, ed., "Receipt Book of Judah Hays, 1759–1760," *PAJHS*, vol. XXXIV (1935), pp. 117–134, and Peter Jay Day Book, pp. 224, 242 and 245 ff. and Peter Jay Ledger, p. 189, in the New-York Historical Society Library. In the Ledger is an account of a tax agreement with John Jay. See Will of Judah Hays, pp. 118–121.

[8] Aaron Louzada (1693–1764), a merchant of New York and New Jersey, was a frequent contributor to the Congregation along with his brother Moses. He died at Bound Brook, New Jersey on December 27, 1764, and was brought to New York for burial. *PAJHS*, vol. XXI (1913), pp. 10, 16, 19, 21, 27 and 29; *Portraits*, pp. 239–240.

[9] Both Levy Maduro and Cohen Henriques, well known Jewish residents of Curaçao, ran an advertisement in Dutch and English as "Testamentary Executors," of Moses Michael in which they requested that "all persons having charge against said estate to deliver vouchers in 6 months from the 1st day Nov. 1740 . . ." *New-York Weekly Journal*, December 1, 1740. See also issues of December 8, 15 and 22.

All what is before written the Testator declared to be his Testament last and utmost Will and desire willing and desiring that the same after his decease shall be firm and of effect bee is as Tystament Codicil gift in case of death or among the living as so is [can] best Subsist the Tystator Praying hereon the uttmost benefit of Law and that hereof by me the Secretary shall bee made and delivered all in form.

This done and witnessed at Curacoa Present NICHOLAS HENRICUS and LAWRENCE LAAN[10] as witnesses.

The minute hereof is duly Signed.

which I witness
(signed) A. POTTEY Secry.

New York 26 March 1740

Translated from a Dutch Coppy Signed by ALBERT POTTEY Secretary of Curacoa.

s/ ABRAH. GOUVENEUR[11]

[10] Laurens Laan, a clerk, succeeded Potteij as Secretary of Curaçao. Schiltkamp, *op. cit.*, pp. 141, 143 and 314.

[11] Abraham Gouverneur, was commissioned on July 15, 1732 as translator and interpreter of foreign languages. *Calendar*, p. 22.

XV

LUIS [LEWIS] GOMEZ[1]

[1740]

In the Name of God Amen the Twenty fourth day of December in the third year of the Reign of our Sovering Lord GEORGE THE SECOND of Great Britain France and Ireland King Defender of the faith etc Anno Domino one Thousand Seven hundred and thirty; I LEWIS GOMEZ of the City of New York and Merchant being in good health of body and blessed be God of Perfect Memory Do make this my last will and Testament in manner and forme following (vizt) First I bequeath my soule to God who geave it me and body to the Earth to be decently Interrd, And for the disposeall of such worly Estate as it hath Pleased God to bestow upon me I do give Devise and bequeath the Same as followeth: First I do hereby revoake and made null void and of no Effect all other and former wills and Testaments heretofore by me maid and Published either by word or in writeing; *Item,* it is my will and Pleasure that all my Just Debts Leggaces and funerall Expenses be honestly Paid and Satisfied in convenient time after my Decease *Item* I give and bequeath unto my Eldest Son MORDECAI GOMES one pare of Silver Adornements for the five Books of Moses weying Thirty nine ounces or thereabouts in full satisfaction of his being my Eldest Son or (heire at Law) *Item* I give and bequeath to my Loving Sister ELLENOR GOMES the yearly annuale sum of Twenty five Pounds Current money of New York to be paid her by my Sons out of my Estate five pounds Each yearly which amounts to the above said sum of Twenty five pounds and allso one Negrow wench which She

[1] Original Will no. 104, HDC; Will Liber 13, p. 368; *NYHSC*, vol. III (1895), pp. 292–293. Born in 1660, possibly in Madrid, Gomez died in New York on March 31, 1740. One of the most important of early New York merchants, he had a rich and varied career. Made freeman of the city on February 12, 1706, he built up a considerable mercantile interest. In 1734, he lived in the Montgomerie Ward. Gomez had a deep commitment to Shearith Israel and was one of its original founders and one of the purchasers of the burial ground. Gomez married Esther Marchaze (d. 1718). He had six sons, Mordecai (1688–1750), Jacob (d. 1722), Daniel (1695–1769), David (1697–1769), Isaac (1705–1770), and Benjamin (1711–1772). *Burghers*, p. 87; NYAL, vol. 1721–1734, Montgomerie Ward, Feb. 27, 1734; *Minutes*, vol. III (1905), pp. 447–448; *PAJHS*, vol. XXI (1913), pp. 7–8, 187 and 195; *Portraits*, p. 220; Directory, pp. 43–44, Conveyance Liber 32, cp. 28–29, New York County Clerk's Office, 31 Chambers Street, New York City. It is possible a seventh son also named Lewis existed, but died prior to this will. See Inventory of Joseph Bueno, HDC which indicates a Lewis Gomez and Lewis Gomez, Jr. purchased goods. As one of the executors of Joseph Bueno's will, he was involved in litigation. See *Gideon v. Gomez, et. al.* (1709), MCP, file 1676–1710, Sept. 6, 1709, MCM, vol. 1704–1710, pp. 414 and 416; *Gomez v. Tongrolon* (1709), MCM, vol. 1704–1710, pp. 424–425 and 428–431. He was involved in numerous other actions. See especially *Gomez v. Breton* (1724), MCP, file 1711–1724, Dec. 22, 1724; MCM, vol. 1723–1728, pp. 147, 150, 186, 195 and 334–335.

Shall Chuse and at her decease it shall desend to my sons; the above Said mony to be paid her upon Every first Day of May from and after my Decease for and During her Naturall Life or in case she sees cause to live with my family than in Stead of the said anuely Sum of Twenty five Pounds She Shall have a Sufficient Maintainance out of my Said Estate; which Shall be in her choyce: the rest of my Estate Reale and personall I give Devise and bequath to my Deare and Loving Children Viz MORDECAI, DANIEL, DAVID, ISAAC and BENJAMIN GOMEZ[2] to be Equally Divided amongst them share and Share alike To have and to Hold to Each of them my said five Children an even and Equale fifth part thereof and to Each of their Heires and Assignes for ever And for the better Enableing my Executors to perform and Execute this my Last will; It is my will and Desire that after my Decease my Executors hereafter named or Such of them as Shall be then Living Shall Dispose of my Reale Estate to the heighest bidder, and the Consideration mony from thence ariseing togeather with the Rest of my Estate to be Divided as aforesaid and in Case of the Decease of any of my Children before they attaine marrige the portion or portions of the Deceased Shall Decend to the Survivours of my Said Children by Even and Equall portion; Executors of his my Last will I make and appoint my five Loving Sons MORDECAI GOMEZ, DANIEL GOMEZ, DAVID GOMEZ, ISAAC GOMEZ and BENJAMIN GOMEZ; In Witness whereof I have hereunto Sett my hand and Seale the Day and year first above written.

Signed Sealed and Published s/ LUIS GOMEZ [seal]
in the Presents of us 1740
s/ T. BRAINES[3]
s/ FRED. WILLEMEZ[4] May 7th Sworn & saw the other two sign
s/ JAMES BROWN[5]

MORDECAI GOMEZ, DANIEL GOMEZ DAVID GOMEZ Executors Sworn (power to ISAAC GOMEZ and BENJAMIN GOMEZ who are absent)

[2] See Wills of Mordecai, David, Isaac, and Benjamin Gomez, *infra*, pp. 84–91, and 125–137.

[3] Thomas Braines was appointed Surrogate of Queens County on December 8, 1759. *Calendar*, p. 53.

[4] Frederick Williams, a baker, was made freeman of the city on February 23, 1725. *Burghers*, p. 106.

[5] James Brown, a perriwig maker, was made freeman on August 26, 1712, and James Brown, a cordwainer, was also thus named. *Ibid.*, pp. 91 and 130.

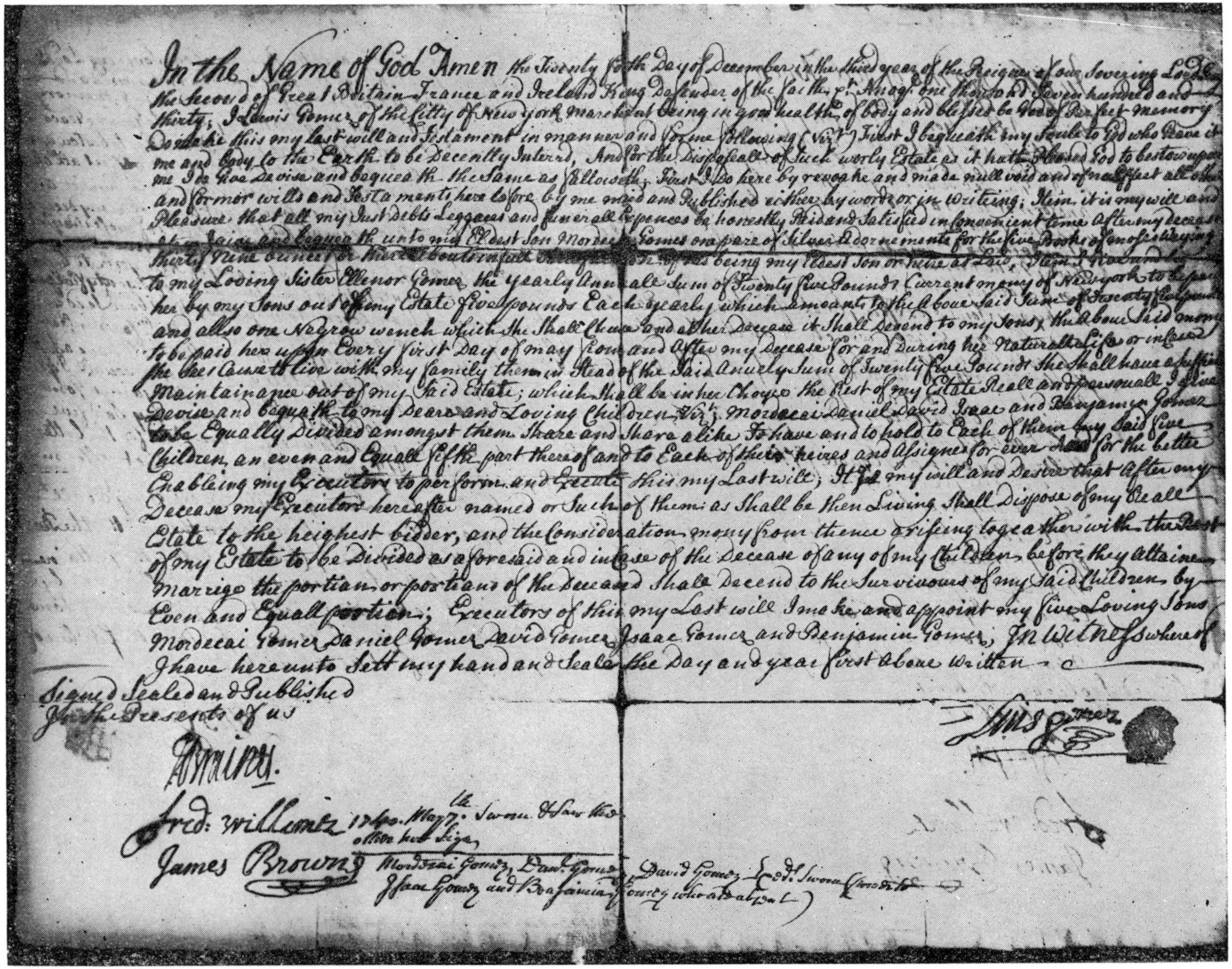

In the Name of God Amen the Twenty forth Day of December in the third year of the Reigne of our Soveraing Lord [illegible]
the Second of Great Britain France and Ireland King Defender of the Faith &c. Annoq. one thousand Seven hundred and
thirty, I Lewis Gomez of the Citty of New york marchant being in good health of body and blessed be God of Perfect memory
Do make this my last will and Testament in manner and forme following (Viz.) First I bequeath my Soule to God who Gave it
me and body to the Earth to be Decently Interd, And for the Dispofeall of Such worly Estate as it hath Pleased God to bestow upon
me I Do Give Devise and bequeath the Same as followeth, First I Do here by revoake and made null void and of no Effect all other
and former wills and Testaments here tofore by me made and Published either by word or in writeing; Item it is my will and
Pleasure that all my Just debts Leggaces and funerall Expences be honestly Paid and Satisfied in Conveenient time after my decease
[illegible] Give and bequeath unto my Eldest Son Mordecai Gomez one pare of Silver Adornements for the five Books of Mosses Weying
thirty Nine ounces [illegible] being my Eldest Son or heire at Law, Item I [illegible]
to my Loving Sister Ellenor Gomez the yearly Annuale Sum of Twenty five Pounds Current mony of New york to be pa[id]
her by my Sons out of my Estate five Pounds Each yearly which amounts to the Above Said Sum of Twenty five Pounds
and allso one Negrow wench which she Shall Chuse and at her decease it Shall Decend to my Sons, the Above Said mony
to be paid her upon Every first Day of may from and After my decease for and During her Naturall Life or in Case
she [illegible] to live with my family then in Stead of the Said Anuely Sum of Twenty five Pounds she Shall have a suffi[cient]
Maintainance out of my Said Estate; which Shall be in her Choyce the Rest of my Estate Reall and Personall I Give
Devise and bequath to my Deare and Loving Children Viz. Mordecai Daniel David Isaac and Benjamin Gomez
to be Equally Divided amongst them Share and Share alike To have and to hold to Each of them my Said five
Children an even and Equall fifth part thereof and to Each of their heires and Assignes for ever [illegible] for the better
Enableing my Executors to perform and Execute this my Last will; It [is] my will and Desire that after my
Decease my Executors hereafter named or Such of them as Shall be then Living Shall Dispose of my Reall
Estate to the heighest bidder, and the Consideration mony from thence arifeing togeather with the Rest
of my Estate to be Divided as aforesaid and in Case of the Decease of any of my Children before they attaine
marrige the portian or portians of the Deceased Shall Decend to the Survivours of my Said Children by
Even and Equall portion; Executors of this my Last will I make and appoint my five Loving Sons
Mordecai Gomez Daniel Gomez David Gomez Isaac Gomez and Benjamin Gomez, In Witness whereof
I have hereunto Sett my hand and Seale the Day and year first Above Written

Signed Sealed and Published
In the Presents of us

[illegible]

Fred: willemez 1740 May 7th Sworn & Saw the [illegible]

James Brown

Mordecai Gomez, Dan.l Gomez David Gomez [illegible] Sworn [illegible]
Isaac Gomez and Benjamin Gomez [illegible]

Luis Gomez

XV. LUIS [LEWIS] GOMEZ [1740]

XVI

SAMUEL MYERS COHEN[1]

[1743]

In the Name of God Amen.

I SAMUEL MYERS COHEN of the City of New York Merchant being now bound on a voyage to England[2] and Considering the Danger of the Seas and certainty of Death and uncertainty of this Life and being willing to settle my worldly affairs have made this my last Will and Testament in manner and form following Viz^{t}:

Imprimis

I bequeath my soul unto God that gave it trusting and alone depending on his mercy for my Eternal Salvation and as for that worldly Estate which it hath Pleased him to bless me with I do by this my last Will give and dispose thereof as follows.

[1] Will Liber 15, p. 107; *NYHSC*, vol. III (1895), p. 405. Samuel Myers Cohen (c. 1708 — Sept. 21, 1743), a merchant, was naturalized on July 12, 1729 and as Samuel Myers, shopkeeper, was made freeman of the city on October 6, 1730. A month before he was elected constable of the Dock Ward, but his place was taken by Christopher Nicholson. *Burghers*, p. 114; *Colonial Laws*, vol. II, p. 513; *Minutes*, vol. IV, pp. 27 and 30. He was *shoḥet, bodek*, and *parnas* of Congregation Shearith Israel. *PAJHS*, vol. XXI (1913), pp. 4, 6, 11, 13–14, 26 and 29; *Portraits*, pp. 228–230. Cohen's first marriage was to Rachel Asher Levy, widow of Samuel Levy (d. 1719 — see Will of Samuel Levy, *American Jewish Historical Quarterly* [=*AJHQ*], vol. LV, no. 3 (March, 1966), p. 342) sometime in 1729 or 1730. Rachel died October 22, 1732 at age 41. Indenture dated Oct. 17, 1732 made by Samuel Myers Cohen and Rachel Myers Cohen to Jacob Franks, Conveyance Liber 12, pp. 356–358, Office of the Secretary of State, Albany, New York. Two daughters, Richa and Rebecca, were born of this marriage. His second marriage was to Rachel Michael, daughter of Moses Michael and Catherine Hacher, who also bore him two daughters Elkaley and Hyah. See Will of Moses Michael (*AJHQ*, vol. LV, no. 3, p. 359); Orders in Chancery, May 13, 1740–March 30, 1770, pp. 4–5, Clerk's Office of the Court of Appeals, Albany. In 1739, Cohen lived on Duke Street in a two story house with a "large yard and Grass-plot, and pump with good water." *Weekly Journal*, Aug. 25 and Sept. 1, 1740. For business dealings, see extensive entries from 1737–1744, Peter Jay Day Book and entries of Feb. 14, 1742 and April 14, 1743, William DeWitt Day Book (1739–1752), both in the New-York Historical Society Library. Cohen was part owner of the ship *London*. NOL, CO 5/1226, June 20, 1743. For litigation in which he was involved see *Samuel Myers v. Goulding* (1730), MCM, vol. 1728–1731, p. 185; *Cohen v. Ten Eyck* (1732), MCM, vol. 1731–1736, p. 106; *Cohen v. Bennett* (1743), MCM, vol. 1742–1748, p. 46.

[2] Notice of Myers Cohen's voyage to England was published in the *Weekly Journal* of August 25 and September 1, 1740. He embarked a year later shortly after this will was drawn. See Abigail Franks to Naphtali Franks, Sept. 6, 1741, Oct. 18, 1741, and June 3, 1742, Abigail Franks Letters. He had various business and legal activities in 1743 in New York, indicating a return to New York by that year. See *supra*, note 1, and the Entry of July 14, 1743, William DeWitt Day Book, wherein it appears, "Mr. Samuell Mirs and his brother to shafe [shave] . . . £0.17.0."

Item

I will that all those just Debts and demands which I owe to any Person or Persons whatsoever be satisfied and Paid as soon as Possible by my Executors hereafter named.

Item

It is my will and Pleasure and I do hereby give and bequeath unto my beloved Wife RACHAEL[3] and to her assigns all my silver Plate all the Furniture of my House all my wearing & Aparel and all those negroes Slaves[4] I have which I shall die possessed of.

Item

It is my will and pleasure that all my Real and Personal Estate (except what I have before disposed of to my wife) be sold and disposed of to the best advantage within such time as shall by my Executors or the Major part of them or the survivors of them or the Major part of such survivors be thought convenient and for the doing executing and perfect finishing whereof I do by these presents Give Grant Will and Transfer to my said Executors or the Major part of them or the survivors of them or the Major part of such survivors free power and authority to Grant Alien bargain sell convey and acquire in fee simple all or any part or parcell of what Real Estate I shall die seized of to any person or persons and their heirs for ever.

Item

It is my Will and Pleasure that the sum of two hundred Pounds New York Money be put out at Interest on Good and Sufficient security and that the Interest money thereby arising shall be employed and laid out for and toward the maintainence and support of my Brother EMANUEL[5] for and during his life and that the said sum of two hundred pounds at the decease of my said Brother EMANUEL shall return and may be accounted as part of my General Estate hereafter by me disposed.

[3] After the death of Samuel Myers Cohen and sometime in 1744, Rachel married Jacob Levy. As late as Feb. 28, 1744, she is still known as Rachel Cohen, but by December 18, 1744, one of the executors of the estate of Samuel Myers Cohen is Jacob Levy and Rachel Cohen is now the latter's wife. *Johnston v. Cohen* (1744), MCM, vol. 1742–1748, p. 111; Levy *et al. v.* Ewetse (1744), *ibid.*, p. 193; Indenture of Rachel Levy, *et al.* to Samuel Macoun, *Town Records of Oyster Bay* (New York, 1930), vol. V, p. 355. She is reported to have died of fright in August, 1749, caused by the sound of a fire alarm. *New York Revised Weekly Post-Boy*, Aug. 21, 1749.

[4] Cohen owned at least two slaves, Windsor and Hereford, both of whom were implicated in the "Negro Plot" of 1741, but who were released. *PAJHS*, vol. XXVII (1920), pp. 384–385.

[5] Possibly the Emanuel Myers Cohen referred to as a member of Shearith Israel in 1744, who was a donor to the Congregation during 1737–1745. *PAJHS*, vol. XXI (1913), pp. 45, 48 and 131–132.

Item

I do hereby Give and bequeath unto my three Sisters named ESTHER, RACHAL now the wife of SALOMON BUNN[6] and BILAH the sum of twenty five Pounds New York money Each to be paid them and each of them by my Executors.

Item

I do hereby Give and bequeath unto my Niece ROSE BUNN[7] the sum of One Hundred Pounds New York money to be paid her at the day of her marriage provided always that she marries with the consent and approbation of my Wife otherwise not.

Item

I do give and bequeath the sum of twenty five pounds New York money to and for the use of the Synagogue now frequented and belon[g]ing to the people called Jews *and* whereof I at present am a Member.

Item

I do hereby give and bequeath to each and every of MR. JACOB FRANK'S children[8] a mourning Ring of the Value of forty shillings Sterling and I do hereby also give and bequeath unto CAPTAIN WILLIAM WALTON and to his wife[9] each a Ring of the same value.

Item

I do hereby give and bequeath unto each & every of my Executors the sum of twenty five pounds New York money for a mourning suit.

Item

It is my Will and pleasure that the Remainder of my Estate be divided equally between my beloved wife RACHEL and my four Daughters namely ELKALEY,[10] HIAH, REBECHA and RICHA[11] share and share alike and if it

[6] Solomon Bunn donated to Shearith Israel in 1741 and 1747. *Ibid.*, pp. 44-45 and 55. His name is also spelled Boon, Bun, etc. Rachel and Solomon were married sometime prior to December, 1735. Abigail Franks to Naphtali Franks, December 12, 1735, Abigail Franks Letters [Friedman Collection, American Jewish Historical Society].

[7] Rosa Bunn, became the wife of Joseph Simon. Morris Jastrow, Jr., "Joseph Simon of Lancaster, Pennsylvania," *PAJHS*, vol. I (1905), p. 122; vol. XXXIII (1934), p. 210.

[8] Jacob Franks (1688-1769) and his wife Abigail Levy Franks (1696-1756) had seven children, three sons and four daughters, in 1741 — David Franks (1720-1794), Moses Franks (1719-1789), Naphtali Franks (1715-1796), Phila Franks (1722-1811), Richa Franks, Rebecca, and Abigail. Two other children Sara (d. 1733) and Aaron (d. 1738) died earlier. See Abigail Franks Letters [Friedman Collection, American Jewish Historical Society]. These letters also reveal the friendship of the Franks family with Samuel Cohen, who had been married to Abigail's aunt.

[9] A William Walton, carpenter, was made freeman in August, 1698. *Burghers*, p. 68. For a reference to a Capt. William Walton see *Minutes*, vol. III, pp. 163 and 167.

[10] Elkaley (1735-1765) married Myer Myers (1723-1795), a noted gold and silversmith. See Will of Moses Michael, *supra*, pp. 59-60, note 3.

[11] Rebecca married Mathias Bush in 1764 in Philadelphia and Richa (1731-1801) married Bernard Gratz in December, 1760. *PAJHS*, vol. XXXIII (1934), pp. 202 and 210.

shall happen that my wife now is or at any time before my Death shall prove to be pregnant with Child that then and in such case the Child or Children of which she shall so prove to be pregnant shall come in for & be entitled to an equal share or a dividend of my Estate with my wife and other children before by me named. And it is further my will and pleasure that each particular Child's Share of my Estate be by my Executors put out at Interest on good and sufficient security and that the Interest money thereby ariseing be employed and laid out for and toward the maintainance & bringing up of each respective child and that the principal sum so put out at Interest be paid to each respective child when they shall marry or arrive at the age of Eighteen years which shall first happen.

Item

I do hereby nominate and appoint my dear and loving wife RACHEL my executrix and my Brother ABRAHAM MYERS COHEN[12] and MESSRS. JACOB WALTON and WILLIAM WALTON JUNR[13] my Executors of this my last Will and Testament. And lastly I do declare this to be my last Will & Testament and I do hereby revoke and make null and void all former & other Wills and Testaments by me heretofore made and this only to be and stand in force. In witness whereof I have hereunto put my Hand and Seal this fourth day of August 1741.

S. MYERS COHEN [L. S.]

Signed Sealed published and declared to be the last Will & Testament of the Testator in the presence of us JOHANNA KALSALL, MARGRIT GOUVERNEUR,[14] ANTHONY WHITE.[15]

[12] Abraham Myers Cohen, a shopkeeper, was made freeman January 10, 1738. He was elected and sworn as constable of the East Ward in 1744. *Minutes*, vol. V, pp. 128 and 132. For biography of Abraham and his wife, see *Portraits*, p. 250.

[13] Jacob and William Walton, Jr., sons of William Walton, were New York merchants. *NYHSC*, vol. IV (1896), p. 484. For references to Jacob see *Minutes*, vol. VII, pp. 106 and 150 and to William, Jr. *ibid.* vol. VII, pp. 38, 106 and 403. The latter was made freeman in 1737. David T. Valentine, *History of the City of New York* (New York, 1853), p. 378. For litigation involving the executors of the estate, see *Cohen v. Wyley* (1744), MCM, vol. 1742–1748, p. 80; *Johnston v. Cohen* (1744), *ibid.*, p. 111. See also deed, dated Jan. 6, 1746, of Rachel Levy, widow of Samuel Myers Cohen, Abraham Myers Cohen, Jacob and William Walton, as executors of the estate of Samuel Myers Cohen, to Samuel Macoun of nineteen acres in Oyster Bay. *Town Records of Oyster Bay, op. cit.*, vol. V, p. 355.

[14] Margrit Gouverneur was the daughter of Isaac Gouverneur and the sister of the second wife of Lewis Morris. *NYHSC*, vol. VI (1898), pp. 168–169.

[15] Anthony White, gentleman, was made freeman on November 7, 1738. *Burghers*, p. 137.

XVII

JOSHUA ISAACS[1]

[1744]

In the Name of God Amen

I JOSHUA ISAACS of the Cyty & province of New York Merchant being in perfect health mind & memmory Yet Calling to mind the Mortallity of my body knowing It is appointed for all men to dye, have thought fitt to make this my Last will & testament, that, when ever it shall be the will & pleasure of the almighty God to call me from here, I humbly Recommend My Soul, unto his holly hands & Care & desire my body may be buryed In Our Jews burying Ground in said New York among my relation & friends, at the discretion of my Executors & Touching the World Estate wherewith It hath pleased God to bless me with (after all my Just & Lawfull Debts are paid Which I desire may be done as Soon as possible) I give devise & bequeath the same in Manner & form following

Whereas I did at the time of my Marriage give unto my wife HANNAH[2] a Bill of Dowry for the Sum of Five hundred pounds Current Money of this province payable at my demise which I will be paid her unless she shall & will sooner accept of the one third of my estate which desire may be at her Choice, but at the time of my demise If my real & personall estate (after my Just & Lawfull debts are paid) shall amount to Twelve hundred fifty pounds (besides my household goods & Utensills) that then I will & give also unto my sd wife HANNAH all my Household goods & Utensills as aforesaid & If it Should not amount to said sum, I will she have the use of them during her Widdowhood & then to return to my Child or Children,[3] I also appoint my said wife HANNAH One of the Execurix of this My last will & Testament

[1] Original Will in Museum of the City of New York, Will Liber 15 p. 245; *NYHSC*, vol. IV (1896), pp. 11–12. Joshua Isaacs (d. July, 1744), a merchant, had considerable business dealings with Peter Jay. Entry of April 23, 1742, Peter Jay Day Book, p. 261, see also pages 232, 250, 265, *et passim*. For examples of litigation, see *Isaacs v. Peterson* (1744), MCM, vol. 1742–1748, p. 146; *Isaacs v. Tuttle, ibid.* He was also active in congregational affairs and often contributed money. At his death he owed £9.14.3. *PAJHS*, vol. XXI (1913), pp. 27, 31 and 48.

[2] Hannah Levy Isaacs (1723–1751), daughter of Moses Levy, married Joshua a few days before December 20, 1741. Abigail Franks to Naphtali Franks, December 20, 1741, Abigail Franks Letters.

[3] Grace Isaacs (d. 1781) married Nathan Hart. *Portraits*, pp. 315 and 503. At the time of Joshua's death, she was his only child. Another child, Joshua, was born posthumously.

Item

I desire that fifty pounds be given to our Congregation of Jews at New York which said Sum I will & put out to use by them, & the Yearly Income of the same to be yearly for ever Imployed For the Support of our Hebrew School at said New York to teach poor Children the Hebrew tongue[4]

Item

I desire that the sum of Five pounds be paid to each of my brothers & Sisters[5] for to buy Mourning

Item

I give & bequeath unto my daughter GRACE, all the residue both of my real & personall Estate, unless at the time of my demise, that I should have any more Children Lawfully begotten by me in the body of my said wife HANNAH,[6] that then my will is that all my said Estate is given unto my said Daughter GRACE equally divided amongst my said Children & paid to them if, Daughter or Daughters, at the time of their Marriage or aged, & if a Son or Sons at the time of their being at full age & my will is that the same be put out to use as soon as may be for her his or their Support & bringing up till that time & In Case (which God forbid) any of them should dye before their Marriage or Age as aforesaid that then his her or their devide be equally devided amongst the Surviving Children or Child, & in Case (which God forbid) all my Children Should dye before their being so Married or of age as aforesaid, that then my will is that the Residue of my said estate so given unto my daughter GRACE or Children be equally divided amongst, my Brothers & Sisters, & in Case of any or either of their deaths to their Heir or Heirs.

I also further Appoint JACOB FRANKS Merchant[7] of this City MR. SOLOMON ISAACS Merchant[8] of Boston & MR. JOSEPH SIMSON[9] of this

[4] A Hebrew school was established by the Congregation soon after the synagogue was built in 1730. The first teacher was Moses Lopez de Fonseca. In 1737, David Machado was made *ḥazzan* and he promised to

> "keep a publick school in due form for Teaching the hebrew Language, either the whole morning or afternoon as he shall think most proper, and any poor that shall be thought unable to pay for their children's Learning they shall be taught gratis [*PAJHS*, vol. XXI (1913), pp. 35–36]."

It was this school which seems to have attracted the testator.

[5] Joshua had two brothers, Solomon and Asher, and three sisters, Rebecca, Rachel, and Judith. See Will of Solomon Isaacs, *infra*, pp. 103–106.

[6] Joshua Isaacs was born after his father's death on September 17, 1744, and died in 1810. A merchant, he served in the Revolutionary Army, and was an "honored elder" of the Congregation. *Portraits*, pp. 317–318.

[7] See Will of Samuel Levy, *supra*, p. 29, note 6.

[8] Solomon Isaacs was the testator's brother. See Will of Solomon Isaacs, *infra*, pp. 103–106.

[9] Joseph Simson was Joshua's brother-in-law, being married to his sister Rebecca. See Wills of Joseph Simson, *infra*, pp. 201–203, and Solomon Isaacs, *infra*, pp. 103–106.

Cyty Joyntly with said Wife Executors[10] to this my Last will & testament & I further Impower them to sell & Convey any of my real estate for the Bennifit of my said wife & Children awarding to their Discretion Rattifieing this & no other to be my Last will & testament:
Dated In New York this 13th July 1744

s/ JOSHUA ISAACS [seal]

Witness
DAVID MACHADO[11]
JACOB PINTO[12]
SAMUELL PINTO[13]
MYER MYERS[14]

6th August 1744
DAVID MACHADO Sworn Witness &
HANNAH ISAACS Executors power reserved
JACOB FRANKS to SOLOMON ISAACS
JOSEPH SIMSON

Be it Remembered that on the Sixth day of November in the Year of Our Lord One thousand Seven hundred and forty four JACOB PINTO and MYER MYERS two of the Witnesses to the within Will Personally Came before me JOHN SMYTH duly authorized to Prove Wills & Qualify Executors in the Eastern Division of New Jersey and they being duely Sworn on the Five Books of Moses, did Depose that they were present and Saw JOSHUA ISAACS the Testator in the within Writing named Sign & Seal the Same & heard him Publish, Pronounce & Declare the Same to be his Last Will & Testament, & that at the Doing thereof the said Testator was of Sound Mind and Memory to the best of their knowledge & Understanding, and they & each of them Signed as an Evidence in the Testators Presence.

s/ JOHN SMYTH

Be it also Remembered that at the Same time JACOB FRANKS, JOSEPH SIMSON and HANNAH ISAACS three of the Executors in the Within Will

[10] These executors obtained a summons against Daniel Dumont for £19. Mayor's Court Writ Book, 1736–1746, June 21, 1746 copied in Oppenheim Collection, Shelf 3D, Case 4. This writ book is unfortunately missing from the County Clerk's Office.

[11] See Will of Rachel Luis, *supra*, p. 51, note 2, and *supra*, p. 70, note 4.

[12] Jacob Pinto donated to the Synagogue between 1736 and 1747. *PAJHS*, vol. XXI (1913), pp. 45 and 53.

[13] Samuel Pinto (1728–1744) was also a donor to the Congregation in 1750. *Ibid.*, p. 63. See also *Portraits*, pp. 248, 260, 472 and 480.

[14] See Will of Samuel Myers Cohen, *supra*, p. 67, note 10.

and Testament named, personally Came before me & were Sworn to the due Execution and performance thereof according to Law.

s/ JOHN SMYTH

Secretary's Office New York August 6 1744

Be it Remembered that on the Day & Year above written personally appeared before me GEORGE JOSEPH MOORE[15] being thereunto delegated & appointed DAVID MACHADO one of the Subscribing Witnesses to the written Will and made Oath on Five Books of Moses that he saw the within named JOSHUA ISAACS Sign Seal publish & declare the within to be his last Will & Testament & also that at the Time thereof he was of Sound & disposing mind & memory to the best of his knowledge And also that he saw the other Subscribing Witnesses Sign their Names in his presence & in the presence of the Testator.

s/ GEO. JOS. MOORE DS

Be it Remembered that on the same Day also personally appeared before me delegated as aforesaid HANNAH ISAACS, JACOB FRANKS & JOSEPH SIMSON three of the Executors within named & were duly Sworn to the due Execution & performance of the Said Will

s/ GEO. JOS. MOORE DS

[15] George Joseph Moore, Deputy Secretary of the Province, was appointed in 1741 by the Court of Chancery as a guardian. *Minutes*, vol. V, pp. 60–61.

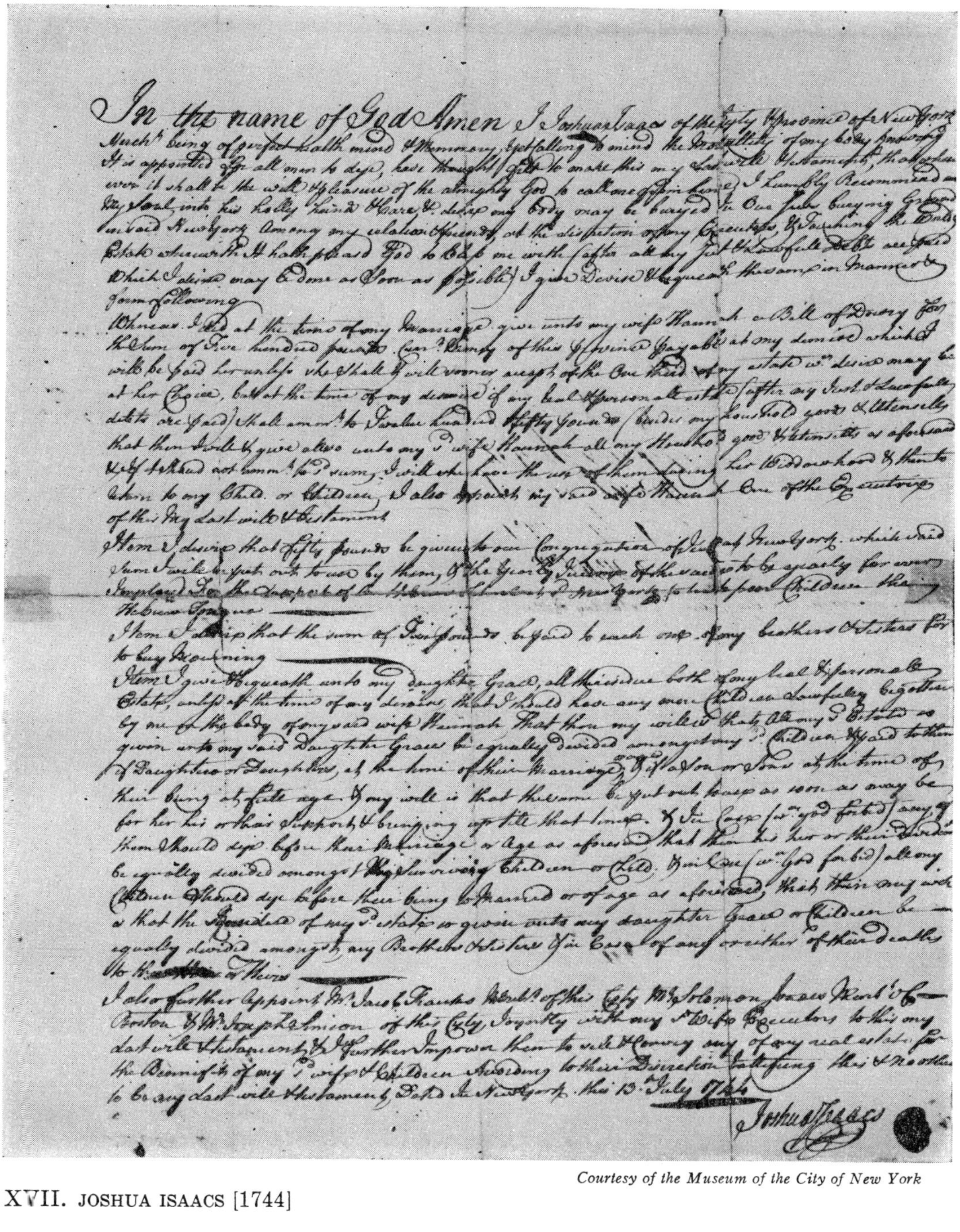

In the name of God Amen I Joshua Isaacs of the City & province of New York Merch[t] being of perfect health mind & memmory, & calling to mind the mortallity of my body knowing it is appointed for all men to dye, have thought fitt to make this my last will & testament, that when ever it shall be the will & pleasure of the almighty God to call me from hence I humbly Recommend my Soul into his holly hands & care & desire my body may be buryed in Our Jews burying Ground in said New york among my relations & friends at the discretion of my Executors, & touching the Wordly Estate wherewith it hath pleased God to bless me with (after all my just & lawfull debts are paid which I desire may be done as soon as possible) I give devise & bequeath the same in manner & form following

Whereas I did at the time of my marriage give unto my wife Hannah a Bill of Dowry for the sum of Five hundred pounds Curr[t] money of this province payable at my demise which will be paid her unless she shall & will rather accept of the One third of my estate w[ch] desire may be at her Choice, but at the time of my demise if my real & personal estate (after my just & lawfull debts are paid) shall amou[t] to Twelve hundred & fifty pounds (besides my household goods & utensills) that then I will & give also unto my s[d] wife Hannah all my household goods & utensills as aforesaid & if it should not amou[t] to s[d] sum, I will she have the use of them during her widowhood & then to return to my Child or Children, I also appoint my said wife Hannah one of the Executors of this my last will & testament

Item I devise that fifty pounds be given to our Congregation of Jews at New York which said sum I will be put out to use by them, & the yearly Interest thereof to be yearly for ever imployed for the support of the Hebrew School in s[d] New York to teach poor Children the Hebrew Tongue

Item I devise that the sum of Ten pounds be paid to each one of my brothers & sisters for to buy mourning

Item I give & bequeath unto my daughter Grace, all the residue both of my real & personal Estate, unless at the time of my demise, that I should have any more Children lawfully begotten by me on the body of my said wife Hannah. That then my will is that all my s[d] Estate so given unto my said Daughter Grace be equally divided amongst my s[d] Children & paid to them if Daughter or Daughters, at the time of their Marriage, & if a son or sons at the time of their being at full age & my will is that the same be put out to use as soon as may be for her his or their support, & bringing up till that time. & in Case (w[ch] God forbid) any of them should dye before their marriage or age as afores[d] that then his her or their share be equally divided amongst the surviving Children or Child. & in Case (w[ch] God forbid) all my Children should dye before their being married or of age as aforesaid, that then my will is that the Residue of my s[d] estate so given unto my daughter Grace or Children be equally divided amongst my Brothers & sisters & in Case of any or either of their deaths to their [illegible] or heirs

I also further appoint M[r] Jacob Franks Merch[t] of this City M[r] Solomon Isaacs Merch[t] of Boston & M[r] Joseph Simson of this City jointly with my s[d] wife Executors to this my last will & testament, & I further impower them to sell & convey any of my real estate for the benefit of my s[d] wife & Children According to their discretion ratifying this & no other to be my last will & testament, Dated in New York this 13th July 1744

Joshua Isaacs

Courtesy of the Museum of the City of New York

XVII. JOSHUA ISAACS [1744]

Courtesy of the Museum of the City of New York

XVII. JOSHUA ISAACS [1744]

XVIII

ISAAC LEVY[1]

[1745]

In the Name of God Amen The Twenty Seventh Day of August Anno Domini One Thousand Seven hundred and Forty five, I ISAAC LEVY being Sick & Weak but of perfect Mind & Memory, calling to Mind ye Mortality of my Body, Do therefore make and ordain this my last Will and Testament, Vizt, first & principally I resign my Soul to Almighty God, & my Body to be buried according to ye Jewish Custom; My Worldly Estate I devise & dispose of in manner following Vizt. To my Daughter RITSY of ye City of New York in ye province of New York, I bequeath, after my lawful Debts are paid, The Sum of Three hundred pounds of Said New-York Currency; To my Grandchildren JOSEPH MOSES, COLLMAN COLMANS, & BYLA COLMANS, Two hundred pounds equally divided between them; To my Nephew DAVID HART, Three hundred pounds, New York Currency; And whatever there be more, I bequeath to My said Daughter RITSY & Said Nephew DAVID HART equally to be divided between them; And I do appoint my Said Daughter RITSY, & Said Nephew DAVID HART to be my Executors of this my last Will and Testament, and that they Shall pay to my Said Grandchildren the above mentioned Sum of Two hundred pounds of Said New York Currency equally to be divided among them at ye Day of Marriage, or if not married before, at the Age of one and Twenty Years. Also to MARY DRUMMY[2] Widdow of said New York, The Sum of Ten pounds Said New York Currency, Also to MARY CANNON[3] of Said New York, Twenty Shillings, any Thing to ye contrary before mentioned notwithstanding. And I do revoke all other wills hereto-

[1] Original Will no. 308, HDC; Will Liber 15, p. 455; *NYHSC*, vol. IV (1896), pp. 56–57. Isaac Levy, a shopkeeper, was made freeman in November, 1740 and elected constable three years later. *Burghers*, p. 142; Minutes of the Court of General Sessions, vol. 1722–1743, p. 304, New York County Clerk's Office. Isaac Levy is a common name and it is difficult to identify who is referred to. An Isaac Levy contributed in 1737 to the building of a wall around the Jewish cemetery on "Fresh Water," part of the Chatham Street burial ground. *PAJHS*, vol. XXI (1913), pp. 37–38. There are a number of Levy cases on record, possibly all or some relate to our Isaac. See for example, *Levi v. Vanderbogart*, (1735), Minutes of the Supreme Court, vol. 1732–1739, p. 179; *Levy v. Bradford* (1737), New York Supreme Court Narrative, William Bradford Manuscripts, New-York Historical Society Library. The inventory of the shop goods of Levy taken September 18, 1745 is in the New-York Historical Society Library and a copy in the American Jewish Historical Society Library.

[2] Mary Drummy was a litigant in the case of *Machado v. Drummy* (1739), MCM, vol. 1736–1742, pp. 257 and 259.

[3] Mary Cannon referred to is possibly the daughter of John Cannon, Jr. and Jerusha, his wife. *NYHSC*, vol. IV (1896), p. 59.

fore made, confirming this to be my last Will and Testament. In witness whereof I have hereunto Set my Hand and Seal the Day abovementioned.

his
ISAAC X LEVY
mark

[seal]

Signed, Sealed, published pronounced, & declared by the Said ISAAC LEVY to be his last Will and Testament in presence of us.

s/ DAVID MACHADO[4]
s/ JOB STAPLES
s/ ELLNOR MASS

Secretarys Office New York September the 18th 1745

Then personally appeared before me JOHN CATHERWOOD[5] thereunto delegated and appointed DAVID MACHADO (a person professing the Jewish Religion) one of the Subscribing Witnesses to the above Will of ISAAC LEVY And being Sworn on the five Books of Moses Declared that he saw the said ISAAC LEVY Sign Seal publish & declare the above Writing to be his last Will and Testament and that at the Time thereof He was of sound and Disposing Mind and Memory to the best of his the Said Witness's Knowledge And Declared further that he saw JOB STAPLES and ELEANOR MASS sign as Witnesses to the same in presence of the Testator. JOB STAPLES another of the Subscribing Witnesses to the said Will of ISAAC LEVY also appeared before me the said JOHN CATHERWOOD and being sworn on the Holy Evangelists of Almighty God Declared that he saw the same Executed as aforesaid and that the Testator at the Time thereof was of sound Mind and Memory to the best of his Knowledge And further that he saw the said DAVID MACHADO and ELEANOR MASS sign as Witnesses to the same Will in presence of the Testator Then and there also appeared before me the said John JOHN CATHERWOOD, RITSY LEVY and DAVID HART, (persons professing the Jewish Religion) the Executors in the said Will named and were Sworn on the five Books of Moses to the true Execution and performance of the same Will.

[4] See Will of Joshua Isaacs, *supra*, p. 70, note 4.

[5] John Catherwood was a merchant who became Secretary to Governor George Clinton by 1748. William Johnson to John Catherwood, April 17, 1746, *William Johnson Papers* (Albany, 1921), vol. I, p. 49. See also pp. 69–70, 153 and 167.

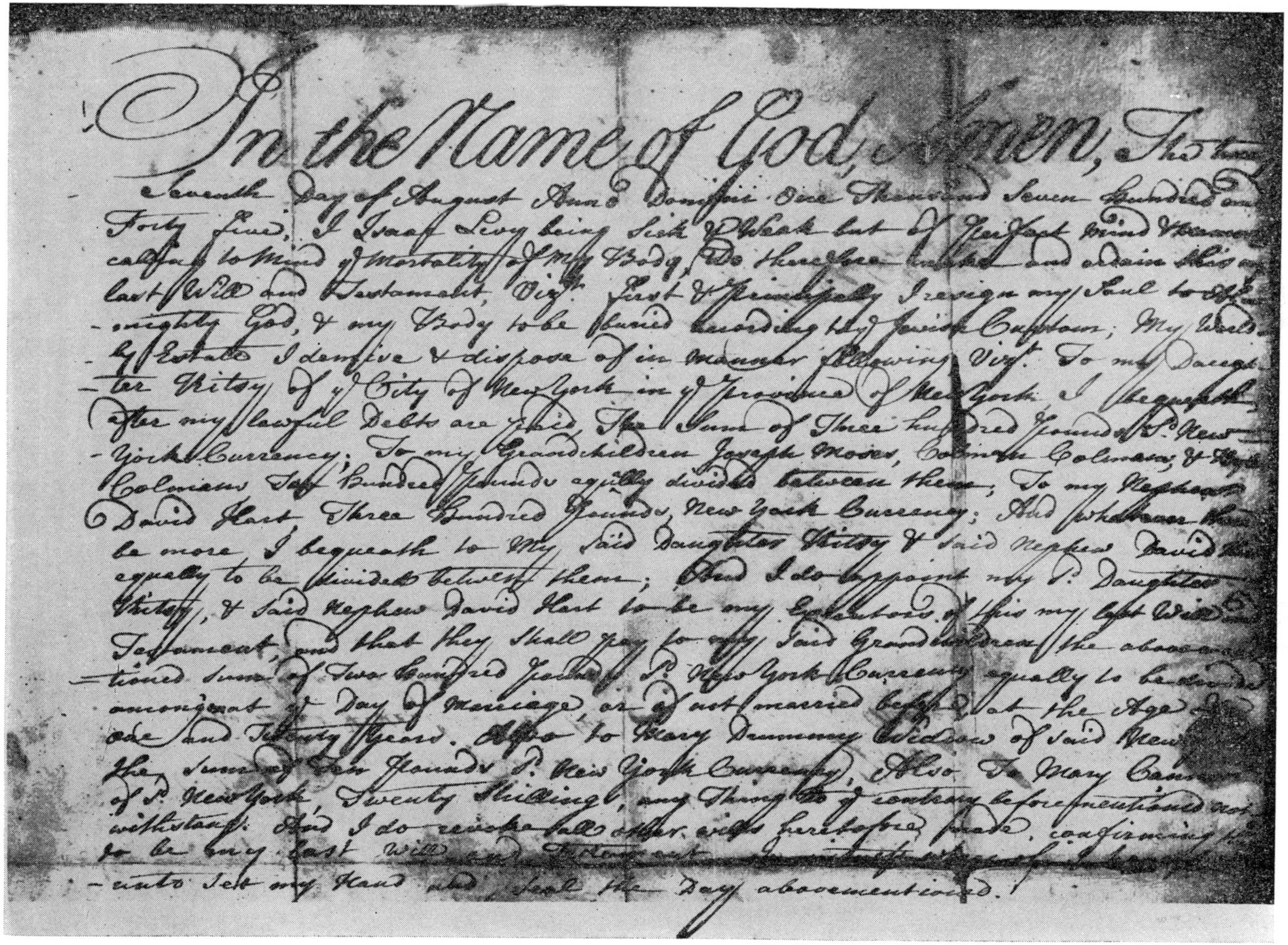
In the Name of God, Amen, The
Seventh day of August Anno Domini One Thousand Seven Hundred and
Forty five, I Isaac Levy being Sick & Weak but of Perfect Mind & memory
calling to Mind ye Mortality of my Body, Do therefore make and ordain this my
last Will and Testament, Viz. First & Principally I resign my Soul to Al-
mighty God, & my Body to be buried according to ye Jewish Custom; My Worl-
dly Estate I demise & dispose of in manner following Viz. To my Daugh-
ter Kitsy of ye City of New York in ye Province of New York I bequeath,
after my lawful Debts are paid, The Sum of Three hundred Pounds Sd. New
York Currency; To my Grandchildren Joseph Moses, [illegible] Colman, & [illegible]
Colman Two Hundred Pounds equally divided between them; To my Nephew
David Hart, Three Hundred Pounds, New York Currency; And whatever there
be more I bequeath to my said Daughter Kitsy & said Nephew David
equally to be divided between them; And I do appoint my S. Daughter
Kitsy, & said Nephew David Hart to be my Executors of this my last Will and
Testament, and that they shall pay to my said Grandchildren the above men-
tioned Sum of Two Hundred Pounds S. New York Currency equally to be divided
amongst at ye Day of Marriage, or if not married before at the Age of
one and Twenty Years. Also to Mary Drummy Widow of said Hen
the Sum of Ten Pounds S. New York Currency, Also To Mary Cam
of S. New York Twenty Shillings, any Thing to ye contrary beforementioned not-
withstanding. And I do revoke all other wills heretofore made, confirming this
to be my last Will and Testament. [illegible] here-
unto set my Hand and Seal the Day abovementioned.

XVIII. ISAAC LEVY [1745]

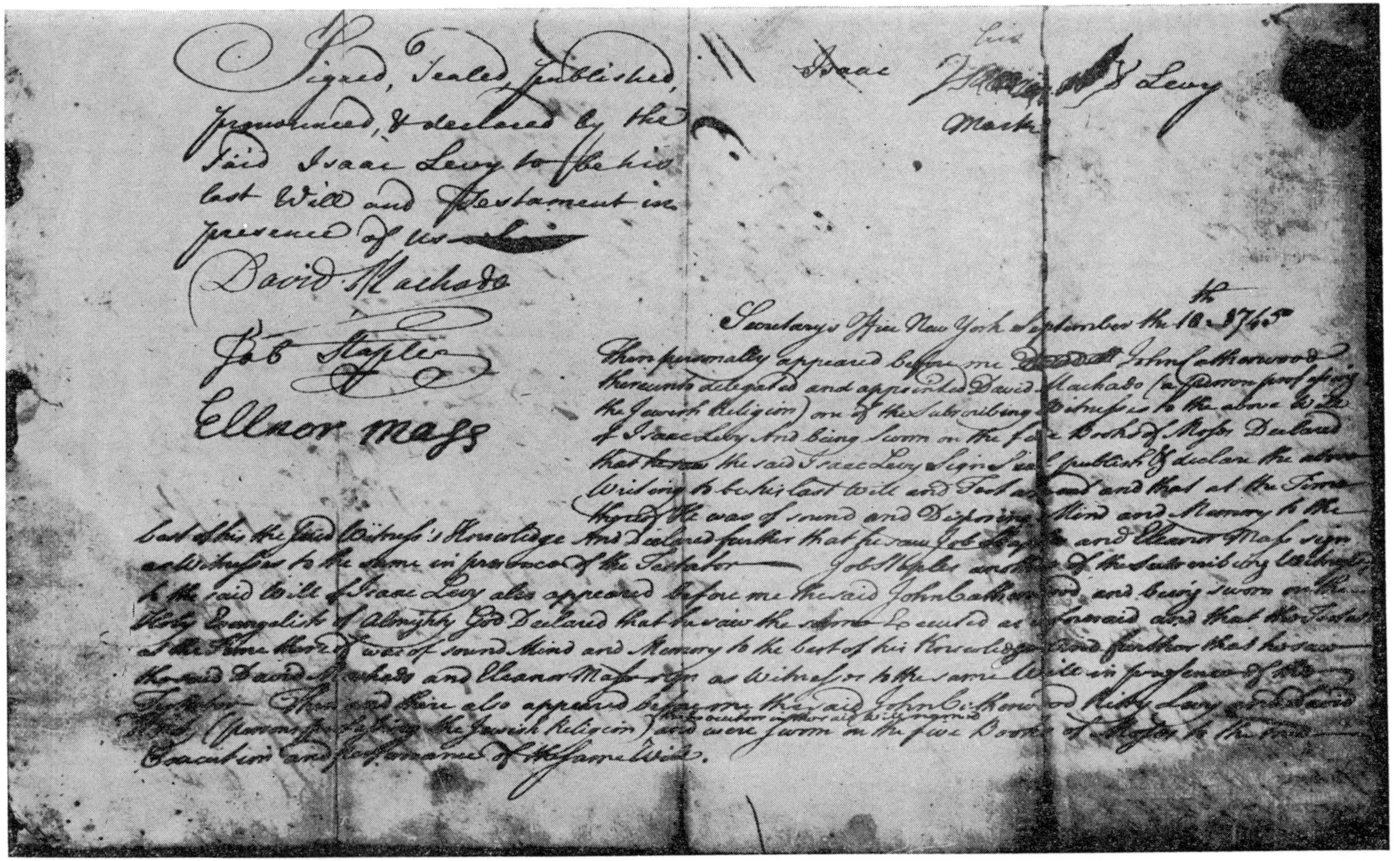

Signed, Sealed, published, pronounced, & declared by the said Isaac Levy to be his last Will and Testament in presence of us

David Machado

Job Stapler

Ellnor Mass

Isaac his Levy
Mark

Secretary's Office New York September the 18th 1745

Then personally appeared before me John Catherwood thereunto delegated and appointed David Machado (a person professing the Jewish Religion) one of the Subscribing Witnesses to the above Will of Isaac Levy And being Sworn on the five Books of Moses Declared that he saw the said Isaac Levy Sign Seal publish & declare the above Writing to be his last Will and Testament and that at the Time thereof He was of sound and Disposing Mind and Memory to the best of his the said Witness's Knowledge And Declared further that he saw Job Stapler and Elleanor Mass sign as Witnesses to the same in presence of the Testator — Job Stapler another of the Subscribing Witnesses to the said Will of Isaac Levy also appeared before me the said John Catherwood and being sworn on the Holy Evangelists of Almighty God Declared that he saw the above Executed as aforesaid and that the Testator at the Time thereof was of sound Mind and Memory to the best of his Knowledge And further that he saw the said David Machado and Eleanor Mass sign as Witnesses to the same Will in presence of the Testator — Then and there also appeared before me the said John Catherwood Hetty Levy and David Hays (persons professing the Jewish Religion) the executors in the said Will named and were Sworn on the five Books of Moses to the true Execution and performance of the same Will.

XVIII. ISAAC LEVY [1745]

XIX

SIMJA DE TORRES[1]

[1746]

New York SS.

In the Name of God Amen I SIMJA DE TORES latte of Jamaica Widow being indisposed, and weak in body but of sound mind and memorey and knowin the Certenty of death and the Uncertanity of Its Approch doe make and ordain this to be my last will and Testement in manner following

Imprimes

I recomend my Soul to Almighty God Craveing pardon and forgiveness of my Sins and my bodey to the Earth to be decentley Buried acording to the manner of the Jews and att the discretion of my Executors hereafter mentioned

Item

I will and desier that all my Just deabtes and funeral Expenses, be first paid.

Item

I give and bequeath to the Tresurer of the Sinegoge for the use of the sinegoge of New York the Sum of five pounds currentmuney of this province to be paid one mounth after my deces.[2]

[1] Original Will no. 339, HDC; Will Liber 16, p. 50; *NYHSC*, vol. IV (1896), p. 103. Simja da Silva de Torres (1677–Oct. 23, 1746) was in 1728 one of the first contributors for the purchase of the new burial ground in New York City at the Fresh Water (now Chatham near Roosevelt Street). She was the wife of Joseph de Torres (d. 1724) and seems to have had something of a slave trading career. *Portraits*, pp. 468–469; *PAJHS*, vol. XXI (1913), p. 8. On July 19, 1742, she imported three Negro slaves at the same time as Manaseh Pevera (Pereira, d. 1741 in Jamaica) imported one slave. Entry of July 19, 1742, vol. XI, Manifest Books, 1740–1768, New York State Library, Albany [=Manifest Books]. On March 19, 1728, she brought another three slaves via the ship *Duke of Portland* for which she paid a duty of £5.5. One was under four years old and "one for my person." Item 611, vol. I, Entry Books, 1728–1766, New York State Library [=Entry Books]. Microfilm copies of the Manifest and Entry Books are in the Paul Klapper Library, Queens College. For reference to Pereira, see List of Wills on record in the Office of the Island of Jamaica 1731–1750, Copy in Oppenheim Collection, Box # 5, American Jewish Historical Society Library [=LWJ].

[2] This legacy was paid by her executors Daniel and Moses Gomez to the Parnas Abraham Rodrigues Rivera with the notation that Simja wished an *Escaba* [memorial prayer] recited every *Roshodes* [new moon] on the day she died. *PAJHS*, vol. XXI (1913), pp. 51 and 55.

Item

My will is that my Executtors Shall remit to the tresureres for the time being of the sinegoge of Kingston In Jamaica five pounds Current muney of Jamaica one mounth after my deceas.

Item

I give to the poor of my nation of new York five pounds to be devided acording to the discretion of my Executors

Item

I give and bequeth unto my brother SAMUEL DA SILVA the Sum of five pounds current muney of Jamaica which he maye demand and receive three mounths after my deceas,

Item

I give unto my Nease REBECA DA SILVA[3] daughter of my brother SAMUEL DA SILVA one Negrow Girle to the Value of fiften pounds, to be purchased by my Executors orders, on or before one year after my deceas in her Name and for her and her heairs for Ever.

Item

I give and bequeth unto my nease RACHEL DA SILVA daughter of my Brother JOSUAH DA SILVA[4] deceased one negro gireal to the Value of fiften pounds to be purchesed by my executors orders, on or before one year after my deceas in her name and for her and her heairs for Ever,

Item

I give and bequeth unto my Nease SIMJA DA SILVA daughter to my said deceased brother JOSUAH DA SILVA one negro gireal to the Value of fiften pounds to be purchased by my Executors orders, on or before one year after my decease in her name and for her and her heairs for Ever.

Item

I give and bequeth all the Resedue of my Easttate both Real and personal of what manner so Ever unto my Dear and Loving Grandson MOSES GOMEZ the Son of DANIEL GOMEZ[5] of this Citty merchant to him

[3] Rebecca da Silva was in New York in 1729. Entry Books, vol. II, item 1516.

[4] Joshua da Silva died in 1735 in Jamaica. LWJ.

[5] Moses Gomez (1728–1789) was the son of Daniel Gomez (1695–1784) and grandson of Lewis Gomez (see Will). Daniel married Rebecca de Torres (1701–Oct. 14, 1729), daughter of Simja and her husband Joseph in 1724. Daniel and Rebecca had two children, Joseph who died in 1734 and Moses mentioned herein (see Will of Moses Gomez, *infra*, pp. 189–191). N. Taylor Phillips, "Notes on the Genealogy of the Gomez Family in America," *PAJHS*, vol. XVII (1909), pp. 197–198.

and his heairs for Ever to be put in posesion of the Same att the day of his Mariage[6] or att the Age of Twenty one Years which shall first happen

Item

My will is in case Itt should (God for bid) happen that my said Grandson Should dey before his mariage or arive to the Eage of twenty one years In such a case I give and bequeath unto my Son DANIEL GOMEZ[7] all my Eastate Real and personal to him and his heairs for Ever. Lastely I do hearby constitute and apoint My Said Loving Son DANIEL GOMEZ and his son my Dear and Loving Grandson MOSES GOMEZ to be the Executtors, of This my last Will and Testament Hereby Revoekeing and Disanulling all former Wills Testements legacis and beque[s]ts by me heretofore made Ratifying and Confirming this and no other to be my last Will and Testament. In Witness whereof I have hereto sett my hand & seal this Sixtenth day of February in the Sixtenth Year of his majesty's Reign one Thousend Seven hundred forty-tow & three

Singed Sealed published pronounced
and Declared by the Testetares as
her Last will and Testament in the
presence of us the subscribers and
subscribed by us in presence of each other

her
SIMJA X DE TORES
mark

DANIEL BONTECOU[8]
DAVID GOMEZ[10] seal
SAMUEL BURLING[9]

Secretarys Office New York November the 13th 1746
Then and there personally appeared before me GOLDSBROW BANYAR[11] thereunto delegated & appointed DANIEL BONTECOU One of the subscribing Witnesses to the within written Instrument signed with the Mark of SIMJA DE TORES and Declared on the Holy Evangelists that He saw the said SIMJA DE TORRES sign Seal publish & declare the said within written Instrument to be her last Will & Testament That at the Time thereof She was of Sound and disposing Mind & Memory to the best of his Knowl-

[6] Moses Gomez married his first cousin Esther Gomez, daughter of Isaac and Deborah Gomez on May 14, 1755. *Ibid.*; Will of Moses Gomez, *infra*, pp. 189–191.

[7] Although Simja refers to Daniel as her son, he was her son-in-law.

[8] Daniel Bontecou, shopkeeper, was made an executor of Dennis Rich shipwright on June, 1748. *NYHSC*, vol. IV (1896), p. 462.

[9] Samuel Burling may have been the son of Mary and William Burling or the son of Edward and Anna Burling. *Ibid.*, pp. 166 and 268.

[10] See Will of David Gomez, *infra*, pp. 125–127.

[11] Goldsbrow Banyar was appointed Probate Judge on October 12, 1753. He also held the office of Register of the Court of Chancery in that year. *Calendar*, pp. 41, 60 and 75. At the time of the probate of this will, he was Deputy Secretary but the date of his commission is not apparent.

edg And that he together with SAMUEL BURLING & DAVID GOMEZ signed their Names as witnesses thereto in the presence of each other and of the Testatrix.

Sworn before me
s/ GEO BANYAR D Secry

At the Time & place abovementioned also appeared before me the said GOLDSBROW BANYAR, DANIEL GOMEZ and MOSES GOMEZ the Executors in the within written last Will and Testament of SIMJA DE TORES named & appointed And were duely sworn (on the five Books of Moses) to the true Execution and performance of the said Will.

Sworn the day & year above Written
Before me

s/ GEO BANYAR DSecry

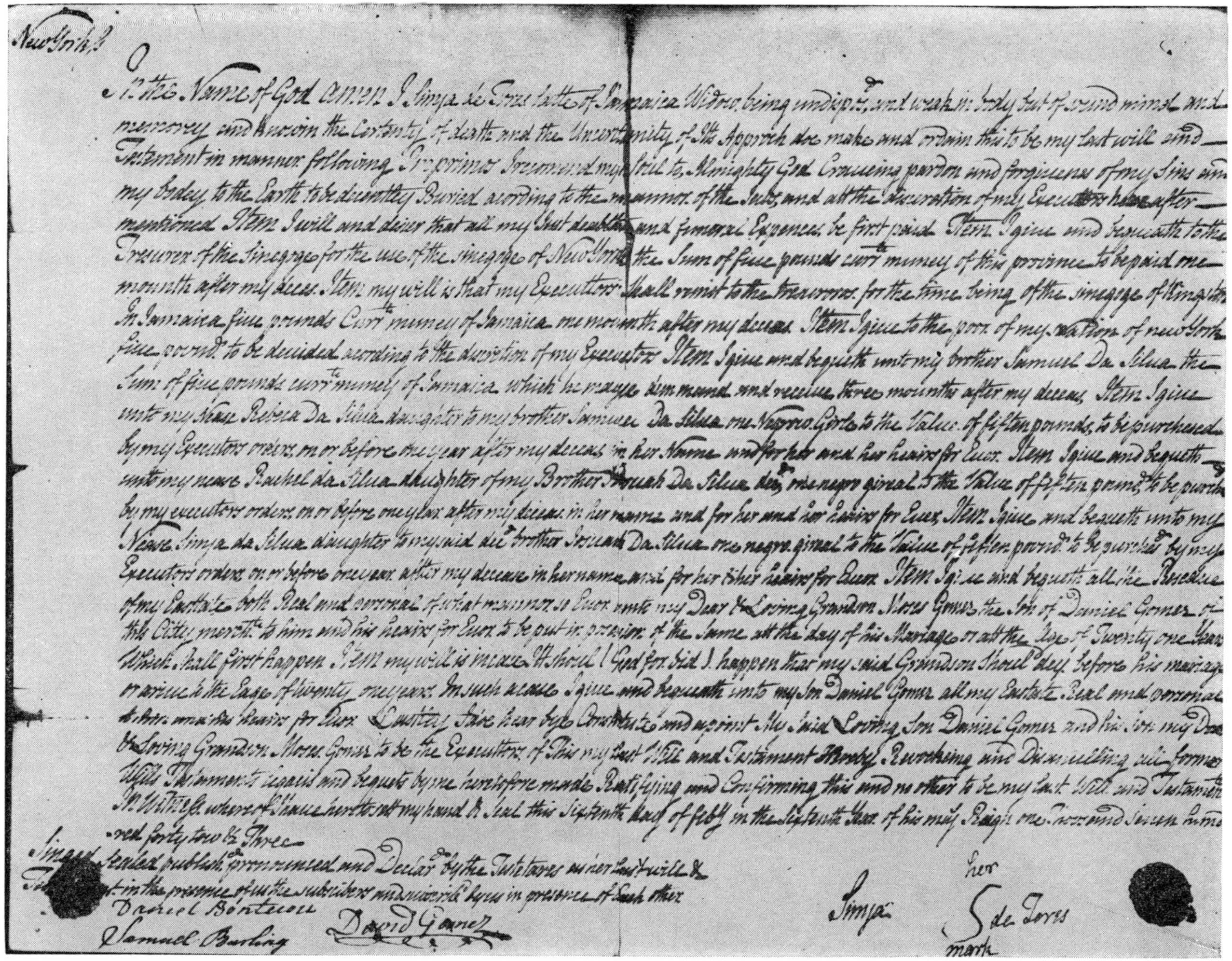

New York ss

In the Name of God Amen I Simja de Torres late of Jamaica Widow being indisposed and weak in body but of sound mind and memory and knowing the certainty of death and the uncertainty of its approch doe make and ordain this to be my last will and Testament in manner following Imprimis I recommend my soul to Almighty God Craveing pardon and forgiveness of my Sins and my body to the Earth to be decently Buried according to the manner of the Jews and att the discretion of my Executors here after mentioned Item I will and desier that all my Just debts and funeral Expences be first paid Item I give and bequeath to the Treasurer of the Sinegoge for the use of the Sinegoge of New York the Sum of five pounds curr.t money of this province to be paid one mounth after my deces Item my will is that my Executors shall remit to the Treasurer for the time being of the Sinegoge of Kingston In Jamaica five pounds Curr.t money of Jamaica one mounth after my decease Item I give to the poor of my Nation of New York five pounds to be decided according to the discretion of my Executors Item I give and bequeath unto my brother Samuel Da Silva the Sum of five pounds curr.t money of Jamaica which he maye demand and receive three mounths after my decease Item I give unto my Niece Rebeca Da Silva daughter to my brother Samuel Da Silva one Negro Girle to the Value of fifteen pounds to be purchased by my Executors orders on or before one year after my decease in her Name and for her and her heirs for Ever Item I give and bequeath unto my neece Rachel da Silva daughter of my Brother Jeosuah Da Silva dec.d one negro girl to the Value of fifteen pounds to be purch by my executors orders on or before one year after my decease in her name and for her and her heirs for Ever Item I give and bequeath unto my Neece Simja da Silva daughter to my said dec.d brother Jeosuah Da Silva one negro girl to the Value of fifteen pounds to be purches by my Executors orders on or before one year after my decease in her name and for her & her heirs for Ever Item I give and bequeath all the Residue of my Estate both Real and personal of what manner so Ever unto my Dear & Loving Grandson Moses Gomez the son of Daniel Gomez of this City merch.t to him and his heirs for Ever to be put in posesion of the same at the day of his Marriage or att the Age of Twenty one Years which shall first happen Item my will is in case It should (God forbid) happen that my said Grandson should dey before his marriage or arrive to the Age of twenty one years In such a case I give and bequeath unto my Son Daniel Gomez all my Estate Real and personal to him and his heirs for Ever Lastly I doe hear by Constitute and appoint My said Loving Son Daniel Gomez and his son my Dear & Loving Grandson Moses Gomez to be the Executors of This my last Will and Testament hereby Revoking and Disanulling all former Wills Testaments legacis and bequests by me heretofore made Ratifying and Confirming this and no other to be my last Will and Testament In Witness whereof I have hereto set my hand & Seal this Sixteenth day of feb.y in the Sixteenth Year of his maj.y Reign one Thousand seven hundred forty two & Three

Signed Sealed publish.d pronounced and Declar.d by the Testatrex as her last will & Testament in the presence of us the subscribers who in her presence & in presence of each other
Daniel Bonteau
Samuel Burling
David Gomez

Simja her S mark de Torres

XIX. SIMJA DE TORRES [1746]

XX

MORDECAI GOMEZ[1]

[1750]

In the Name of God Amen I MORDECAY GOMEZ of The City of New York Merchant being in good health of body and of Sound and disposing Mind Memory and Understanding (Thanks be to God) But Considering the uncertainty of This Mortal life and Certainty of death Do Make and Ordain this my last Will and Testament in Manner and form following That is To Say I Committ my Precious and immortal Soul into The hands of God who gave it To me and my body to The Earth to be buried in the Jews Burying Ground according To the Jewish Custom at the Discretion of my Executors hereinafter Named and as To Such Worldly Estate wherewith It hath pleased God to bless me I Do give devise and Dispose thereof as followeth (To witt)

Imprimis

I will That all my Just Debts and funeral Charges be well and Truly paid and Satisfied

Item

I do give devise and bequeath unto my beloved wife REBECCA GOMEZ[2] All That My Dwelling house and Lott of Ground thereunto belonging Scituate

[1] Original Will no. 523, HDC; Will Liber 17, p. 272; *NYHSC*, vol. IV (1896), p. 45. Mordecai Gomez (1688–November 1, 1750), the son of Lewis Gomez (See Will), was made freeman on June 7, 1715 and was elected collector of the East Ward in 1723. On November 3, 1734 he was appointed Spanish interpreter in the Admiralty Court. *Calendar*, p. 23; *Burghers*, p. 93; *Minutes*, vol. III, p. 327. Gomez was very active in congregational affairs and was among those who petitioned for a Jewish burial ground. *PAJHS*, vol. XXI (1913), pp. 5, 7, *et passim*; *Minutes*, vol. IV, p. 437. He married Hester Campos (1695 — d. Sept. 29, 1736) and she bore him three sons, Moses, Isaac, and Jacob. Conveyance Liber 32, cp. 28–29, New York City Register's Office, 31 Chambers Street, New York City. Unless otherwise indicated references to Conveyance Libers are to be found in this office. In 1741 he married Rebecca, daughter of Abraham de Lucena. *Portraits*, p. 235. For examples of his very active mercantile career, see NOL, CO 5/1224, 1225, *passim*; Entry and Manifest Books, *passim*. For examples of his very extensive litigation, see *Gomez v. Owen* (1728), MCP, file 1725–1729, Feb. 27, 1728; *Gomez v. Goulding*, MCM, vol. 1723–1728, p. 530. In 1746, the Assembly due to fear of smallpox in the house of Sir Peter Warren, met in Mordecai's house, probably in Greenwich Village. *Gazette*, Nov. 5, 1750; "Necrology of Henry S. Hendricks," *PAJHS*, vol. XLIV (1954), p. 59. For other biographical references, see *Portraits*, pp. 213–214 and 234–237; *PAJHS*, vol XVII (1909), p. 197.

[2] Rebecca (1714–1801), daughter of Abraham de Lucena was married to Gomez on May 4, 1741. Their marriage contract was recorded in Conveyance Liber 32, cp. 205. *Portraits*, pp. 286–287.

and being on The Dock in The East Ward of The City of New York[3] between The house of DANIEL BLOOM[4] and house now in The Occupation of The Widdow of JOHN LAWRENCE[5] which Said house and Ground is Now in The Tenure and Occupation of LAWRENCE BURROWS[6] as my Undertenant *To Hold* The Said Dwelling house and Lott of Ground unto my Said Wife REBECCA GOMEZ for and During the Term of her Natural Life and not Longer and from and imediately after her decease I do Give devise and bequeath The Said Dwelling house and Lott of Ground unto my Sons ABRAHAM GOMEZ[7] and MOSES GOMEZ[8] and To my Daughters HESTER GOMEZ[9] and RACHEL GOMEZ[10] *To Hold* one full and equal fourth part thereof unto my Said Son ABRAHAM GOMEZ his heirs and assigns for ever one other full and Equal fourth Part thereof unto my Said Son MOSES GOMEZ his heirs and Assigns for ever one other full and Equal fourth part thereof unto my Said Daughter HESTER GOMEZ her heirs and assigns for Ever and The Remaining one full and equal fourth part thereof unto my Said Daughter RACHEL GOMEZ her heirs and assigns for ever

Item

I do give devise and bequeath unto my Son ISAAC GOMEZ[11] his Executors

[3] The house given to Rebecca was purchased by Gomez in 1733. At that time it was described as being between the houses of Francis Child and Samuel Payton. Conveyance Liber 31, cp. 469–470. Child and Payton must have transferred title to their houses to Daniel Bloom and John Lawrence or his widow. The house was on Water Street between Wall Street and Maiden Lane. *NYHSC*, vol. IV (1896), p. 312.

[4] Daniel Bloom, a merchant, became a freeman on April 10, 1744. *Burghers*, p. 149.

[5] There were at least two John Lawrences living during this period. Perhaps it was the Lawrence, barber, made freeman on September 7, 1725 or perhaps the Lawrence, butcher, made freeman on December 12, 1732. *Ibid.*, pp. 107 and 121.

[6] Lawrence Burrows is probably the Laurence Burros, "perriwiggmaker," made freeman on March 4, 1746. *Ibid.*, p. 155.

[7] Abraham Gomez (1742–1808) was the son of Mordecai's second marriage. He was a subscriber to the Congregation Shearith Israel and was proposed as a trustee. *Portraits*, pp. 235 and 312; *PAJHS*, vol. XVII (1909), p. 197; *ibid.*, vol. XXI (1913), pp. 79 and 132.

[8] Moses Gomez (1744–1826) married Esther Lopez. Like Abraham, he was the son of Mordecai and Rebecca. Moses held a number of positions in the Congregation including that of *parnas*. *PAJHS*, vol. XXI (1913), pp. 111 and 126, *et passim*. Mordecai had another son Moses, born January 2, 1716 by his first wife Hester, who died in Jamaica. *PAJHS*, vol. XVII (1909), p. 197.

[9] Hester Gomez (1743–1775), daughter of Mordecai and Rebecca, married Uriah Hendricks, a merchant, on June 30, 1762. She was known most often as Eve Esther. Although she died at an early age, she left eight children. *Ibid.*

[10] Rachel Gomez (1739–1809), also daughter of Rebecca, married Abraham Waage, a merchant, on July 4, 1770. She died in England. *Ibid.*; *Dictionary*, p. 46.

[11] Isaac Gomez, son of Mordecai and his first wife, Hester, was born in New York on July 14, 1718 and died in Curaçao on November 9, 1764. He married Esther Jessurun of Curaçao. *Ibid.*, p. 44; *PAJHS*, vol. XVII (1909), p. 197; Conveyance Liber 32, cp. 28–29. Mordecai divides his property between his two sets of children by his two wives. For a description of some of his property, see deed made by Rebecca Gomez, widow, Abraham Waag[e] and Rachel, his wife, Uriah Hendricks and Esther, his wife, to Moses Gomez, Jr. Conveyance Liber 32, cp. 35–39.

Administrators and Assigns my five Books of Moses and one pair of Silver Ornaments Thereunto belonging weighing about Thirty Nine Ounces[12]

Item

I do give devise and bequeath unto my Grandaughter HESTER GOMEZ[13] now In Jamaica Daughter of my Son MOSES GOMEZ[14] deceased The Sum of one hundred Pounds current money of New York To be paid out of my Estate

Item

I will That my Said grandaughter Shall have and Enjoy To her Self her heirs and assigns for ever All That one full and Equal Third part of my Dwelling house Store house and lott of ground (The Water Lot excepted) wherein I now live Scituate and being in Queens Street in The City of New York[15] bounded on The East by The house and Ground late of JOHN STEPHENS[16] deceased on The West by The house and Ground now In the Occupation of WILLIAM BRADFORD, JUNIOR[17] and on The South by The East River or harbour which did belong to and was The Property of my deceased wife HESTER GOMEZ

Item

I do give devise and bequeath unto my Son ISAAC GOMEZ and To his heirs and assigns for ever on other full and Equal third Part of my Said Dwelling house Store house and Lott of Ground (The Water Lott Excepted)

Item

I do give devise and bequeath unto my son JACOB GOMEZ[18] and To his

[12] The Five Books of Moses had been given to Mordecai by his father Lewis Gomez (see Will). For another exchange of Torahs see *supra*, Will of Joseph Bueno de Mesquita, p. 15, note 1.

[13] Hester Gomez was the mother of Mrs. Flamenge of Jamaica. *PAJHS*, vol. XVII (1909), p. 197.

[14] Moses Gomez was the oldest son of Mordecai and Hester. He was born January 2, 1716 and probably died sometime after 1730. The last reference to him in the Congregation is dated August 1730. *Ibid.*, vol. XXI (1913), pp. 23 and 25; Conveyance Liber 39, cp. 28–29.

[15] For a description of his dwelling and stone house in the East Ward, see NYAL, Feb. 23, 1734.

[16] Probably John Stephens, Esq. who died intestate and letters of administration of his estate issued to his wife Belinda, April 14, 1743. *NYHSC*, vol. III (1895), p. 403.

[17] William Bradford, Jr. was the son of William Bradford, New York's first printer. A pewterer by that name was made freeman on November 13, 1719. *Burghers*, p. 99.

[18] Jacob Gomez (1720–1763) was the son of Mordecai's first marriage. Conveyance Liber 32, cp. 28–29; *PAJHS*, vol. XVII (1909), p. 197; *Dictionary*, p. 44.

heirs and assigns for ever The remaining one full and equal Third part of my Said Dwelling house Store house and Lott of Ground (The Water Lott Excepted)

Item

I will and order That my Said Wife REBECCA GOMEZ with her Children Shall live in hold and enjoy, my Said Dwelling house Store house and Lott of Ground for and during one year from and after my decease and not Longer free of all Rent

Item

I do give devise and bequeath unto my Sons ISAAC GOMEZ and JACOB GOMEZ All That my Dwelling house and lot and Piece of Ground and all buildings Thereon Scituate and being in The Sloat[19] in The East Ward of The City of New York which I Purchased from SARAH HYER Widow and Executrix of GARRET HYER[20] deceased *To Hold* one full and Equal half part Thereof unto my Said Son ISAAC GOMEZ his heirs and Assigns for ever and The other one full and Equal half Part thereof unto my Said Son JACOB GOMEZ his heirs and Assigns for ever

Item

I do give devise and bequeath unto my Said Sons ISAAC GOMEZ and JACOB GOMEZ Their Executors Administrators and Assigns Equally To be divided between Them my Two Negro Men Slaves called LEVANT and FRANK and my Negro Woman Slave called PERLA and also my Two [Snuff] Mills and also The one full and Equal half Part of all my household Stuff and furniture of What Nature or kindsoever (Plate excepted)

Item

I do give devise and bequeath unto my Said wife REBECCA GOMEZ her Executors Administrators and Assigns The other one full and Equal half part of all my Said household Stuff and furniture (plate excepted)

Item

I do give devise and bequeath unto my Said wife REBECCA GOMEZ my Said Sons ABRAHAM GOMEZ and MOSES GOMEZ and my Said Daughters HESTER GOMEZ and RACHEL GOMEZ and to their Executors Administrators and Assigns equally To be divided betwen Them my Negro Woman Slave

[19] The "Sloat" was a narrow lane at the rear of lots on Hanover Square. Present day Beaver Street is part of this area. *NYHSC*, vol. IV (1896), p. 312.

[20] Garret Hyer, cooper, died between 1741 and December, 1746. For abstract of his will, see *ibid.*, p. 104.

called HANNAH my Negro Boy Slave called PASCUAL and my Negro girl Slave called CELIA

Item

I do give devise and bequeath unto my Said Two Sons ABRAHAM GOMEZ and MOSES GOMEZ and my Said Daughters HESTER GOMEZ and RACHEL GOMEZ All Those my Five houses and lotts of Ground thereunto belonging Scituate and being in The North Ward of The City of New York[21] containing in Breadth from Kips Street up Annes Street and in The rear Ninety foot More or less and in length on both Sides Two hundred and four foot More or less and also another house and lott of Ground in Dye Street bounded Southerly by The Rope Walk of EVERT PELLS[22] Easterly by The house and Ground of ABRAHAM GORDEN Westerly by The house and Ground belonging To JOHN RYCKMAN[23] and Northerly by Dye Street aforesaid Now in the Occupation of ABRAHAM LYON[24] To hold one fourth Part Thereof unto my Said Son ABRAHAM GOMEZ his heirs and assigns for Ever one Other fourth part thereof unto my Said Son MOSES GOMEZ his heirs and Assigns for ever One other fourth part thereof unto my Said Daughter HESTER GOMEZ her heirs and Assignes for ever And The Remaining one fourth part thereof unto my Said Daughter RACHEL GOMEZ her heirs and Assigns for ever which last Mentioned Lott of Ground contains in Breadth fourteen foot and In Length Eighty five foot

Item

I do give Devise and bequeath unto my Mother in Law RACHEL DE LUCENA The Sum of Ten Pounds Current Money of New York per annum during her Natural life which I will and desire shall be Paid her yearly during her Natural Life aforesaid by my Executors out of my Estate

Item

I do give and devise unto The Manager or Ruler of The Synagougue in New York for The use of The Same Synogouge The Sum of Twenty five Pounds current money of New York which I will and desire Shall be paid in One Month after my decease out of my Estate

[21] For description of these lots and transfer of part to Moses Gomez, Jr., see Conveyance Liber 39, cp. 35–39.

[22] Evert Pells (Pelse) was a ropemaker, *Minutes*, vol. IV, pp. 437–438; *Burghers*, p. 120.

[23] John Rychman was elected assesor in the Bowery Ward. *Minutes*, vol. II, pp. 89 and 286.

[24] Abraham Lyon, "(a Jew) Baker," was made freeman of New York on May 29, 1750. *Burghers*, p. 169.

Item

I do give devise and bequeath all The Rest Residue and Remainder of all My whole Estate Real and personal whatsoever and Wheresoever unto my Said Wife REBECCA GOMEZ my Said Sons ISSAC GOMEZ, JACOB GOMEZ, ABRAHAM GOMEZ, and MOSES GOMEZ and my Said Daughters HESTER GOMEZ and RACHEL GOMEZ *To Hold* one full and Equal Seventh part thereof unto my Said Wife REBECCA GOMEZ her heirs Executors Administrators and Assigns for ever, One other full and Equal Seventh part thereof unto my said Son ISAAC GOMEZ his heirs Executors Administrators and Assigns for ever, One other full and equal Seventh part Thereof unto my Said Son JACOB GOMEZ his heirs Executors Administrators and Assigns for ever, One other full and Equal Seventh part Thereof unto my Said Son ABRAHAM GOMEZ his heirs Executors Administrators and assigns for ever, one other full and Equal Seventh part thereof unto my Said Son MOSES GOMEZ his heirs Executors Administrators and Assigns for ever; One other full and Equal Seventh part Thereof unto my Said Daughter HESTER GOMEZ her heirs Executors Administrators and assigns for Ever and The Remaining one full & Equal Seventh Part thereof unto my Said Daughter RACHEL GOMEZ her heirs Executors Administrators and assigns for ever *And In Case It* Shall so happen That any or either of my Said Two Sons ABRAHAM and MOSES and my Two Daughters HESTER and RACHEL Shall dye before he she or They Shall attain to The Age of Twenty one years without having Lawfull Issue Then and In Such Case my Will is That his her or Their Respective Part of my Estate herein given and bequeathed Shall fall To The Survivor or Survivors of Them To hold as aforesaid And in Case all my Said four Children ABRAHAM, MOSES, HESTER and RACHEL Shall happen to dye before They Attain To The age of Twenty one Years without lawfull Issue Then and In Such Case my Will is That all Their parts of my Estate Real and personal herein given and bequeathed unto Them Shall fall to my Said wife REBECCA GOMEZ and my Said Two Sons ISAAC and JACOB GOMEZ To Hold To Each of Them one full and Equal third part thereof and To Each of Their heirs Executors Administrators and Assigns for ever And Lastly I do Nominate and appoint My Said Wife REBECCA GOMEZ, My said Son ISAAC GOMEZ, and my four Brothers DANIEL GOMEZ,[25] DAVID GOMEZ,[26] ISAAC GOMEZ,[27] and BENJAMIN GOMEZ[28] Executors of this my last Will and Testament hereby Revoking all other Wills by me at any Time heretofore Made declaring This only To be my last Will and Testament *In*

[25] See Will of Simja de Torres, *supra*, p. 80, note 5.

[26] See *infra*, Will of David Gomez, pp. 125–127.

[27] See *infra*, Will of Isaac Gomez, pp. 129–131.

[28] See *infra*, Will of Benjamin Gomez, pp. 135–137.

Witness Whereof I The Said MORDECAY GOMEZ have hereunto Set my hand and Seal The Third day of May in The year one Thousand Seven hundred and fifty.

s/ MORDY GOMEZ [seal]

Signed Sealed Published and Declared by
the Said MORDECAY GOMEZ as and for his
last Will and Testament in The presence
of us who Subscribed our Names as Witnesses
thereto in the presence of The Testator
The Words (Son, Sons) being Interlined and
the The Words (Breadth-Third) being wrote on
a Razed place all done before Execution & The
Word Two being Wrote on a Razed Place before
Execution.

s/ SARAH GRIFFITH[29]
s/ MARY CADMIS
s/ CORNELIUS CADMIS[30]
s/ JAMES EMOTT[31]

City of New York Ss Be It Remembred That on the twelfth day of November 1750 appeared before me GOLDSBROW BANYAR hereunto authorized JAMES EMOTT of the said City Gentn who being duely sworn on the Holy Evangelists on his Oath declared That he saw MORDECAI GOMEZ late of the said City Merchant deceased In his lifetime Sign and Seal the within written Instrument purporting to be the Will of the said MORDECAI GOMEZ and heard him publish and declare the same to be & Contain his last Will and Testament That at the time thereof He was of sound and disposing Mind and Memory to the best of his the Deponents Knowledge and Belief That he the Deponent and SARAH GRIFFITH, MARY CADMIS and CORNELIUS CADMIS Subscribed their Names as Witnesses to the said Will in the Testator's presence.

s/ GEO BANYAR

City of New York } *Ss. Be It Also Remembred* That on the twenty first day of December 1750 also appeared before me the said GOLDSBROW BANYAR, REBECCA GOMEZ, DANIEL GOMEZ, DAVID GOMEZ, ISAAC GOMEZ and BENJAMIN GOMEZ Five of the Executors in the within

[29] Sarah Griffith witnessed a will on January 11, 1750 along with James Emott, another witness to this will. *NYHSC*, vol. IV (1896), p. 330.

[30] Cornelius Cadmis was also witness to a will dated February 16, 1760. *Ibid.*, vol. VI (1898), p. 361.

[31] James Emott, attorney at law, often appeared as witness to wills and probably drew the wills he witnessed. He was made freeman on August 3, 1698. *Burghers*, p. 63.

written Will of Mordecai Gomez named and appointed and were duely sworn to the true Execution and Performance of the said Will [Isaac Gomez Son of Testator & the other Executor of his Will being absent]

Before me
s/ Geo Banyar

City of New York } *Ss. Be It Also Remembred* That on the twelfth day of June one thousand seven hundred and Fifty one Isaac Gomez, son of the within named testator Mordecai Gomez deceased and one of the Executors of his Will appeared personally and was duely sworn to the true Execution and Performance of the said Will Before me

s/ Geo Banyar

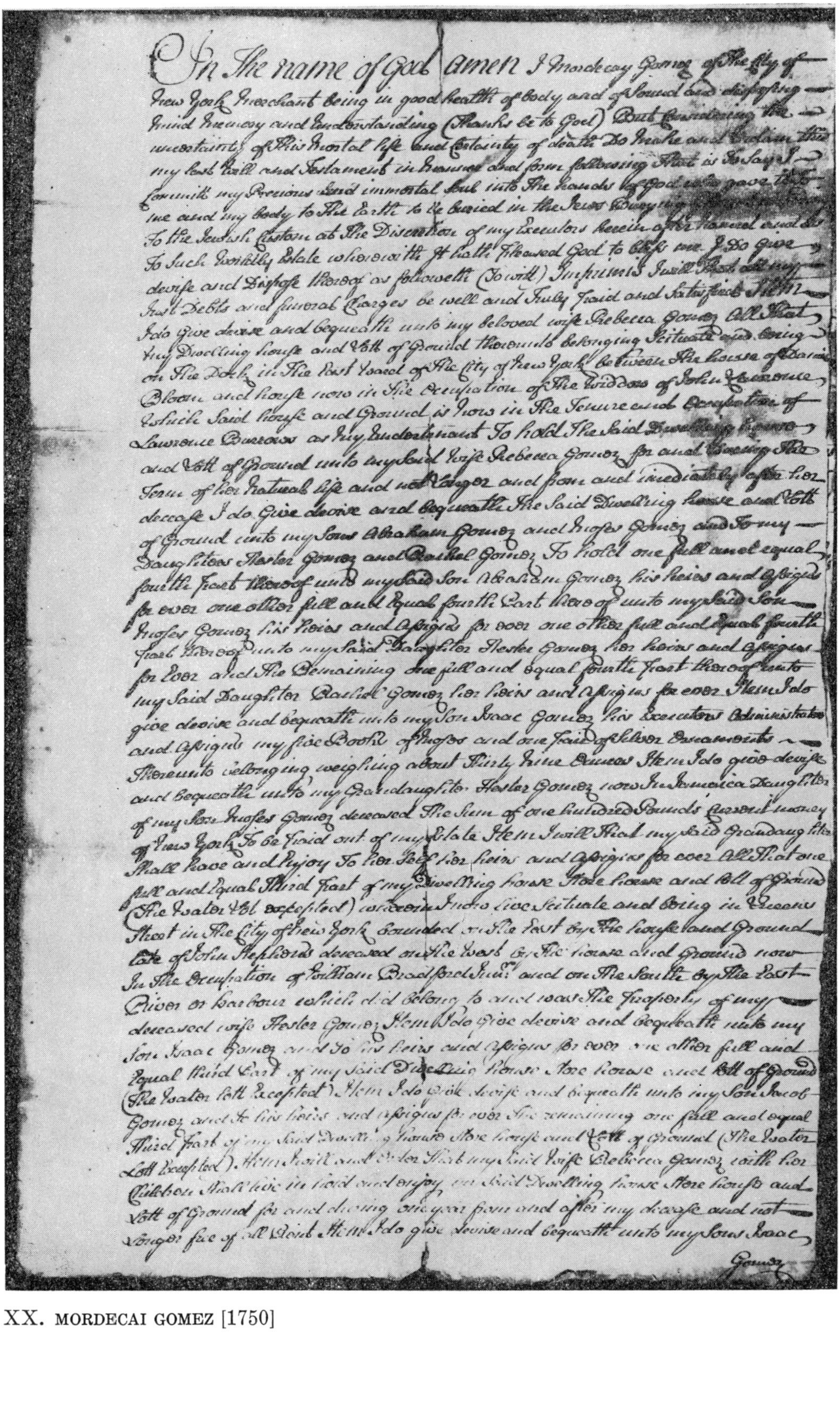

In The name of God amen I Mordecay Gomez of The City of New York Merchant being in good health of body and of Sound and disposing Mind Memory and Understanding (Thanks be to God) But Considering the uncertainty of This Mortal life and Certainty of death Do Make and Ordain this my last Will and Testament in Manner and form following That is To Say I Commit my Precious and immortal Soul into The hands of God who gave it to me and my body to The Earth to be buried in the Jews burying place according To the Jewish Custom at The Discretion of my Executors herein after named and as To Such Worldly Estate wherewith It hath Pleased God to bless me I Do give devise and Dispose thereof as followeth (To wit) Imprimis I will That all my Just Debts and funeral Charges be well and Truly Paid and Satisfied Item I do give devise and bequeath unto my beloved wife Rebecca Gomez All That my Dwelling house and Lott of Ground thereunto belonging Scituate and being on The Dock in The East Ward of The City of New York between The house of Daniel Bloom and house now in The Occupation of The widdow of John Lawrence which Said house and Ground is Now in The Tenure and Occupation of Lawrence Burrows as my Undertenant To hold The Said Dwelling house and Lott of Ground unto my Said wife Rebecca Gomez for and During The Term of her Natural life and not Longer and from and imediately after her decease I do Give devise and bequeath The Said Dwelling house and Lott of Ground unto my Sons Abraham Gomez and Moses Gomez and To my Daughters Hester Gomez and Rachel Gomez To hold one full and equal fourth Part thereof unto my Said Son Abraham Gomez his heirs and Assigns for ever one other full and Equal fourth Part thereof unto my Said Son Moses Gomez his heirs and Assigns for ever one other full and Equal fourth Part thereof unto my Said Daughter Hester Gomez her heirs and Assigns for Ever and The Remaining one full and Equal fourth Part thereof unto my Said Daughter Rachel Gomez her heirs and Assigns for ever Item I do give devise and bequeath unto my Son Isaac Gomez his Executors Administrators and Assigns my Five Books of Moses and one Pair of Silver Ornaments Thereunto belonging weighing about Thirty Nine Ounces Item I do give devise and bequeath unto my Granddaughter Hester Gomez now In Jamaica Daughter of my Son Moses Gomez deceased The Sum of one hundred Pounds Current money of New York To be Paid out of my Estate Item I will That my Said Granddaughter Shall have and Enjoy To her Self her heirs and Assigns for ever All That one full and Equal Third Part of my Dwelling house Store house and Lott of Ground (The Water Lot excepted) wherein I now live Scituate and being in Queens Street in The City of New York bounded on The East by The house and Ground late of John Stephens deceased on The West by The house and Ground now In The Occupation of William Bradford Junr and on The South by The East River or harbour which did belong to and was The Property of my deceased wife Hester Gomez Item I do give devise and bequeath unto my Son Isaac Gomez and To his heirs and Assigns for ever one other full and Equal third Part of my Said Dwelling house Store house and Lott of Ground (The Water Lott Excepted) Item I do give devise and bequeath unto my Son Jacob Gomez and to his heirs and Assigns for ever The remaining one full and equal Third Part of my Said Dwelling house Store house and Lott of Ground (The Water Lott Excepted). Item I will and Order That my Said wife Rebecca Gomez with her Children Shall live in hold and enjoy my Said Dwelling house Store house and Lott of Ground for and during one year from and after my decease and not Longer free of all Rent Item I do give devise and bequeath unto my Sons Isaac

Gomez

XX. MORDECAI GOMEZ [1750]

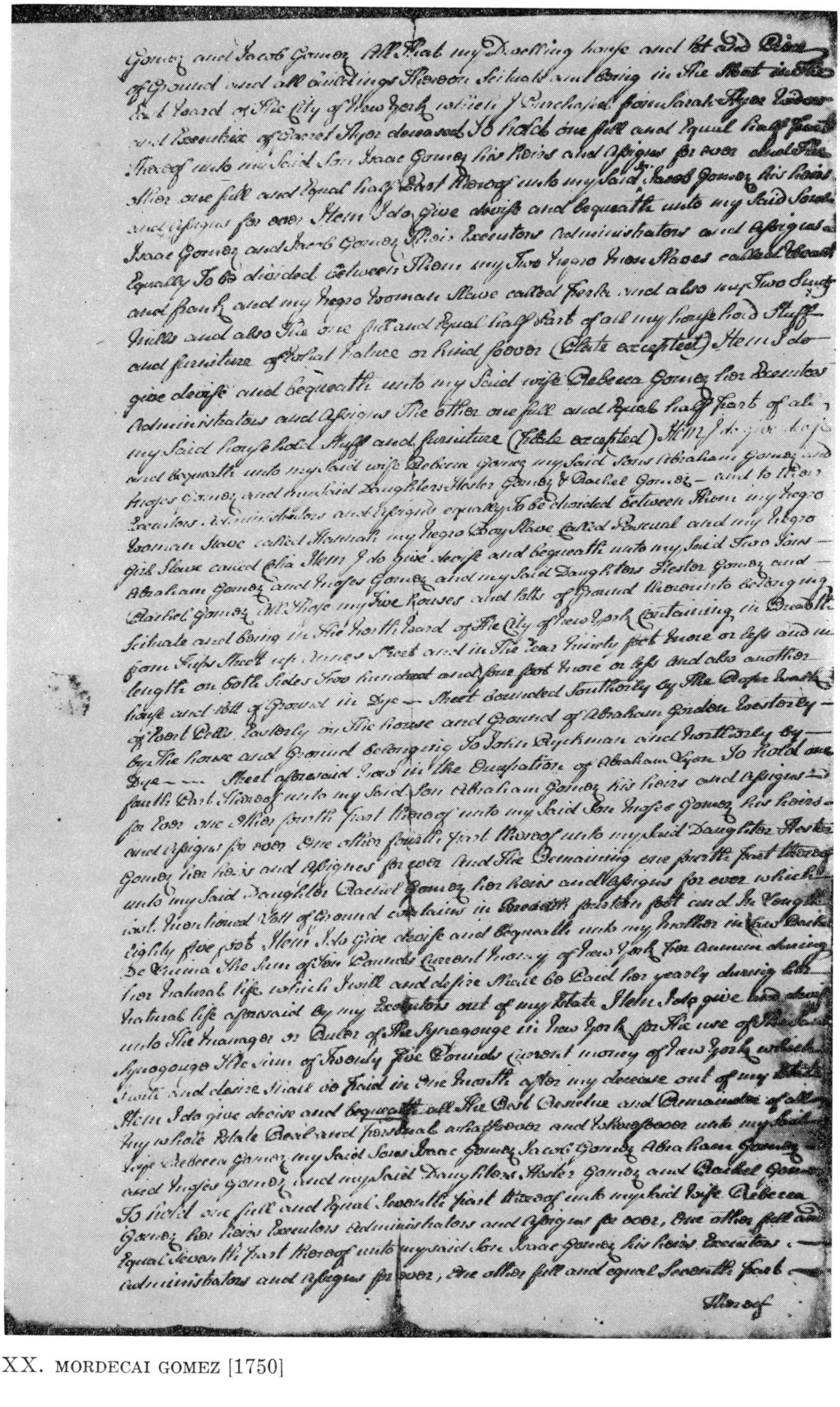
Gomez and Jacob Gomez All That my Dwelling house and lot and Piece
of Ground and all buildings Thereon Scituate and being in The Street in the
East Ward of The City of New York which I Purchased from Sarah Myer Widow
and Executrix of Garret Myer deceased To hold one full and Equal half part
Thereof unto my Said Son Isaac Gomez his heirs and Assigns for ever and The
other one full and Equal half part thereof unto my Said Son Jacob Gomez his heirs
and Assigns for ever Item I do give devise and bequeath unto my Said Sons
Isaac Gomez and Jacob Gomez Their Executors Administrators and Assigns
Equally To be divided between Them my Two Negro Man Slaves called Quash
and Frank and my Negro Woman Slave called Bella and also my Two Snuff
Mills and also The one full and Equal half part of all my household Stuff
and furniture of what Nature or kind soever (Plate excepted) Item I do
give devise and bequeath unto my Said wife Rebecca Gomez her Executors
Administrators and Assigns The other one full and Equal half part of all
my Said household Stuff and furniture (Plate excepted) Item I do give devise
and bequeath unto my Said wife Rebecca Gomez my Said Sons Abraham Gomez and
Moses Gomez and unto said Daughters Hester Gomez & Rachel Gomez — and to Their
Executors Administrators and Assigns equally To be divided between Them my Negro
Woman Slave called Hannah my Negro Boy Slave called Pascual and my Negro
Girl Slave called Celia Item I do give devise and bequeath unto my Said Two Sons —
Abraham Gomez and Moses Gomez and my Said Daughters Hester Gomez and —
Rachel Gomez All Those my Two houses and lotts of Ground thereunto belonging
Scituate and being in The North Ward of The City of New York Containing in Breadth
from Dyes Street up Nassau Street and in The Rear Thirty feet more or less and in
length on both Sides Two hundred and four feet more or less and also another
house and lott of Ground in Dye — Street bounded Southerly by The [illegible]
of Peter Bells Easterly by The house and Ground of Abraham Gordon Westerly —
by The house and Ground belonging To John Ryckman and Northerly by —
Dye — — Street aforesaid Now in The Occupation of Abraham Lyon To hold one
fourth Part Thereof unto my Said Son Abraham Gomez his heirs and Assigns and
for Ever one other fourth Part thereof unto my Said Son Moses Gomez his heirs and
and Assigns for ever One other fourth Part thereof unto my Said Daughter Hester
Gomez her heirs and Assigns for ever And The Remaining one fourth part thereof
unto my Said Daughter Rachel Gomez her heirs and Assigns for ever which
last Mentioned Lott of Ground contains in Breadth fourteen feet and In Length
eighty five feet Item I do give devise and bequeath unto my brother in Law Bachi
De Vienna The Sum of Ten Pounds Current money of New York per annum during
her Natural life which I will and desire Shall be Paid her yearly during her
Natural life aforesaid by my Executors out of my Estate Item I do give and devise
unto The Manager or Ruler of The Synagogue in New York for The use of The Said
Synagogue The Sum of Twenty five Pounds Current money of New York which
I will and desire Shall be Paid in One Month after my decease out of my Estate
Item I do give devise and bequeath all The Rest Residue and Remainder of all
my whole Estate Real and Personal whatsoever and wheresoever unto my Said
wife Rebecca Gomez my Said Sons Isaac Gomez Jacob Gomez Abraham Gomez —
and Moses Gomez and my Said Daughters Hester Gomez and Rachel Gomez
To hold one full and Equal Seventh part thereof unto my Said wife Rebecca
Gomez her heirs Executors Administrators and Assigns for ever, One other full and
Equal Seventh part thereof unto my said Son Isaac Gomez his heirs Executors —
Administrators and Assigns for ever, One other full and equal Seventh part —
thereof

XX. MORDECAI GOMEZ [1750]

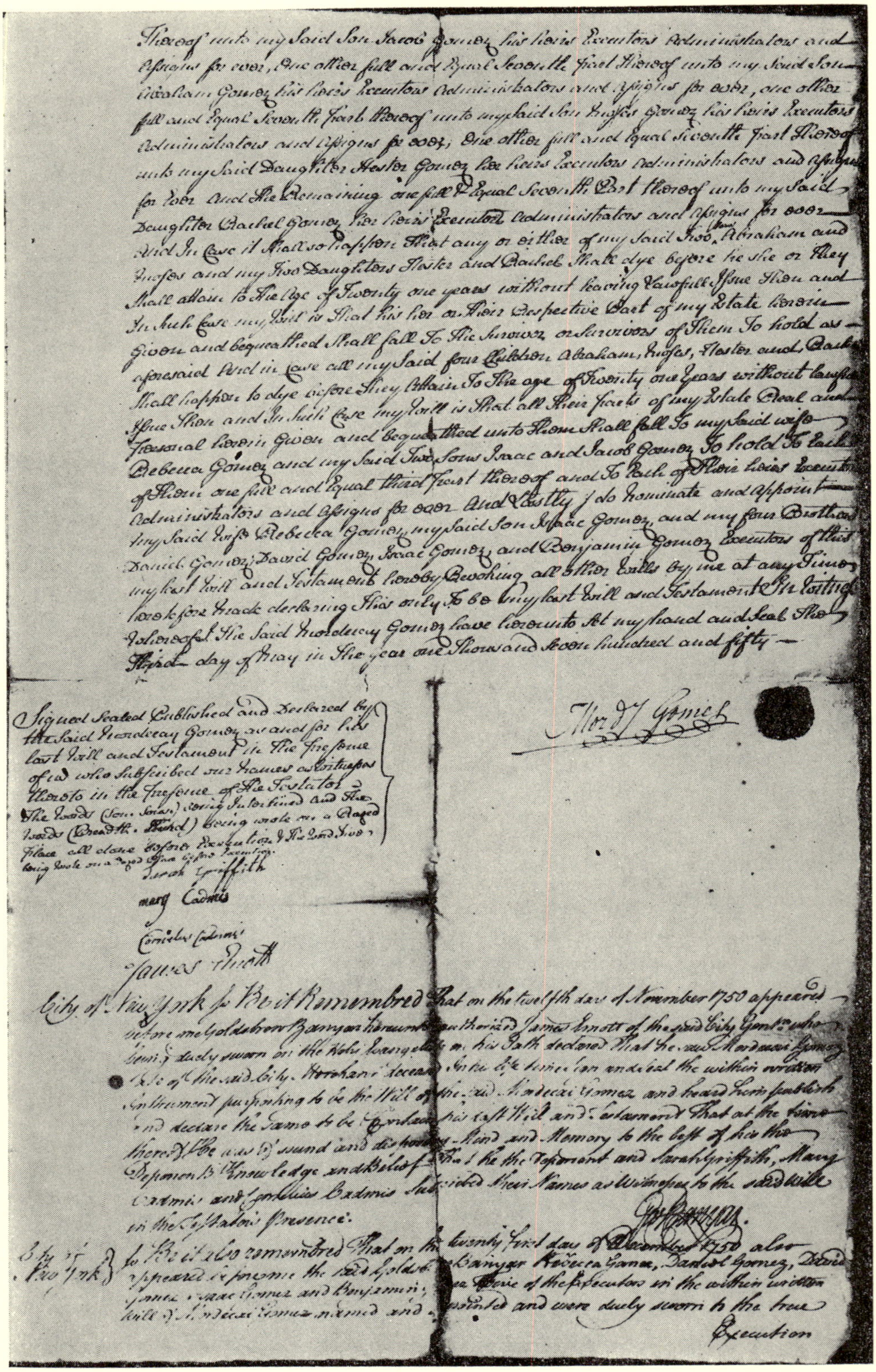
Thereof unto my Said Son Jacob Gomez his heirs Executors Administrators and Assigns for ever, One other full and Equal Seventh Part thereof unto my Said Son Abraham Gomez his heirs Executors Administrators and Assigns for ever, one other full and Equal Seventh Part thereof unto my Said Son Moses Gomez his heirs Executors Administrators and Assigns for ever; One other full and Equal Seventh Part thereof unto my Said Daughter Hester Gomez her heirs Executors Administrators and Assigns for ever And the Remaining one full & Equal Seventh Part thereof unto my Said Daughter Rachel Gomez her heirs Executors Administrators and Assigns for ever And In Case it Shall so happen that any or either of my Said two Sons Abraham and Moses and my two Daughters Hester and Rachel Shall dye before he she or they Shall attain to the Age of Twenty one years without leaving Lawfull Issue then and In Such Case my Will is that his her or their Respective Part of my Estate herein Given and bequeathed Shall fall to the Survivor or Survivors of them to hold as aforesaid And in Case all my Said four Children Abraham, Moses, Hester and Rachel Shall happen to dye before they Attain to the age of Twenty one Years without Lawful Issue then and In Such Case my Will is that all their Parts of my Estate Real and Personal herein Given and bequeathed unto them Shall fall to my Said wife Rebecca Gomez and my Said Two Sons Isaac and Jacob Gomez To hold to Each of them one full and Equal third Part thereof and to Each of their heirs Executors Administrators and Assigns for ever And Lastly I do Nominate and Appoint my Said wife Rebecca Gomez, my Said Son Isaac Gomez, and my four Brothers Daniel Gomez, David Gomez, Isaac Gomez, and Benjamin Gomez Executors of this my last Will and Testament hereby Revoking all other Wills by me at any Time heretofore made declaring this only to be my last Will and Testament In Testimony whereof I the Said Mordecay Gomez have hereunto Set my hand and Seal the Third day of May in the year one Thousand seven hundred and fifty —

Signed Sealed Published and Declared by the Said Mordecay Gomez as and for his last Will and Testament in the Presence of us who Subscribed our Names as Witnesses thereto in the Presence of the Testator The words (Son Isaac) being Interlined and the words (Breadth. Third) being wrote on a Rased Place all done before Execution & the word two being wrote on a rased place before Execution.

Sarah Griffith

Mary Cadmis

Cornelius Cadmis

James Emott

Mord. Gomez

City of New York ss Be it Remembred That on the twelfth day of November 1750 appeared before me Goldsbrow Banyar hereunto authorized James Emott of the said City Gent. who being duly sworn on the Holy Evangelists on his Oath declared That he saw Mordecai Gomez late of the said City Merchant deceased in his life time sign and seal the within written Instrument purporting to be the Will of the said Mordecai Gomez and heard him publish and declare the same to be [illegible] his last Will and Testament That at the time thereof he was of sound and disposing Mind and Memory to the best of his this Deponents Knowledge and Belief And that he the Deponent and Sarah Griffith, Mary Cadmis and Cornelius Cadmis Subscribed their Names as Witnesses to the said Will in the Testators Presence.

Gw Banyar

City of New York ss Be it also remembred That on the twenty first day of December 1750 also appeared before me the said Goldsbrow Banyar Rebecca Gomez, Daniel Gomez, David Gomez, Isaac Gomez and Benjamin [illegible] some of the Executors in the within written Will of Mordecai Gomez named and [illegible] and were duly sworn to the true Execution

XX. MORDECAI GOMEZ [1750]

XXI

PHILLIP ISAACS[1]

[1756]

In the Name of God Amen.

I PHILLIP ISAACS of East Chester in the Province of New York Merchant being of sound Mind and Memory, and considering the Uncertainty of this frail and transitory Life, *Do* therefore make and ordain this my last Will and Testament, That is to Say,

First, after all my just Debts be paid and discharged, I give and bequeath to ISAACS ISAACS[2] of the City of New York Gentleman all that I shall be possest of either in Goods Money or Debts owing to me at the time of My Death.

Likewise, I make and ordain the Above Named ISAACS ISAACS to be Executor of this my last Will and Testament, hereby utterly disallowing and revoking all former Wills by me made. *In Witness* whereof I have hereunto set my Hand and Seal the Nineteenth day of October in the Year of our Lord One Thousand Seven Hundred and fifty five and in the Twenty Ninth Year of his Majesty's Reign.

Signed, Sealed, published, and declared, by the Said as his last Will and Testament in the presence of us the Subscribers.	Mark of s/ PHILLIP PI ISAAC [seal]

s/ NAPHTALY HT. MYERS[3]
s/ JOHN HUESTIS
the Mark of × ELIZABETH HUESTIS

[1] Original Will no. 968, HDC; Will Liber 19, p. 377; *NYHSC*, vol. V (1897), p. 96. Very little is known of Philip Isaacs. He made contributions to Shearith Israel in 1738 and 1747 and in 1728 contributed six shillings towards the purchase of the burial ground. He was a resident of New York during the 1720's. NYAL, South Ward, March 1, 1726. *PAJHS*, vol. XXI (1913), pp. 9, 39, 53 and 55. Possibly he is related to the Isaacs family of Connecticut. Leon Huhner, "Jews of New England (Other than in Rhode Island) Prior to 1910," *PAJHS*, vol. XI (1903), pp. 88–89. For escapades of Ralph Isaacs, possible relative, convert to Christianity and graduate of Yale, see Rollin G. Osterweis, "The House of Ralph Isaacs, Jr.," *The Connecticut Antiquarian*, vol. VII (1955), pp. 18–25; Kenneth Scott, "A 'Dust' at Yale and a 'Blessing' for President Clap," *The Connecticut Historical Society Bulletin*, vol. XXIII (1958), pp. 46–49.

[2] Isaac Isaacs was a member of a New York Masonic Lodge as well as *Ḥatan Beresith* in 1754 and *Parnas Residente* in 1756–1757. There is a record of a contribution to the Congregation in 1750. *PAJHS*, vol. XXI (1913), pp. 64, 70, 73 and 211; Samuel Oppen-

City of New York Ss. Be it Remembered that on the first day of March one thousand seven hundred and fifty six personally came and appeared before me JOHN GODBY thereunto delegated and appointed NAPTHALI HART MYERS of the City of New York Merchant who being of the Jewish Profession was duly sworn on the five Books of Moses and on his Oath declared that he did see PHILIP ISAACS set his hand mark and Seal the within written Instrument purporting to be the Will of the said PHILIP ISAACS bearing date the nineteenth day of October 1755 and heard him publish and declare the same to be and contain his last Will and Testament. That at the time thereof, he the said PHILIP ISAACS was of sound disposing mind and memory to the best of the knowledge and belief of him the Deponent and that his name Subscribed to the said Will is of his proper hand Writing which he Subscribed as a Witness to the said Will in the Testators presence and that he the Deponent saw JOHN HUESTIS Subscribe his Name and ELIZABETH HUESTIS set her hand mark as Witnesses thereto in the Testators presence.

s/ JNO. GODBY[4]

Be It Also Remembred that on the first day of March 1756 ISAAC ISAACS the Executor of the within written Will of PHILIP ISAACS likewise appeared before me the said JOHN GODBY and being of the Jewish Profession was duly sworn on the five Books of Moses to the true Execution and performance of the said Will by taking the oath of an Executor as by Law appointed.

Before me

s/ JNO. GODBY

---

heim, "Jews and Masonry in the United States before 1810," *ibid.*, vol. XIX (1910), p. 33. There is a record of an Isaac Isaacs in Jamaica, New York, during the 1760's and of a person so named in Norwalk in 1763. It is not known whether this is one or two Isaacs or whether either of these was the Isaac mentioned in the will, nor is the relation to Philip apparent. Jacob R. Marcus, *Early American Jewry, 1649–1794*, vol. I (Philadelphia, 1951), p. 51; William Alexander Papers, Box 1A, New-York Historical Society Library, List of "Recoverable Outstanding Debts, November 4, 1763."

[3] Naphtali Hart Myers (1711–1788) was a prominent New York, London, Newport, and Philadelphia merchant. He was frequently involved in the affairs of the Congregation and was *parnas* in 1754. *PAJHS*, vol. XXI (1913), pp. 49, 50, 70 *et passim*; *Dictionary*, p. 128.

[4] John Godby was appointed a clerk of the Court of Chancery on September 29, 1752. *Calendar*, p. 39.

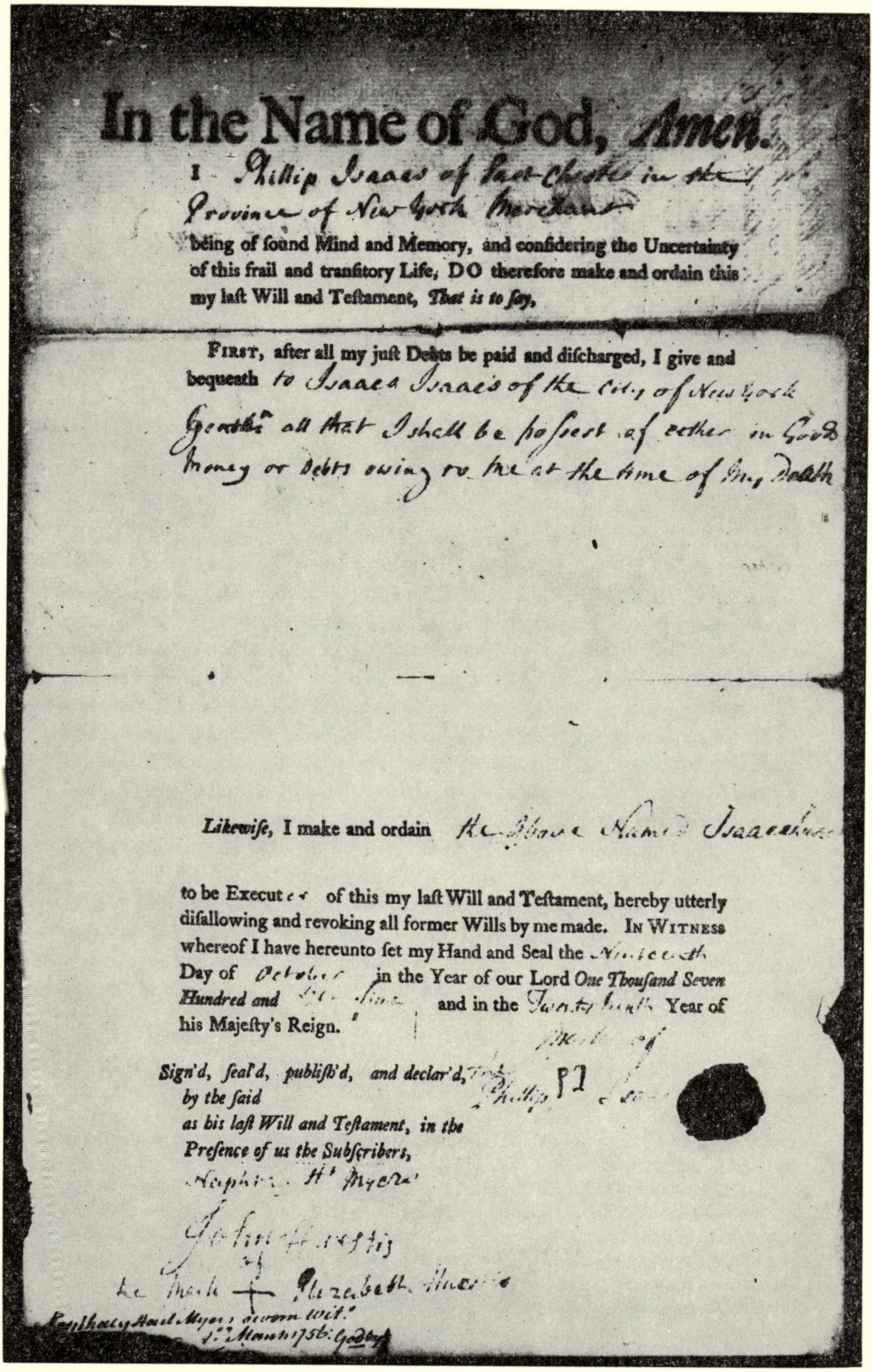

In the Name of God, *Amen.*

I Phillip Isaacs of East-Chester in the Province of New York Merchant being of sound Mind and Memory, and considering the Uncertainty of this frail and transitory Life, DO therefore make and ordain this my last Will and Testament, *That is to say,*

FIRST, after all my just Debts be paid and discharged, I give and bequeath to Isaacs Isaacs of the City of New York Gentlm all that I shall be possest of either in Goods money or Debts owing to me at the time of my Death

Likewise, I make and ordain the above Named Isaacs Isaacs

to be Executor of this my last Will and Testament, hereby utterly disallowing and revoking all former Wills by me made. IN WITNESS whereof I have hereunto set my Hand and Seal the Nineteenth Day of October in the Year of our Lord *One Thousand Seven Hundred and* fifty five and in the Twenty ninth Year of his Majesty's Reign.

Sign'd, seal'd, publish'd, and declar'd, by the *said* as *his last Will and Testament, in the Presence of us the Subscribers,*

his mark Phillip PI Isaacs

Naphtaly H. Myers

John Harris

her mark + Elizabeth Harris

Naphtaly Hart Myers sworn wit. 1st March 1756 Godfrey

XXI. PHILLIP ISAACS [1756]

XXII

ABRAHAM MENDES SEIXAS[1]

[1756]

To All and Singular the Faithfull in Christ to whom these our present Letters Testimonial shall come or whom the matters herein written do or may hereafter in any wise concern, THOMAS by divine providence ARCHBISHOP OF CANTERBURY primate of all England and Metropolitan Send Greeting, in our Lord God everlasting and will that undoubted faith be given to these presents and do make known and will that it be hereby made known to you that on searching the registry of our prerogative Court of Canterbury in the Archives thereof there well and faithfully preserved and kept we have discovered and plainly found amongst other things in the same that on the seventh day of April in the year of our Lord, one thousand seven hundred and thirty-eight at London before the worshipfull ROBERT CHAPMAN Doctor of Laws, Surrogate to the right Worshipfull JOHN BETTERSWORTH Doctor of Laws, Master keeper or Commissary of our prerogative Court of Canterbury lawfully constituted the last Will and Testament of ABRAHAM MENDES SEIXAS otherwise MIGUEL PACHECO DA SILVA late of the Parish of St. Dunstan Stepney in the County of Middlesex, deceased (having whilst living and at the time of his death Goods, Chattels or Credits in diverse Dioceses or Jurisdictions sufficient to found the jurisdiction of our Prerogative Court of Canterbury aforesaid) was proved approved and registred and administration of all and singular the goods, chattels and credits of the said deceased and any way concerning his will was granted to RODRIGO PACHECO and DANIEL MENDES SEIXAS Executors named in the said will, they being first sworn well and faithfully to administer the same and to make a true and perfect inventory of all and singular the said Goods, Chattels and Credits and to exhibit the same into the registry of the prerogative Court of Canterbury on or before the last day of October then next ensuing and also to

[1] The probating of wills in the London, England area was the prerogative of the Archbishop of Canterbury and therefore the language and format of wills by Jews had to conform to established procedures of the Prerogative Court of Canterbury. This applied also to wills made by Jews and the language used does not imply that the maker of the will had been converted to Christianity.

Will Liber 20, p. 37; *NYHSC*, vol. V (1897), pp. 115–116. Abraham Mendes Seixas, his Marrano name being Miguel Pacheco da Silva (d. 1738) was a London merchant and member of the Mahamed, the governing board, of the Sephardic congregation of London in 1730 and 1735. *Portraits*, p. 346. There is no record of his coming to New York, although he must have had assets in the province which is the reason for the appointment of Isaac Mendes Seixas as administrator of the property of Abraham. Seixas apparently had a claim against the Depeyster family for goods sold and delivered here. "Items Relating to Seixas Family," *PAJHS*, vol. XXVII (1920), pp. 350–352.

render a just and true account thereof. The true Tenor of which said will follows in these words and is such to wit, translated out of Portuguese:

In the Name of the Blessed God Creator of Heaven and earth I ABRAHAM MENDES SEIXAS otherwise MIGUEL PACHECO DA SILVA being in my perfect understanding though incapable of making my will with my own hand for want of sight and by reason of other infirmities have caused these presents to be made which I desire shall be deemed as my last will not only to declare herein some of my concerns but also to dispose of my Estate as I shall think best And therefore I do declare that I was lawfully married once[2] of which Matrimony I had three Children who are all of them alive at this day to wit JUDITH who is married with RODRIGO PACHECO,[3] ISAAC[4] who is at this time a single man and REBECCA at this time also married with DANIEL MENDES SEIXAS[5] And as I have given unto the husbands of my said daughters their Marriage Portions I therefor leave unto each one of my said daughters a legacy of twenty pounds Sterling as a token of my love and unto my said Son ISAAC I leave or bequeath only fifty pounds sterling for reasons better known to myself unto ESTHER DA SILVA who is at present in my Company I leave or bequeath fifty pounds Sterling and also all the Cloth and Linnen she hath in use unto

[2] Abigail Mendes Seixas, the wife of Abraham died in 1739. *Ibid.*, p. 169.

[3] Rodrigo Pacheco (1711–1749) married Judith (d. 1738), Abraham's daughter, probably in England in May, 1732. He had a prominent career as an English and New York merchant. *Dictionary*, p. 139; *Portraits*, p. 346; Leon Huhner, "Will of Jews on File in the Surrogates at the City of New York, 1754–1760," *PAJHS*, vol. XII (1904), p. 166. He was made freeman of the city on November 11, 1712 and was appointed colonial agent of the province in 1731. *Burghers*, p. 91; *Colonial Laws*, vol. II, p. 731. For his extensive business career see Naval Office Lists, Public Records Office, London [NOL], *passim*, Entry and Manifest Books, *passim*. He left New York late in 1726 or early 1727. *New York Gazette*, Oct. 10, 1726. When he returned, he became involved in a bitter and long court battle in the case of *Pacheco et al. v. Rene Het* (1726–1730), Chancery Minutes, vol. III, *passim*, New York County Clerk's Office; James Alexander Papers, Box 3, New-York Historical Society Library. Perhaps fearful of the consequences of this case, he left for England though he maintained property here. NYAL, South Ward, Feb. 18, 1732 and Feb. 24, 1733.

[4] Isaac Mendes Seixas (1709–1781) had a long career as merchant in New York, Connecticut, and Rhode Island. At the time this will was written he was twenty-eight years old and unmarried, probably to the chagrin of his father. He later married Rachel Levy (1719–1797) daughter of Moses Levy (see Will) in May, 1740. Abigail Franks to Naphtali Franks, July 6, 1740, Abigail Franks Letters; N. Taylor Phillips, "The Levy and Seixas Families of New York and Newport," *PAJHS*, vol. IV (1896), pp. 189–204; *Ibid.*, vol. XXVII (1920), pp. 161 and 169–170. Seixas was very much involved in congregational activities. *Ibid.*, vol. XXI (1913), pp. 42, 45, 49, *et passim*. After his marriage he went to live in New Jersey and became a shopkeeper there. Abigail Franks to Naphtali Franks, Nov. 9, 1740, Abigail Franks Letters. In 1747 he was elected constable of the South Ward in New York City, but he is declared ineligible as not being a freeman or freeholder. *Minutes*, vol. V, pp. 200 and 202.

[5] Daniel Mendes Seixas (d. 1758) was a member of the London Mahamad several times between 1741 and 1758. He married Rebecca in 1736. *PAJHS*, vol. XII (1904), p. 166; *ibid.*, vol. XXVII (1920), p. 169.

my son in law DANIEL MENDES SEIXAS I leave or bequeath eighty pounds sterling and I do hereby nominate my said two Sons in Laws RODRIGO PACHECO and DANIEL MENDES SEIXAS or the Survivour of them or the Executor or Administrator of the Survivour of them to be Executors of this my Testament and Administrators of all my Estate for them my said Executors to dispose of the effects which shall be found unto me belonging or appertaining in the manner following my said Executors and Administrators or the Survivour of them or the Executor or Administrator of the Survivour are to do their endeavours to take in or recover all my effects and out thereof pay my lawful debts and the legacies above mentioned and the rest and residue of my said effects or the produce thereof I Leave unto my said Executors or unto the Survivour of them or to the Executor or Administrator of the Survivour of them in trust for them to place it out at Interest as they shall think best and thereof to make use in the manner following my said Executors or the Survivour of them or the Executor or Administrator of the Survivour of them are to give or allow unto my said Son during his life the sum of thirty pounds Sterling every year in two equal or half yearly payments on Condition that my said son shall never alienate Mortgage or Sell the same annuity or yearly income upon pain (in case he should) that my said Executors shall forever after remain free or exempted from giving or allowing him the said sum of thirty pounds a year but apply the same to their own use and in case my said son shall marry with the approbation of my said Executors or the Survivor of them in writing it shall then remain to the choice of my said Executors either to give my said son the said annual Sum of thirty pounds Sterling or to deliver unto him all the whole amount of my Estate on Condition that in case my said son shall have Children of such Matrimonies approved of by my said Executors in such case my said Executors by the death of my said Son shall be obliged to divide all the said whole amount of my Estate amongst my said sons said Children (excepting my Executors shall happen to have done it before in the manner by me mentioned above) so and as if my said Estate belonged to and was the Estate of my said Son but in case he should not have children of that Matrimony so by them approved, or if he shall happen to marry without their approbation though he should then have children in such case he shall only enjoy the said annuity of thirty pounds a year under the conditions above declared during his life and by his death the whole amount of my Estate shall devolve to my said daughters JUDITH and REBECCA and to their heirs and in case the income of my said Estate shall be less than the said thirty pounds Sterling my said Executors shall not be obliged to give unto my said son any more then what my said Estate by them administered shall bring in but if it shall produce more than the said sum of thirty pounds it shall remain to the choice or discretion of my said Executors either to give the same to my said son or to make addition thereof to the whole Estate I also declare that if at any time both my Executors shall be minded not to take the trouble of the Execution of this my Testament, it shall remain to their choice in such case either to deliver the said Estate to my said Son, or to make a Deposit thereof in the Court of Chancery in this Kingdom to be there disposed of in the manner I mention above.

Done in Bethnal Green on the sixth day of March, one thousand and seven hundred and thirty-seven, eight.

ABRAHAM MENDES SEIXAS

Read and signed in our presence ABRA^M DE MESQUITA,[6]
PIEMENTAL,[7] ISAAC MUSSAPHIX[8]

Faithfully translated from the portugese original hereunto annexed according to the best of my skill and knowledge which after Examination I attest in London this tenth day of April 1738.

JOHN DA COSTA Notary Public 1738

In faith and testimony of all and singular which premises we have caused these our Letters Testimonial to issue forth and to be Corroborated and Confirmed by affixing thereto the seal of our said prerogative Court of Canterbury (which we use in this behalf) Given at London as to the time of the aforesaid search and the sealing of these presents the twenty fourth day of January in the year of our Lord one thousand seven hundred and fifty and the fourth year of our Translation L.S. W^M LEGARD, PET^R ST. ELORY, HEN. STEVENS Deputy Rigesters SIR CHARLES HARDY Knight,[9] Captain General and Governour in Chief in and over the Province of New York and the Territories depending thereon in America and Vice Admiral of the same. To ISAAC MENDES SEIXAS of the City of New York, Merchant, Attorney of DANIEL MENDES SEIXAS of the City of London, Merchant Surviving Executor of ABRAHAM MENDES SEIXAS, otherwise MIGUEL PACHECO DA SILVA, late of the Parish of St. Dunstan Stepney, in the County of Middlesex, Merchant, deceased, Sendeth Greeting, Whereas the said ABRAHAM MENDES SEIXAS otherwise MIGUEL PACHECO DA SILVA made his last Will and Testament in writing bearing date the Sixth day of March 1737/8 and thereby appointed RODRIGO PACHECO and DANIEL MENDES SEIXAS Executors thereof and soon after died. Which said will was afterwards at London on the Seventh day of April

[6] Abraham de Mesquita was possibly the brother or other relative of Joseph Bueno de Mesquita (see Will, *supra*, pp. 15–20).

[7] Possibly one of several contemporary Pimentals, including Isaac, Jacob, or Jael. Arthur P. Arnold, "Anglo-Jewish Wills and Letters of Administration," *Anglo-Jewish Notabilities* (London, 1949), p. 29.

[8] Possibly Isaac Mussaphia related to Esther Mussaphia whose will was proved in England in 1736. *Ibid.*, p. 195.

[9] Charles Hardy, Knight was appointed Governor on September 3, 1755 and served until June, 1757. *Civil List*, p. 150.

one thousand seven hundred and thirty-eight duly proved, approved, and registered in the prerogative Court of Canterbury and administration of all and Singular the Goods, Chattels, and Credits of the said deceased and any way concerning his will Granted to RODRIGO PACHECO and DANIEL MENDES SEIXAS Executors named in the said Will as by the Letters Testimonial under the seal of the prerogative Court of Canterbury (to which these presents are annexed) may appear. And whereas the said DANIEL MENDES SEIXAS now surviving Executor of the the last will and Testament of the said ABRAHAM MENDES SEIXAS otherwise MIGUEL PACHECO DA SILVA by Letters or Power of Attorney bearing date the twenty ninth day of January, 1750, did among other things authorize and impower you the said ISAAC MENDES SEIXAS to take if necessary letters of administration out of the prerogative Court of this province with the will of the said ABRAHAM MENDES SEIXAS otherwise MIGUEL PACHECO DA SILVA thereto annexed as by the said Letter or power of Attorney may appear I desiring therefore that the Goods, Chattels and Credits which were of the said ABRAHAM MENDES SEIXAS otherwise MIGUEL PACHECO DA SILVA, deceased, in this Province, may be well and faithfully administered converted and disposed of according to the true intent and meaning of his said Will hereunto annexed. Do grant unto you the said ISAAC MENDES SEIXAS during the absence of the said DANIEL MENDES SEIXAS, surviving Executor as aforesaid full power to collect Levy recover and receive all and singular the Goods, Chattells, Rights and Credits of the said deceased and the same to administer and dispose of according to the tenor and effect of his said will and as the Law directs being first in due form of Law to fulfill the will of the said deceased and to pay his debts and legacies as far forth as his Goods, Chattells and Credits will thereto extend and the Law bind you. And also to make or cause to be made a true and perfect Inventory of all and singular the Goods, Chattels and Credits of the said deceased, which have or shall come to your hands possession or knowledge, and to exhibit the same into the Registry of the prerogative Court of this Province on or before the twenty fifth day of December next ensuing and to render a just and true account when thereunto required And I do by these presents Nominate Constitute and appoint you the said ISAAC MENDES SEIXAS administrator of all and singular the Goods, Chattells and Credits which were of the said ABRAHAM MENDES SEIXAS otherwise MIGUEL PACHECO DA SILVA deceased, together with his said will annexed, during the absence of the said DANIEL MENDES SEIXAS, surviving Executor as aforesaid.

In testimony whereof I have caused the prerogative seal of the province of New York to be hereunto affixed at the City of New York the twenty fifth day of June one thousand seven hundred and fifty six.

GEO. BANYAR, D. Secr'y

XXIII

SOLOMON ISAACS[1]

[1757]

In the Name of God and by his permission I SOLOMON ISAACS of Charles Town and Province of South Carolina being sound of Body and perfect memory and understanding do make and publish this to be and Contain my last will and Testament & after paying all my just and Lawfull Debts, I give and Bequeath the remainder of my Estate in manner following, Whatever Effects or moneys due to me that are in the hands of my Brother ASHER I bequeath to him & his heirs forever. I likewise bequeath to my brother ASHER and to my sister JUDITH and to my Sister REBECCA[2] and to my sister RACHEL and to the heirs of my Brother JOSHUA,[3] each an Equal part of the rest of my Estate to be Equally divided amongst those five & their heirs Executors, or assigns. The part or share of my Brother JOSHUA's heirs I desire may be left in trust to my Executors to be let out at Interest, and the yearly Income or part thereof to be paid yearly towards the support of said Children but in Case of the demise of said heirs of my Brother JOSHUA before they arrive to be of Age then their share or part (with what may become due thereon), to be given and Equally shared between SOLOMON ISAACS[4] the son of my Brother ASHER and SOLOMON SIMSON[5] the son of JOSEPH & my Sister REBECCA SIMSON each share and share alike (and to their heirs), but on the demise of either of those two before they arrive to be of age, then the whole to go to the survivor, and his heirs, And I do hereby appoint (and desire) Mr. JOHN SAVAGE[6] of Charles Town Merchant & my Nephew SAMPSON SIMSON[7] of New York Merchant to be the Executors of this my last Will and

[1] Will Liber 20, p. 294; *NYHSC*, vol. V (1897), p. 179. Solomon Isaacs, son of Joseph and brother of Joshua Isaacs (see Will) was a merchant in Freehold, New Jersey, Boston, and in Charleston. In 1730, he contributed to Shearith Israel in New York. *Portraits*, p. 317; *PAJHS*, vol. XXI (1913), pp. 21, 25, 33 and 35; *ibid.*, vol. XXIII (1915), p. 84; *Dictionary*, p. 69. The testator who conducted business under the name of Solomon Isaac & Co. was involved in a lawsuit in 1748 in South Carolina. The inventory of his estate was filed in that state. Barnett A. Elzas, *The Jews of South Carolina* (Philadelphia, 1905), pp. 28-29, 40n. and 41.

[2] Rebecca Isaacs, was the wife of Joseph Simson. See the latter's will, *infra*, pp. 201-203; Will of Sampson Simson, *infra*, p. 139, note 3.

[3] See Will of Joshua Isaacs, *supra*, pp. 69-70, notes 2, 3 and 5.

[4] This may be the storekeeper Solomon Isaacs who died of yellow fever in New York in 1798. Samuel Oppenheim, "Jews Who Died of Yellow Fever in the Epidemic in New York in 1798," *PAJHS*, vol. XXV (1917), p. 123.

[5] See Will of Sampson Simson, *infra*, p. 141, note 15.

[6] John Savage is left a mourning ring by Sampson Simson. (See *infra*, Will, p. 140.)

[7] *Ibid.*, p. 141.

Testament. In witness whereof I have hereunto set my hand and seal this twenty-sixth day of August and in the year one thousand and seven hundred fifty one.

SOL ISAACS L.S.

Signed Sealed published & delivered by the Testator to be his last will and testament in presence of us who at his request have hereunto set our hands as witnesses.

THOMAS OLIVE WILLIAM ELLIS JNO. PAINE

South Carolina

By his Excellency WILLIAM HENRY LYTTELTON Esquire Captain General and Governor in Chief in and over the said Province and Ordinary of the same, personally appeared before me, WILLIAM ELLIS, one of the witnesses to the within will who being duly sworn upon the Holy Evangelists of Almighty God maketh oath and saith that he was present & saw SOLOMON ISAACS, the testator sign, seal, publish, pronounce and declare the same to be and contain his last will and testament. That he then of sound mind memory & understanding to the best of this Deponents knowledge and belief, that he himself signed his name as a witness thereto, in the presence and at the request of the said Testator and also saw THOMAS OLIVE, and JOHN PAINE do the same. Given under my hand this fourteenth day of January, 1757.

W. H. LYTTLETON

Whereas I SOLOMON ISAACS on the Twenty sixth day of August one thousand seven hundred & fifty one did duly Execute my last will and testament, wherein I did nominate Constitute and appoint Messrs. JOHN SAVAGE and SAMPSON SIMSON Executors of my said last Will and Testament, But being at present, very weak and low but of perfect mind & memory for several Good Reasons moving me thereto, I do by these presents nominate and appoint PETER BACOT to be another of my Executors to act in conjunction with the before named JOHN SAVAGE and SAMPSON SIMSON, each of whom is hereby declared to be invested with equal power and authority to act in the affairs which concern my Legatees before named to the best of their interest and with the Consent and approbation of my other Executors and farther I do hereby give and bequeath to ELIZABETH TOOKENMAN the sum of two hundred Spanish Dollars or the value of them in Current money of this Province and Likewise I give to JOHN HOLMES the sum of one hundred Spanish Milled Dollars of the value of them in Currency of South Carolina aforesaid. In witness whereof I have hereunto set my hand and seal this twentieth day of December in the year one thousand seven hundred and fifty six.

his
SOLOMON X ISAACS L.S.
mark

Signed Sealed & published [the word (did) in the first line of this Codicil & (South) mentioned in the fourth line from the bottom being scratched out & interlined] as a Codicil to this my last will and Testament in presence of us who at his request have hereunto set our hands as witnesses.

RICHARD FOWLER JOHN FOWLER JOHN WIMER

South Carolina

By his Excellency WILLIAM HENRY LYTTELTON Esquire Captain General and Governor in Chief in and over the said Province and ordinary of the same Personally appeared before me, JOHN FOWLER, one of the witnesses to the above Codicil of the last Will & Testament of SOLOMON ISAACS who being duly sworn upon the Holy Evangelists of Almighty God maketh oath & saith that he was present and saw the Testator set his mark and seal & publish pronounce and declare the same to be a Codicil to his last will and Testament. That he was then of sound mind memory and understanding to the best of this deponents knowledge and belief that he himself signed his name as a witness thereto at the request and in the presence of the Testator and also saw RICHARD FOWLER and JOHN WIMER do the same at the same time qualified PETER BACOT Executor.
Given under my hand this 14th January 1757

W. H. LYTTELTON

Secretary's Office A true copy taken from the original will and probates kept in this office Examined & Certified by

JOHN MURRAY Deputy Secretary

JAMES DELANCEY[8] Esquire his Majesty's Lieutenant Governor and Commander in Chief in and over the Province of New York and the Territories depending thereon in America To all to whom these presents shall come or may concern Greeting Whereas SOLOMON ISAACS late of Charles Town in the province of South Carolina, deceased, made his last will and Testament in writing bearing date the twenty-sixth day of August 1751 and the twentieth day of December 1756 and thereby appointed JOHN SAVAGE, SAMPSON SIMPSON and PETER BACOT Executors thereof, as by the said will duly proved before the Governor of the said Province of South Carolina and the certificate thereof under the Great Seal of the said Province hereto annexed, may appear Know ye therefore that the said deceased, having whilst he lived, and at the time of his death, Goods, Chattels and Credits within this province by means whereof the proving and registring his said will and the granting administration of all and singular the said Goods, Chattels and Credits and also the auditing allowing and final dis-

[8] James DeLancey, a Judge of the Supreme Court and a Chief Justice was appointed Lieutenant Governor on October 27, 1747. He died in 1761. *Calendar*, p. 34.

charging the account thereof belonging unto me The said will is proved and Certified as aforesaid is now approved of and allowed of by me, and Administration of all and singular the said Goods, Chattels and Credits of the said deceased and any way concerning his will is now granted unto SAMPSON SIMPSON of the City of New York Merchant one of the Executors in the said Will named and appointed being first sworn well and faithfully to administer the same, and to make and exhibit a true and perfect inventory of all singular the said Goods Chattels and Credits and also to render just and true account thereof when thereunto required.

In testimony whereof I have caused the prerogative seal of the province of New York to be hereunto affixed the Eighteenth day of July one thousand seven hundred and fifty-seven.

GEO. BANYAR, Deputy Secretary

1.

2.

3.

4.

5.

6.

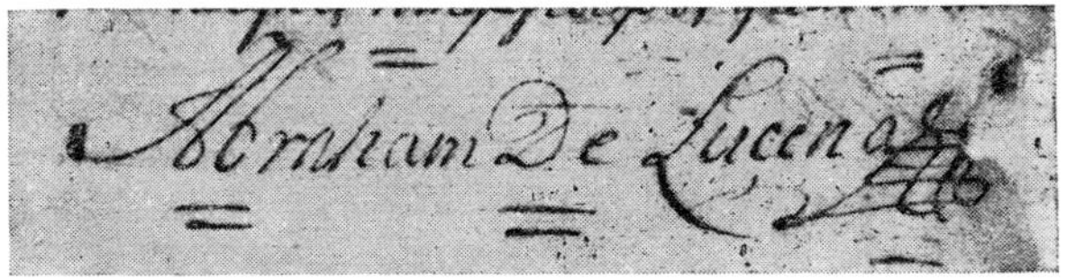

SIGNATURES, MARKS AND SEALS OF EARLY NEW YORK WILLS (1704–1799)

1. JOSEPH NUNEZ (1704)
2. ESTER BROWN (1708)
3. JOSEPH BUENO (1708)
4. ESTER PINHEIRO (1710)
5. SAMUEL LEVY (1719)
6. ABRAHAM DE LUCENA (1725)

7.

8.

9.

10.

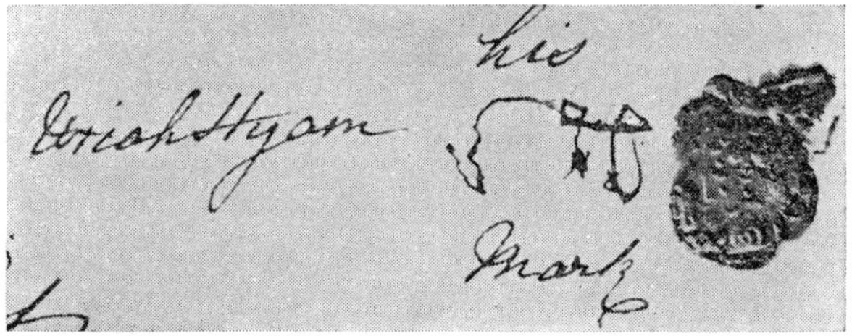

11.

SIGNATURES, MARKS AND SEALS OF EARLY NEW YORK WILLS (1704–1799)

7. MOSES LEVY (1728) 9. RACHEL LUIS (1737)

8. MICHAEL [MICKALLS] MICHAELS (1736) 10. URIAH HYAM (1740)

11. LUIS GOMEZ (1740)

12.

13.

14.

15.

16.

17.

SIGNATURES, MARKS AND SEALS OF EARLY NEW YORK WILLS (1704–1799)

12. Isaac Levy (1745)
13. Simja de Torres (1746)
14. Mordecai Gomez (1750)
15. Phillip Isaacs (1756)
16. Judah Hays (1764)
17. David Gomez (1769)

18.

20.

19.

21.

22.

SIGNATURES, MARKS AND SEALS OF EARLY NEW YORK WILLS (1704–1799)

18. Isaac Gomez (1770)
19. Benjamin Gomez (1772)
20. Sampson Simson (1774)
21. Esther Benzaken (1790)
22. Manuel Myers (1799)

SEAL OF PHILLIP ISAACS [1756] (*enlarged*)

SEAL OF ISAAC GOMEZ [1770] (*enlarged*)

MONOGRAM OF MICHAEL MICHAELS [1736] (*enlarged*)

MONOGRAM OF SAMPSON SIMSON [1774] (*enlarged*)

XXIV

AARON HART[1]

[1763]

To All and singular the faithfull in Christ to whom these our present Letters Testimonial shall come or whom the matters herein written do or may hereafter in any wise Concern THOMAS by divine Providence ARCHBISHOP OF CANTERBURY Primate of all England and Metropolitan send greeting in our Lord God Everlasting and will that undoubted faith be given to these presents and do make none and will that it be hereby known to you that on searching the Registry of our Prerogative Court of Canterbury in the Archives thereof there well and faithfully preserved and kept we have discovered and plainly found amongst other things in the same that on the twenty seventh day of November in the year of our Lord One thousand seven hundred and Sixty two at London before the worshipfull ANDREW COTTER DUCAREL Doctor of Law Surrogate to the right worshipfull SIR EDWARD SIMPSON Knight Doctor of Laws Master keeper or Comissary of our Prerogative Court of Canterbury lawfully Constituted the last will and Testament [of] AARON HARTE late of the Parish of St. Mary White Chappel in the County of Middlesex deceased having whilst he lived and at the time of his death Goods Chattels and Credits in divers Dioceses or Jurisdictions sufficient to found the jurisdiction of our Prerogative Court of Canterbury aforesaid was proved approved and Registered and Administration of all and singular the goods Chattels and Credits of the said deceased and any way concerning his will was granted to NATHAN SALOMONS One of the Executors named in the said Will he having been first sworn well and faithfully to administer the same and to make a true and perfect Inventory of all and singular the said Goods Chattels and Credits and to exhibit the same into the Registry of our Prerogative Court of Canterbury on or before the last day of May next ensuing and also to render a just and true account thereof Power reserved of makeing the like Grant to BARENT GOMPERTZ[2] the

[1] Will Liber 24, p. 178; *NYHSC*, vol. VI (1898), pp. 266–268. This is one of a number of Anglo-Jewish wills recorded in New York, not because of family ties, but because assets were located here. Like Joseph Israel Levy, little is known about the testator. It is possible that he was related to Aaron Hart (1670–1756), chief rabbi of the Great Synagogue in London, whose brother Moses built the synagogue at his own expense. It is probable, however, that he was the Aaron Hart (1724–1762) who was a Commissary in Canada and a resident of New York for a while. Albert M. Hyamson, "Dictionary of Anglo-Jewish Biography," *Anglo-Jewish Notabilities* (London, 1949), p. 29. At his death he was called "an eminent Jew merchant." London *Gentleman's Magazine*, vol. XXXII (1762), p. 627.

[2] The will of Barent Gompertz was probated in England in 1768. Arnold, *op. cit.*, p. 29.

other Executor named in the said will when he shall apply for the same the true tenor of which said will follows in these words and is such to wit: In the name of God amen I AARON HART of Newstreet otherwise Somerset Street White Chappel London Merchant being of Sound mind Memory and Understanding but sick in body do make this my last will and Testament, and first I recommend my soul to God hoping forgiveness of my sins and my body I Commit to the Earth to be decently Interred as I shall direct: I desire to be buried in Linnen and to have a Herse 4 Mourning Coaches and six Others and a Marble Stone shall be put on me to the amount of ten or twelve pounds and I desire and order that ten persons may come to read every morning and evening for one month after my decease for which I desire my Executors hereafter named will give them twenty shillings each and first after all my just debts and funeral Expenses shall be paid I leave and bequeath unto my daughter RACHEL HART six hundred pounds for a Marriage portion when she shall arrive at the Age of twenty one years or day of Marriage provided she marries with the Consent of my Executors hereafter mentioned but in Case she should die before she attains the age of twenty one years or day of marriage then it shall go to my three sons NAPHTALY,[3] HYAM[4] and SAMUEL HART[5]

Item
I also leave and bequeath to my said daughter when she shall marry as aforesaid a second best bed of my house

Item
I leave and bequeath unto my dear wife six hundred pounds in the following manner Three hundred and sixty nine pounds which is at New York and the reaminder in Cash besides the furniture of my house Except Silver.

Item
I also leave my dear wife a silver Teapot a silver Coffee Pott and a small silver Tea Equipage

Item
I leave to Each of my three sons NAPHTALY, HYAM and SAMUEL HART when they shall arrive at the Age of twenty one years six hundred

[3] Possibly the Naphtali Hart (1716–1786), a merchant, who appears to have been in New York in 1739. "Gomez Ledger," *PAJHS*, vol. XXVII (1920), p. 246. He was also *parnas* of the Newport Synagogue in 1761. *Ibid.*, pp. 181–183. It does not appear likely, however, that this was the Naphtali referred to since the will written in 1762 seems to indicate that the testator's children were not yet twenty-one.

[4] The will of a Hyam Hart was probated in England in 1838. Arnold, *op. cit.*, p. 165.

[5] Possibly the Samuel Hart whose will was probated in England in 1768, *ibid.* or less likely the Samuel Hart, who was a *parnas* of Shearith Israel in 1761. Samuel and Naphtali are mentioned together in the "Gomez Ledger" in 1739. *PAJHS*, vol. XXVII (1920), pp. 183 and 246.

pounds Each and in Case any of my three sons should happen to die before he attains the age of twenty one years it shall go to my other sons or the Survivors and Survivor of them share and share alike

Item

I leave and bequeath unto the two single Children of Mr. SIMON JONAS LEVY which he had by my sister BAYLA twenty pounds Each for a Legacy

Item

I leave and bequeath unto the married daughter of Mr. SIMON JONAS LEVY the sum of five pounds for a legacy

Item

I leave and bequeath unto Mr. MOSES MYER and his wife the sum of twelve guineas as a Legacy

Item

I leave and bequeath unto Mr. BENJAMIN ALEXANDER, JUNIOR the sum of five Guineas as a Legacy.

Item

I leave to Mrs. ROSE COHEN my wifes Mother the sum of twenty pounds as a legacy and five pounds for mourning

Item

I leave and bequeath to my Servant a mourning Gown and the remainder of my Estate and Effects (if any) I leave and bequeath unto my three sons NAPHTALY, HYAM and SAMUEL HART share and share alike when they shall Attain their Respective ages of One and twenty years It is my will and pleasure that my Children shall live with their said Mother till they attain their respective ages of twenty one years my daughter the day of Marriage if she should marry before she attains the said age of twenty one Years and that all my Effects be sold as soon as possible and be put out in the funds and the Interest thereof shall be for their Maintenance and be paid unto their Mother quarterly But in Case my said wife should marry again then they shall be maintained by my Executors and I do hereby nominate and appoint for Executors of this my last will and Testament Mr. NATHAN SALOMONS[6] and Mr. BARENT GOMPERTZ hereby revoking all former wills by me heretofore made thus done in London the 21st day of November 1762 AARON HART LS Signed sealed published and declared by the said Testator to be his will and Testament in the presence of us JOS JACOBUS, PHINEAS NETTO[7] I the underwritten

[6] Possibly the Nathan Salomons whose will was probated in England in 1793. Arnold, *op. cit.*, p. 218.

[7] Phineas Netto is probably Phineas Nieto, possibly son of David Nieto, a rabbi and distinguished Jewish scholar of eighteenth century England. David's father was Rabbi Phineas Nieto of Venice. Vivian D. Lipman, *Three Centuries of Anglo-Jewish History* (London, 1961), p. 51.

do declare to have writ the six on Eracement PHINEAS NETTO In faith and testimony of all and singular which Premises we have caused these our Letters Testimonial to issue forth and to be Corroborated and Confirmed by affixing thereto the seal of our said Prerogative Court of Canterbury which we use in this behalf Given at London as to the time of the aforesaid Search and the sealing of these presents the sixteenth day of June in the year of Our Lord one thousand seven hundred sixty three and in the sixth year of our translation WM LEGARD HEN. STEPHENS JOHN STEVENS Deputy Registers Extracted by PHILIP CRESPIGNY in Doctors Commons London 16th June 1763.

CADWALLADER COLDEN[8] Esquire his Majesty's Lieutenant Governor and Commander in Chief of the province of New York and the Territories depending thereon in America. To ACHESON THOMSON of the City of New York Merchant Attorney of NATHAN SOLOMONS one of the Executors of the last will and Testament of AARON HART late of the City of London Merchant decease sendeth Greeting. *Whereas* the said AARON HART in his lifetime made his last will and Testament in writing bearing date the twenty first day of November 1762 and thereby appointed NATHAN SOLOMONS and BARENT GOMPERTZ Executors thereof and soon after dyed. And whereas the said will was afterwards to wit on the 27th day of November in the year of our Lord 1762 at the City of London duly proved and administration of all and singular the goods Chattels and Credits of the said deceased and any way concerning his will was granted unto the said NATHAN SOLOMONS one of the Executors as aforesaid as by an Exemplification of the said will and the proceedings thereupon under the seal of the prerogative Court of Canterbury hereunto annexed may more fully appear and whereas the said NATHAN SOLOMONS and BARENT GOMPERTZ Executors of the said AARON HART are both absent beyond the seas and whereas the said Testator had whilst living and at the time of his death Goods Chattels and Credits within this Province: I therefore desiring that the Goods Chattels and Credits which were of the said Testator may be well and faithfully administered converted and disposed of according to the true Intent and meaning of his said will do grant unto you the said ACHESON THOMSON (during the absence of the said Executors) full power to Collect levy Recover and receive all and singular the Goods Chattels and Credits of the said Testator that are or shall be found within this Province and the same to administer and dispose of according to the tenor and Effect of the said will and as the Law directs being first in due form of Law to fulfill the will of the said deceased and to pay his debts and Legacies as far forth as his Goods Chattels and Credits will

[8] Cadwallader Colden served as Lieutenant Governor at various periods from 1761 to 1775. He was a noted politician, historian, and scientist of the period. He served also as surveyor-general, boundary commissioner, Master of the Court of Chancery, and member of the Governor's Council. *Civil List*, pp. 150, 162, 187, 208 and 236.

thereunto Extend and the Law bind you and also to make or Cause to be made a true and perfect Inventory of all and singular the Goods Chattels and Credits of the said deceased which have or shall come to your hands possession or knowledge and to Exhibit the same into the Registry of the Prerogative Court of this province on or before the seventeenth day of March next ensuing and to render a just and true account thereof when thereunto required and I do by these presents nominate Constitute and appoint you the said ACHESON THOMPSON Administrator of all and singular the Goods Chattels and Credits which were of the said AARON HART deceased with his will annexed during the absence of his Executors as aforesaid In Testimony whereof I have Caused the prerogative seal of the province of New York to be hereunto affixed at the City of New York the seventeenth day of September one thousand seven hundred and sixty three.

GEO. BANYAR Dep. Secry.

XXV

JUDAH HAYES[1]

[1764]

In the Name of the Eternal God of Israel Amen I JUDAH HAYES of the City of the City of New York Merchant being a little indisposed at present but injoying the free Exercise of my Understanding as in a Season of Health think it is proper to make my Will and it is in these Words,

Imprimus

I order my Remains to be interred in such a Manner and at such an Ex-

[1] Original Will no. 1659A, HDC; Will Liber 24, p. 464; *NYHSC*, vol. VI (1898), pp. 339–340. Judah Hayes (1703–August 19, 1764), a merchant was probably born in Holland and arrived sometime before 1729, the year in which he was naturalized. On December 2, 1735, he was made freeman of New York and in September, 1746, was elected constable, a position frequently served by Jews. *Colonial Laws*, vol. II, p. 513; *Burghers*, p. 129; *Minutes*, vol. IV, pp. 346 and 351. Hayes had a long, if not perfectly happy, relationship with the Congregation. He first appears in its Minutes when he donated £2 toward the building of the Mill Street Synagogue in 1728. In 1750, he was elected *parnas*. In June of 1760 Judah lodged a complaint against his brother-in-law Judah Mears. *PAJHS*, vol. XXI (1913), pp. 10, 22, 27, 60, 81–84 and 211. Hayes married Rebecca Michaels sometime in 1734, and Mears married her sister, Johevit Michaels. Abigail Franks to Naphtali Franks, June 9, 1734, Abigail Franks Letters (Friedman Collection, American Jewish Historical Society); Will of Moses Michal, *supra*, pp. 59–61. They carried on a feud over the seating of their daughters in the women's gallery of the synagogue. Mears was fined forty shillings and when attempts at reconciliation proved unsuccessful, Hayes was also fined this amount and given ten days to consider relenting or face exclusion from the congregation. He appears to have acquiesced, although he seems to be a very argumentative fellow. At any rate, he is often involved in litigation particularly in the Mayor's Court. For example, see *Hays v. Hunt* (1730), MCM, vol. 1728–1731, p. 487; *Campanell v. Hays* (1733), MCP, file 1730–1740, Nov. 1, 1733. In the latter case Asher Campanell sued for work done as Judah's storekeeper and servant. *Jacob Hays v. Judah Hays* (1736), MCP, file 1730–1740, March 19, 1736; *Hays v. Man* (1739), MCP, file 1730–1740, March 1, 1739; *Annely and Lewis v. Hays* (1742), MCP, file 1741–1749, Jan. 31, 1742. For his business activities, see Entries of August 29, 1737, August 9, 1738, April 23, 1740, Day Book of Peter Jay, at pp. 171, 193, 224 *et passim*. He seems to have dealt almost entirely in cloths, linens, rugs, etc. in his business dealings with Jay. For other business activities, see Mary Alexander Papers, Box 8, New-York Historical Society Library for a bill of exchange dated August 26, 1758 of £110 made by Francis Legge and signed by Hayes; William Alexander Papers, Box 1A, List of "Recoverable Outstanding Debts, November 4, 1763," New-York Historical Society Library. According to the last record Judah owed £2.9 at that time to Alexander. See also Manifest Books, vol. XX, January 13 and 27, 1748; vol. XV, September 28, 1748; vol. XI, July 19, 1742; vol. VIII, August 20, 1741; Entry Books, vol. IV, item 85; vol. V, item 1017; vol. VI, item 1437; *PAJHS*, vol. XXXIV (1937), pp. 117–122. Hayes lived and carried his business in the city. In 1741, he moved to the house of Joseph Murray, noted attorney, "opposite to Cortlandt's Market, where Persons may [be] supply'd with All Sorts of Goods, wholesale or retale." *Weekly Journal*, May 4 and June 27, 1741. At this time, he may have resided in the house of Mrs. Sims. Abigail Franks to Naphtali Franks, June 21, 1741, Abigail Franks Letters (Friedman Collection, American Jewish Historical Society). He lived for a time in Westchester as well and had litigation in Fairfield, Connecticut. *PAJHS*, vol. XI (1903), p. 89. For other material, see *Portraits*, pp. 471–474.

pence as my Wife in her Discretion shall think proper to direct And I bequeath to her absolutely all my Plate & Linnin and all my Household Furniture.

Secondly

Having frequently taken very just Offence at the Disobedience and General Conduct of my Son MICHAEL[2] who owes me above four hundred Pounds and having no opinion of his Prudence I have sometimes resolved to give him no Part of my Estate. But by the Advice of a Friend and upon mature Consideration thinking it my Duty to make some Provision for him I do herby forgive his Debt and ordain that the Capital Sum of three hundred pounds New York Money be [put] out at Interest upon Land and personal Security by my Executors who are also directed annually within twenty Days after the Interest becomes due to give the said MICHAEL a Power to demand and receive the same to his own Use & upon Default of Payment I direct them to sue for the same and put out the Capital in other Hands for the Preservation of the annual Interest for his Use during Life.

Thirdly

The said Capital and all other my Estate both real and personal I devise & bequeath to my Wife[3] and the Rest of my Children[4] (except my Daughter RACHEL to whom I give only five Shillings as she married contrary to my will & desire)[5] equally to be divided between them; my Wife taking no more than one of the Children and each to hold his or her Part of the Real Estate as Tenants in Common in Fee Simple And what I have above devised & bequeathed to my Wife is in Lieu of her Dower.

Fourthly

The share of such of my Children as may die before full Age unmarried and without Issue I devise & bequeath to the surviving Children to be equally divided between such Survivors as Tenants in Common in Fee Simple.

[2] The Michael Hays of Westchester (see Will) is the son of Jacob Hays, and nephew of Judah. Little is known of the son of Judah, although in September, 1746, a person with this name witnessed the enactment of "good and wholesome Laws" of the Congregation and in 1786 was elected *shamas*. *PAJHS*, vol. XXI (1913), pp. 6, 51 and 149; *Portraits*, p. 471.

[3] Rebecca Michaels (d. April 9, 1801), daughter of Moses Michaels, married Judah about 1734. *Dictionary*, p. 113.

[4] Rebecca and Judah had many children — three sons and seven daughters, all of whom were living at the time this will was written except for a son Meleg who died on February 26, 1759 and for a daughter Basha Hays who died on March 4, 1741. *Portraits*, pp. 466 and 472. Besides Michael, Moses, and Rachel specifically mentioned by name in the will, there were alive at this time Caty, Jossie (d. March 14, 1808), Phila (1738–1808), Sarah (b. 1764), and Reyna (1743–1787), *Dictionary*, pp. 57–60.

[5] Rachel Hays (d. May 2, 1768 in Quebec) married Levy Michaels (1723–1815) in 1759. He was a Canadian merchant and fur trader. *Ibid.*, pp. 59 and 112. Jacob R. Marcus, *American Jewry-Documents Eighteenth Century* (Cincinnati, 1959), p. 89.

Fifthly

I impower my Executors and the Major Part of them and the Survivor or Survivors of them to sell all my real Estate & turn the same into Money for the more easy Distribution of my Estate & Compliance with this Will and I ordain that the Share of each Child under Age at my Decease be put out at Interest for his or her maintainance till full Age or if a Girl till Mariage or full Age when the Capital Share shall be paid to them respectively.

Sixthly

Notwithstanding any Thing in my Will to the contrary I devise and bequeath & ordain that the share and Estate of my Daughter now the Wife of ABRAHAM SARZADAS[6] be put out at Interest by my Executors as soon as the same can be liquidated after the Settlement of my Estate that the Annual Interest when received be paid to her as long as she lives And that her Receipt Covert or Discovert shall be their Discharge And that after her Death leaving issue the said Interest be employed to maintain [ ] when the Capital shall be given to such Issue in equal Shares.

Lastly

I revoke all former Wills & declare this only to be my last Will & Testament Whereof I appoint my Wife REBECCA my son MOSES M. HAYES[7] and WILLIAM SMITH JUNIOR[8] to be the Executors. *In testimony* whereof I have hereunto set my Hand & Seal this twenty Second Day of July in the year according to the Christian Account of Time One Thousand Seven hundred & Sixty three.

Signed sealed & published by the Testator as his last Will in the Presence of us who subscribed our Names as Witnesses thereto at his Request & in his Presence and in the Presence of each other. The words [ordain] in the first side and [be] in the last being first interlined and the Word [Fifthly] wrote on an erasure in the Second side.

s/ JUDAH HAYES

[seal]

s/ JOSSEPH JESURUN PINTO[9]
s/ ABRAHAM BURJEAU[10]
s/ GEOR. CLINTON[11]

City of New York Ss. Be it remembered that on the twenty Seventh day of August one thousand Seven hundred and Sixty four Personally came and appeared before me EDWARD SMITH thereunto duely authorized JOSEPH JESURUN PINTO of the City of New York and being duely Sworn on his oath declared that he did see the within named JUDAH HAYES Sign and

[6] Caty Hays married Abraham Sarzadas in New York City in 1753 and Jacob Jacobs in 1775. *Dictionary*, p. 59. The *Dictionary* incorrectly mentions that she is married to

Seal the within written Instrument purporting to be the Will of the Said JUDAH HAYES bearing date the twenty Second day of July 1763 and heard him publish and declare the same as and for his last Will and Testament; that at the time thereof he the said JUDAH HAYES was of sound disposing mind and memory to the best of the knowledge and belief of him the Deponent, that the Name of him the Deponent Subscribed to the Said Will is of his own proper hand writing which he subscribed as a Witness to the Said Will in the presence of the Testator; and that he the Deponent likewise Saw ABRAHAM BURJEAUX and GEORGE CLINTON the other Witnesses to the said Will subscribe their Names as Witnesses thereto in the Testators presence

s/ EDW^{D}. SMITH[12]

City of New York Ss. Be it also remembered that on the said twenty Seventh day of August 1764 REBECCA HAYES and MOSES M. HAYES two of the Executors of the within Will of JUDAH HAYES likewise appeared before me the said EDWARD SMITH and were duely Sworn to the true Execution and performance of the said Will by severally taking the Oath of an Executor as by Law appointed before me

s/ EDW^{D}. SMITH

---

an Abraham Lazarus. There is no reference to a Abraham Lazarus in New York at this time. The confusion seems to occur because in the original will the name is written twice, once as Larzadas, the other as Sarzadas. The second spelling is undoubtedly correct. Unfortunately and another example of the shortcoming of the *Abstracts*, this name is incorrectly printed therein and has been followed. *NYHSC*, vol. VI (1898), p. 340. Abraham Sarzadas was made freeman on July 17, 1753, and is mentioned as donating to the synagogue. *PAJHS*, vol. XXI (1913), pp. 51, 67 and 79; *Burghers*, p. 178.

[7] Moses M. Hayes (1739–1805), a merchant, was granted power of attorney for James Walsh and the former in turn assigned this power to Hayman Levy. The instrument was recorded July 30, 1764. Conveyance Liber 27, cp. 17–19. He was *parnas* in 1768. *PAJHS*, vol. XXI (1913), pp. 97 and 101, see also references at pp. 79, 94, 102, 103 and 211.

[8] William Smith, Jr. (1728–1793) was a noted attorney. Interestingly, his father William Smith made a vicious anti-Semitic speech in the Assembly questioning the right of Jews to vote. These feelings seem not to have been accepted by the son, who probably acted as attorney in drawing the will. I.N.P. Stokes, *Iconography of Manhattan Island* (New York, 1895–1928), vol. IV, p. 553.

[9] Joseph Jesurun Pinto (b. 1729) was *ḥazzan* of Shearith Israel in 1758, 1759, 1762–1765. In 1766 his passage, as well as that of his family, was paid to London. *PAJHS*, vol. XXI (1913), pp. 79, 86, 91–92 and 208.

[10] Abraham Burjeaux, possibly Abraham Bargeau, mariner, was made freeman on November 22, 1743. *Burghers*, p. 149.

[11] George Clinton, possibly the Clinton, appointed County Clerk of Ulster on July 8, 1752, and later Surrogate of Ulster County on January 25, 1762. *Calendar*, pp. 39 and 65.

[12] Edward Smith together with Goldsbrow Banyar was commissioned Judge of Probate for New York on June 7, 1762. *Ibid.*, p. 60.

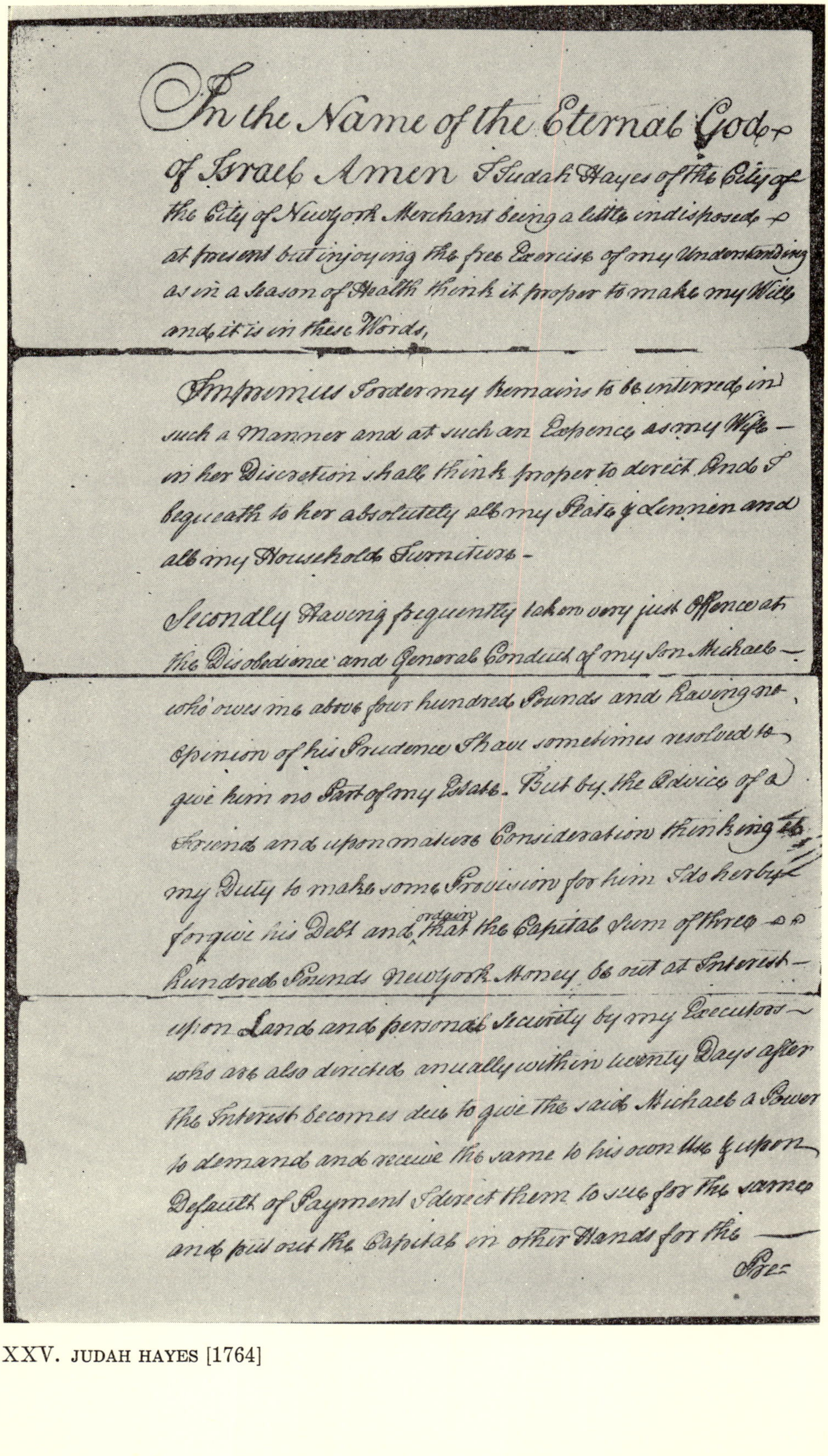

In the Name of the Eternal God of Israel Amen I Judah Hayes of the City of the City of New York Merchant being a little indisposed at present but injoying the free Exercise of my Understanding as in a Season of Health think it proper to make my Will and it is in these Words,

Imprimis I order my Remains to be interred in such a Manner and at such an Expence as my Wife in her Discretion shall think proper to direct And I bequeath to her absolutely all my Plate & Linnen and all my Household Furniture –

Secondly Having frequently taken very just Offence at the Disobedience and General Conduct of my Son Michael – who owes me above four hundred Pounds and having no opinion of his Prudence I have sometimes resolved to give him no Part of my Estate. But by the Advice of a Friend and upon mature Consideration thinking it my Duty to make some Provision for him I do herby forgive his Debt and ordain that the Capital Sum of three hundred Pounds New York Money be out at Interest – upon Land and personal Security by my Executors – who are also directed anually within twenty Days after the Interest becomes due to give the said Michael a Power to demand and receive the same to his own use & upon Default of Payment I direct them to sue for the same and put out the Capital on other Hands for the —

Pre-

XXV. JUDAH HAYES [1764]

Reservation of the annual Interest for his Use during
Life.

Thirdly; The said Capital and all other my Estate both real and personal I devise & bequeath to my Wife and the Rest of my Children (excepting my Daughter Rachel to whom I give only five Shillings as she married contrary to my will & desire) equally to be divided between them, my Wife taking no more than one of the Children and each to hold his or her Part of the Real Estate as Tenants in Common in Fee Simple And what I have above devised & bequeathed to my Wife is in Lieu of her Dower.—

Fourthly; The Share of such of my Children as may die before full Age unmarried and without Issue I devise & bequeath to the surviving Children to be equally divided between such Survivors as Tenants in Common in Fee Simple.—

Fifthly; I impower my Executors and the Major Part of them and the Survivor or Survivors of them to sell all my real Estate & turn the same into Money for the more easy Distribution of my Estate & Compliance with this Will And I ordain that the Share of each Child under Age at my Decease be put out at Interest for his or her Maintainance till full Age or if a Girl till Marriage or full Age when the Capital Share shall be paid to them respectively.—

Sixthly notwithstanding any thing in my Will to the contrary I devise and bequeath & ordain that the Share and Estate of my Daughter now the Wife of Abraham
Sarzadas

XXV. JUDAH HAYES [1764]

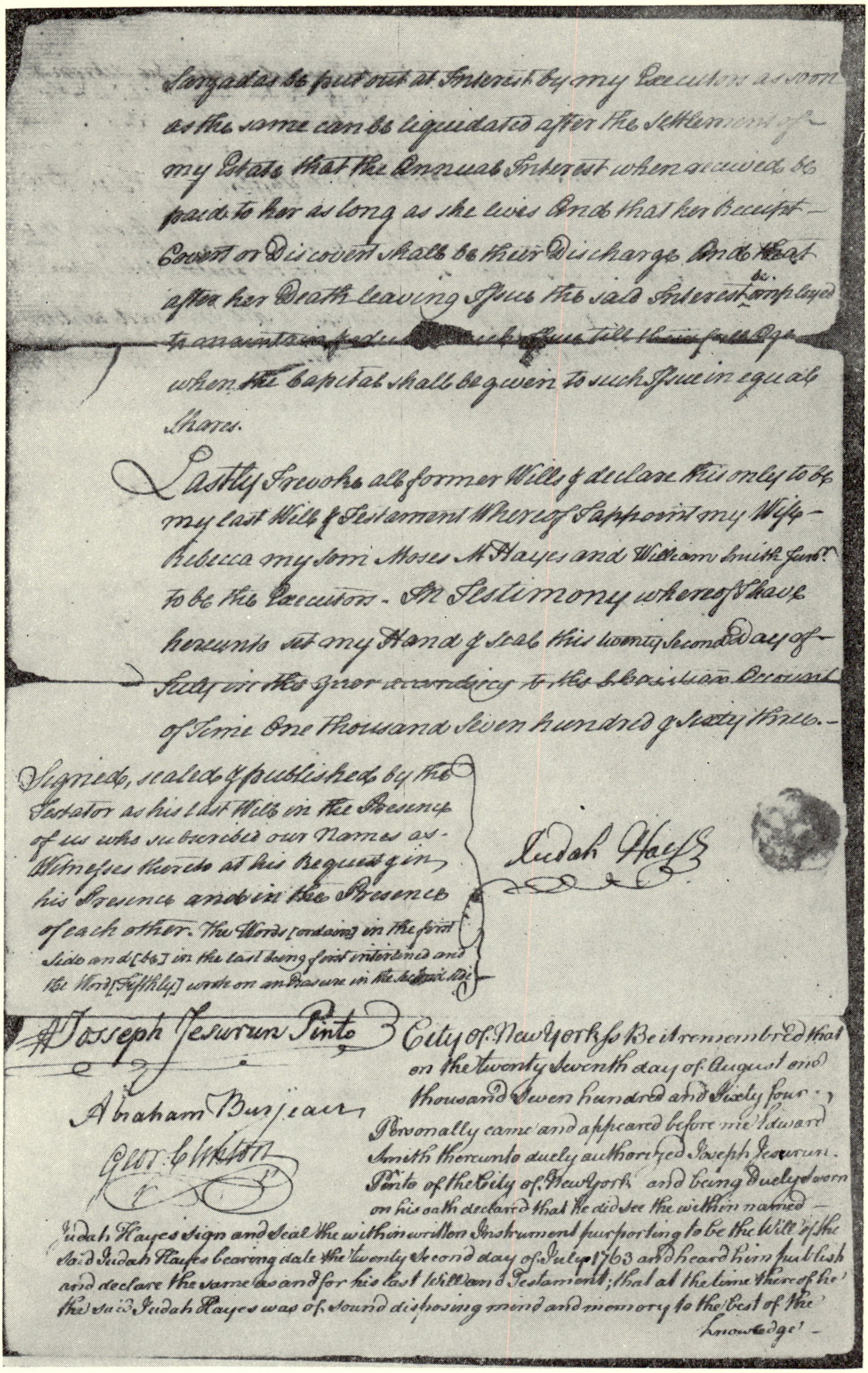

Sarzadas be put out at Interest by my Executors as soon as the same can be liquidated after the Settlement of my Estate that the Annual Interest when received be paid to her as long as she lives And that her Receipt Covert or Discovert shall be their Discharge And that after her Death leaving Issue the said Interest be employed to maintain [illegible] such Issue till their full Age when the Capital shall be given to such Issue in equal Shares.

Lastly I revoke all former Wills & declare this only to be my last Will & Testament Whereof I appoint my Wife Rebecca my Son Moses M. Hayes and William Smith Junr. to be the Executors — In Testimony whereof I have hereunto set my Hand & Seal this twenty Second day of July in the year according to the Christian Account of Time One thousand Seven hundred & Sixty three —

Signed, sealed & published by the Testator as his last Will in the Presence of us who subscribed our Names as Witnesses thereto at his Request & in his Presence and in the Presence of each other. The Words [ordain] in the first Side and [be] in the last being first interlined and the Word [Fifthly] wrote on an Erasure in the second Side

Judah Hayes

Joseph Jesurun Pinto

Abraham Busjeau

Geor. Elliston

City of New York ss Be it remembred that on the twenty seventh day of August one thousand seven hundred and Sixty four; Personally came and appeared before me Edward Smith thereunto duely authorized Joseph Jesurun Pinto of the City of New York and being duely sworn on his oath declared that he did see the within named Judah Hayes sign and seal the within written Instrument purporting to be the Will of the said Judah Hayes bearing date the twenty second day of July 1763 and heard him publish and declare the same as and for his last Will and Testament; that at the time thereof he the said Judah Hayes was of sound disposing mind and memory to the best of the knowledge —

XXV. JUDAH HAYES [1764]

XXVI

DAVID GOMEZ[1]

[1769]

In the Name of God, Amen. I [DAVID] GOMEZ of the Citty of New York Merchant being of Perfect mind and memory do make this my last Will and Testament Annulling and Revokeing all [Wills here] tofore made and done by me.

Imprimis

My soul to the Almighty God my Creators I humbly resigne and my body to the Earth to be deacently Enter[red] Touching the Distribution of my Temporal Estate I dispose of as follows.

Item

It is my will that all my just debts and funerall Charges be duly [paid.]

Item

I give and bequate unto my loving Brother ISAAC GOMEZ[2] and his Heirs for ever, my part of the Silver Ornaments or *Remoniems* of the five books of Moses [which] I had by my deceased Wife out of the Estate of my Mother in law Mrs. LELONAH DE LYON

Item

I give and bequate unto the Synagoge of this City the Sum [£10] Current Money of New York to be paid the Wardens thereof for the use of it[3]

Item

It is my Will that all my Estate both Real and Personal [may be] disposed of Either by Private or Public Sale.

[1] Original Will no. 2207, HDC; Will Liber 27, p. 87; *NYHSC*, vol. VII (1899), p. 270. David Gomez (August 14, 1697–July 15, 1769), son of Lewis Gomez, married Rebecca de Leon Sielva of the Barbadoes (d. 1761), sister of Deborah de Leon, wife of Isaac Gomez, his brother. *Portraits*, p. 470; *PAJHS*, vol. XVII (1909), p. 198. David, a merchant, had an interesting career. He appears in court as early as 1720 in *Gomez v. Graves* (1720), MCP file 1711–1724, Jan. 14, 1720. See also agreement recorded on March 3, 1739 between Egbert van Borsum and Mordecai, Daniel and David to settle a suit in Supreme Court. Conveyance Liber 32, cp. 100. He appears frequently in the records with his brother Mordecai as an importer and exporter of flour, biscuits, and pork. Entry of May 3, 1734, NOL CO 5/1225; Entry of April 6, 1738, NOL CO 5/1226; Entry Books, vol. I, item 619. In 1723, he presented a petition to prevent selling of "not marketable" flour in the city. *Minutes*, vol. IV, pp. 169–170. During 1733 and 1734, he lived in the house of Lewis Gomez. NYAL, Feb. 24, 1733 and Feb. 27, 1734. David had an intense interest in Shearith Israel, although he paid a fine of £10 when he declined the office of *parnas*. *PAJHS*, vol. XXI (1913), p. 61, see also pp. 10–11, *et passim; Portraits*, pp. 474–475. For a description of some of David's property on Queen Street and "the use of the alley in back of Burlings Slip," see Conveyance Liber 38, cp. 370–372.

[2] See *infra*, Will of Isaac Gomez, pp. 129–131.

[3] The sum has been torn in the original will, but the Minutes of Shearith Israel indicate that ten pounds were left in the will to the synagogue for which his executors on August 14, 1769 requested an Escaba be made for him twice a year. *PAJHS*, vol. XXI (1913), p. 104.

Item

I give and bequate unto my loving nephew MATTATHIAS GOMEZ[4] the Son of my brother ISAAC GOMEZ and unto his Heirs & Assigns for ever the Sum of One hundred and fifty Pounds Current Money of New York to be paid him by Executors out of my Estate

Item

After all my legacys be paid I give and bequate and Devoise unto my loving brother DANIEL GOMEZ[5] One Quarter part part of all my Estate both Real and Personal and unto him his Heirs and Assigns for ever.

Item

I give and bequate and Devoise unto my loving brother ISAAC GOMEZ One Quarter part of all my Estate both Real and Personal and unto him his Heirs and Assigns for ever.

Item

I give and bequate and Devoise unto my loving brother BENJAMIN GOMEZ[6] One Quarter part of all my Estate both Real and Personal and unto him his Heirs and Assigns for ever.

Item

The remaining Quarter part of all my Estate both Real and Personal I give bequate and Devoise unto my loving Neice ESTHER GOMEZ[7] the Wife of MOSES GOMEZ[8] the Son of DANIEL GOMEZ and unto her Heirs and Assigns for Ever and unto my Neice RACHEL GOMEZ the Wife of MATTATHIAS GOMEZ[9] the Son of ISAAC GOMEZ and unto her Heirs and Assigns for Ever and unto MORDECAY GOMEZ the Son of ISAAC GOMEZ, JUNIOR[10] deceased and unto his Heirs and Assigns for Ever to be Shared among them Share and Share alike. The propotion of said Quarter part of my Estate that may be coming to MORDECAY GOMEZ I desire it may be put out at Interest for him untill he doth attaine the Lawfull age of Twenty One Years to be paid him togeather with the Interest that may Accrue thereon and lastly *I Do Make Nominate and Appoint* my three loving brothers DANIEL GOMEZ, ISAAC GOMEZ, and BENJAMIN GOMEZ to be Executors of this my last Will and Testament. *In Witness* hereof

[4] See *infra*, Will of Mattathias Gomez, pp. 151–154.

[5] See *supra*, Will of Simja de Torres, p. 80, note 5.

[6] See *infra*, Will of Benjamin Gomez, pp. 135–137.

[7] Esther was the daughter of his brother Isaac. See Will of Isaac Gomez, *infra*, p. 130, note 4; *supra*, Will of Simja de Torres, p. 81, note 6.

[8] See *infra*, Will of Moses Gomez, pp. 189–191.

[9] See *infra*, Will of Mattathias Gomez, pp. 151–154.

[10] The Mordecai Gomez referred to here is possibly the son of Isaac Gomez, the son of Mordecai Gomez, David's brother. In the elder Mordecai's marriage contract to Rebecca De Lucena, Isaac is referred to as Isaac Gomez, Jr. See Conveyance Liber 32, cp. 205. This Isaac Gomez, Jr., who died in Curaçao in 1764 would be the nephew of David Gomez and Mordecai David's grandnephew. See *supra*, Will of Mordecai Gomez, p. 85, note 11. Since both his brother and his brother's son were not alive at this time, the testator may have wished to leave a legacy to his brother's grandchild.

I have hereunto sett my hand and Seal this Twenty fifth day of April in Year One Thousand Seven Hundred and Sixty five

Signed, Sealed, published and delivered
in the presence of us s/ DAVID GOMEZ

the words among them being interlined
and the words and devoise and assigns
being wrote on raised pacles [*sic!*] all done
before signed, Sealing and executing
of this

[seal]

s/ WM. BUTLER[11]
s/ THO^s. PEARSALL
s/ JAMES PARSONS[12]

City of New York Ss: Be it Remembered that on the fourteenth day of August, One Thousand, Seven hundred and Sixty nine, personally came and appeared before me FRANCIS CHILD thereunto duly Authorized, JAMES PARSONS of the said City Merchant, and being duly Affirmed, on his Affirmation declared, that he did see DAVID GOMEZ Sign and Seal the within written Instrument purporting to be the Will of the said DAVID GOMEZ, bearing date the twenty fifth day of April One thousand Seven hundred and sixty five and heard him publish and declare the same as and for his last Will and Testament: That at the time thereof he the said DAVID GOMEZ was of Sound disposing Mind and Memory, to the best of the knowledge and belief of him the Affirmant, and that his Name Subscribed to the said Will is of his proper hand writing which he Subscribed as a Witness to the said Will in the Testators presence, And that he the Affirmant, saw WILLIAM BUTLER and THOMAS PEARSALL the other Witnesses to the said Will subscribe their Names as Witnesses thereto in the Testators presence.

s/ FRAN CHILD[13]

City of New York Ss: Be it also Remembered that on the said 14th day of August 1769. DANIEL GOMEZ, ISAAC GOMEZ, and BENJAMIN GOMEZ, the Executors of the withim written Will of the said DAVID GOMEZ, and were duly Sworn to the true Execution and performance of the said Will, by severally taking the Oath of an Executor, as by Law appointed.

Before me
s/ FRAN CHILD

[11] William Butler, a scrivener, was made a freeman on January 31, 1769. *Burghers*, p. 218. Perhaps, it was he who drew the will for David Gomez.

[12] James Parsons, a merchant and Quaker, witnessed another will in April, 1760. *NYHSC*, vol. VIII (1900), p. 14.

[13] Francis Child was appointed Judge of Probate Court on April 26, 1769, and, in 1789, was elected as a Member of Assembly. *Calendar*, p. 73; *Civil List*, p. 284. He was a neighbor of Mordecai Gomez (see *supra*, Will, note 3).

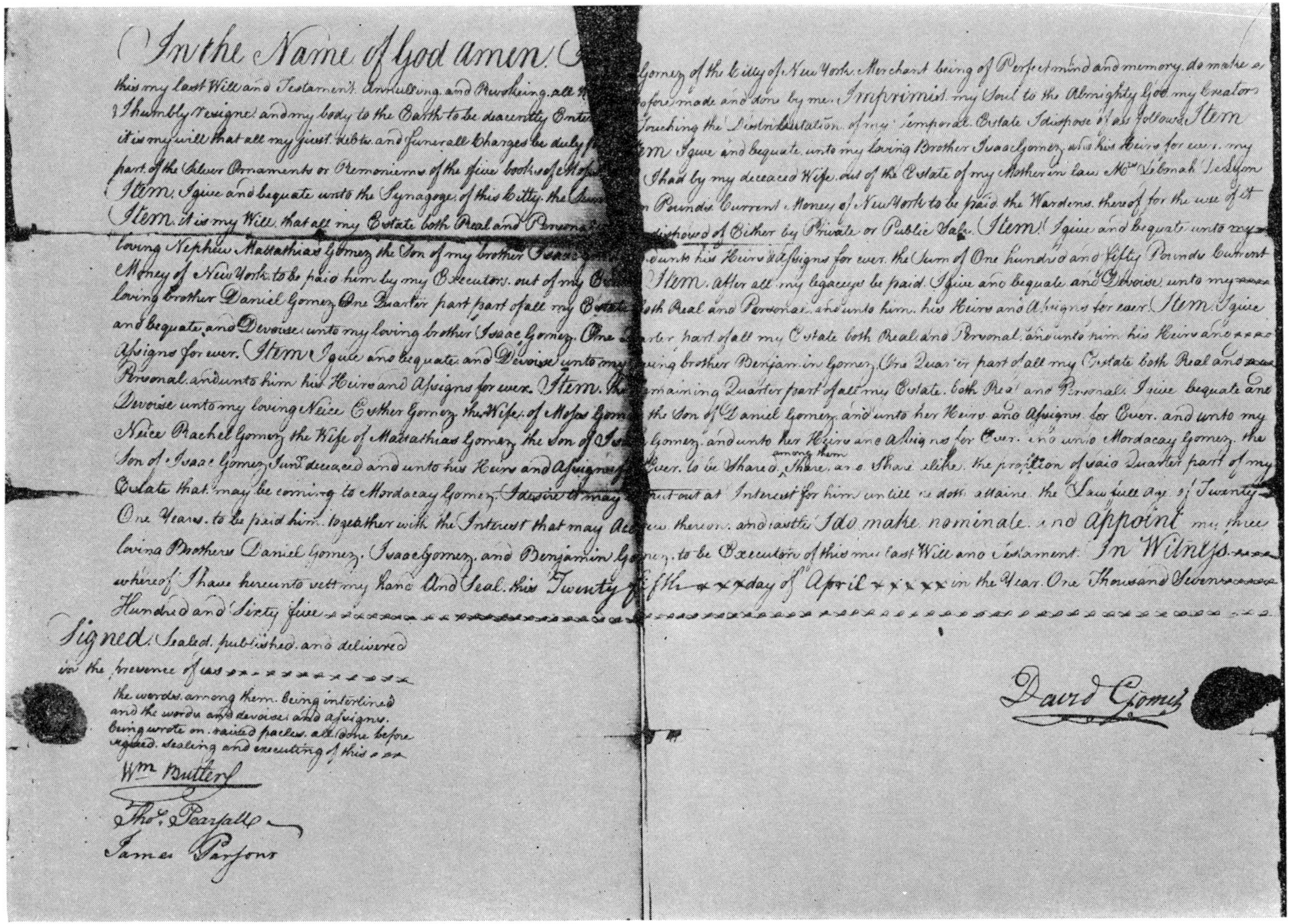

In the Name of God amen [illegible] Gomez of the Citty of New York Merchant being of Perfect mind and memory do make a
this my last Will and Testament Annulling and Revoking all [illegible] before made and don by me. Imprimis my Soul to the Almighty God my Creator
I humbly resigne and my body to the Earth to be decently Enter[illegible] Touching the Distribution of my Temporal Estate I dispose of as follows Item
it is my will that all my just debts and funerall Charges be duly [illegible] Item I give and bequeath unto my loving Brother Isaac Gomez and his Heirs for ever my
part of the Silver Ornaments or Ceremonies of the five books of Moses [illegible] I had by my deceased Wife out of the Estate of my Mother in law Mrs [illegible]
Item I give and bequeath unto the Synagogue of this Citty the Sum [illegible] Pounds Current Money of New York to be paid the Wardens thereof for the use of it
Item it is my Will that all my Estate both Real and Personal [illegible] disposed of Either by Private or Public Sale. Item I give and bequeath unto my
loving Nephew Mattathias Gomez the Son of my brother Isaac [illegible] unto his Heirs & Assigns for ever the Sum of One hundred and Fifty Pounds Current
Money of New York to be paid him by my Executors out of my [illegible] Item after all my legacys be paid I give and bequeath and Devise unto my
loving brother Daniel Gomez One Quarter part part of all my Estate both Real and Personal and unto him his Heirs and Assigns for ever Item I give
and bequeath and Devise unto my loving brother Isaac Gomez One Quarter part of all my Estate both Real and Personal and unto him his Heirs and
Assigns for ever. Item I give and bequeath and Devise unto my [illegible] brother Benjamin Gomez One Quarter part of all my Estate both Real and
Personal and unto him his Heirs and Assigns for ever. Item The remaining Quarter part of all my Estate both Real and Personal I give bequeath and
Devise unto my loving Neice Esther Gomez the Wife of Moses Gomez the Son of Daniel Gomez and unto her Heirs and Assigns for Ever and unto my
Neice Rachel Gomez the Wife of Mattathias Gomez the Son of Isaac Gomez and unto her Heirs and Assigns for Ever and unto Mordacay Gomez the
Son of Isaac Gomez Junr deceased and unto his Heirs and Assigns for Ever to be Shared among them Share and Share alike the proportion of said Quarter part of my
Estate that may be coming to Mordacay Gomez I desire it may be put out at Interest for him untill he doth attaine the Lawfull Age of Twenty
One Years to be paid him togeather with the Interest that may Accrew thereon and lastly I do make nominate and appoint my three
loving Brothers Daniel Gomez Isaac Gomez and Benjamin Gomez to be Executors of this my last Will and Testament In Witness
whereof I have hereunto sett my hand And Seal this Twenty fifth day of April in the Year One Thousand Seven
Hundred and Sixty five

Signed Sealed published and delivered
in the presence of us

the words among them being interlined
and the words and devise and assigns
being wrote on raised places all done before
signing sealing and executing of this

Wm Butterf
Thos Pearsall
James Parsons

David Gomez

XXVI. DAVID GOMEZ [1769]

XXVII

ISAAC GOMEZ[1]

[1770]

In the Name of God Amen I Isaac Gomez of the City of New York Merchant being in as good State of Health as I have been for sometime past but of sound and disposing mind memory and Understanding blessed be God for the same. Yet reflecting on the uncertainty of Life I have thought proper to settle my temporal Affairs by this my last Will and Testament in manner and form following (that is to say) I recommend my Immortal Soul to the Mercy of my great Creator and my Body I commit to the Earth to be decently interred And after the Payment of all my just Debts and funeral Expenses I do settle and dispose of the rest of my Estate in manner and form following (that is to say) First I do give and bequeath unto my beloved Wife Deborah Gomez[2] an annuity of One hundred and fifty pounds Current Money of New York to be paid to her out of my Estate yearly and every year for and during the Term of her Widowhood I do also give and bequeath unto my said Wife the Use and possession of my Dwelling House and Lot of Ground situate in Queen's Street of the City of New York[3] wherein I now dwell and reside And also of all my Furniture Plate and Jewels with as many of my Slaves as are necessary to attend her *To Hold* the same to her my said Wife as long as she shall remain my Widow and no longer

Item

It is my Will and I do declare that what I have herein given to my said Wife is and shall be in full Bar of her Dower and Right of thirds in and to my Estate.

[1] Original Will no. 2207 B, HDC; Liber 27, p. 324; *NYHSC*, vol. VII (1899), p. 337. Isaac Gomez (July 13, 1705–August 29, 1770), son of Lewis Gomez, married Deborah de Leon of Barbadoes, sister of Rebecca, David Gomez' wife. Several children died young, except Esther (1739–1822) and Mattathias (see Will). *PAJHS*, vol. XVII (1909), p. 198. As were the other members of his family, Isaac was deeply involved in congregational affairs. In 1757 and 1762, he was elected *parnas*. *PAJHS*, vol. XXI (1913), pp. 74 and 86. See also pp. 10, 21, 38, *et passim*. For his business activity, which was not nearly as extensive as his brothers', see Entry Books, vol. I, item 1230; vol. II, items 1604 and 1855. In 1763, he and his brother Benjamin bought a still house from Jean Peak and George Willis which was located in the Montgomerie Ward fronting on Ferry Street. Conveyance Liber 36, cp. 333–336. For the legacy left by his brother David, see Conveyance Liber 38, cp. 370–372 which included part of a house and lot 24 feet wide and 69 feet long, located on Queen Street.

[2] Deborah de Leon (1713–1801) married Isaac in 1738. In 1770, she asked the permission of the *parnassim* and elders to have vacant burial ground next to her husband set aside for her. This request was granted. *PAJHS*, vol. XXI (1913), p. 161; *ibid.*, vol. XXVII (1920), p. 288.

[3] This may have been the house and lot left to him by his brother David. See *supra*, note 1. The Gomez family had considerable property throughout the city, some on Queen Street. Lewis Gomez also left property located on this street. Conveyance Liber 32, cp. 146–147 and 213.

Item

At and immediately upon the decease of my said Wife I give and bequeath unto my Daughter ESTER GOMEZ[4] if she shall then be living or to her legal Representatives in Case of her Death the Sum of Six Hundred Pounds Current Money aforesaid Together with one half of my Plates and Jewels excepting the Silver Ornaments belonging to my five Books of Moses called by us Rimonaim.

Item

I give and bequeath to the Ruler of the Jewish Synagogue in this City the Sum of Fifteen pounds Current Money aforesaid to be paid unto him by my Executor within one month after my Decease for the Use of the said Synagogue.[5]

Item

All the Rest Residue and Remainder of my Estate both real and personal of what Nature or kind soever and wheresoever I do give devise and bequeath unto my Son MATTATHIAS GOMEZ[6] his Heirs Executors Administrators and assigns forever *To have and to Hold* the same unto him my said Son MATTATHIAS GOMEZ his Heirs Executors Administrators and Assigns to his and their sole and only proper Use Benefit and Behoof for ever

Item

Lastly I do nominate constitute and appoint my said Son MATTATHIAS GOMEZ to be sole Executor of this my last Will and Testament hereby revoking and annulling all former and other Wills and Dispositions of my Estate at any time heretofore made And declaring these presents only to be and contain my last Will and Testament *In Testimony* whereof I have hereunto set my hand and Seal this Sixteenth Day of February One Thousand Seven Hundred and Sixty nine.

s/ ISAAC GOMEZ [seal]

Signed Sealed published and declared by the
said ISAAC GOMEZ as and for his last Will
and Testament. In the Presence of us who sub-
scribed our Names as Witnesses thereto In the
Presence and at the Request of the Testator

s/ JONATHAN MORRELL[7]
s/ JOHN DUNLAP[8]
s/ MOSES SMITH

[4] Esther Gomez married Moses Gomez (see Will), son of Daniel and her first cousin on May 14, 1755. She and Moses had five children, three of whom died in infancy. *PAJHS*, vol. XVII (1909), p. 198; *ibid.*, vol. XXVII (1920), p. 287.

[5] On September 28, 1770, Mattathias Gomez paid to the *parnas* Benjamin Gomez, his uncle, the willed £15 for the use of the synagogue for which an "*Escaba* is to be made for said Isaac Gomez Yearley on the Sabbath before the *Sepher* is taken out. Every year as also *Roshodeses* and *Kipur*." *Ibid.*, vol. XXI (1913), p. 108.

City of New York Ss. Be it Remembered that on the first Day of October one thousand seven hundred and Seventy personally came and appeared before me GOLDSBROW BANYAR thereunto duly authorized JOHN DUNLAP of the City of New York Merchant and being duly Sworn on his Oath Declared that he saw ISAAC GOMEZ sign and Seal the aforewritten Instrument purporting to be the Will of the said ISAAC GOMEZ bearing date the Sixteenth Day of February One thousand seven hundred and sixty Nine, and heard him publish and declare the same to be and Contain his last Will and Testament. That at the time thereof he the said ISAAC GOMEZ was of sound disposing Mind and Memory to the best of the knowledge and belief of him the Deponent and that his Name Subscribed to the said Will is of his proper hand writing which he Subscribed as a Witness to the said Will in the presence of the Testator, and that he the Deponent likewise saw JONATHAN MORRELL and MOSES SMITH the other witnesses to the said Will subscribe their Names as Witnesses thereto in the Testators presence.

City of New York Ss. Be it also remembered that on said first Day of October 1770 MATTATHIAS GOMEZ sole Executor of the within will of ISAAC GOMEZ likewise appeared before me the Said GOLDSBROW BANYAR and was duly sworn to the true Execution and performance of the said Will by taking the oath of an Executor as by Law appointed Before me.

Memorandum that on the twenty third day of October in the year of our Lord one thousand seven hundred and seventy JONATHAN MORRELL one of the evidences to the execution of the foregoing will appeared before me JOHN SMYTH duely authorized to prove wills and qualify executors in the province of New Jersey, and he being duely sworn on the Holy Evangelists of Almighty God on his oath declared that he was present and did see ISAAC GOMEZ the testator in said foregoing will named sign and seal the same and heard him publish pronounce & declare it to be his last will and testament, that at the time of doing thereof the said ISAAC GOMEZ was of sound mind and memory to the best of the deponent's knowledge and as he verily believes, and that JOHN DUNLAP and MOSES SMITH the other evidences were also present and signed as evidences to the execution of said foregoing will as he the deponent did in the presence of the said ISAAC GOMEZ. Also at the same time MATTATHIAS GOMEZ the executor in said will named came before me and was duely qualified to the execution & performance thereof by taking the oath of an executor as by law appointed.

s/ JOHN SMYTH

---

[6] See Will of Mattathias Gomez, *infra*, pp. 151–154.

[7] Jonathan Morrell was elected constable of the East Ward and was fined when he refused to serve. *Minutes*, vol. VI, pp. 222 and 226.

[8] John Dunlap, merchant, was made freeman on July 23, 1753. *Burghers*, p. 178.

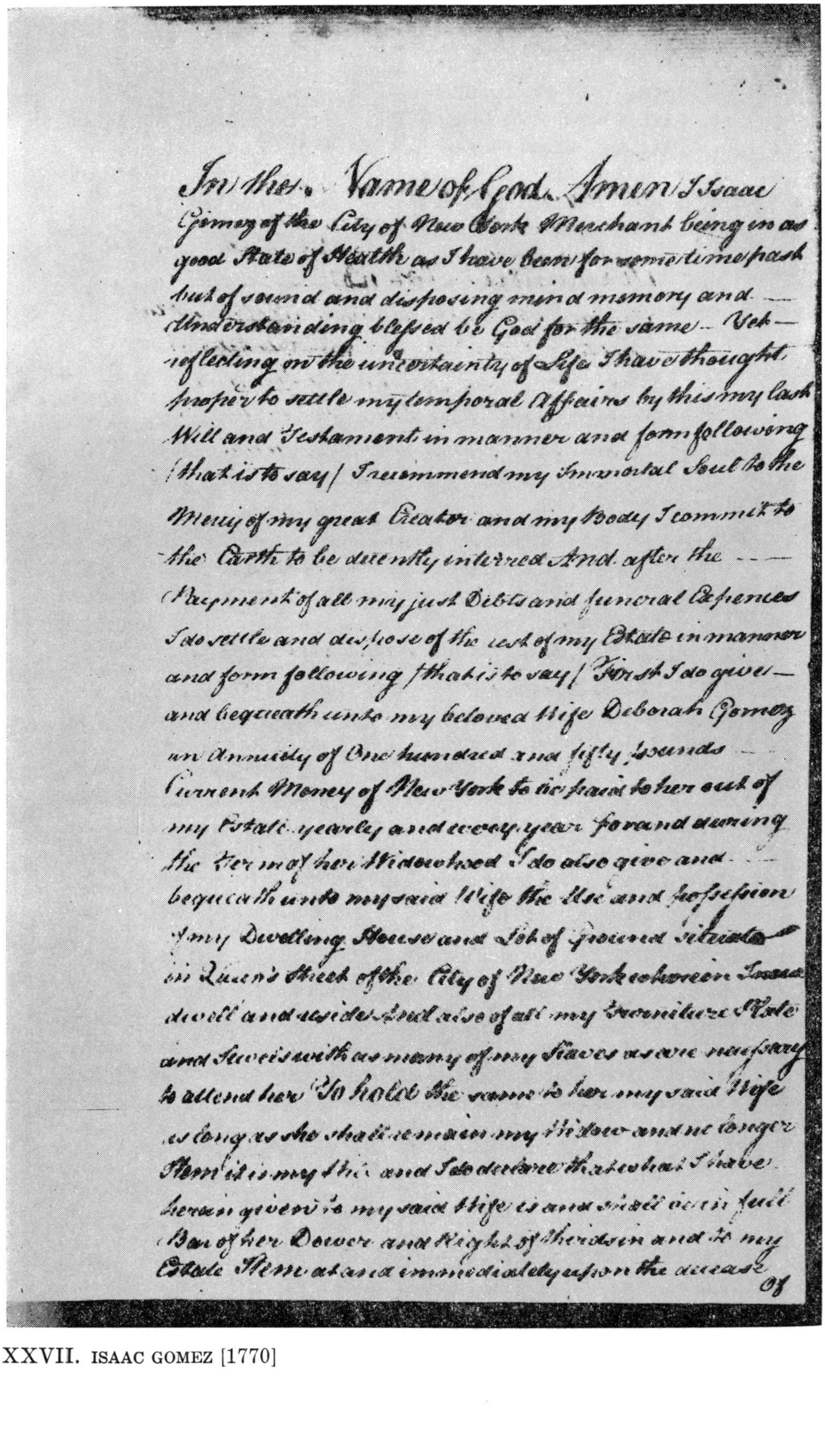
In the Name of God Amen I Isaac
Gomez of the City of New York Merchant being in as
good State of Health as I have been for some time past
but of sound and disposing mind memory and —
Understanding blessed be God for the same — Yet —
reflecting on the uncertainty of Life I have thought
proper to settle my temporal Affairs by this my last
Will and Testament in manner and form following
(that is to say) I recommend my Immortal Soul to the
Mercy of my great Creator and my Body I commit to
the Earth to be decently interred And after the — —
Payment of all my just Debts and funeral Expences
I do settle and dispose of the rest of my Estate in manner
and form following (that is to say) First I do give —
and bequeath unto my beloved Wife Deborah Gomez
an Annuity of One hundred and fifty pounds —
Current Money of New York to be paid to her out of
my Estate yearly and every year for and during
the Term of her Widowhood I do also give and —
bequeath unto my said Wife the Use and possession
of my Dwelling House and Lot of Ground situate
in Queen's Street of the City of New York wherein I now
dwell and reside And also of all my Furniture Plate
and Service with as many of my Slaves as are necessary
to attend her To hold the same to her my said Wife
as long as she shall remain my Widow and no longer
Item it is my Will and I do declare that what I have
herein given to my said Wife is and shall be in full
Bar of her Dower and Right of Thirds in and to my
Estate Item at and immediately upon the decease
of

XXVII. ISAAC GOMEZ [1770]

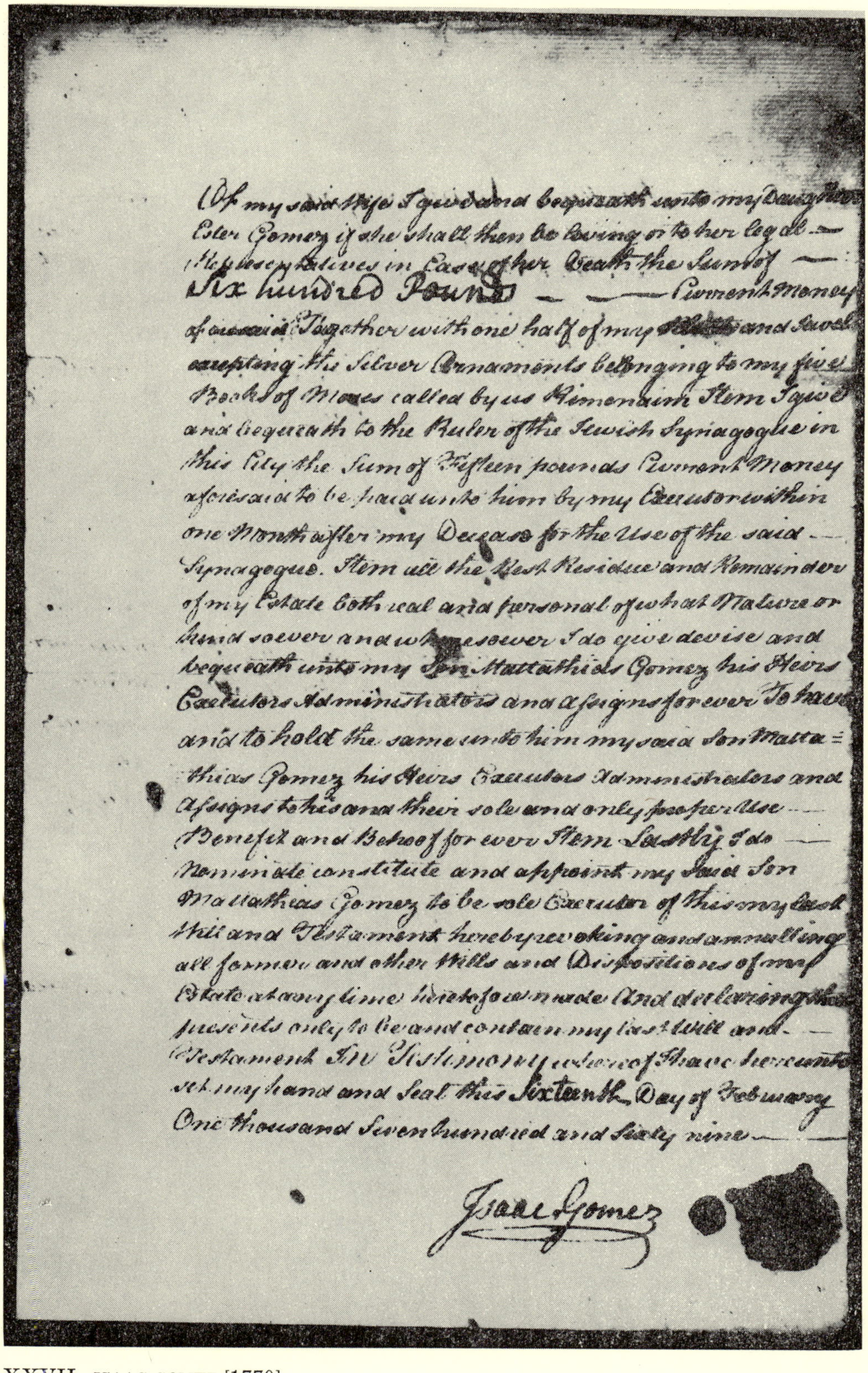
(Of my said Wife I give and bequeath unto my Daughter
Ester Gomez if she shall then be living or to her legal —
Representatives in Case of her Death the Sum of —
Six hundred Pounds — —— Current Money
of aforesaid Together with one half of my [illegible] and Jewels
excepting the Silver Ornaments belonging to my five
Books of Moses called by us Rimonim Item I give
and bequeath to the Ruler of the Jewish Synagogue in
this City the Sum of Fifteen pounds Current Money
aforesaid to be paid unto him by my Executor within
one Month after my Decease for the Use of the said —
Synagogue. Item all the Rest Residue and Remainder
of my Estate both real and personal of what Nature or
kind soever and wheresoever I do give devise and
bequeath unto my Son Mattathias Gomez his Heirs
Executors Administrators and Assigns for ever To have
and to hold the same unto him my said Son Matta=
thias Gomez his Heirs Executors Administrators and
Assigns to his and their sole and only proper Use —
Benefit and Behoof for ever Item Lastly I do —
Nominate constitute and appoint my said Son
Mattathias Gomez to be sole Executor of this my last
Will and Testament hereby revoking and annulling
all former and other Wills and Dispositions of my
Estate at any time heretofore made And declaring these
presents only to be and contain my last Will and
Testament In Testimony whereof I have hereunto
set my hand and Seal this Sixteenth Day of February
One thousand Seven hundred and Sixty nine —

Isaac Gomez

XXVII. ISAAC GOMEZ [1770]

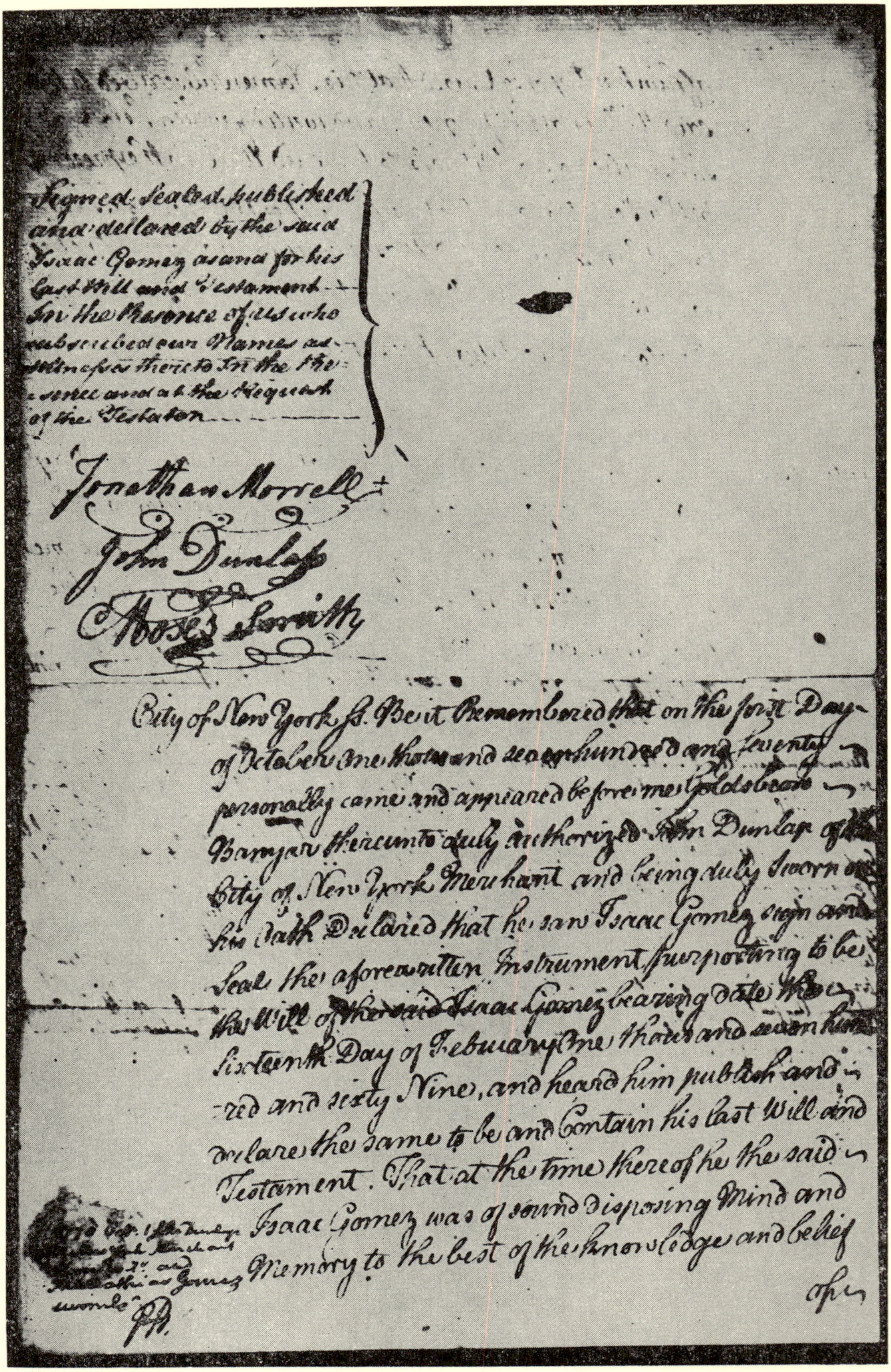
Signed Sealed published and declared by the said Isaac Gomez as and for his last Will and Testament In the Presence of us who subscribed our Names as Witnesses thereto In the Presence and at the Request of the Testator

Jonathan Morrell
John Dunlap
Moses Smith

City of New York ss. Be it Remembered that on the first Day of October One thousand seven hundred and Seventy personally came and appeared before me Goldsbrow Banyar thereunto duly authorized John Dunlap of the City of New York Merchant and being duly Sworn on his Oath Declared that he saw Isaac Gomez sign and Seal the aforewritten Instrument purporting to be the Will of the said Isaac Gomez bearing date the Sixteenth Day of February One thousand seven hundred and sixty Nine, and heard him publish and declare the same to be and Contain his last Will and Testament. That at the time thereof he the said Isaac Gomez was of sound disposing Mind and Memory to the best of the knowledge and belief of

XXVII. ISAAC GOMEZ [1770]

XXVIII

BENJAMIN GOMEZ[1]

[1772]

New York Ss.

In the Name of God Amen, I BENJAMIN GOMEZ of the Citty of New York Merchant being at this time in perfect health sound of mind & memory do publish & declare this Instrument of Writing to be my last Will & testament in the manner & form following Vizt. First & principally I recomend my Soul to God & my body to be decently Interred my Just debts & funeral charges to be paid. I give devise & bequeath as follows. *Item.* I give devise & bequeath unto my granddaughters DEBORAH GOMEZ[2] & ESTHER GOMEZ[3] both daughters of MATTATHIAS[4] & RACHEL GOMEZ[5] When they shall Severley attain the Age of Twenty One Years or day of Marriage Which shall first happen One hundred & Fifty pounds current money of the province of New York to Each of them. *Item* I give devise & bequeath unto the Sinogague in the City of New York the sum of Ten pounds current money aforesaid to be paid to the Ruler thereof one month after desease for the Use of the Same.[6] *Item,* I give devise & bequeath unto my daughter RACHEL GOMEZ Wife of MATTATHIAS GOMEZ all my Household furniture plate Jewels linnen with my two Slaves ISHMAEL & JENNEY to her & her heirs forever. Allso all the Rents & proffitts of my Estate both Real & personal during her Natural life & after her desease the principal Sum of what moneys I die possest of & that shall be due oweing & belonging unto me I direct to be put Out at Intrest on good Security by my other Executor MATTATHIAS

[1] Original Will no. 2207A, HDC; Will Liber 28, p. 307; *NYHSC*, vol. VII (1900), p. 63. Benjamin Gomez (April 11, 1711–August 8, 1772), son of Lewis Gomez, married Esther Nunes of the Barbadoes who died sometime before this will was written. As his family, he, too, was active in congregational affairs and served three terms as *parnas* in 1760, 1766 and 1770. He first appears in the synagogue records on November, 1728 when he is recorded as donating £1 toward the building of the first temple of Shearith Israel. *PAJHS*, vol. XXI (1913), pp. 10, 107, 199 and 211. For examples of his trading activity, see Entry Books, vol. I, item 1233, vol. II, item 1436. Benjamin used his house "opposite Col. Depeyster's Treasurer" to sell a wide variety of cloths, rum, sugar and molasses. Two advertisements run in the *New York Mercury* for 1761 and in the *New York Gazette* are quoted in *Portraits*, pp. 476–477. As part of his business interest he and his brother Isaac bought a still house near the "New Chapple" in the Montgomerie Ward. Conveyance Liber 36, cp. 333–336.

[2] Deborah Gomez (1766–1783) never married and died in Philadelphia. *PAJHS*, vol. XVII (1909), p. 198.

[3] Esther Gomez (1768–before 1807) married a Mr. Meeks and died in Virginia. *Ibid.*, *Dictionary*, p. 44.

[4] See Will of Mattathias Gomez, *infra*, pp. 151–154.

[5] Rachel Gomez (d. April 16, 1776 in Newark, New Jersey) married her first cousin Mattathias, son of Isaac Gomez, on February 6, 1765. *PAJHS*, vol. XVII (1909), p. 198; *ibid.*, XXVII (1920), pp. 282–283, *Portraits*, p. 503.

[6] For record of bequest given to synagogue, see *PAJHS*, vol. XXI (1913), p. 114.

GOMEZ hereafter Named. to be divided with the Intrest that may Accrue thereon as follows (to witt) I give devise & bequeath the Same as allso all the Real Estate I shall die Seized of unto my grandsons ISAAC GOMEZ[7] & BENJAMIN GOMEZ[8] both sons of MATTATHIAS & RACHEL GOMEZ & to such of my grand[sons] as may hereafter be born of my daughter RACHEL GOMEZ by this Marriage with MATTATHIAS GOMEZ & to their heirs & Assignes for Ever When they shall respectively attain the Age of Twenty One Years to be divided Equally Amoung them share and share alike, And in case any of my said Grandsons Should happen to die Under the Age of Twenty One Years, & without lawfull Issue that then in Such a case I give & devise the part of my Estate herein before intended to Such Grandson their Maintenance thereout being allowed unto the Survivors of my Said Grandsons & to their heirs & assignes for Ever Equally to be divided Amoung them Share & Share alike, I allso hereby confirm the freedom given to my Mustie Wench KATTEY to be made free from the Yoke of Slavery[9] after the desease of my daughter RACHEL GOMEZ As a Reward for her fidelity & faithfull Services to my said daughter. And lastly I Nominate & apoint my daughter RACHEL GOMEZ & her husband MATTATHIAS GOMEZ to be Executors to this my last Will & Testament. in Wittness Whereof I the said BENJAMIN GOMEZ have set my hand & seal this third day of January One Thousand Seven Hundred & Seventy

s/ BENJ^A. GOMEZ [seal]

Signed Sealed published & declared
by the testator as his last Will &
Testament in the presence of Us.

s/ CHRIS^R. P. YATES[10]
s/ THOS. W. W. BEAVEN
s/ ELIAS JONES

[7] Isaac Mattathias Gomez (1767–1810), son of Mattathias and Rachel, was a cripple who died unmarried. He was by profession a broker with an office at 32 Maiden Lane. *New York Directory and Register, 1790* (New York, 1790) [=Directory], p. 43; *PAJHS*, vol. XVII (1909), p. 198. He was one of the first Jews to sit as a juror in the Mayor's Court. See MCP, file 1791, Panel of Jurors, August 30, 1791. On this list, he is referred to as a bookseller. For congregational activities, see *PAJHS*, vol. XXI (1913), pp. 160–161 and 170.

[8] Benjamin Gomez (1769–1828) married Charlotte, daughter of Uriah Hendricks and Esther Gomez. The couple had four children. He was a bookseller, bookbinder, and publisher, perhaps the first of Jewish origin, as well as lottery agent, grocer, and tobacconist. He was elected *parnas* of Shearith Israel on five occasions in 1802, 1803, 1811, 1812 and 1813. *PAJHS*, vol. XXI (1913), pp. 198 and 212; *Portraits*, pp. 432–434. He was also an early Jewish juror in New York City. MCP, file 1792, Panel of Jurors, Jan. 10, 1792. Among his other activities Benjamin was also a pawnbroker. *Minutes of the Common Council, 1784–1831* (New York, 1927) [=MCC], vol. V, p. 427.

[9] Gomez also manumitted another slave, this was John Saint John. See document, dated May 7, 1765, in Conveyance Liber 37, cp. 218–219.

[10] Christopher P. Yates may have been the eldest son of Johannes Yates of the Manor Rensselaerswyck. *NYHSC*, vol. VIII (1900), p. 349.

City of New York Ss. Be it remembered that on the twenty second day of September One thousand Seven hundred and Seventy Two personally came and appeared before me EDMUND FANNING[11] Surrogate of the Province of New York THOMAS W. W. BEAVANS of said City Gentleman and being duly Sworn on his Oath declared that he did See BENJAMIN GOMEZ sign and Seal the within written Instrument purporting to be the Will of the said BENJAMIN GOMEZ bearing date the third day of January One thousand Seven hundred and Seventy, and heard him publish and declare the Same as and for his last Will and Testament that at the time thereof he the Said BENJAMIN GOMEZ was of Sound & disposing mind & memory to the best of the knowledge and belief of him the Deponent and that his name Subscribed as a Witness to the said Will is of his own proper hand writing which he Subscribed as a Witness to the said Will in the Testators presence and that the Deponent likewise saw CHRISTOPHER P. YATES and ELIAS JONES the other Witnesses to the said Will Subscribe their names as Witnesses thereto in the Testators presence.

s/ EDMUND FANNING Surr

City of New York Ss Be it remembered that on the said twenty second day of September MATTATHIAS GOMEZ Executor and RACHEL GOMEZ Executrix of the within written Will of BENJAMIN GOMEZ likewise appeared before me the said EDMUND FANNING, and were duly Sworn to the true Execution and performance of the said Will by Severally taking the Oath of an Executor as by Law appointed before me.

s/ EDMUND FANNING Surr

[11] Edmund Fanning was appointed register and principal surrogate of the Prerogative Court in 1771 and served until 1774. *Civil List,* p. 223.

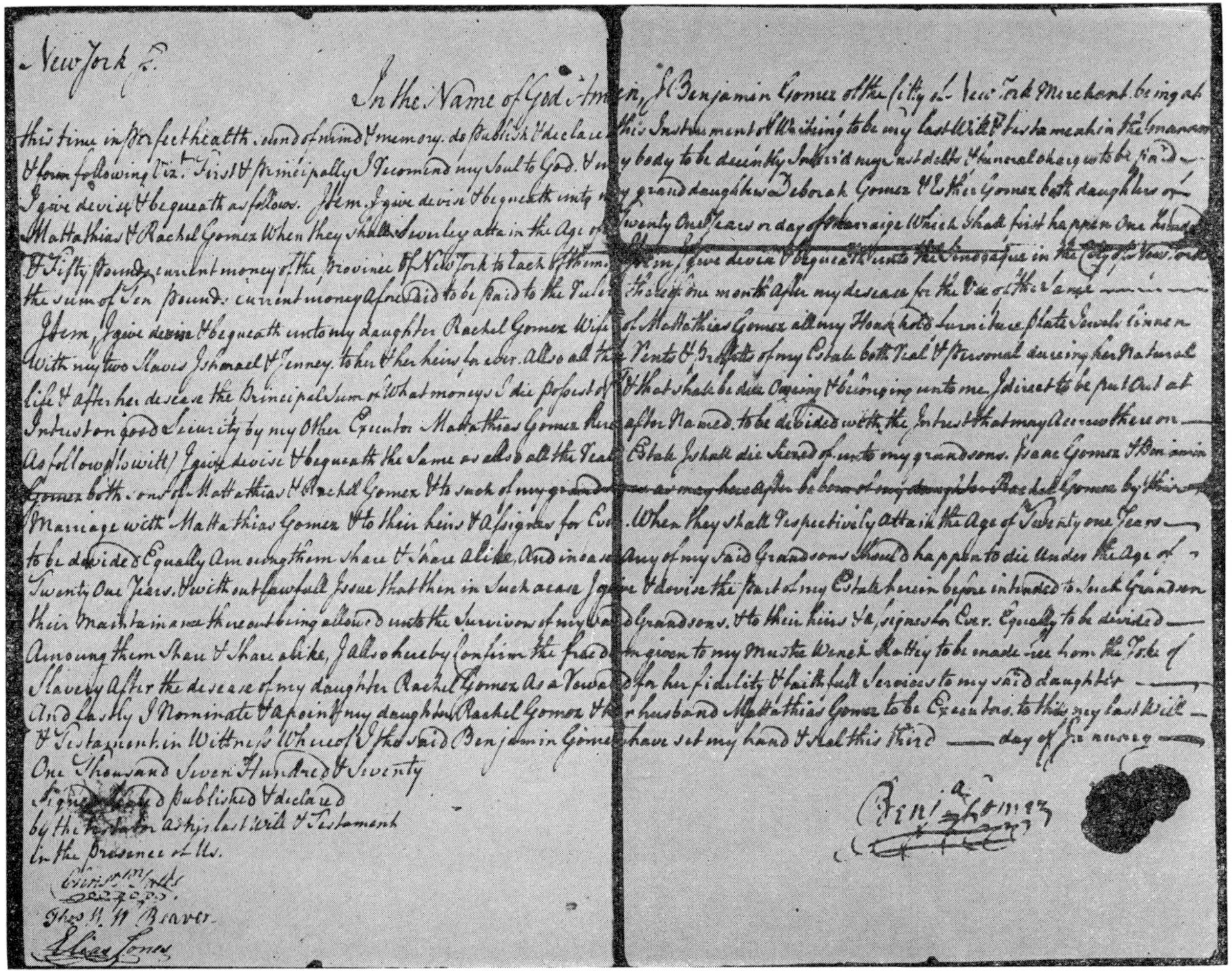

New York ss.

In the Name of God Amen, I Benjamin Gomez of the City of New York Merchant being at this time in perfect health sound of mind & memory do Publish & declare this Instrument of Writing to be my last Will & Testament in the manner & form following Viz. First & Principally I Recommend my Soul to God & my body to be decently Interr'd my just debts & funeral charges to be paid — I give devise & bequeath as follows. Item I give devise & bequeath unto my grand daughters Deborah Gomez & Esther Gomez both daughters of Mattathias & Rachel Gomez When they Shall Severally attain the Age of Twenty One Years or day of Marraige Which Shall first happen One Hundred & Fifty Pounds current money of the Province of New York to each of them. Item I give devise & bequeath unto the Sinagogue in the City of New York the sum of Ten Pounds current money aforesaid to be paid to the Parnas thereof one month after my decease for the use of the same —

Item I give devise & bequeath unto my daughter Rachel Gomez Wife of Mattathias Gomez all my Household furniture Plate Jewels Linnen With my two Slaves Ishmael & Jenney to her & her heirs for ever. Also all the Rents & Profits of my Estate both Real & Personal during her Natural life & after her decease the Principal Sum or What moneys I die Possest of & What shall be due Owing & belonging unto me I direct to be put Out at Interest on good Security by my Other Executor Mattathias Gomez here after Named. to be divided with the Interest that may accrue thereon — As follows (to witt) I give devise & bequeath the Same as also all the Real Estate I shall die Seized of unto my grandsons Isaac Gomez & Benjamin Gomez both sons of Mattathias & Rachel Gomez & to such of my grandsons as may hereafter be born of my daughter Rachel Gomez by their Marriage with Mattathias Gomez & to their heirs & Assignes for Ever. When they shall Respectively attain the Age of Twenty one Years — to be divided Equally Amoung them Share & Share alike, And in case any of my said Grandsons should happen to die Under the Age of Twenty One Years & without lawfull Issue that then in Such a case I give & devise the Part of my Estate herein before intended to such Grandson their Maintainance thereout being allowed unto the Survivors of my said Grandsons & to their heirs & Assignes for Ever. Equally to be divided — Amoung them Share & Share alike, I allso hereby Confirm the freedom given to my Mustee Wench Hatty to be made free from the Yoke of Slavery After the decease of my daughter Rachel Gomez As a Reward for her fidelity & faithfull Services to my said daughter — And Lastly I Nominate & appoint my daughter Rachel Gomez & her husband Mattathias Gomez to be Executors to this my last Will — & Testament in Witness Whereof I the said Benjamin Gomez have set my hand & Seal this third — day of January One Thousand Seven Hundred & Seventy

Benjamin Gomez

Signed Sealed published & declared
by the Testator as his last Will & Testament
in the Presence of Us.

Thos. Beaver
Elias Jones

XXVIII. BENJAMIN GOMEZ [1772]

XXIX

SAMPSON SIMSON[1]

[1774]

In the Name of God, and by his Permission, I SAMPSON SIMSON of the City of Newyork, being in a poor State of Health, but in usual Soundness of Mind and Understanding do make this my Sole Will, and after paying all my just Debts, I give and bequeath, the Remainder of my Estate in the Manner following,

To my Honored Father,[2] One Hundred Pounds a year and every year, during his Life.

To my Honored Mother,[3] One Hundred Pounds a year and every year during her Life.

To my Nephews, BENJAMIN JACOBS[4] & JOSEPH JACOBS.[5] Three Hundred Pounds each. They to account for what my Self and Brother have already advanced them.

[1] Original Will no. 2693 A, HDC; Will Liber 29, p. 44; *NYHSC,* vol. VIII (1900), pp. 156–157. Sampson Simson (1725–August 29, 1773) was a prominent merchant of New York who was deeply committed to Shearith Israel. In 1757, he was elected *parnas,* in 1761 an assistant, and in 1764 and 1769 re-elected *parnas.* He was also chosen for other offices. *PAJHS,* vol. XXI (1913), pp. 74, 77–79, 85, 88, 108 *et passim.* His business activities included a close connection to the New York Chamber of Commerce, being one of the drafters of its constitution. He and his brother Solomon owned a store on Stone Street, on which street he resided when he died. At his death, he was eulogized as upright, liberal, kind, tender, and a "real Friend to the Liberties of his Country." *Portraits,* p. 282; *Dictionary,* p. 161; *NYHSC,* vol. VIII (1900), p. 157. He held land also in Oyster Bay. *Oyster Bay Town Records* (New York, 1929), vol. VII, p. 150. He was named as an executor of the will of Aaron Louzada in 1764. George J. Miller, "Early Jews in Middlesex County, New Jersey," *PAJHS,* vol. XXXV (1936), p. 254. He also served as the executor of the estate of Newell Harris, and was sued in this capacity by James Magra, Harris' physician, because of Harris' alleged failure to pay Magra his fee for curing him of the "flux and disorder." *Magra v. Simson, executor of Harris* (1756), MCP, file 1753–1756, November 26, 1756. Interestingly he later served as witness to the will of James Magra. *NYHSC,* vol. XI (1903), p. 191.

[2] See *infra,* Will of Joseph Simson, pp. 201–203.

[3] Rebecca Isaacs Simson, daughter of Joseph Isaacs, married Joseph Simson sometime in 1722 in Wilton, Connecticut. As wife of Simson, "of ye town of Oysterbay," she bought a house and lot in that town on June 13, 1726. *Oyster Bay Town Records, supra,* vol. IV, pp. 260–261. The Simsons invested heavily in that area. *Portraits,* p. 339; *Dictionary,* p. 68; *PAJHS,* vol. XXXIII (1934), p. 202; Samuel Oppenheim, "Will of Nathan Simson, a Jewish Merchant in New York before 1722 and Genealogical Notes concerning Him and Joseph Simson," *ibid.,* vol. XXV (1917), pp. 87–91.

[4] Benjamin Jacobs (1744–1824) was the son of Sara and Raphael Jacobs (d. 1796). Sara (1727–1767) was the daughter of Joseph Simson and sister to Sampson and Solomon. See *Michael J. Hays v. Benjamin Jacobs* (1772), MCP, file 1772, August 31, 1772, in which Hays sued Benjamin claiming that he found Jacob Moses as a purchaser of a house and lot owned by Raphael Jacobs, Benjamin's father. He claimed a fee of £10 and sued for £19 damages.

[5] Joseph Jacobs, brother of Benjamin, was born in New York City in 1746 and died in 1831. The Register of Congregation Shearith Israel, p. 35.

To my Nephew ABRAHAM JACOBS,[6] Three Hundred Pounds to be paid to him within one year after he becomes of Age with all my Wearing Apperal, except such as my Father Mother and Brother, or either of them may choose to take for themselves or the Poor.

To my Niece JUDITH JACOBS,[7] Three Hundred Pounds to be paid to her, within One year after her Marriage Provided it be with the Consent of my Father Mother and Brother or the Survivors or Survivor of them otherwise to pay her in lieu thereof Twenty Five Pounds a year, and every year, during her Life to begin from the time of her Coming of Age, towards her Support and Mantainance. I also give her all my Rings.

To RICHA the Widow of DAVID JACOBS,[8] Fifty Pounds, for the use of her Self and Children. To SAMUEL LEVY and his Wife Fifty Pounds[9]

To the Ruler and Members of the Hebrew Congregation in this City for the use of the Synagogue. Twenty Pounds.[10]

To each of my God Sons. Five Pounds a Piece to be laid out for them in Books, at the discretion of my Brother

To MYER MYERS,[11] ASHER MYERS,[12] JOSEPH MYERS,[13] JACOB ROD RIVERA[14] of Newport, JOHN SAVAGE and LIONEL CHALMERS of South Carolina each a Mourning Ring.

All the Rest of my Estate, both Real and Personal whatsoever and wheresoever, with every remainder and Remainders, revertion and Revertions, I give and bequeath Wholy and fully without reserve to

[6] Abraham Jacobs (1755–1834), another son of Raphael, signed the will of James Magra as witness along with his uncle. See *supra*, p. 139, note 1.

[7] Judith Jacobs (1758–1832) was the daughter of Raphael. See *infra*, Will of Manuel Myers, pp. 208–211.

[8] Richa Jacobs was possibly the daughter of Samuel Simson. *Dictionary*, pp. 73 and 161. They had sons, Samuel and Jacob. *PAJHS*, vol. XXVII (1920), pp. 152–153. David Jacobs (d. 1771) was involved in litigation in the case of *Jacobs v. Ramage* (1769), MCP, file 1766–1774, February 8, 1769. M. H. Stern, *op. cit.*, p. 195.

[9] There are a number of contemporary Samuel Levys and it is not clear who is referred to. It may have been the Samuel Levy who in 1772 contritely agreed to pay his *Sedakah* bill. *PAJHS*, vol. XXI (1913), p. 114.

[10] Solomon Simson presented the £20 legacy and requested a yearly *Escaba*. *Ibid.*, p. 116.

[11] See *supra*, Will of Samuel Myers Cohen, p. 67, note 10.

[12] Asher Myers (1725–1789), possibly the brother of Myer Myers, was a brazier, and was made a freeman on September 30, 1755, and elected Constable of the Dock Ward. He was very much interested in synagogue activities and was elected *parnas* in 1765 and 1771. *PAJHS*, vol. XXI (1913), pp. 70 and 88–89; *ibid.*, vol. XXXIII (1934), p. 203; *Burghers*, p. 183; *Minutes*, vol. VI, pp. 6 and 33.

[13] References to Joseph Myers are made in several entries in the Minutes of the congregation. *PAJHS*, vol. XXI (1913), pp. 63, 79 and 85; *Dictionary*, p. 126.

[14] Jacob Rodriques Rivera (1717–1789), son of Abraham, was a very wealthy merchant and especially involved in the spermaceti candle business. *Ibid.*, p. 149; *Portraits*, pp. 196 and 402–403.

my Beloved Brother SOLOMON SIMSON[15] for his Use, out of which, as moneys comes into his Hands, I desire him to put Three Hundred Pounds at Interest on good Security for Each of his Children,[16] those he has already, and those that he may have hereafter. The Principal and Interest to be given or used at his discretion. And I do hereby appoint my Honored Father JOSEPH SIMSON Executor, my Honored Mother REBECCA SIMSON, Executrix, and my beloved Brother SOLOMON SIMSON, Executor, to this my Sole Will, desiring him to be the Acting Executor.

I having intended to write this myself, but finding my self weak, desired my Brother to do it for me which he has done from my Mouth, and I having fully examined the same, do desire and order that it may pass and be held in good and firm to all intents and purposes therein mentioned, as if it had been wrote every word and letter with my own hand and that it may require no other proof or authority then my hand and Seal hereunto Subscribed and fixed this Thirtyeth Day of July, one Thousand Seven Hundred and Seventy Three.

s/ SAMPSON SIMSON [seal]

City of New York Ss. Be it also remembered that on the Eighteenth day of January One thousand Seven hundred and Seventy Four MYER MYERS of said City Goldsmith personally appeared before me the Said JOHN GRUEMLY and being Sworn on his Oath declared that he has carefully perused and examined a written paper dated the Thirtyeth day of July One thousand Seven hundred & Seventy three mentioned to be the last Will and Testament of SAMPSON SIMSON late of said City Merchant deceased, and that part of said Will at the latter end thereof beginning with the words I haveing and ending with the word Three as also the Signature thereunto Subscribed are to the best of this Deponents knowledge and belief the proper hand writing of the Said SAMPSON SIMSON, having been conversant with, and having Several times Seen the Said SAMPSON SIMSON write and Sign his name in his life time, and further Saith not

Sworn before me s/ MYER MYERS

s/ JN° GRUMLY

City of New York Ss. Be it remembered that on the Eighteenth day of January One thousand seven hundred and Seventy four, WILLIAM

[15] Solomon Simson (1738–1801) married Sarah Mears, daughter of Judah and Johevit Mears on October 26, 1768. A prominent merchant, he was in partnership with his brother Sampson, and was active in politics and congregational activities. In 1786, he lived at 31 Broad Street. *Portraits*, pp. 282–284; *Directory, 1786*, p. 40; *PAJHS*, vol. XXI (1913), pp. 79, 90, 103 *et passim*. For one of many court involvements, see *Benedict v. Simson* (1785), MCP, file 1785, Nov. 26, 1785.

[16] Solomon's children were Rebecca (1769–1854), Jochabed (1771–1814), Joseph (1779–1842), Sampson (1780–1857), Helena (1773–1819); Frumet (July, 1774). *PAJHS*, vol. XXXIII (1934), p. 202; *Portraits*, p. 282. See also *infra*, Will of Joseph Simson, pp. 201–203.

CLAJON Gentleman and DANIEL BLOUIN[17] of said City Merchant personally appeared before me JOHN GRUMLY thereunto duly authorized, and being severally Sworn on their Oaths declared, that they and each of them have Carefully examined a Certain written paper dated the Thirtyeth day of July One thousand Seven hundred and Seventy three mentioned to be the last Will and Testament of SAMPSON SIMSON, late of said City Merchant deceased, and that part of the said Will beginning at the latter end thereof with the words I haveing and ending with the word Three as also the Signature thereunto Subscribed are to the best of these Deponents knowledge and belief the proper hand writing of the said SAMPSON SIMSON, Their Cause of knowledge arising from having Several times Seen the Said SAMPSON SIMSON write and Sign his name, and each of these Deponents having often Seen Accoundts depending and Settled with the said SAMPSON SIMSON in his life time.

Sworn before me — s/ WM. CLAJON
JNO GRUMLY — s/ DANIEL BLOUIN

City of New York Ss. Be it remembered that on the Eighteenth day of January One thousand Seven hundred and Seventy four, personally came and appeared before me JOHN GRUMLY thereunto duly authorized SOLOMON SIMSON of said City Merchant, and being duly Sworn on his Oath declared that he did See SAMPSON SIMSON Sign and Seal the within written Instrument purporting to be the Will of the said SAMPSON SIMSON bearing date the Thirtyeth day of July, One thousand seven hundred and Seventy three, and heard him publish and declare the Same as and for his last Will and Testament, That at the time Thereof he the said SAMPSON SIMSON was of sound disposing mind and memory to the best of the knowledge and belief of him the Deponent

s/ JNO GRUMLY

City of New York Ss. Be it also remembered that on the Eighteenth day of January One thousand seven hundred and seventy four SOLOMON SIMSON one of the Executors of the within written will of SAMPSON SIMSON, likewise appeared before me the said JOHN GRUMLY, and was duly Sworn to the true Execution and performance of the said Will by taking the Oath of an Executor as by Law appointed Before me.

s/ JNO GRUMLY

[17] Possibly Daniel Bloom, a merchant, made a freeman on April 10, 1744. *Burghers*, p. 149.

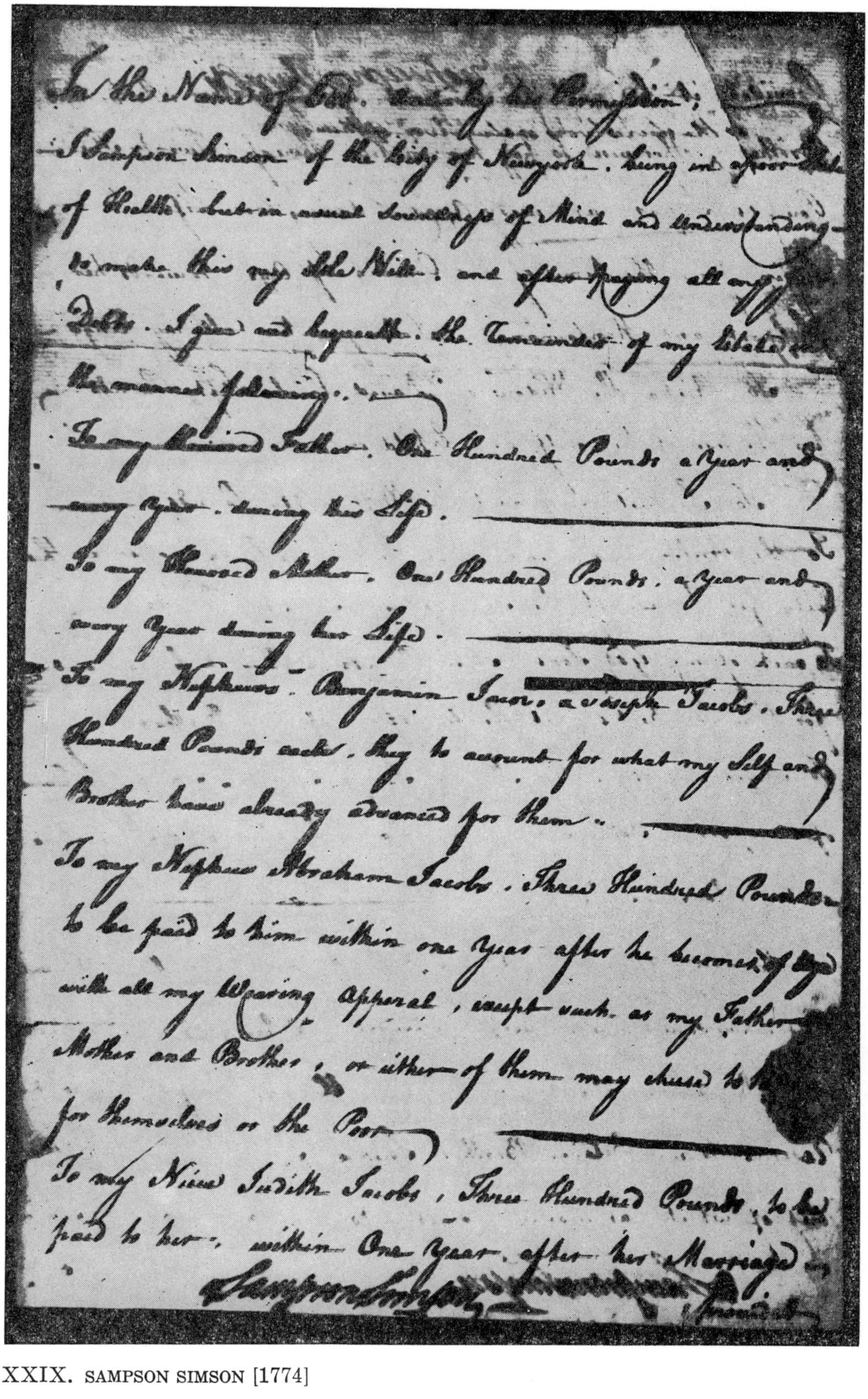
In the Name of God. [illegible] by his Permission;
I Sampson Simson of the City of Newyork. being in a poor State of Health but in sound Senses of Mind and Understanding do make this my Sole Will. and after Paying all my Debts. I give and bequeath. the Remainder of my Estate in the manner following.
To my Honored Father. One Hundred Pounds a Year and every Year. during his Life.
To my Honored Mother. One Hundred Pounds. a Year and every Year during her Life.
To my Nephews. Benjamin Isaac, & Joseph Jacobs. Three Hundred Pounds each. they to account for what my Self and Brother have already advanced for them.
To my Nephew Abraham Jacobs. Three Hundred Pounds to be paid to him within one Year after he becomes of Age with all my Wearing Apparel, except such as my Father Mother and Brother, or either of them may chuse to keep for themselves or the Poor.
To my Niece Judith Jacobs, Three Hundred Pounds, to be paid to her, within One Year. after her Marriage.
Sampson Simson

XXIX. SAMPSON SIMSON [1774]

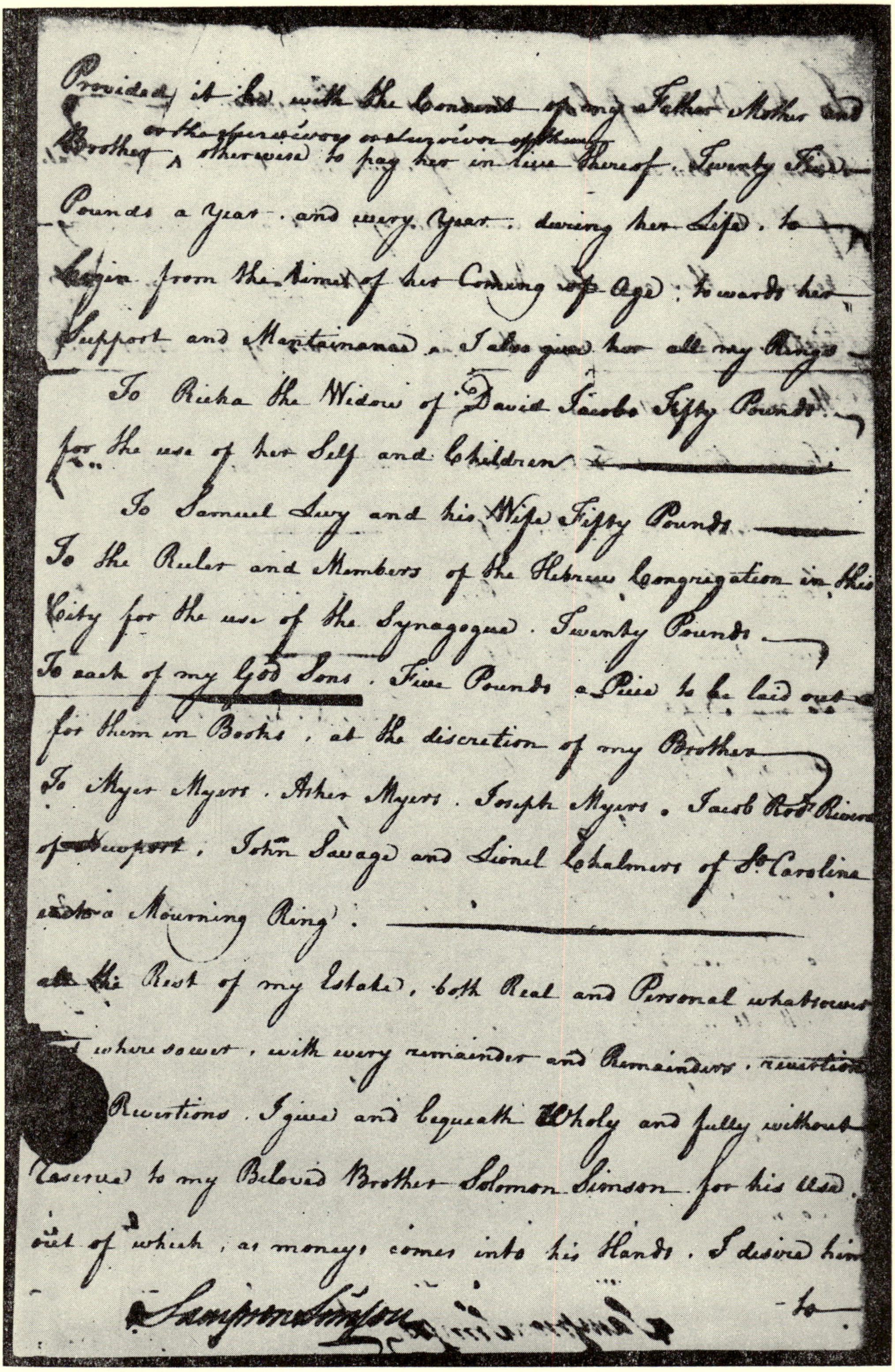
Provided it be with the Consent of my Father Mother and
Brother or the Survivors or Survivor of them otherwise to pay her in lieu thereof Twenty Five
Pounds a Year and every Year during her Life to
begin from the time of her Coming of Age towards her
Support and Maintainance. I also give her all my Rings

To Ricka the Widow of David Jacobs Fifty Pounds
for the use of her Self and Children

To Samuel Levy and his Wife Fifty Pounds
To the Ruler and Members of the Hebrew Congregation in this
City for the use of the Synagogue Twenty Pounds
To each of my God Sons Five Pounds a Piece to be laid out
for them in Books at the discretion of my Brother
To Myer Myers. Asher Myers. Joseph Myers. Jacob Rodr Rivera
of Newport. John Savage and Lionel Chalmers of So Carolina
each a Mourning Ring.

All the Rest of my Estate, both Real and Personal whatsoever
and wheresoever, with every remainder and Remainders, reversion
and Reversions I give and bequeath Wholy and fully without
reserve to my Beloved Brother Solomon Simson for his Use
out of which, as moneys comes into his Hands I desire him
to

Sampson Simson

XXIX. SAMPSON SIMSON [1774]

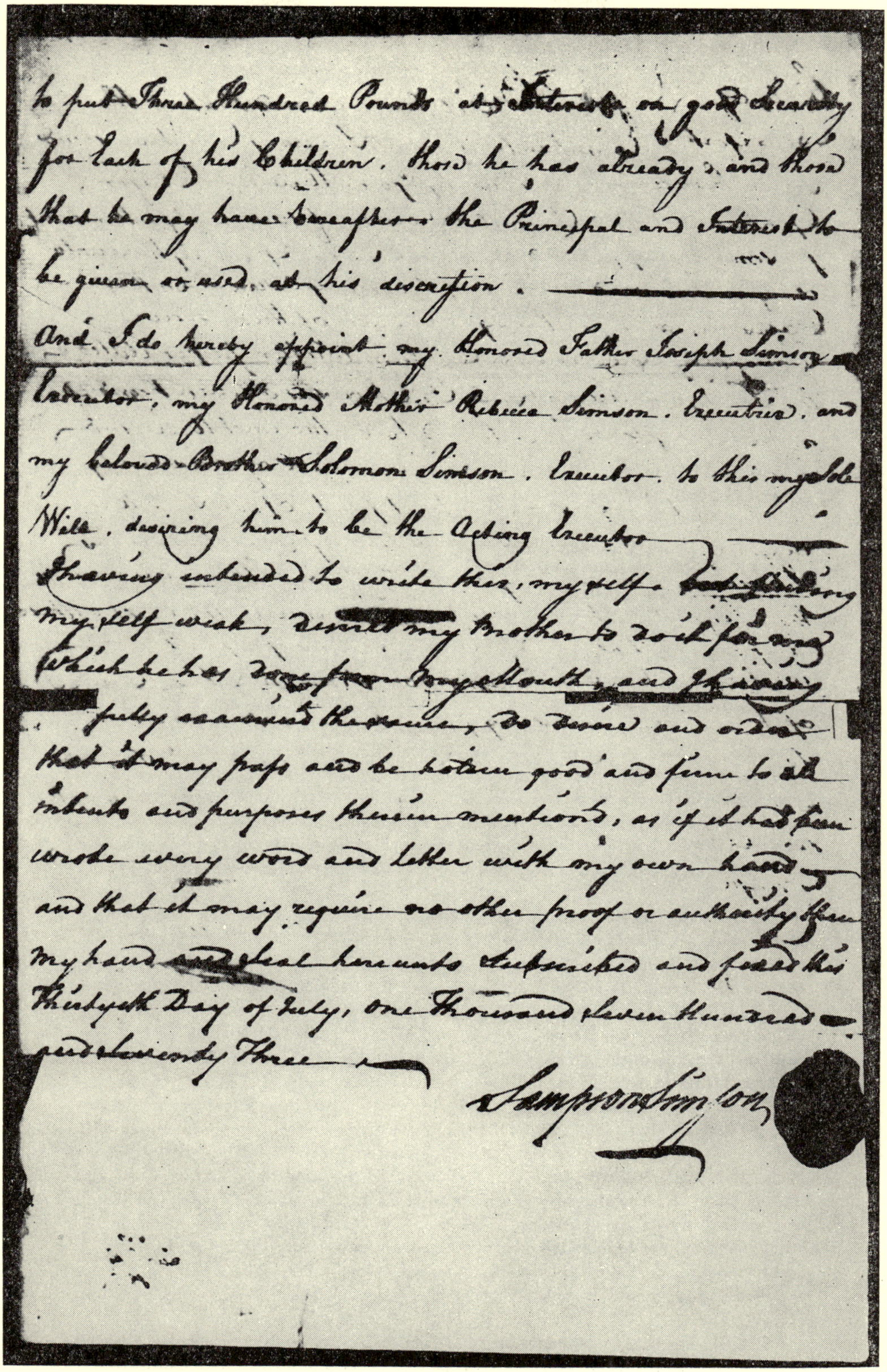
to put Three Hundred Pounds at Interest on good Security
for Each of his Children. those he has already, and those
that he may have hereafter the Principal and Interest to
be given or used at his descretion.
And I do hereby appoint my Honored Father Joseph Simson
Executor, my Honored Mother Rebecca Simson. Executrix. and
my beloved Brother Solomon Simson. Executor. to this my Sole
Will. desiring him to be the Acting Executor
I having intended to write this, my self but finding
my self weak, desired my brother to do it for me
Which he has done from my Mouth, and I having
fully examined the same, do sine and order
that it may pass and be taken good and firm to all
intents and purposes therein mentioned, as if it had been
wrote every word and letter with my own hand
and that it may require no other proof or authority than
my hand and Seal hereunto subscribed and fixed this
Thirtyeth Day of July, one Thousand Seven Hundred
and Seventy Three
Sampson Simson

XXIX. SAMPSON SIMSON [1774]

XXX

ISAAC ADOLPHUS[1]

[1774]

In the Name of God Amen, I ISAAC ADOLPHUS of the City of New York merchant, Do make, and ord[ain this] my last Will and Testament, in manner and form foll[owing] that is to say, after all my Just Debts are paid and discharged, I give devise, and bequeath unto BENJ[AMIN] ETTING[2] the Sum of twenty five pounds; also I give [and] bequeath unto the Widow HETTY HAYS,[3] the Sum of Tw[enty] five pounds; and unto my Executors for the use of the Synagogue, in the City of New York, the sum of ten pounds[4] Likewise my will further is, that my Executors, within some

[1] Original Will no. 2620, HDC; Will Liber 29, p. 164; *NYHSC,* vol. VIII (1900), p. 197. Isaac Adolphus (1725–September 7, 1774) arrived in New York sometime about 1750 from Amersfoort, Holland. He became a merchant and was made a freeman on August 15, 1758. *Burghers,* p. 191. His wife Charity Hays (1722–1773), daughter of Michael Hays and sister of Judah and Jacob Hays, died fifteen months before him of a "Sore throat disorder." *Portraits,* p. 245; *NYHSC,* vol. VIII (1900), p. 197. From his residence on Burling Slip, he conducted a dry goods establishment. He was very much concerned with the condition of Peck and Beekman's slips and signed a petition asking the Common Council to clean Beekman slip in Montgomerie Ward. *Minutes,* vol. VII, pp. 77–78. He was elected *Ḥatan Torah* of Shearith Israel in 1758 and 1764, and *parnas* in 1766 and 1767. As a dutiful husband, he paid the *parnas* Hayman Levy £5 as a legacy for his wife who was to have *Ashet Hiel* ([אשת חיל] a woman of worth at the beginning of the memorial prayer) every *Rosh Ḥodes. PAJHS,* vol. XXI (1913), pp. 79, 88, 92, 93, 115 and 211. In 1767, he sent Aaron Lopez four double sets of *Tsitsiths* (having no extra *tephilin* to spare) via Abraham I. Abrahams. Jacob R. Marcus, *American Jewry Documents Eighteenth Century* (Cincinnati, 1959), pp. 91–92. Interestingly, Isaac died the very day that he drew his will. His Hebrew name was Abraham Isaac son of Ephraim Reine, just how this translates to Adolphus is not known. For further biography, see *Portraits,* pp. 115 and 244–245.

[2] Benjamin Etting (d. May 24, 1778), a goldsmith, was a nephew and business partner of Adolphus. He was the son of Asher Etting (d. circa 1752) and Ritzel Adolphus (d. 1761), sister of Isaac. Benjamin made freeman on February 7, 1769, aided the Revolutionary cause from Norwalk. *Burghers,* p. 225; *Dictionary,* pp. 5 and 35; Malcolm H. Stern, *Americans of Jewish Descent* (Cincinnati, 1960), p. 5. Solomon Solis-Cohen, "Notes Concerning David Hays and Esther Etting his wife, and Michael Hays and Reuben Etting their Brothers, Patriots of the Revolution," *PAJHS,* vol. II (1894), p. 66. Interestingly, the testator, his uncle, took an oath of allegiance to the Crown in 1741 along with twenty-eight other Jews, including David, Daniel, and Mordecai Gomez and Samuel Myers Cohen. Oath of allegiance, April 27, 1741, New-York Historical Society Library.

[3] Hetty Adolphus Hays (d. September 1783), sister of Isaac Adolphus, married Jacob Hays (d. September, 1760), Isaac's brother-in-law. *Dictionary,* pp. 6 and 58; Stern, *op. cit.,* pp. 5 and 75. The Hays family was quite poor. In 1751, Jacob Hays and his family were given £10 by the congregation. *Ibid.,* vol. XXI (1913), p. 64. In 1774, after having purchased a quarter of lamb, seemingly not properly killed, she was ordered to clean all utensils used in the house, otherwise to be looked upon as a "*Treffo* House." Mrs. Hays complied and her house was publicly declared as being "*Coshair.*" *Ibid.,* pp. 123, 124 and 219.

[4] The £10 was paid by Hayman Levy, as executor, to the *parnas residente* Isaac Moses for which Adolphus was entitled to a *Hascaba* said at *Areb Kippur* [Eve of Yom Kippur]

Short time after my decease, Sell and dispose of all my whole Estate, as well Real, [and personal] and all the monies thence arising, after payment of my Just Debt, funeral expenses, and the several Legacies above mentioned, I do Give, devise, and bequeath unto my Brothers, and Sisters JACOB ADOLPHUS, PHILIP ADOLPHUS, EZEKIAL ADOLPHUS, ESTER SAMUELS, MINIKE [MOSES], HANNAH WORMS, GELLAH ABRAHAMS,[5] and my Nephews MOSES ETTING[6] and MICHAEL ISRAEL[7] to be Equally divided between them Share and Share alike To hold the said several and respective parts and Shares unto my said Brothers, Sisters, and Nephews and to them severally and to their several and respective Executors administrators and assigns for ever and Lastly I do hereby Constitute and appoint my Brother PHILIP ADOLPHUS and my Good friends HAYMAN LEVY,[8] MYER MYERS,[9] and ISAAC MOSES[10] to be Executors of this my last Will and Testament hereby revoking all former Wills by me made *In Witness* whereof I the said ISAAC ADOLPHUS have (after interlining MINIKE MOSES's name on the other side hereof) hereunto Set my hand & Seal this Seventh day of September in the year one thousand seven hundred and Seventy four.

Signed, Sealed, published, and declared by the said ISAAC ADOLPHUS, as and for his last Will and Testament, in the presence of us, who subscribed our names as Witnesses thereto, in the presence, and at the request of the said Testator. (the words [and MICHAEL ISRAEL] being interlined before sealing and publishing hereof }

s/ JOHN BERRIEN[11]
s/ JN: D. CRIMSHEIR[12]

Proved by JNO. BERRIEN of the City of New York, merchant JNO. D. CRIMSHERE Esq. (and by BENJAMIN SEIXAS[13] Saddler who was sworn on the five books of Moses being a Jew) & Qualifed HAYMAN LEVY, MYER MYERS & ISAAC MOSES & PHILIP ADOLPHUS Exrs. Sept 13: 1774 all Jews

---

and *Ros Ḥodes*. £5 was also donated for the building of Walls and supporting the ground of the *Bet Ḥaim*, even though this sum does not appear in the will.

[5] This list of Isaac Adolphus' brothers and sisters is difficult to annotate. A check of standard sources reveals nothing. It is supposed that these people were not residents of New York, though Philip Adolphus was sworn as executor in New York.

[6] Moses Etting (d. *circa* 1778) was a merchant and son of Asher Etting, nephew of Isaac, who died in Easton, Pennsylvania. *PAJHS*, vol. II (1894), p. 66.

[7] Michael Israel was a member of the congregation in 1783. *Ibid.*, vol. XXI (1913), pp. 142, 148–149 and 159.

[8] See *infra*, Will of Hayman Levy, pp. 165–178. See David Franks to Bernard Gratz, Nov. 22, 1780, Gratz Papers, Historical Society of Pennsylvania for reference to executors of Isaac Adolphus.

[9] See *supra*, Will of Samuel Myers Cohen, p. 67, note 10.

[10] Isaac Moses (1742–1818) first mentioned in the Minutes as *Ḥatan Beresheet* in 1768, was *parnas* four times in 1775, 1789, 1790 and 1792. *PAJHS*, vol. XXI (1913), pp. 101

City of New York } *Ss.* Be it Remembered that on the Thirteenth day of September One Thousand Seven Hundred and Seventy four Personally came and appeared before me CARY LUDLOW Esq.[14] thereunto duly Authorised and appointed JOHN BERRIEN of the City of New York Merchant, and JOHN D. CRIMSHIER of the said city attorney at Law and BENJAMIN SEIXAS of the same City Sadler and Severally Sworn did Depose and Say And First the Said JOHN BERRIEN & JOHN D. CRIMSHIER for themselves Severally swore that they were present and heard ISAAC ADOLPHUS Publish and declare the annexed written Instrument purporting to be the Will of the Said ISAAC ADOLPHUS bearing date the Seventh day of September one Thousand Seven hundred and Seventy Four as and for his Last Will and Testament That at the Time thereof He the Said ISAAC ADOLPHUS was of Sound Disposing Mind & Memory to the Best of the Knowledge of them the Depenants and thet their names Severally Subscribed as Witnesses to the Said Will are of their [ ] Hands Writing which they severelly subscribed as Witness to the Said Will in the Testators presence & in the presence of each other and the said BENJAMIN SEIXAS [ ] Saith That he was also present and heard the Said ISAAC ADOLPHUS Publish & Declare the Said Annexed Instrument purporting to be the Will of the Said ISAAC ADOLPHUS bearing date the said Seventh day of September as and for his Last Will and Testament and that at the Time thereof he the Said ISAAC ADOLPHUS was of Sound Disposing Mind & memory to the [best] of the Knowledge and Belief of him the Deponent and he also Saw the before named JOHN BERRIEN and JOHN D. CRIMSHIER Subscribe there names as witnesses to the Said Will in the Testators presence.

s/ CARY LUDLOW Surr.

City of New York Ss.

Be it also Remembered That on the day and year above written Personally appeared before me the Said CARY LUDLOW, HAYMAN LEVY, MYER MYERS, ISAAC MOSES, and PHILIP ADOLPHUS the Executors in the said Will named and Severally Sworn to the True Execution and performance of the Said Will by Severally taking the Oath of an Executor as by Law appointed.

s/ CARY LUDLOW Surr.

---

and 212. For other congregational activities, see *ibid.*, pp. 103, 106, 111, *et passim.* He was an auctioneer who resided at 37 Dock Street. *Directory, 1786*, p. 38.

[11] John Berrian, boatman was made freeman on May 29, 1750. He was another signer of the petition along with Isaac Adolphus and others asking for the clearing of Beekman Slip. *Minutes*, vol. VII, pp. 77–78; *Burghers*, p. 169.

[12] John Dutton Crimshier was licensed attorney on June 26, 1766 and on August 8 of that year he was made a notary public for the province. *Calendar*, pp. 67–68.

[13] See *infra*, Will of Hayman Levy, pp. 165–178.

[14] Cary Ludlow was appointed a Master of the Court of Chancery in 1755. *Civil List*, p. 208.

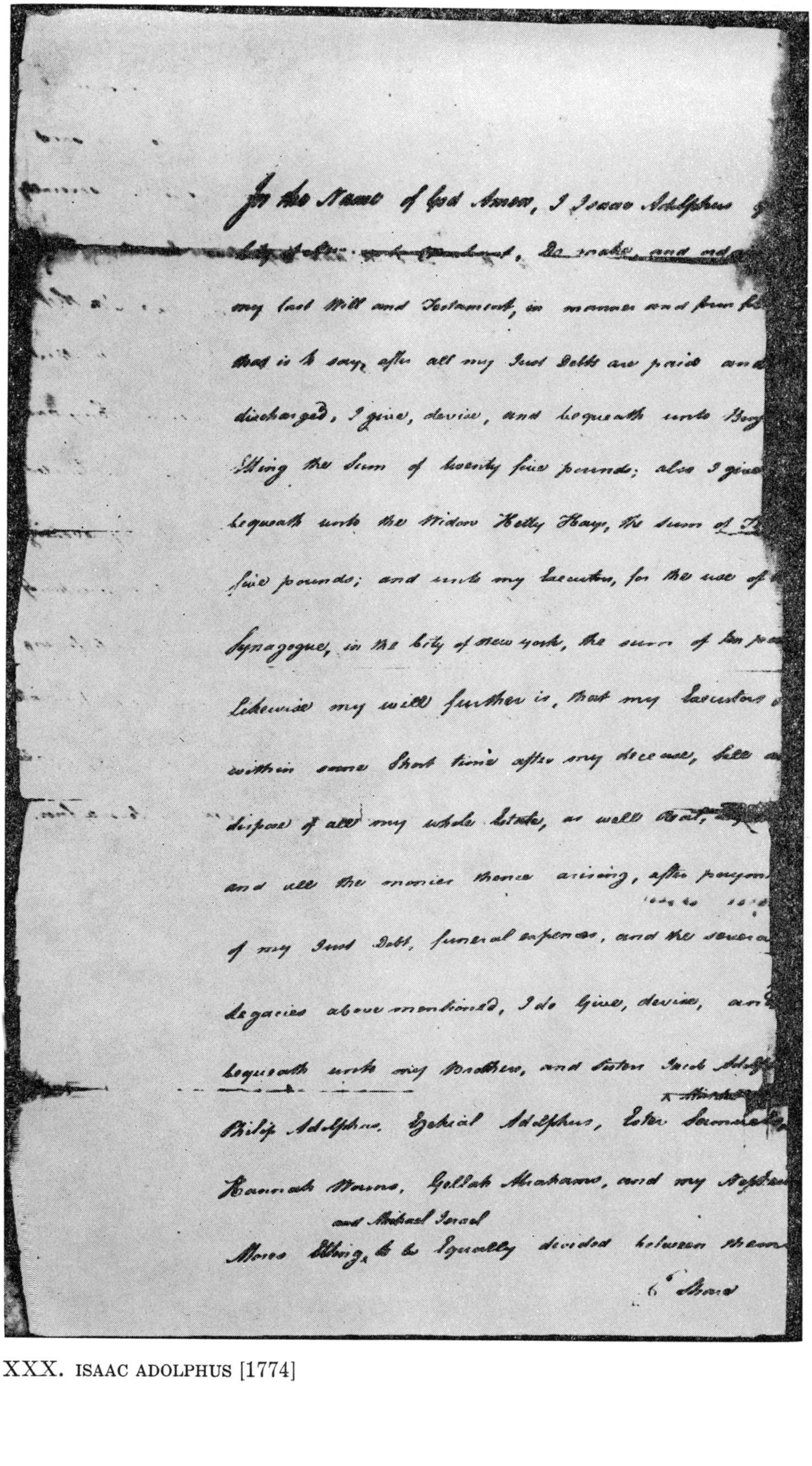

In the Name of God Amen, I Isaac Adolphus of
City of New York, Merchant, Do make, and ord
my last Will and Testament, in manner and form fo
that is to say, after all my Just Debts are paid and
discharged, I give, devise, and bequeath unto Benj
Etting the Sum of twenty five pounds; also I give
bequeath unto the Widow Hetty Hays, the sum of T
five pounds; and unto my Executors, for the use of
Synagogue, in the City of New York, the sum of ten po
Likewise my will further is, that my Executors
within some Short time after my decease, Sell an
dispose of all my whole Estate, as well Real, as
and all the monies thence arising, after paym
of my Just Debts, funeral expences, and the severa
Legacies above mentioned, I do Give, devise, and
bequeath unto my Brothers, and Sisters Jacob Adolph
Philip Adolphus, Ezekiel Adolphus, Ester Samuel
Hannah Moses, Yellah Abrahams, and my Nephew
and Michael Israel
Moses Etting, &c Equally divided between them
6 Share

XXX. ISAAC ADOLPHUS [1774]

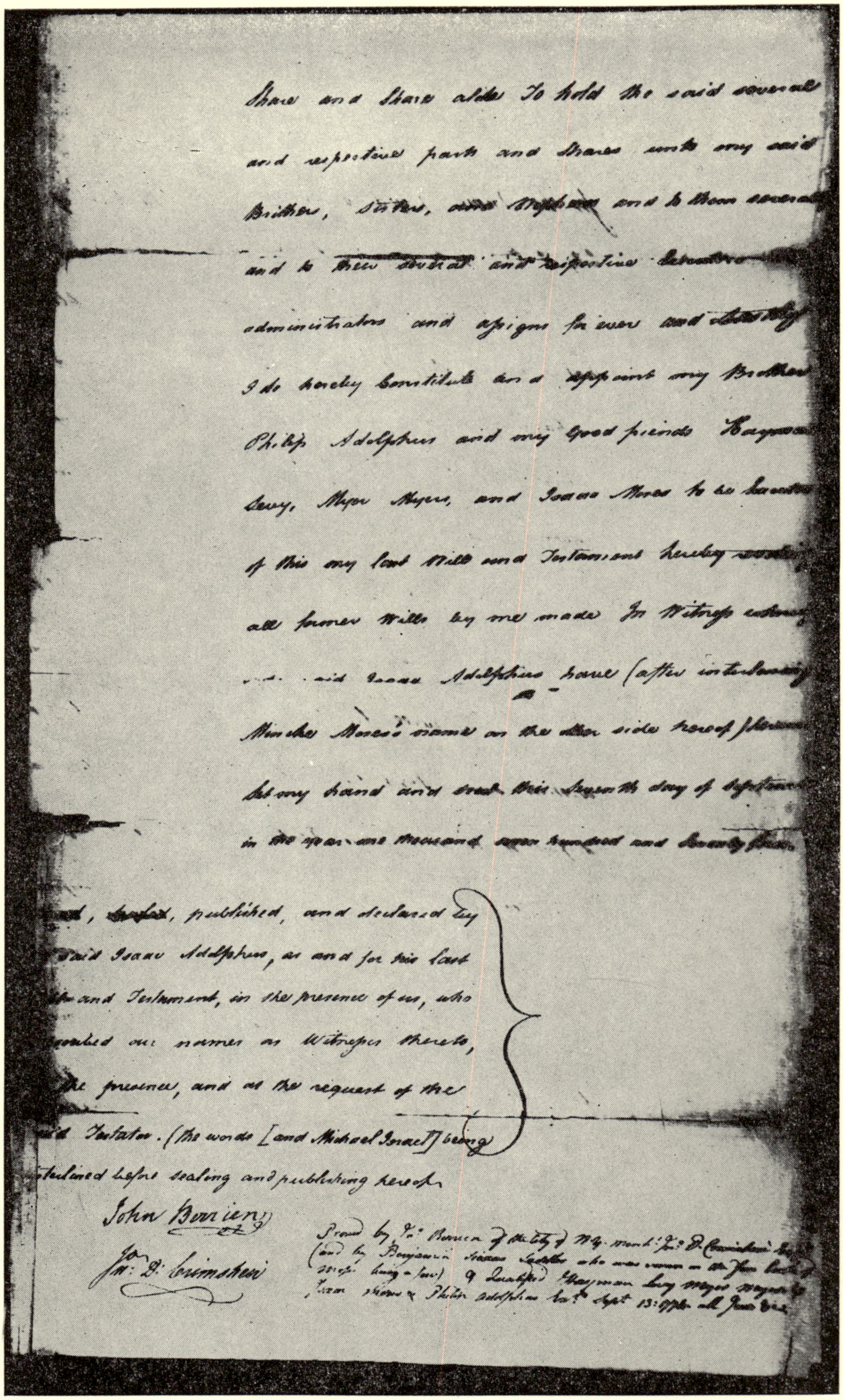
Share and Share alike To hold the said several
and respective parts and Shares unto my said
Brother, Sisters, and Nephew and to them severally
and to their several and respective Executors
administrators and assigns for ever and lastly
I do hereby Constitute and appoint my Brother
Philip Adolphus and my Good friends Hayman
Levy, Myer Myers, and Isaac Moses to be Executors
of this my last Will and Testament hereby revoking
all former Wills by me made In Witness whereof
I the said Isaac Adolphus have (after interlining
Mincke Moses's name on the other side hereof) hereunto
set my hand and seal this Seventh day of September
in the year one thousand seven hundred and seventy four

Signed, Sealed, published, and declared by
the said Isaac Adolphus, as and for his last
Will and Testament, in the presence of us, who
subscribed our names as Witnesses thereto,
in his presence, and at the request of the
said Testator. (the words [and Michael Israel] being
interlined before sealing and publishing hereof

John Berrien

Jn: D: Crimshier

Proved by Jn. Berrien of the City of N.Y. merch. & Jn. D. Crimshier Esq.
(and by Benjamin Isaacs Seixas who was sworn on the Five Books of
Moses being a Jew) & Qualified Hayman Levy Myer Myers
Isaac Moses & Philip Adolphus Exrs. Sept. 13: 1774 all Jews [illegible]

XXX. ISAAC ADOLPHUS [1774]

XXXI

MATTATHIAS GOMEZ[1]

[1784]

In the Name of the God of Israel! I MATTATHIAS GOMEZ of the Township of the Northern Liberties in the County of Philadelphia in Pennsylvania, Merchant being sick and weak in Body, but through the Goodness of God of sound disposing Mind and Memory, and considering the Certainty of Death and the Uncertainty of the Time thereof, do make and put in Writing this my last Will and Testament, in Manner and Form following, that is to say; *First,* I do recommend my Soul to the Almighty and Eternal God and my body to the Earth to be decently interred according to the Order of the Jews at the Discretion of my Executors hereinafter named. And it is my Will that all my just Debts and Funeral Expences be fully paid, and satisfied as soon as may be convenient after my Decease.

Item

I do nominate and appoint my loving Mother DEBORAH GOMEZ,[2] my Brother in Law MOSES GOMEZ[3] and his son DANIEL GOMEZ[4] to be the Executors of this my last Will and Testament.

Item

I do Give and Bequeath unto my four Children, DEBORAH GOMEZ,[5] ISAAC GOMEZ,[6] ESTHER GOMEZ,[7] and BENJAMIN GOMEZ[8] their Heirs and Assigns for Ever, to be equally divided between them when they shall respectively

[1] Original Will no. 3226, HDC; Will Liber 36, p. 185, *NYHSC*, vol. XII (1904), pp. 154–155. Mattathias Gomez (d. May 5, 1786), son of Isaac Gomez (see Will) married his cousin Rachel Gomez, daughter of Benjamin Gomez (see Will) on February 6, 1765. They had six children. Very active in congregational activities, he was elected *Ḥatan Beresheet* (one chosen to commence the annual reading of the Pentateuch which begins on *Simḥat Torah*) in September, 1764, and was *parnas* during 1774–1775. During the Revolutionary War he located himself along with other Jews in Philadelphia and he might not have returned. *PAJHS*, vol. XVII (1909), pp. 197–198; *ibid.*, vol. XXI (1913), pp. 183 and 212. Register of Congregation Shearith Israel, pp. 26, 38 and 41a.

[2] Deborah Gomez was the wife of Isaac Gomez, see footnote 2 of the latter's will, *supra*, p. 129.

[3] Moses Gomez, son of Daniel Gomez, married Esther Gomez, Mattathias' sister. See *supra*, Will of Simja de Torres, p. 81, note 7, and *infra*, Will of Moses Gomez, pp. 189–191.

[4] Daniel Gomez (1759–1784) served in the Revolutionary Army as a member of the Philadelphia militia. *Portraits*, p. 481.

[5] See *supra*, Will of Benjamin Gomez, p. 135, note 2.

[6] See *supra*, Will of Benjamin Gomez, p. 136, note 7.

[7] See *supra*, Will of Benjamin Gomez, p. 135, note 3.

[8] See *supra*, Will of Benjamin Gomez, p. 136, note 8.

attain to the Age of twenty one Years, Two full equal and undivided third parts (the whole into three equal parts to be divided) of, in and to a certain Messuage or Tenement and Lot of Ground on Queen Street in the Fly in the City of New-York;[9] Also two Messuages or Tenements and Lots of Ground on Golden Hill[10] in the said City of New-York; Also one full equal and undivided half part (the whole into two equal parts to be divided) of and in a Distillery House and Lot of Ground with the Stills and Utensils thereunto belonging Situate on Ferry Street in the said City of New-York;[11] Also my House and Lot of Ground situate on Queen Street in the Fly in the City of New-York aforesaid which was devised to me by my late Father ISAAC GOMEZ deceased, after the Decease of my Mother the said DEBORAH GOMEZ, together with their and every of their Rights, Members and Appurtenances.

Item

I Give and Bequeath unto my Eldest Son ISAAC GOMEZ and his Heirs my *Sepher* or the five Books of Moses wrote on Parchment, with *Rimonims* or Ornaments of Silver.[12]

Item

I do hereby authorize and direct my said Executors and the Survivors of them to let or demise all my Messuages, or Tenements and Lots of Ground from Year to Year, during the Minority of my said Children for the best Rent or Rents that can be gotten; and the Rents so issuing shall be applied to the Support and Maintenance of my said loving Mother DEBORAH GOMEZ in Lieu and Stead of the Annuity of One hundred and fifty Pounds York Currency given to her by my late Father ISAAC GOMEZ for and during the Term of her natural Life; And also for the Support, Maintenance and Education of my said four Children till they shall attain to the Age of twenty one Years respectively, And in Case the Rents aforesaid should prove insufficient to answer that Purpose; then and in such Case but not otherwise, I do authorize and direct my said Executors and the Survivors of them to grant, bargain and sell all or any of my Houses and Lots of Ground in the City of New-York, and all my Estate, Right,

[9] See *supra*, Will of Isaac Gomez, p. 129, note 3, for reference to Queen Street property. Though the property was left to Mattathias' mother for life, it somehow was transferred to Mattathias. The "Fly," also known as Smith's Valley, was along the East River at present Pearl Street between Wall Street and Peck Slip.

[10] Possibly the house and ground purchased by Isaac Gomez from Elizabeth Axon on May 2, 1752. The property was bounded by Gold Street and the French Church. Conveyance Liber 34, cp. 21.

[11] For reference to a still house purchased by Isaac and Benjamin Gomez in 1763 which may be the distillery house in question. See *supra*, Will of Benjamin Gomez, p. 135, note 1.

[12] These Five Books of Moses were given by Isaac Gomez to Mattathias who now bequeaths them to his eldest son Isaac. See Will of Isaac Gomez, *supra*, p. 130. The handing down of the Torah was a family tradition carried out from Lewis Gomez, if not before, to the present testator.

Title and interest of, in or to any of them, for the best Price or Prices that can be gotten, and to sign, seal, acknowledge and deliver sufficient Deed or Deeds to the Purchaser or Purchasers thereof, his, her or theire Heirs and Assigns for Ever: And the Moneys arising from such Sale or Sales after deducting incidental Charges, shall be applied to the Support and Maintenance of my said Mother and Children in manner and form aforesaid. *And* all the remainder and residue of my Estate both Real and Personal, I do Give and Bequeath unto my said four Children, DEBORAH, ISAAC, ESTHER, and BENJAMIN, their Heirs, Executors, Administrators and Assigns, to be equally divided between them part and Share alike when they do respectively attain to the Age of twenty one Years: But if either of them my said Children shall happen to depart this Life in his or her Minority, Intestate and without lawful Issue, then the Part, Share Portion or Bequest of him or her so dying shall descend and go to the Survivors of them, part and Share alike as Tenants in common to be equally divided between them when they do respectively attain the Age of Twenty one Years as aforesaid. And I do nominate and appoint my said Executors and Survivors of them to be the Guardians of the Persons and Estate of my said Children during each of their Minorities as aforesaid, hereby revoking all former Wills and Testaments heretofore by me made and do declare this only to be my last Will and Testament. *In Witness* whereof I the Said MATTATHIAS GOMEZ, the Testator, have hereunto set my Hand and Seal, the Twentyeth day of April in the Year one Thousand Seven hundred and eighty one.

Signed, Sealed, pronounced published & declared by the said MATTATHIAS GOMEZ, the Testator, as and for his last Will & Testament in the Presence of us who have subscribed our Names hereunto as Witnesses in his Presence and at his Request.

s/ MATTATHIAS GOMEZ

[seal]

s/ WALTER BICKER[13]
s/ SAM COOPERTHWAIT
s/ THO^{S}. FRANKLIN, JUN.[14]

City of New York SS. Be It Remembered that on the second day of January in the year of our Lord one thousand seven hundred and eighty four personally came and appeared before me THOMAS TREDWELL[15] Judge of the Court of Probates of the State of New York WALTER BICKER

[13] Walter Bickers was made freeman on June 7, 1768. *Burghers*, p. 215.

[14] Thomas Franklin, Jr., ironmonger, made freeman on June 20, 1787. *Ibid.*, p. 279.

[15] Thomas Tredwell, appointed Judge of the Court of Probate on March 13, 1778. *Civil List*, p. 224.

of the said City Hatter and being duly sworn on his oath declared that he did see Mattathias Gomez sign and seal the aforegoing written instrument purporting to be the will of the said Mattathias Gomez bearing date the twentieth day of April in the year ~~of our Lord~~ one thousand seven hundred and eighty one and heard him publish and declare the same as and for his last will and testament that at the time thereof he the said Mattathias Gomez was of sound disposing mind and memory to the best of the knowledge and belief of him the deponent that his name subscribed to the said will is of his own proper hand writing which he subscribed as a witness to the said will in the presence of the testator and that he the deponent saw Samuel Cooperthwait and Thomas Franklin, Junior the other witnesses to the said will subscribe their names as witnesses thereto in the testator's presence.

s/ Thomas Tredwell, Judge of Probates

City of New York SS. Be It Also Remembered that on the same second day of January one thousand seven hundred and eighty four Moses Gomez one of the Executors of the aforegoing written will of Mattathias Gomez deceased likewise appeared before me the said Thomas Tredwell and was duly sworn to the true execution and performance of the said will.

s/ Thomas Tredwell, Judge of Probates

City of New York SS. Be It Also Remembered that on the seventh day of January in the year of our Lord one thousand seven hundred and eighty four Daniel Gomez one other of the Executors of the preceding will of Mattathias Gomez, likewise appeared before me the said Thomas Tredwell and was duly Sworn to the true execution and performance of the said will.

s/ Thomas Tredwell, Judge of Probates

In the Name of the God of Israel!

I Mattathias Gomez of the Township of the Northern Liberties in the County of Philadelphia in Pennsylvania, Merchant, being sick and weak in Body, but through the Goodness of God of sound disposing Mind and Memory, and considering the Certainty of Death and the Uncertainty of the Time thereof, do make and put in Writing this my last Will and Testament in Manner and Form following, that is to say; First, I do recommend my Soul to the Almighty and Eternal God and my Body to the Earth, to be decently interred according to the Order of the Jews at the Discretion of my Executors herein after named. And it is my Will, that all my just Debts and Funeral Expences be fully paid and satisfied as soon as may be convenient after my Decease. Item, I do nominate and appoint my loving Mother Deborah Gomez, my Brother in Law Moses Gomez and his Son Daniel Gomez to be the Executors of this my last Will and Testament. Item, I do Give and Bequeath unto my four Children, Deborah Gomez, Isaac Gomez, Esther Gomez and Benjamin Gomez their Heirs and Assigns for Ever, to be equally divided between them when they shall respectively attain to the Age of twenty one Years; Two full equal and undivided third parts (the whole into three equal parts to be divided) of, in and to a certain Messuage or Tenement and Lot of Ground situate on Queen Street in the Fly in the City of New-York; Also two Messuages or Tenements and Lots of Ground on Golden Hill in the said City of New-York; Also one full equal and undivided half part (the whole into two equal parts to be divided) of and in a Distillery House and Lot of Ground with the Stills and Utensils thereunto belonging situate on Ferry Street in the said City of New-York; Also my House and Lot of Ground situate on Queen Street in the Fly in the City of New-York aforesaid which was devised to me by my late Father Isaac Gomez deceased, after the Decease of my Mother the said Deborah Gomez, together with their and every of their Rights Members and Appurtenances. Item, I Give and Bequeath unto my Eldest Son Isaac Gomez and his Heirs my Sepher or the five Books of Moses

wrote

XXXI. MATTATHIAS GOMEZ [1784]

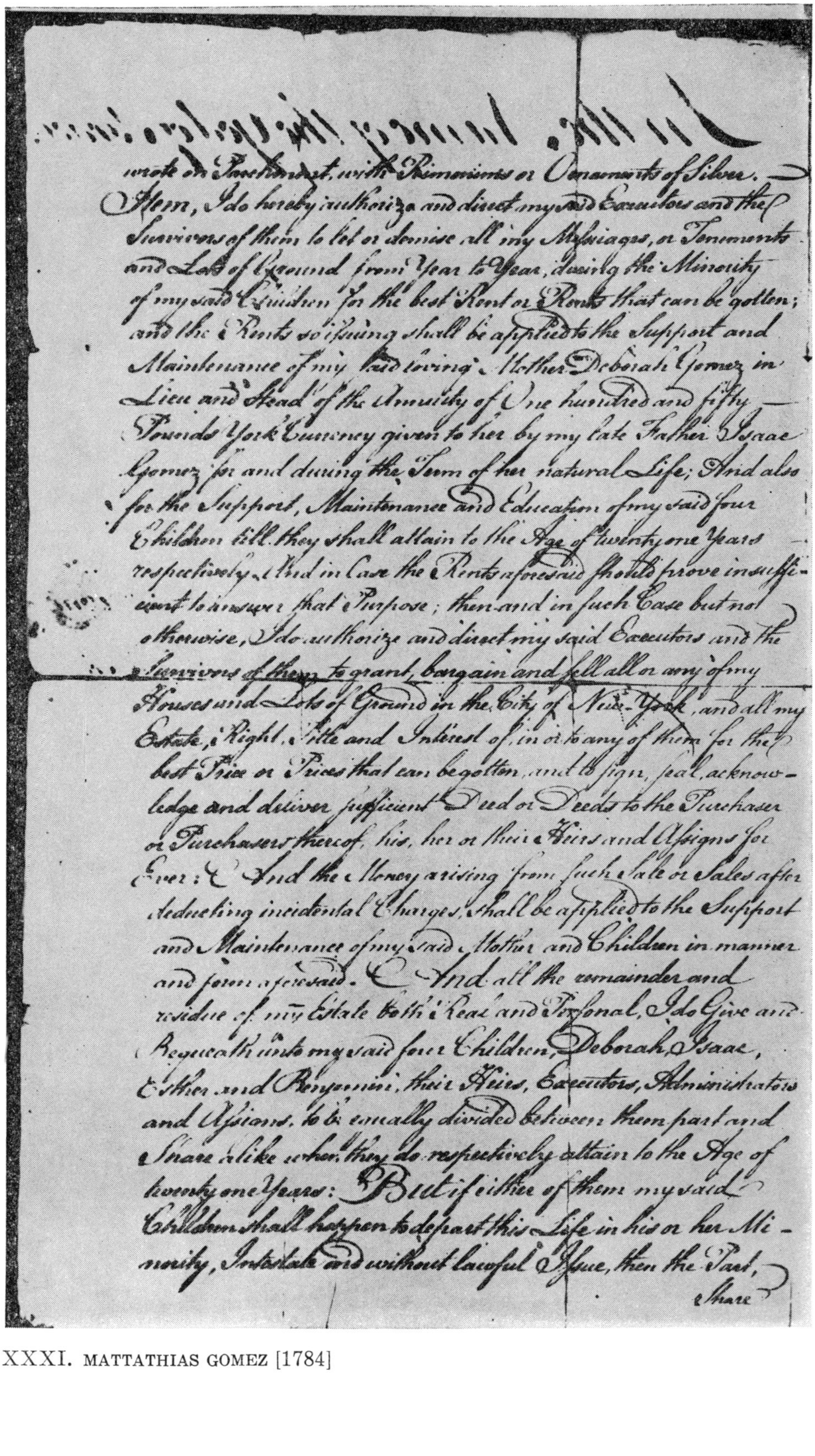

XXXI. MATTATHIAS GOMEZ [1784]

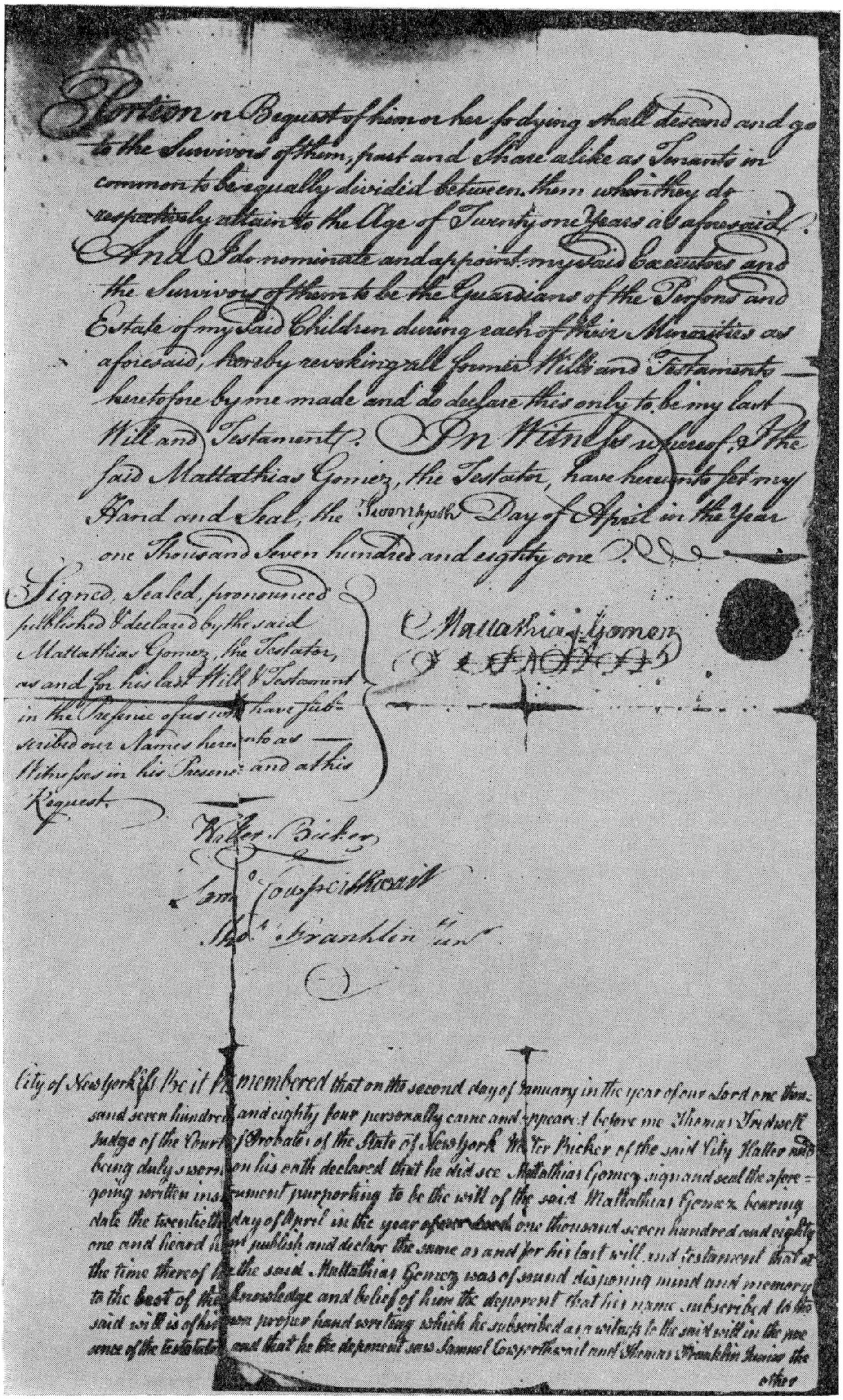

Portion or Bequest of him or her so dying shall descend and go to the Survivors of them, part and Share alike as Tenants in common to be equally divided between them when they do respectively attain to the Age of Twenty one Years as aforesaid. And I do nominate and appoint my said Executors and the Survivors of them to be the Guardians of the Persons and Estate of my said Children during each of their Minorities as aforesaid, hereby revoking all former Wills and Testaments heretofore by me made and do declare this only to be my last Will and Testament. In Witness whereof, I the said Mattathias Gomez, the Testator, have hereunto set my Hand and Seal, the Twentyeth Day of April in the Year one Thousand Seven hundred and eighty one

Signed, Sealed, pronounced published & declared by the said Mattathias Gomez, the Testator, as and for his last Will & Testament in the Presence of us who have subscribed our Names hereunto as Witnesses in his Presence and at his Request.

Mattathias Gomez

Walter Bicker

Saml. Cowperthwait

Thos. Franklin Junr.

City of New York ss. Be it Remembered that on the second day of January in the year of our Lord one thousand seven hundred and eighty four personally came and appeared before me Thomas Tredwell Judge of the Court of Probates of the State of New York Walter Bicker of the said City Hatter and being duly sworn on his oath declared that he did see Mattathias Gomez sign and seal the afore-going written instrument purporting to be the will of the said Mattathias Gomez bearing date the twentieth day of April in the year of our Lord one thousand seven hundred and eighty one and heard him publish and declare the same as and for his last will and testament that at the time thereof he the said Mattathias Gomez was of sound disposing mind and memory to the best of the knowledge and belief of him the deponent that his name subscribed to the said will is of his own proper hand writing which he subscribed as a witness to the said will in the presence of the testator and that he the deponent saw Samuel Cowperthwait and Thomas Franklin Junior the other

XXXI. MATTATHIAS GOMEZ [1784]

XXXII

ISAAC LEVY[1]

[1785]

I ISAAC LEVY of New York in the Province of New York do declare this to be my last Will and Testament revoking and annulling all former Wills & Testaments of every Sort Kind or Nature by me made whatsoever. My Will is that all my real Estate of every kind & denomination at my decease shall become the Property of my Son ASHER[2] & my daughter ESTHER[3] otherwise called HENRIETTA & I do give the same to them as also all my personal Estate I give & bequeath to them my said Son ASHER & my Daughter ESTHER otherwise called HENRIETTA both borne of ELIZABETH PUE, My Will is that all my real & personal Estate shall be equally divided between them at the times they respectively become of Age & on Conditions hereafter mentioned. My Will is that in Case of

[1] Albany Will L48, Clerk's Office of the Court of Appeals, Albany, New York; Will Liber 38, p. 231, *NYHSC*, vol. XIII (1905), pp. 228–229. Isaac Levy (July 19, 1706–March, 1777), son of Moses Levy (see Will) and his first wife Rebecca Asher, was a prominent merchant who at various times lived in New York City, Philadelphia, Boston, and London. Probably born in London, he remained there as a merchant until sometime in 1727 when he appeared in the Supreme Court as plaintiff (though he is identified as a resident of London). *Levy v. Sommans* (1727), Minutes of Supreme Court, vol. 1723–1727, p. 241, New York County Clerk's Office. See also pp. 252, 265 and 283, and vol. 1727–1732, pp. 3, 18 and 21. In 1728, he filed charges of assault in the case of *Levy v. Silvester* (1728), MCP, file 1725–1729, Dec. 7, 1728, MCM, vol. 1728–1731, pp. 121 and 149–150. Other cases in which he was involved in New York are *Soumans v. Isaac Levy and Executors of Nathan Simpson* (1730), Chancery Minutes, vol. 1720–1748, pp. 64–66, New York County Clerk's Office; *Levy v. Fowler* (1730), Minutes of Supreme Court, vol. 1727–1732, p. 248; *Levy v. Bradford* (1734), *ibid.*, vol. 1732–1739, p. 109; narrative form of *Levy v. Bradford* in 1737 in William Bradford Manuscripts, New-York Historical Society Library. In June 1737 and 1738, he was in New York to settle business affairs with his step-mother Grace Mears Levy. Abigail Franks to Naphtali Franks, Abigail Franks Letters. See also action of *David Hays, et al. v. Nathan Levy et al.* (1738), Chancery Decrees before 1800, File H, No. 19, Clerk's Office of the Court of Appeals, Albany. Sometime in 1741, he returned to England and seems to have remained there until 1750 when he appears again in a court case with his brother Nathan. *Nathan and Isaac Levy v. Marks* (1750), MCM, vol. 1750–1751, p. 9. In 1761, he seems to be in Philadelphia. Abigail Franks Letters (Lee M. Friedman Collection, American Jewish Historical Society), *passim*; Edwin Wolf, 2nd, and Maxwell Whiteman, *The History of the Jews of Philadelphia from Colonial Times to the Age of Jackson* (Philadelphia, 1957), p. 44. For business activities, see *ibid.*, pp. 22–26; NOL CO 5/1222, entry of June 5, 1721 reveals that Levy, as part owner of the *Crown Gally* of London, brought 117 slaves from Africa; *ibid.*, entry of July 21, 1721 reveals that, as part owner of the *Postillion*, he brought to London a varying cargo including elephants' teeth, pitch and logwood, etc. See also Entry Books, vol. I, items 706 and 1244; vol. II, item 1920 *et passim*. For the testator's congregational activities, see *PAJHS*, vol. XXI (1913), pp. 8, 22–23, 25 and 38.

[2] Asher Levy (d. Aug. 1785) possibly was in Philadelphia in 1783. Herbert Friedenwald, "Jews in the American Revolution," *PAJHS*, vol. X (1902), p. 165. For Asher Levy's will, see Will Book T, pp. 183–184, Registry of Wills, City Hall, Philadelphia.

[3] Esther Henrietta Levy married Matthias Williamson. Will of Asher Levy, *ibid.*

the death of either my said Son or Daughter before he or She become of Age of Twenty One Years that then in such case the whole of my real & Personal Estate I give to the Surviver, & in Case both die before they become of Age of Twenty One years that then & in such Case I give all my real & personal Estate to my Brother SAMSON LEVY[4] & my Sister RACHEL SEIXAS Wife of ISAAC SEIXAS[5] equally to be divided between them. My Will is that neither my Son nor Daughter shall Marry or enter into Matrimonial Contract before the Age of Twenty one years, My Will is that in Case my Son or Daughter marry or enter into Matrimonial contract before he or She become of Age that then he or She so Marrying or entering into Matrimonial Contract shall have no Share or part of my Estate but the Share of he or She that doth marry or enter into matrimonial Contract shall be given to the other that doth not marry contrary to this my Will & if they both marry or enter into matrimonial Contract before the Age of Twenty one years that then & in such Case I give my whole Estate real and personal to my said Brother SAMSON LEVY and my Sister RACHEL SEIXAS, My Will is & I appoint my said Brother SAMSON LEVY his Son MOSES LEVY[6] & My Son ASHER LEVY to be my Executors of this my Last Will and Testament and during my Son ASHERS Minority or till he becomes of Age my Will is that my Brother SAMSON LEVY & his Son MOSES LEVY do act as my Executors. — ISAAC LEVY |Seal| Signed & Sealed as the Last Will and Testament of ISAAC LEVY in the presence of us the Twenty Second of October one thousand seven hundred and seventy six. WALTER SHEE, BENJ^N^. CONDY. EDMUND NIKELL

GEORGE CAMPBELL Esquire Register for the Probate of Wills & Granting Letters of Administration in and for the City & County of Philadelphia. —

To all whom it may Concern

Greeting —

These are to Certify that the foregoing writing is an Exemplification and true Copy from the Original Will Examined allowed and Filed in the Registers Office at Philadelphia — Given under the Seal of Office the

8th day of November A.D. 1785

s/ GEO. CAMPBELL Esqr.

[4] Samson Levy (1722–1781) was the son of Grace Mears and Moses Levy and Isaac's half-brother. Perhaps this conditional legacy was an attempt to salve a conscience growing out of his controversy with his step-mother. For Samson's congregational activities, see *PAJHS*, vol. XXI (1913), pp. 45, 53 and 55. See also *supra*, Will of Moses Levy, pp. 37–38, note 8. Wolf and Whiteman, *op. cit.*, pp. 388–389. For Philadelphia property, see Conveyance Libers I 9, cp. 85, and D 15, cp. 413, Department of Records, City Hall, Philadelphia.

[5] Isaac Mendes Seixas (September 5, 1709–November 3, 1782) married the testator's half sister Rachel Levy sometime before July 6, 1740. See *supra*, Will of Abraham Mendes Seixas, p. 99, note 4.

[6] Moses Levy (1756–1826) graduated from the University of Pennsylvania in 1772 and was admitted to the bar. He became an Episcopalian. Wolf and Whiteman, *op. cit.*, pp. 31, 43 and 63.

City of New York SS: Be it Remembered that I have admitted JOSHUA ISAACS[7] of the City of New York Merchant a Creditor of ISAAC LEVY formerly of the same place but late of the City of Philadelphia Merchant deceased Administrator of the said ISAAC LEVY with his will annexed (the Executors of the said Will being all absent from this State) and the said JOSHUA ISAACS having been duly sworn and given bond before me this day given under my hand the sixteenth day of November in the year of our Lord one thousand seven hundred and eighty-five.

s/ THOMAS TREDWELL Judge of
Probates

[7] Possibly Joshua Isaacs (1744–1810), the son of Joshua (see Will), who served in the Revolutionary Army. *Portraits*, p. 317, *Dictionary*, p. 68. A Joshua Isaacs listed as a merchant in 1786 was located at 8 Water Street, New York City. *Directory, 1786*, p. 34. He was arrested during a business visit to South Carolina on the petition of Manuel Myers (see Will). MCP, file 1786, Petition of Joshua Isaacs.

XXXIII

JOSEPH ISRAEL LEVY[1]

[1786]

In the name of God amen I JOSEPH ISRAEL LEVY Living in Calcutta in the Kingdom of Bengall Inhabitant being in Badly Health and of Sound and Disposing mind and memory and Considering the Perels and Other uncertainties of this transitory Life (do for avoiding controversies after my Decease make Publish and Declare this my Last will and testament in manner following (that is to say) first I Recommend my Soul to God that give it and my Body to the Earth as it shall Please God to Order and as for and concerning all my worldly Estate and Effects I give bequeath and Dispose thereof as followeth that is to Say unto my Daughter ABEGAEL ISRAEL LEVY one thousand Peunds Sterling at the time of my Decease to be left in the Hands of Mr. ABRAHAM LEVY merchant in London to be applied to the Best advantge that is to Say that money to be Put to Land Interest and that Interest to be for the use of Bring her up untill she is Twenty one years of age or in Case of her Decease that money is to go to my mother and I give unto my mother ROSEY ISRAEL — Living in Houndsdetch near algate London five hundred Peunds Sterling more and in Case of my mother and my Daughters Decease as it shall Please God there money is to go to my Brothers and Sisters I Likewise give five Hundred Peunds Sterling more unto the Jews Collige[2] in Jerusaelm and unto they Poor widow and Poor fatherless and motherless Children in London two Hundred Peund Sterling more. I further more give unto the mother of my Child named JABECA five Hundred arcot Rupees and two Slave girls and the Garden and the House with everything belonging unto her to be Payd her here by my Executors at the time of my Decease and the Other amount of all Such Sum and Sums of money Lands Tenements Goods Chattels and Estate whatsoever as shall be any ways due owing or belonging unto me at the time of my Decease I do give Devise and bequeath the Same unto my Brothers and Sisters in London or Elsewhere Each to have Eagael and I do hereby naminate and appoint Mr. ABRAHAM

[1] Albany Will L-38; Will Liber 39, p. 34; *NYHSC*, vol. XIII (1905), pp. 331–332. Little is known of Joseph Israel Levy in American and English sources. His will was published in England in 1785. Arnold, *op. cit.*, p. 178. See *infra*, Will no. XXXV, pp. 186–188 of Joseph Israel Levy [1789], particularly footnote 1 on page 186.

[2] There is no evidence of a Jews' College in Jerusalem in the eighteenth century. Probably the testator referred to a *yeshivah* or similar school.

LEVY merchant in London and Mr. CHARLES WESTON Mr. JOSEPH POLLARD and ROBERT BROWN to be my true and Lawfoll Executors joinly of this my Last will and Testament hereby Revoking all former and Other wills Testaments and deeds of Gifts by me at any time heretofor made and I do Ordain and Ratify this Presents to Stand and be for and as my only Last will and Testament in Witness whereof to this my Said will I have Set my hand and Seal in Calcutta the Second day of January one thousand Seven Hundred and Seventy Two and in the Twelve year of the Reign of his majesty KING GEORGE the THIRD Over Great Britain, etc.

Signed Sealed wher no Stamp Paper was to be had in the Presents of us
s/ ANTH^o^. O BRIEN
s/ JAMES MILLER
this is the Copy

s/ JOSEPH ISRAEL LEVY

[seal]

City of New York SS. Be It Remembered that on the twenty seventh day of April in the year of our Lord one thousand seven hundred and Eighty six personally came and appeared before me THOMAS TREDWELL Judge of the Court of Probates of the State of New York MOSES ISRAEL[3] Gentleman, and on the twenty eighth SOLOMON SIMSON Merchant both of the said City and being duly sworn on their oaths declared that they had often seen JOSEPH ISRAEL LEVY the Testator write, that they Were Well acquainted with his Character and manner of hand writing and that they Verily believe the Name JOSEPH ISRAEL LEVY subscribed to the within Will to be the Proper hand writing of the said JOSEPH ISRAEL LEVY.

s/ THOMAS TREDWELL

City of New York SS. Be It Also Remembered that I have admitted SAMUEL ISRAEL of the City of New York Gentleman a brother and Creditor of JOSEPH ISRAEL LEVY late of Calcutta in the Kingdom of Bengall Merchant Deceased Administrator with his Will annexed of the goods Chattels and Credits of the said JOSEPH ISRAEL LEVY (the Executors of the said Will being Absent beyond Seas) the said SAMUEL ISRAEL having been duly sworn and given bond before me

[3] Possibly the Moses Israel (b. 1762) who attended a meeting of the congregation on December 21, 1783. *PAJHS*, vol. XXI (1913), p. 142; *Dictionary*, p. 70.

Witness My hand this twenty eighth day of April in the year of our Lord one thousand seven hundred and Eighty six

s/ THOMAS TREDWELL

JOSEPH ISRAEL LEVY

The People of the State of New York By The Grace of God Free and Independent To SAMUEL ISRAEL[4] of the City of New York Gentleman & brother of JOSEPH ISRAEL LEVY late of Calcutta in the Kingdom of Bengal Merchant deceased *Send Greeting Whereas* the said JOSEPH ISRAEL LEVY did in his lifetime make his last Will and testament in writing bearing date the second day of January in the year of our Lord one thousand seven hundred and seventy two and

Thereby appointed ABRAHAM LEVY, CHARLES WESTON, JOSEPH POLLARD and ROBERT BROWN Executors of his said Will and soon after died *And Whereas* afterwards on the day of the Date hereof and on the day next preceding the same at the City of New York before THOMAS TREDWELL Esquire Judge of our Court of Probates the said Will was Proved and is now approved and allowed of by us and the aforesaid ABRAHAM LEVY, CHARLES WESTON, JOSEPH POLLARD and ROBERT BROWN the Executors thereof are absent beyond the seas and We desiring that the goods, Chattels and Credits of the said Deceased may be well and faithfully Administered, applied and disposed of according to the true intent and meaning of his said Will (a Copy whereof is herein to annexed) Do grant unto you the said SAMUEL ISRAEL full power during the absence of the said Executors to Collect, levy, recover and receive all and singular the goods, Chattels and credits of the said Deceased and the same to Administer and dispose of according to the Tenor and effect of his said Will and as the law directs you being first duly to fulfil the Will of the said Deceased and to pay his debts and legacies as far forth as his goods, Chattels, and Credits will thereto extend and the law bind you and also to make or Cause to be made a true and perfect Inventory of all and singular the goods, Chattels and Credits of the said Deceased which have or shall come to

[4] Samuel Israel also attended meetings of the congregation in 1783, 1785, and 1786. *PAJHS*, vol. XXI (1913), pp. 148–149 and 159. He was very litigious, see *Israel v. Regensburg* (1785), MCP, file 1785, August, 1785; *Israel v. Hayman Solomon* (1786), MCP, file 1786, July 24, 1786.

your hands, possession or knowledge and to exhibit the same unto the registry of the Court of Probates of this State on or before the twenty eighth day of November next ensuing and also to render a just and true account when thereunto lawfully requested And We do by the presents ordain, depute, constitute and appoint you the said SAMUEL ISRAEL Administrator of all and singular the goods, Chattels and Credits of the said Deceased together with his said Will annexed during the absence of the said Executors.

In Testimony whereof we have Caused the seal of our Court of Probates to be hereunto affixed *Witness* THOMAS TREDWELL Esquire Judge of our said Court at the City of New york the twenty eighth day of April in the year of our Lord one Thousand seven hundred and Eighty six.

s/ DAV[D]. JUDSON
Clk.

XXXIV

HAYMAN LEVY[1]

[1789]

In the Name of God Amen

I HAYMAN LEVY of the City of New York Merchant being of sound and disposing Mind Memory and Understanding to the God of Israel be ascribed the Praise! Do make and ordain this my last Will and Testament in manner and form following (that is to say) *First* I do will and direct that all my just debts be duly paid and satisfied which have been by me contracted since the twenty third day of January which was in the Year One thousand seven hundred and sixty five the time I made a Surrender of all [my] then property for the benefit of my then Creditors *And as for and Concern[ing]* All my Real and Personal Estates I do dispose of the same as hereinafter is mentioned. In consideration of the Love Affection and Fidelity which I have experienced from my dear beloved Wife SLOE LEVY[2] I do Give and devise unto my Said Wife All that my Mess[uage] or Tenement wherein I now dwell situate in Duke Street[3] together with the Lot of Ground leading back into Mill Street whereon the same is erected And all the Store houses Outhouses and other Appurtenances thereunto belonging and now occupied therewith *To Hold* the same and every part and parcel thereof during the term of her natural Life if she shall so long continue my Widow and unmarried But in case she shall

[1] Original Will unnumbered, HDC; Will Liber 40, p. 282; *NYHSC*, vol. XIV (1906), pp. 165–166. Hayman Levy (January 15, 1721–August 20, 1789), a merchant, was made freeman December 20, 1750. One of the most noted of New York Jews, he had a long and noteworthy career. Born in Germany, he made and lost several fortunes. During the Revolution, he left New York City and went to Philadelphia where he joined a militia company. He returned after the war and opened a commission store at 7 Duke Street. *Portraits*, pp. 252–259; *Directory, 1786*, p. 37; *Burghers*, p. 171. He owned considerable property in New York. Conveyance Libers 36, cp. 398, 448–450; 37, cp. 17; 56, cp. 66; 57, cp. 178. His career was a stormy one, as is evidenced in part by his frequent appearance in court. In 1757, he was brought into criminal court for creating a nuisance and was fined. *King v. Levy* (1757), Minutes of the Court of General Sessions, vol. 1742–1760, August 4, 1757, November 2, 1757, and February 9, 1758. See also *Nicholson v. Levi* (1785), MCP, file 1785, October 3, 1785, *Levy v. Van Maaren* (1752), MCP, file 1750–1752, May 13, 1752.

Levy also had a considerable interest in the Synagogue and was elected six times as *parnas*, first in 1760 and the last time in 1788. *PAJHS*, vol. XXI (1913), p. 211. For an extended biography, see *Portraits*, pp. 252–259.

An interesting feature of this will is the interrogatories taken after his death to prove the will. It was finally accepted by the court. *NYHSC*, vol. XIV (1906), p. 166.

[2] Sloe Myers Levy (1728–1811), daughter of Solomon Myers and granddaughter of Myer Myers, married the testator on May 15, 1750. *Portraits*, p. 324; *PAJHS*, vol. IV (1896), p. 210. For reference to her properties, see Conveyance Liber 53, cp. 230 and 232.

[3] Levy resided at 7 Duke Street. *Directory, 1790*, p. 62.

again intermarry or in case she die before the expiration of Ten Years after my decease Then I do Give and devise the said Messuage or Tenement Lot of Ground and Premises as aforesaid unto my Son [ ] SOLOMON HAYMAN LEVY[4] and my Son in Law ISAAC MOSES[5] *Upon Trust* that they the said SOLOMON HAYMAN LEVY and ISAAC MOSES or the Survivor of them or the Executors or Administrators of such Survivor shall and do lease or let out the said hereinbefore devised Messuage or Tenement and Premises during so much of the said Term of ten years after my decease which shall be unexpired at the decease of my said Wife or her intermarriage again whichever shall first happen And by and with the Monies thereby arising shall and place the same in the Capital or Stock in Trade to be established for the support of my said Wife and my [minor] or unmarried Children[6] as hereinafter directed with the residue and remainder of my real and personal Estates And from and after the expiration of the said term of ten years after my decease Then I do Give and devise the said Messuage or Tenement Lot of Ground and Premises hereinbefore devised with their and every of their appurtenances unto and amongst all my Children and to their Heirs and Assigns share and share alike as Tenants in Common Except the equal part or share which will devolve to my Daughter ZIPPORAH[7] which said equal part or share of my said Messuage or Tenement Lot of Ground and Premises with the appurtenances I do Give and devise unto my said Daughter ZIPPORAH for and during the term of her natural Life and after her decease Then I do Give and devise the said equal part or share of my said Daughter ZIPPORAH as aforesaid unto the said SOLOMON HAYMAN LEVY and ISAAC MOSES *Upon Trust* that they the said SOLOMON HAYMAN LEVY and ISAAC MOSES or the Survivor of them or the Executor or Administrator of such Survivor shall and will dispose of the same to the best advantage and place the Monies thereby arising out at Interest for the benefit of all the Children of my said Daughter ZIPPORAH untill her youngest Child[8] shall have at-

[4] Solomon Hayman Levy (1764–1841), married to Rebecca Hendricks, was a frequent contributor to Shearith Israel. *PAJHS*, vol. XXVII (1920), pp. 41, 168 and 185. He was involved in the action of *Levy v. Rowes* (1794), MCP, file 1794, February 25, 1794.

[5] Isaac Moses (1742–1818) was the testator's son-in-law, having married his daughter Reyna. A merchant, he resided at 37 Dock Street. He became a freeman October 22, 1766 as a cordwainer. He too was a frequent contributor to Shearith Israel. *Directory, 1786*, p. 38; *Burghers*, p. 213; *PAJHS*, vol. XXVII (1920), p. 168. See also *supra*, Will of Isaac Adolphus, p. 147, note 10.

[6] Hayman Levy had eleven children. Of these Haya Sara died May 5, 1763; Abraham on September 20, 1767 and Deborah on April 17, 1761. His surviving children were Reyna (1753–1824), Zipporah (1760–1832), Deborah (1762–1821), Isaac (1763-1854), Solomon (1764–1841), Sara (1768–1855), Richea (1770–1788) and Aaron (1771–1852). *PAJHS*, vol. XXVII (1920), p. 168.

[7] Zipporah married Benjamin M. Seixas on January 27, 1779. *Ibid.*, p. 162.

[8] Zipporah and Benjamin's youngest child was Moses B. Seixas (1780–1839). Other children alive at this time included Isaac, Rebecca, Abigail, Abraham, Solomon, and Esther. After this date, nine other children were born and one died in infancy for a total of seventeen. *Ibid.*, p. 163.

tained the age of Twenty one years; and so soon as the youngest Child of my said Daughter ZIPPORAH shall have attained the Age of Twenty one Years Then I do direct my said Trustees to divide the Monies arising by the Sale thereof together with all such Interest as may have accrued thereon (not expended for their use during their minority) to and amongst all such of the Children as shall be living when the Youngest Child shall have attained the Age of twenty one years as aforesaid. *Also* I Give and bequeath unto my said Wife All my Plate Jewells Household and Kitchen furniture for her own sole use and benefit during the term of her natural life or Widowhood as aforesaid And after her decease or intermarriage again which ever shall first happen then the same to be equally divided amongst all such of my Children who shall be living at the decease of my said Wife or her intermarriage as aforesaid or else to be then sold and the Proceeds thereof after deducting all Costs and Charges of Sale to be equally divided between my said Children as aforesaid which Sale shall be made if agreed upon by a Majority but not otherwise Except such part or share (whether divided before or after such Sale) as shall devolve to my Daughter ZIPPORAH which it is my Will and I do hereby direct shall be under the same restrictions and subject to and *Upon* the same Trusts Intents and purposes as the part or Share of my said Daughter ZIPPORAH in my Real Estate hereinbefore devised is subjected to and to and for no other use intent or purpose whatsoever *Also* I Give and bequeath unto my Daughter DEBORAH HAYMAN LEVY the Sum of One Hundred Pounds Current Money of the State of New York (over and above what I do hereinafter Give devise and bequeath to her in equal share with my other Children) to be paid to my said Daughter DEBORAH HAYMAN LEVY by my Executors and Executrix hereinafter named within twelve Months after my decease *Also* I Give and bequeath unto the Congregation of Shearith Israel the sum of Five Pounds of like Current Money to be paid by my said Executrix and Executors hereinafter named within two Months after my decease for the benefit of having an *Escoba* as is usual *And as for and Concerning* all the rest residue and remainder of my Real and Personal Estates I do Give devise and bequeath the same in manner following And I do hereby direct my Executrix and Executors hereinafter named to collect in all the Debts and Sums of Money which shall be due and owing to me at the time of my decease in the most expeditious manner that can be for the benefit of my Estate and to place the same as collected, together with such other of my personal Estate not hereinbefore given and bequeathed which shall come to their hands as a Capital or Stock in trade to be managed as hereinafter is directed for the purposes hereinafter mentioned And I do further direct that my two Sons ISAAC H. LEVY[9] and AARON HAYMAN LEVY shall have the management and carry on Business with the said Capital or Stock in Trade

[9] Isaac H. Levy, shopkeeper, continued to reside at 7 Duke Street after his father's death. *Directory, 1790*, p. 62. He served as a juror in the Mayor's Court on January 10, 1792. MCP, file 1792, Panel of Jurors.

under the firm of Isaac H. Levy and Company[10] and keep a regular set of books of Accounts in that concern during the life time or Widowhood of my said Wife But in case my said Wife should die or intermarry before my youngest Child attains the Age of Twenty one years or being in either of these cases then only until my said Youngest Child attains the Age of Twenty one years or being a Daughter is married under the direction and inspection of my Son SOLOMON HAYMAN LEVY and my son in Law ISAAC MOSES. And it is my Will, and my desire is, that my said Sons ISAAC H. LEVY and AARON HAYMAN LEVY, shall deduct One sixth of the Net Profits arising from such Trade for their Trouble in the Management thereof And the remaining four sixths parts of the Net Profits from such Trade to be appropriated for the support of said Wife during her life or so long thereof only as she continues my widow as aforesaid and of my minor and unmarried Children And for that purpose I do hereby impower my said Son SOLOMON HAYMAN LEVY and my said son in Law ISAAC MOSES to advance or procure to be advanced such Sum or sums of Money and Merchandize as they shall judge proper and also in case they or either of them the said ISAAC H. LEVY or AARON HAYMAN LEVY shall misbehave or act imprudently (whereby my intention appears likely to be frustrated) in this charge committed to their management (which God forbid) then my said wife if my Widow (but not otherwise) my said Son SOLOMON HAYMAN LEVY and my said Son in Law ISAAC MOSES shall by Virtue of this my Will be empowered and I do hereby empower them to withdraw the whole of the said Stock in Trade and Books of Accounts out of the hands of the said ISAAC H. LEVY and AARON HAYMAN LEVY and pursue such measures therewith as they shall judge most conducive to answer my intended purpose for supporting my Wife during her Life or Widowhood as aforesaid and my minor and unmarried Children *And Whereas* the said residue of my Personal Estate may not prove adequate to the purpose of establishing a sufficient Capital or Stock in Trade to answer the intent of supporting my Wife during her Lifetime or her Widowhood as aforesaid and my minor and unmarried Children and it may therefore be found expedient to sell or dispose of a part of my Real Estates not hereinbefore given and devised I do therefore hereby empower my Executrix (if she be then my Widow but not otherwise) and Executors herein named or the Survivors or Survivor of them to sell and dispose of all such parts thereof in Fee Simple as they shall judge proper for that purpose And it is my wish and I do recommend them not to do it but in case the most pressing necessity should require such a measure it being my desire that the same shall continue undivided for the space of Ten years after my decease But should such an expedient be found absolutely necessary, then only such parts thereof to be sold as may be competent to establish a sufficient Capital or Stock in Trade for the purposes aforesaid And should there

[10] Isaac H. Levy and Company had a store at 2 Water Street. In 1807 Aaron went into a partnership with Isaac Moses and Sons. *Directory, 1790*, p. 62; *PAJHS*, vol. XXVII (1920), p. 337.

be no necessity to part with any of my said Estates or being such a part should still remain unsold Then I do Give and devise the whole of such part thereof as is unsold unto the said SOLOMON HAYMAN LEVY and the said ISAAC MOSES or the Survivor of them or the [Executors] or Administrators of such Survivor *Upon* the several *Trusts* and to and for the several Uses Intents and purposes hereinafter mentioned (that is to say) *Upon Trust* that they the said SOLOMON HAYMAN LEVY and ISAAC MOSES or the Survivor of them or the Executors and Administrators of such Survivor shall and will lease out or otherwise appropriate the same to a yearly Income during the natural life or Widowhood of my said Wife or in case of the death or intermarriage of my said Wife during the term of Ten years after my decease, which said yearly income after deducting all costs or charges incident shall every year be added to the Capital or Stock in Trade for the purposes aforesaid so long as such Trade is continued and carried on by Virtue of this my Will *Then Upon This Further Trust* that all the rest and residue of my Real Estates at the expiration of Ten years after my decease in case my said Wife should then be dead or have intermarried (or if then in Life not untill she does die or intermarry) and the whole Stock in Trade [?] shall be accumulated at the decease of my said Wife or her intermarriage which I direct shall be exactly stated from the Books of Accounts of such Copartnery as aforesaid to be kept for that purpose shall be divided in equal proportions to and amongst all my Children at that time living or in case of the death of any Child or Children leaving lawfull Issue then the part or share of the one so dying shall devolve and go to and be divided amongst all the issue of him her or them so dying and to their heirs and assigns forever as Tenants in Common *Except* the part or share which will devolve to my Daughter ZIPPORAH which said part or share of the rest and residue of my Real and Personal Estate as aforesaid I do Give devise and bequeath the same unto my said Daughter ZIPPORAH for and during the term of her natural Life and after her decease Then I do Give devise and bequeath the said equal part or share of the rest and residue of my Real and Personal Estates unto the said SOLOMON HAYMAN LEVY and ISAAC MOSES *Upon Trust* that they the said SOLOMON HAYMAN LEVY and ISAAC MOSES or the Survivor of them or the Executors or Administrators of such survivor shall and will dispose of the same and appropriate the Monies thereby arising in like manner and to and for the like Uses Intents and purposes as I have directed concerning the equal proportion which will devolve to my said Daughter ZIPPORAH or her issue in the Messuage or Tenement and Premises with the Appurtenances wherein I now dwell as given and devised to my said Trustees in the former part of this my Will *And Whereas* I have advanced several sums of money to my Son in Law BENJAMIN SEIXAS[11]

[11] Benjamin M. Seixas (1748–1817), son of Isaac M. Seixas, a saddler, became a freeman on February 8, 1769. He was one of the founders of the New York Stock Exchange and was also prominent in congregational affairs. *Portraits*, p. 378; *Dictionary*, p. 154; *Burghers*, p. 225; *PAJHS*, vol. XXVII (1920), p. 161. For litigation, see *Noyes v. Seixas* (1792), MCP, file 1792, July 10, 1792 (Mr. Wilkins Rules).

as part of portion with my Daughter ZIPPORAH and although I have exonerated and discharged the said BENJAMIN SEIXAS from some Debts due and owing to me, yet no part of such discharge is intended to [effect] the Sums of Money advanced as part of her portion *And Whereas* I have likewise advanced certain Monies and Goods to my said Son SOLOMON HAYMAN LEVY as an outfit for him I do therefore hereby direct and it is my will and desire that said sum and Sums of Monies and the amount of Goods so advanced and for which they do respectively stand indebted to me shall be considered as a part of the residue of my Personal Estate and shall be deducted from the proportions which will fall to the share of my said Daughter ZIPPORAH and my said Son SOLOMON HAYMAN LEVY respectively or their respective issue entitled thereto in case of the Death of either leaving such at the time of the division of my Real or Personal Estate anything in this my Will contained to the contrary thereof in anywise notwithstanding, *And* it is my intent and meaning and I hereby direct that the Gifts Devises and bequests so made to my said Wife in and by this my Will as aforesaid shall be considered in lieu and full compensation of all her Dower or Title of Dower *And Lastly* I do hereby Nominate Constitute and Appoint my loving wife SLOE LEVY so long as she shall continue my Widow and unmarried (but no longer) my Sons ISAAC H. LEVY, SOLOMON HAYMAN LEVY, AARON HAYMAN LEVY (so soon as he shall have attained the Age of Twenty one years) and my Son in law ISAAC MOSES, Executrix and joint Executors of this my Last Will and Testament And I do hereby revoke all former Wills by me at any time heretofore made *In Witness* whereof I the said HAYMAN LEVY have to this my said Last Will and Testament contained in six sides of Paper to the first five sides thereof set my Hand and to the last Side thereof Set my Hand and Seal the day of In the year One Thousand Seven hundred and eighty nine and teenth of the Independence of the United States.

Signed, Sealed, Published and declared by the said HAYMAN LEVY the Testator as and for his last Will and Testament in the presence of us who at his request, in his presence and in the presence of each other have subscribed our names as Witnesses to the same
The word "Wife" being first interlined in the twenty fifth line of the third side).

* * *

EXHIBIT A

On Friday the eleventh day of September one Thousand Seven Hundred and eighty Nine This Instrument was shewn unto STEPHEN PATERSON and GERSHOM SEIXAS[12] and on Thursday the Seventeenth day of September in the same year was shewn unto CHARLES MCKNIGHT[13] and by them severally deposed to in their answers to Interogatories concerning the Testament and last Will of HAYMAN LEVY late of the City of New York merchant Deceased

DAVID GELSTON, Surrogate[14]

* * *

I, DAVID GELSTON Esquire Surrogate of the City and County of New York

The Petition of ISAAC H. LEVY, SOLOMON HAYMAN LEVY and ISAAC MOSES sheweth:

That HAYMAN LEVY, late of the City of New York Merchant, deceased, on or about the twenty ninth day of June last past made his last Will and Testament in writing, and appointed your Petitioners, together with his wife SLOE LEVY, so long as she should continue his widow and unmarried, and his son, AARON HAYMAN LEVY as soon as he should attain the age of twenty one years as Executors thereof

Your Petitioners therefore pray that the same Testament may be duly proved and approved of, and that Letters testamentary thereof may be granted to them in due form of Law — And your Petitioners shall ever pray.

s/ ISAAC H. LEVY
s/ SOLOMON HAYMAN LEVY
s/ ISAAC MOSES

New York
April 2nd 1789

* * *

[12] Gershom M. Seixas (1746-1816), son of Isaac M. Seixas, had a long and distinguished career as spokesman for American Jewry. He was elected *ḥazzan* in 1768 and remained in that office until his death. He was also for many years a trustee of Columbia College. *PAJHS*, vol. XXI (1913), p. 208. See also pp. 100, 103, *et passim*.

[13] Charles McKnight (1750-1791), a physician, died soon after this deposition was taken. See *Barrons v. Mary McKnight, exec. of Charles McKnight decd* (1792), MCP, file 1792, April 3, 1792 (Mr. Boyd's Rules). In his will dated October 13, 1791 and proved December 2, 1791, the doctor left everything to his wife Mary. Will Liber 40, p. 496. He was Port physician and professor of surgery at Columbia College. Martha Lamb and Mrs. Burton Harrison, *History of the City of New York* (New York, 1896), vol. II, p. 284.

[14] David Gelston served as Surrogate of New York County from March 30, 1787 to August, 1801. *Civil List*, p. 359. He had been a delegate to the Continental Congress. *Ibid.*, p. 116.

City and County of New York } *SS.*
Surrogates Office

Interrogatories to be administered to STEPHEN PATTERSON A witness to be produced Sworn and Examined before DAVID GELSTON Esquire Surrogate of the City and County of New York, concerning a certain Written Instrument purporting to be the Testament and last Will of HAYMAN LEVY late of the City of New York Merchant deceased, and produced and offered to be proved as such by ISAAC H. LEVY, SOLOMON HAYMAN LEVY, and ISAAC MOSES three of the Executors in the said Written Instrument or Testament named.

Imprimis — What is your Age? and what is your occupation in Life?

Secondly — Did you know HAYMAN LEVY late of the City of New York Merchant? And how long did you know him? Declare!

Thirdly — Do you know the Instrument of Writing now shewn unto you contained in two sheets of paper connected by a black Seal and marked on the back Exhibit A? declare fully what you know respecting the same.

Fourthly — Did you ever shew the said Instrument of Writing distinguished and Marked as aforesaid "Exhibit A" after the same was engrossed by you? If the same was Ingrossed by you to the said HAYMAN LEVY? Was the same read to him by any person and by whom? and where? as you know and believe, Was it truly read to him and has the same been since altered or is the same Instrument now produced in the words read to him the said HAYMAN LEVY and was the same approved of by him the said HAYMAN LEVY as his last Will and Testament? What did he say upon the same being read to him?

Fifthly — Do you know what was the reason that the said HAYMAN LEVY did not at that time Execute and sign the same? declare fully what you know thereof.

Sixthly — Do you know anything else of and concerning or in relation to the said Instrument Writing Marked as aforesaid Exhibit "A" and now shewn unto you?

* * *

City and County of New York } *Surrogate Office*

Depositions of Witnesses produced, sworn and examined on Interrogatories on Friday, the eleventh day of September in the year of our Lord one Thousand seven hundred and Eighty nine Before me DAVID GELSTON Esquire Surrogate of the City and County of New York concerning a certain written Instrument purporting to be the Testament and last Will of HAYMAN LEVY, late of the City of New York, merchant, deceased, and produced and offered to be proved as such, by ISAAC H. LEVY, SOLOMON HAYMAN LEVY and ISAAC MOSES, three of the Executors in the said written Instrument or Testament named

---

STEPHEN PATERSON of the City of New York being produced, sworn and examined, deposeth as follows

To the first Interrogatory, this deponent saith: That his age is thirty four years; that his occupation in life is that of Scrivener.

To the second Interrogatory, this deponent saith that he was acquainted with the said HAYMAN LEVY for the space of five years last past.

To the third Interrogatory, this deponent saith that he is perfectly acquainted with the paper writing marked Exhibit A now shewn unto him and the same is his own hand writing that in the month of June last past he received Instructions from the said HAYMAN LEVY to draw his last Will and Testament that according to his instructions he made a draft of the same Will and that on shewing the said draft to the said HAYMAN LEVY for his approbation he the said HAYMAN LEVY did after some alterations made by himself approve thereof and delivered the same draft again to this deponent that the same might be by him fairly copied. That thereupon this deponent copied the same according to the directions of the said HAYMAN LEVY and that the said Instrument in writing now shewn unto this deponent marked Exhibit A is the very instrument of writing so by him as aforesaid copied pursuant to the instructions of the said HAYMAN LEVY.

To the fourth Interrogatory this deponent saith that on the Evening of the twentyninth of June last past he shewed the said HAYMAN LEVY the said Instrument in writing now shewn unto him marked Exhibit A purporting to be the last Will and Testament of the said HAYMAN

Levy and that then and there this deponent read the said Instrument in writing justly and truly and in the very words in which it now is unto him the said Hayman Levy and at the time and after reading the same the said Hayman Levy declared his full approbation of the same.

To the fifth Interrogatory this deponent saith, that on showing the said instrument in writing above referred to by him and now shewn unto him marked Exhibit A unto the said Hayman Levy at the time aforesaid to wit on the evening of the twenty ninth of June last past and after the same was read to him by this deponent and by him the said Hayman Levy approved of as his last Will and Testament and that then he said to this deponent that he the said Hayman Levy would then execute the said Instrument in writing as his last will and Testament but that he was desirous to have the same witnessed by this deponent and two Clerks living with Isaac Moses and that it then being late in the day their attendance could not be obtained and that for this reason he the said Hayman Levy would for the present defer signing of his last Will and Testament and the said Hayman Levy then said he would sign the same at some other time.

To the Sixth Interrogatory this deponent answers No.

s/ Step[n] Paterson

Sworn before me
David Gelston

* * *

City and County of New York } *Surrogate Office*

Interrogatories to be administered to Charles McKnight a Witness to be produced and sworn and examined before David Gelston Esquire Surrogate of the City and County of New York Concerning a written Instrument purporting to be the last Will and Testament of Hayman Levy late of the City of New York Merchant Deceased and produced and offered to be proved as such by Isaac H. Levy, Solomon Hayman Levy and Isaac Moses three of the Executors in the said Written Instrument or Testament named.

Imprimis — What is your age? and what is your Occupation in Life?

Secondly — Did you know HAYMAN LEVY late of the City of New York Merchant deceased? and how long did you know him? declare.

Thirdly — Did you know the Written paper or instrument of writing now shewn unto you contained in two sheets of Paper and Connected with a Black Seal and endorsed "Exhibit A"? did you ever see the same and where?

Fourthly — Was the said HAYMAN LEVY desirous to sign or execute the said Written Instrument Marked on the Back thereof Exhibit A. declare fully as the same appeared to you.

Fifthly — Did the said HAYMAN LEVY at this time or at any other time say anything respecting the Written papers now shewn unto you distinguished as aforesaid and marked on the back thereof "Exhibit A" and what did he say? declare fully thereto.

Sixthly — Had the said HAYMAN LEVY his perfect senses and understanding at this time to your belief?

Seventhly — Do you know anything else of or concerning or relative to the said Instrument of Writing marked as aforesaid Exhibit A? If you do declare the same.

Deposition of CHARLES MCKNIGHT, produced sworn and examined on Interrogatories on Thursday the Seventeenth day of September in the year of our Lord one thousand, seven hundred and eighty nine Before me, DAVID GELSTON Esquire, Surrogate of the City and County of New York, concerning a certain written Instrument purporting to be the Testament and Last Will of HAYMAN LEVY late of the City of New York, Merchant, deceased, and produced and offered to be proved as such, by ISAAC H. LEVY, SOLOMON HAYMAN LEVY and ISAAC MOSES, three of the Executors in the said written instrument, or Testament named.

To the first Interrogatory, this deponent saith — that he is a Resident of the City of New York, that his age is thirty-eight that his occupation in Life is that of a Physician.

To the second Interrogatory this deponent saith that he hath known the said HAYMAN LEVY for the four years last past and hath attended him and his family in the line of his profession.

To the third Interrogatory this deponent saith that on the evening of Wednesday the nineteenth day of August last this deponent was sent for to attend the said HAYMAN LEVY then in his last Illness, that on entering the Room this deponent found him in company with the Reverend GERSHOM SEIXAS, apparently in the act of praying and near his dissolution that the said HAYMAN LEVY then held in his left hand the written paper or Instrument now shewn unto this deponent contained in two sheets of papers connected with a black seal indorsed on the back Exhibit A and in his right hand a pen without Ink in the posture or situation of writing.

To the fourth Interrogatory this deponent saith that he fully believes the said HAYMAN LEVY wished to sign or execute the same paper writing now shewn unto him marked Exhibit A as aforesaid as he the said HAYMAN LEVY made every effort his situation would admit of to do the same and in the strongest manner possible at that time evinced his desire therefor.

To the fifth Interrogatory this deponent saith that the said HAYMAN LEVY held the same written paper marked Exhibit A and now shewn unto him in his left hand as this deponent hath above declared and that on this deponents entering the Room and standing by the side of the said HAYMAN LEVY this deponent inquired of the Reverend GERSHOM SEIXAS who at that time was very near the said HAYMAN LEVY what paper that was the said HAYMAN LEVY held in his hand upon which the said GERSHOM SEIXAS answered in the presence and hearing of the said HAYMAN LEVY that the paper he (the said HAYMAN LEVY meaning) held in his hand was his Will (the will of the said HAYMAN LEVY meaning) and that he (the said HAYMAN LEVY meaning) wanted Ink to sign or execute the same and thereupon the said HAYMAN LEVY emphatically said Yes by which this deponent understood and verily believed that the said Instrument of Writing then in the hand of the said HAYMAN LEVY and now exhibited unto this deponent and marked as aforesaid Exhibit A was intended to be declared and expressed by the said HAYMAN LEVY to be his last Will and Testament the said HAYMAN LEVY in a few minutes expired holding the said Instrument of writing marked Exhibit A as aforesaid and now shewn unto this deponent in his left hand and a pen in the other hand.

To the Sixth Interrogatory this deponent saith that the said HAYMAN LEVYS speech from the time he saw him until the time he the said HAYMAN LEVY expired was imperfect but that this deponent has no doubt and is very certain during the whole time aforesaid and until the time he the said HAYMAN LEVY expired, the said HAYMAN LEVY had his full and perfect senses and was of sound disposing mind memory and understanding.

To the Seventh Interrogatory this deponent answers, No.

Sworn before me
DAVID GELSTON

s/ CHARLES MCKNIGHT

* * *

Surrogates Office } *Ss*

Interrogatories to be administered to GERSHOM SEIXAS a witness to be produced sworn and examined before DAVID GELSTON Esquire Surrogate of the City and County of New York concerning a certain instrument purporting to be the Testament and last will of HAYMAN LEVY late of the City of New York Merchant deceased and produced and offered to be proved as such by ISAAC H. LEVY, SOLOMON HAYMAN LEVY and ISAAC MOSES three of the Executors in the said Written Instrument or Testament named.

Imprimis — What is your age? and what is your occupation in Life?

Secondly — Did you know HAYMAN LEVY late of the City of New York, Merchant deceased? and how long did you know him? declare.

Thirdly — Was you present at the last illness of the said HAYMAN LEVY? and what were the circumstances attending the same?

Fourthly — Was CHARLES MCKNIGHT of the City of New York Physician there at that time? or what time? If he was Had the said HAYMAN LEVY any Written paper in his hand at the time the said CHARLES MCKNIGHT came in and what paper was it? and had he any other paper in his hand during the time you was with him?

Fifthly — Had you any Conversation with the said CHARLES MCKNIGHT at this time relative to the said HAYMAN LEVY or concerning the said written Paper and what was the same? declare fully.

Sixthly — Is the Instrument of Writing now Shewn unto you and contained in two sheets of paper Connected by a black Seal and marked on the back "Exhibit A" the same that the said HAYMAN LEVY held in his hand and declared by him to be his Will in manner aforesaid?

Seventhly — Do you know anything else of or concerning or relative to the said Instrument of Writing Marked as aforesaid ("Exhibit A") and now shewn unto you?

* * *

GERSHOM SEIXAS of the City of New York being produced sworn and examined deposeth as follows

To the first Interrogatory this deponent saith that he is upwards of forty years of age and that he is Minister to the Jewish Congregation in this City.

To the second Interrogatory this deponent saith that he hath been acquainted with the said HAYMAN LEVY for upwards of twenty years last past.

To the third Interrogatory this deponent saith that he was present at the last Illness of the said HAYMAN LEVY that on Wednesday evening the nineteenth of August last about half an hour past ten o'clock in the same evening he was called to visit the said HAYMAN LEVY who had suddenly been taken ill that on this deponents entering the room, he found him the said HAYMAN LEVY sitting in a chair with a written paper in one hand and a pen without Ink in the other hand. That upon this deponent inquiring of him what was the matter he the said HAYMAN LEVY earnestly answered I want Ink and at the same time declared and said this is my Will. they will not give me Ink. The said HAYMAN LEVY then holding up the written paper or instrument of writing aforesaid which he then had in his hand and meaning the same as the Will of the said HAYMAN LEVY that the said HAYMAN LEVY again called for Ink and none being brought to him which this deponent attributed to the great confusion of the Family they not being able to find any, the said HAYMAN LEVY began saying the prayers of a dying Person in which this deponent joined him That shortly thereafter on the same evening CHARLES MCKNIGHT of this City Physician came in for a few minutes this deponent retired and on returning found the said HAYMAN LEVY had expired.

To the fourth Interrogatory this deponent saith that he has before said CHARLES MCKNIGHT of the City of New York Physician was present with the said HAYMAN LEVY during part of his last Illness that when the said CHARLES MCKNIGHT entered the room the said HAYMAN LEVY had the written paper before referred to by this deponent in his hand and that the said HAYMAN LEVY held the same until this deponent left him and that the said HAYMAN LEVY had no other paper whatever in his hand during the whole time this deponent was with him.

To the fifth Interrogatory this deponent saith that he had some conversation with the said CHARLES MCKNIGHT at this time respecting the said HAYMAN LEVY and the Instrument of writing aforesaid but that this deponent does not remember the same.

To the Sixth Interrogatory this deponent saith that according to the best of his knowledge and belief the Instrument of writing now shewn unto him contained in two sheets of Paper and connected by a black seal and marked Exhibit A is the same that the said HAYMAN LEVY held in his hand while this deponent was with him in his last Illness and which this deponent hath above mentioned and referred to and which by the said HAYMAN LEVY was declared to be his last will and Testament as this deponent hath above specified and declared.

To the Seventh Interrogatory this deponent answers No.

s/ GERSHOM SEIXAS

Sworn before me
DAVID GELSTON

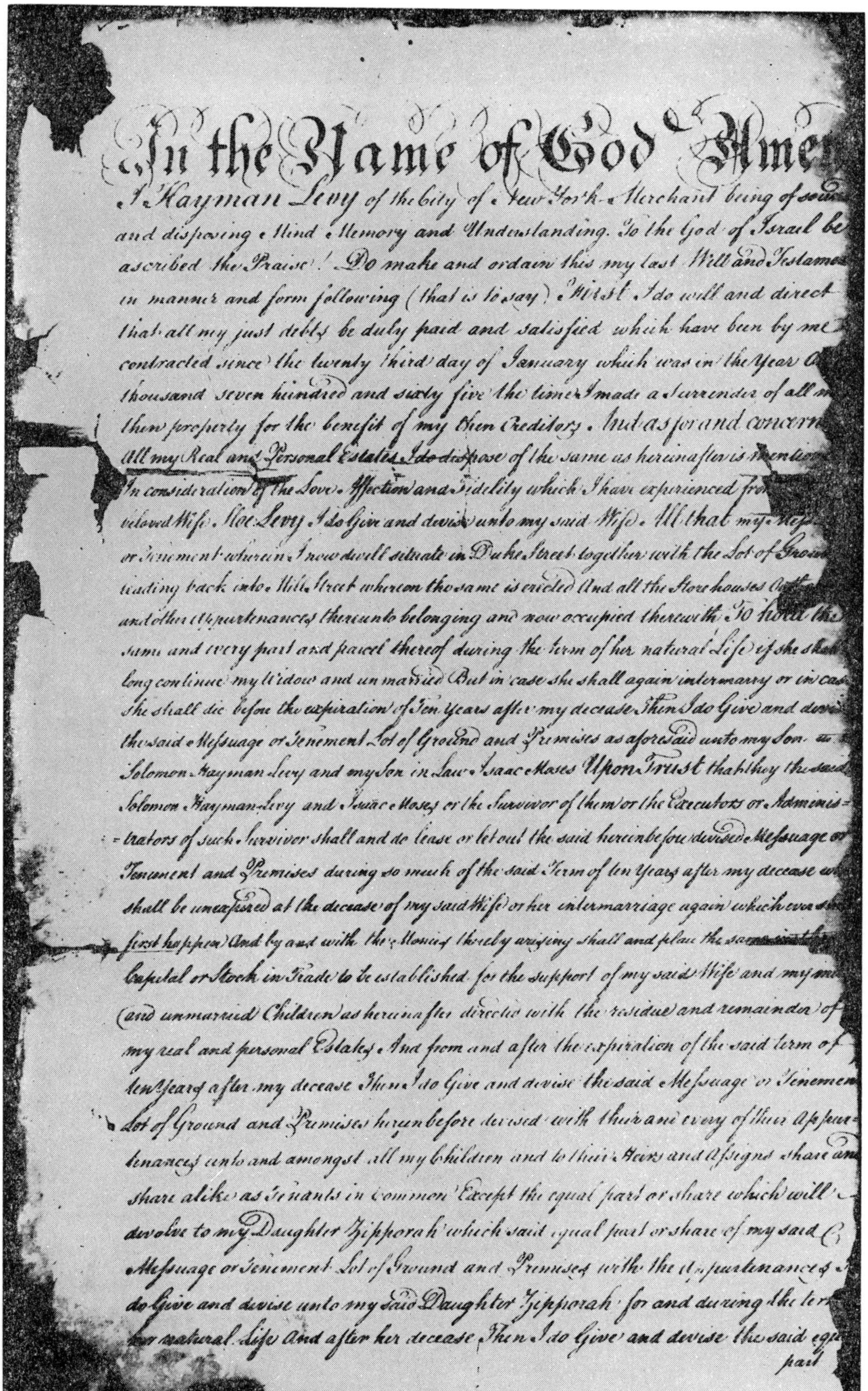

In the Name of God Ame
I Hayman Levy of the City of New York Merchant being of sou
and disposing Mind Memory and Understanding. To the God of Israel be
ascribed the Praise! Do make and ordain this my last Will and Testamen
in manner and form following (that is to say) First I do will and direct
that all my just debts be duly paid and satisfied which have been by me
contracted since the twenty third day of January which was in the Year O
thousand seven hundred and sixty five the time I made a Surrender of all m
then property for the benefit of my then Creditors And as for and concern
All my Real and Personal Estates I do dispose of the same as hereinafter is mention
In consideration of the Love Affection and Fidelity which I have experienced fro
beloved Wife Sloe Levy I do Give and devise unto my said Wife All that my Mess
or Tenement wherein I now dwell situate in Duke Street together with the Lot of Groun
leading back into Mill Street whereon the same is erected And all the Store houses Out
and other Appurtenances thereunto belonging and now occupied therewith To hold the
same and every part and parcel thereof during the term of her natural Life if she shal
long continue my Widow and unmarried But in case she shall again intermarry or in cas
She shall die before the expiration of Ten Years after my decease Then I do Give and devi
the said Messuage or Tenement Lot of Ground and Premises as aforesaid unto my Son
Solomon Hayman Levy and my Son in Law Isaac Moses Upon Trust that they the said
Solomon Hayman Levy and Isaac Moses or the Survivor of them or the Executors or Adminis=
=trators of such Survivor shall and do lease or let out the said hereinbefore devised Messuage or
Tenement and Premises during so much of the said Term of ten Years after my decease w
shall be unexpired at the decease of my said Wife or her intermarriage again which ever sh
first happen And by and with the Monies thereby arising shall and place the sa
Capital or Stock in Trade to be established for the support of my said Wife and my mi
and unmarried Children as hereinafter directed with the residue and remainder of
my real and personal Estates And from and after the expiration of the said term of
ten Years after my decease Then I do Give and devise the said Messuage or Tenemen
Lot of Ground and Premises hereinbefore devised with their and every of their Appur=
tenances unto and amongst all my Children and to their Heirs and Assigns share an
share alike as Tenants in Common Except the equal part or share which will
devolve to my Daughter Zipporah which said equal part or share of my said
Messuage or Tenement Lot of Ground and Premises with the Appurtenances
do Give and devise unto my said Daughter Zipporah for and during the ter
her natural Life And after her decease Then I do Give and devise the said equ
part

XXXIV. HAYMAN LEVY [1789]

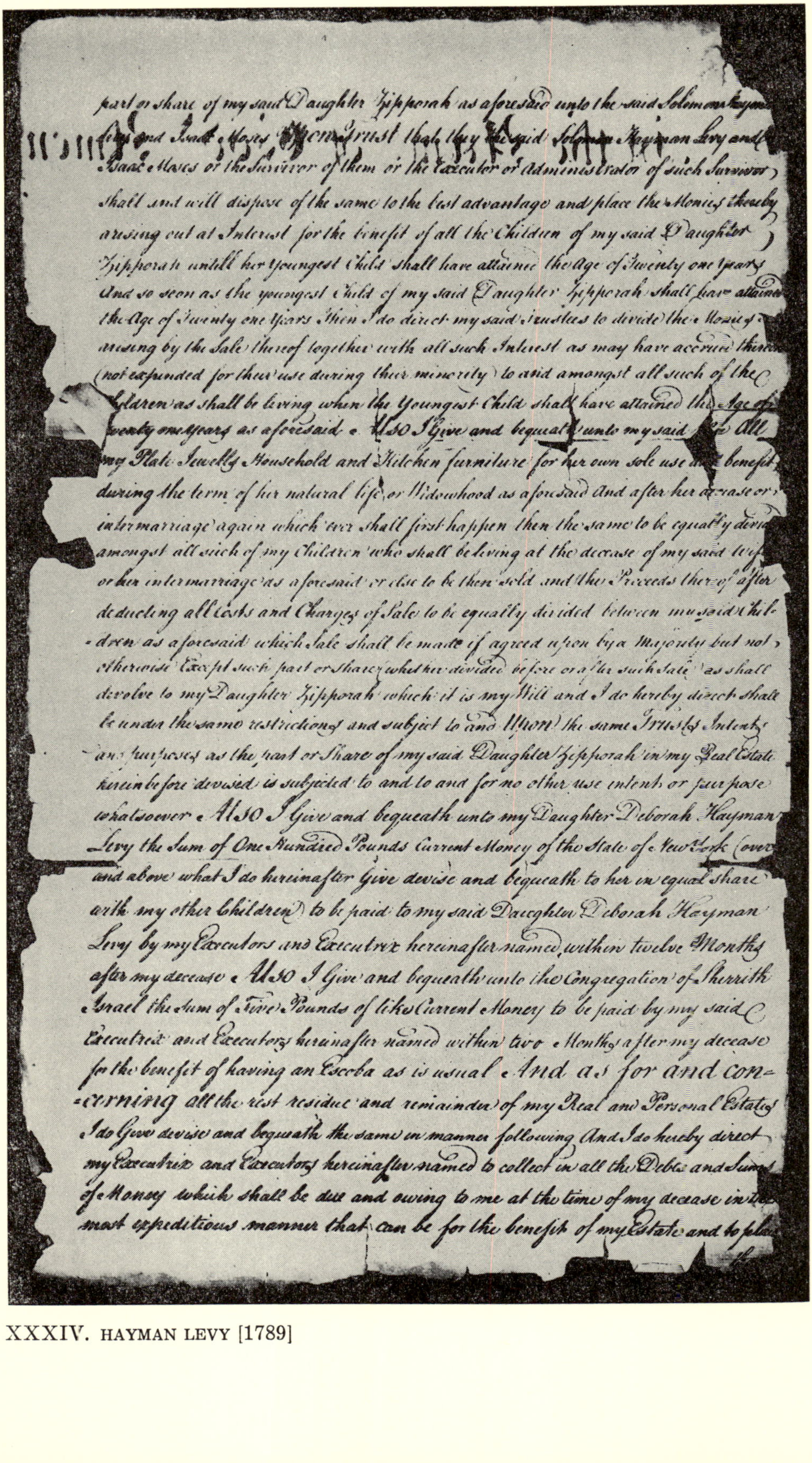

part or share of my said Daughter Zipporah as aforesaid unto the said Solomon Hayman Levy and Isaac Moses Upon Trust that they the said Solomon Hayman Levy and Isaac Moses or the Survivor of them or the Executor or Administrator of such Survivor shall and will dispose of the same to the best advantage and place the Monies thereby arising out at Interest for the benefit of all the Children of my said Daughter Zipporah untill her Youngest Child shall have attained the Age of Twenty one Years And so soon as the youngest Child of my said Daughter Zipporah shall have attained the Age of Twenty one Years Then I do direct my said Trustees to divide the Monies arising by the Sale thereof together with all such Interest as may have accrued thereon (not expended for their use during their minority) to and amongst all such of the Children as shall be living when the Youngest Child shall have attained the Age of Twenty one Years as aforesaid. Also I Give and bequeath unto my said Wife All my Plate Jewells Household and Kitchen furniture for her own sole use and benefit during the term of her natural life or Widowhood as aforesaid And after her decease or intermarriage again which ever shall first happen then the same to be equally divided amongst all such of my Children who shall be living at the decease of my said Wife or her intermarriage as aforesaid or else to be then sold and the Proceeds thereof after deducting all Costs and Charges of Sale to be equally divided between my said Children as aforesaid which Sale shall be made if agreed upon by a Majority but not otherwise Except such part or Share whether divided before or after such Sale as shall devolve to my Daughter Zipporah which it is my Will and I do hereby direct shall be under the same restrictions and subject to and Upon the same Trusts Intents and purposes as the part or Share of my said Daughter Zipporah in my Real Estate hereinbefore devised is subjected to and to and for no other use intent or purpose whatsoever. Also I Give and bequeath unto my Daughter Deborah Hayman Levy the Sum of One Hundred Pounds Current Money of the State of New York (over and above what I do hereinafter Give devise and bequeath to her in equal share with my other Children) to be paid to my said Daughter Deborah Hayman Levy by my Executors and Executrix hereinafter named within twelve Months after my decease. Also I Give and bequeath unto the Congregation of Sherrith Israel the Sum of Five Pounds of like Current Money to be paid by my said Executrix and Executors hereinafter named within two Months after my decease for the benefit of having an Escoba as is usual And as for and concerning all the rest residue and remainder of my Real and Personal Estates I do Give devise and bequeath the same in manner following And I do hereby direct my Executrix and Executors hereinafter named to collect in all the Debts and Sums of Money which shall be due and owing to me at the time of my decease in the most expeditious manner that can be for the benefit of my Estate and to place the

XXXIV. HAYMAN LEVY [1789]

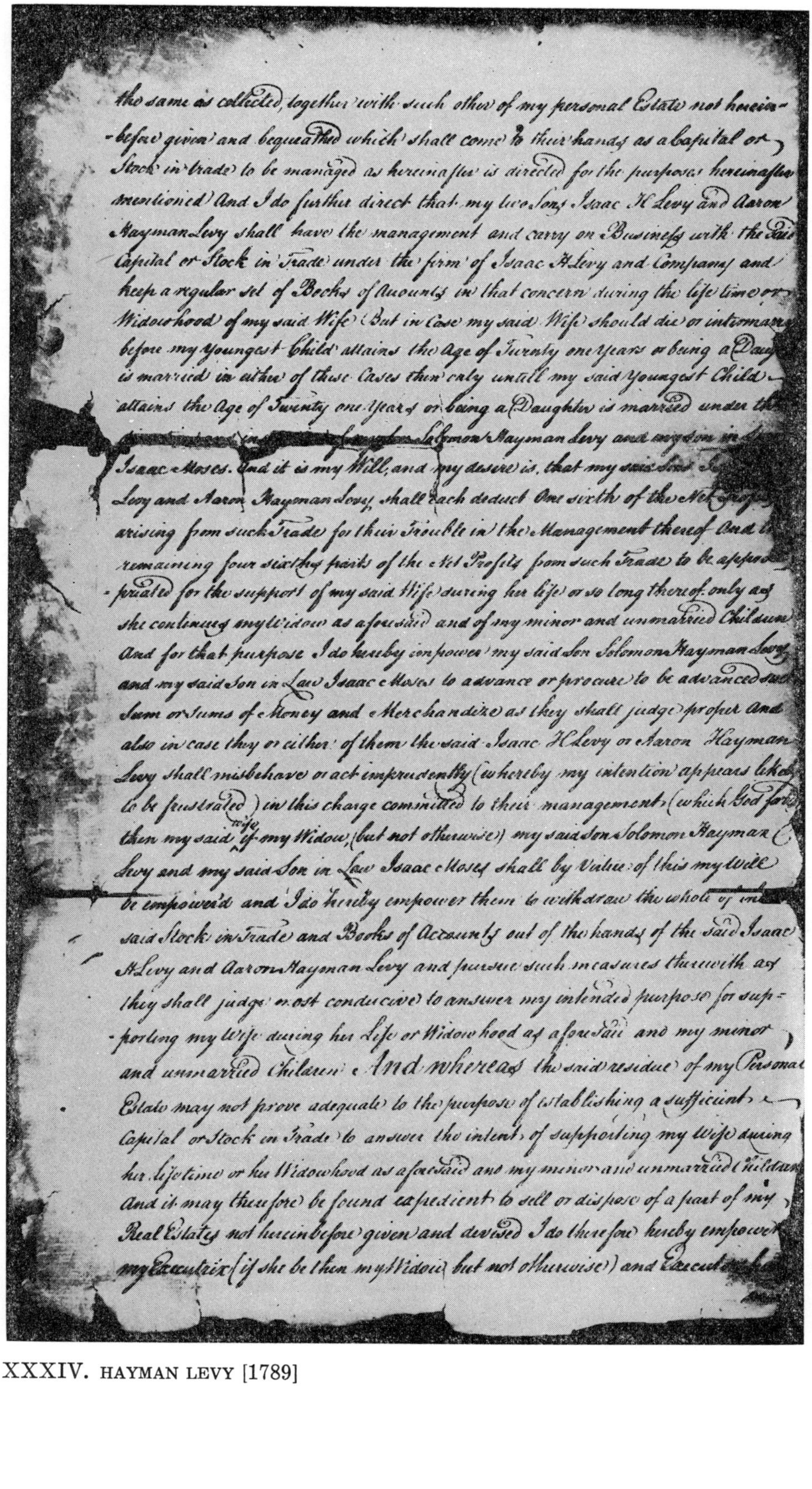
the same as collected, together with such other of my personal Estate not herein-
-before given and bequeathed which shall come to their hands as a Capital or
Stock in trade to be managed as hereinafter is directed for the purposes hereinafter
mentioned And I do further direct that my two Sons Isaac H Levy and Aaron
Hayman Levy shall have the management and carry on Business with the Said
Capital or Stock in Trade under the firm of Isaac H Levy and Company and
keep a regular set of Books of Accounts in that concern during the life time or
Widowhood of my said Wife (But in Case my said Wife should die or intermarry
before my Youngest Child attains the Age of Twenty one Years or being a Daug[illegible]
is married in either of these Cases then only untill my said Youngest Child
attains the Age of Twenty one Years or being a Daughter is married under the
[illegible] Solomon Hayman Levy and my son in L[illegible]
Isaac Moses. And it is my Will, and my desire is, that my said Sons I[illegible]
Levy and Aaron Hayman Levy shall each deduct One sixth of the Net Profi[illegible]
arising from such Trade for their Trouble in the Management thereof And t[illegible]
remaining four sixth parts of the Net Profits from such Trade to be appro-
-priated for the support of my said Wife during her life or so long thereof only as
she continues my Widow as aforesaid and of my minor and unmarried Children
And for that purpose I do hereby impower my said Son Solomon Hayman Levy
and my said Son in Law Isaac Moses to advance or procure to be advanced such
Sum or Sums of Money and Merchandize as they shall judge proper And
also in case they or either of them the said Isaac H Levy or Aaron Hayman
Levy shall misbehave or act imprudently (whereby my intention appears likely
to be frustrated) in this charge committed to their management, (which God for[illegible]
then my said wife if my Widow, (but not otherwise) my said Son Solomon Hayman
Levy and my said Son in Law Isaac Moses shall by Virtue of this my Will
be empower'd and I do hereby empower them to withdraw the whole of th[illegible]
said Stock in Trade and Books of Accounts out of the hands of the said Isaac
H Levy and Aaron Hayman Levy and pursue such measures therewith as
they shall judge most conducive to answer my intended purpose for sup-
-porting my Wife during her Life or Widowhood as aforesaid and my minor
and unmarried Children And whereas the said residue of my Personal
Estate may not prove adequate to the purpose of establishing a sufficient
Capital or Stock in Trade to answer the intent of supporting my Wife during
her lifetime or her Widowhood as aforesaid and my minor and unmarried Children
And it may therefore be found expedient to sell or dispose of a part of my
Real Estates not hereinbefore given and devised I do therefore hereby empower
my Executrix (if she be then my Widow but not otherwise) and Executors he[illegible]

XXXIV. HAYMAN LEVY [1789]

named or the Survivors or Survivor of them to sell and dispose of all such parts
thereof in Fee Simple as they shall judge proper for that purpose And it is my
Wish and I do recommend them not to do it but in case the most pressing
necessity should require such a measure it being my desire that the same shall
continue undivided for the space of Ten Years after my decease But should such
an expedient be found absolutely necessary, then only such parts thereof to be
sold as may be competent to establish a sufficient Capital or Stock in Trade for
the purposes aforesaid And should there be no necessity to part with any of my
said Estates or being such a part should still remain unsold Then I do Give
and devise the whole or [illegible] part thereof as is unsold unto the said Solomon
Hayman Levy and the said Isaac Moses or the Survivor of them or the [illegible]
or Administrators of such Survivor Upon the several Trusts and to and
for the several Uses Intents and purposes hereinafter mentioned (that is to say)
Upon Trust that they the said Solomon Hayman Levy and Isaac Moses
or the Survivor of them or the Executors and Administrators of such Survivor
shall and will lease out or otherwise appropriate the same to a Yearly
Income during the natural Life or Widowhood of my said Wife or in case of
the death or intermarriage of my said Wife during the term of Ten Years after
my decease, which said Yearly income after deducting all Costs and Charges
incident shall every Year be added to the Capital or Stock in Trade for the
purposes aforesaid so long as such Trade is continued and carried on by Virtue
of this my Will Then upon this further trust that all the rest
and residue of my Real Estates at the expiration of Ten Years after my decease
in case my said Wife should then be dead or have intermarried (or if then in
Life not untill she does die or intermarry) And the whole Stock in Trade
shall be accumulated at the decease of my said Wife or her intermarriage
which I direct shall be exactly stated from the Books of Accounts of such
Copartnery as aforesaid to be kept for that purpose shall be divided in equal propor-
tions to and amongst all my Children at that time living or in case of the
death of any Child or Children leaving lawfull Issue then the part or share
of the one so dying shall devolve and go to and be divided amongst all the
issue of him her or them so dying and to their Heirs and assigns for ever as tenants
in Common Except the part or share which will devolve to my Daughter
Zipporah which said part or share of the rest and residue of my Real and
Personal Estate as aforesaid I do Give devise and bequeath the same unto my said
Daughter

XXXIV. HAYMAN LEVY [1789]

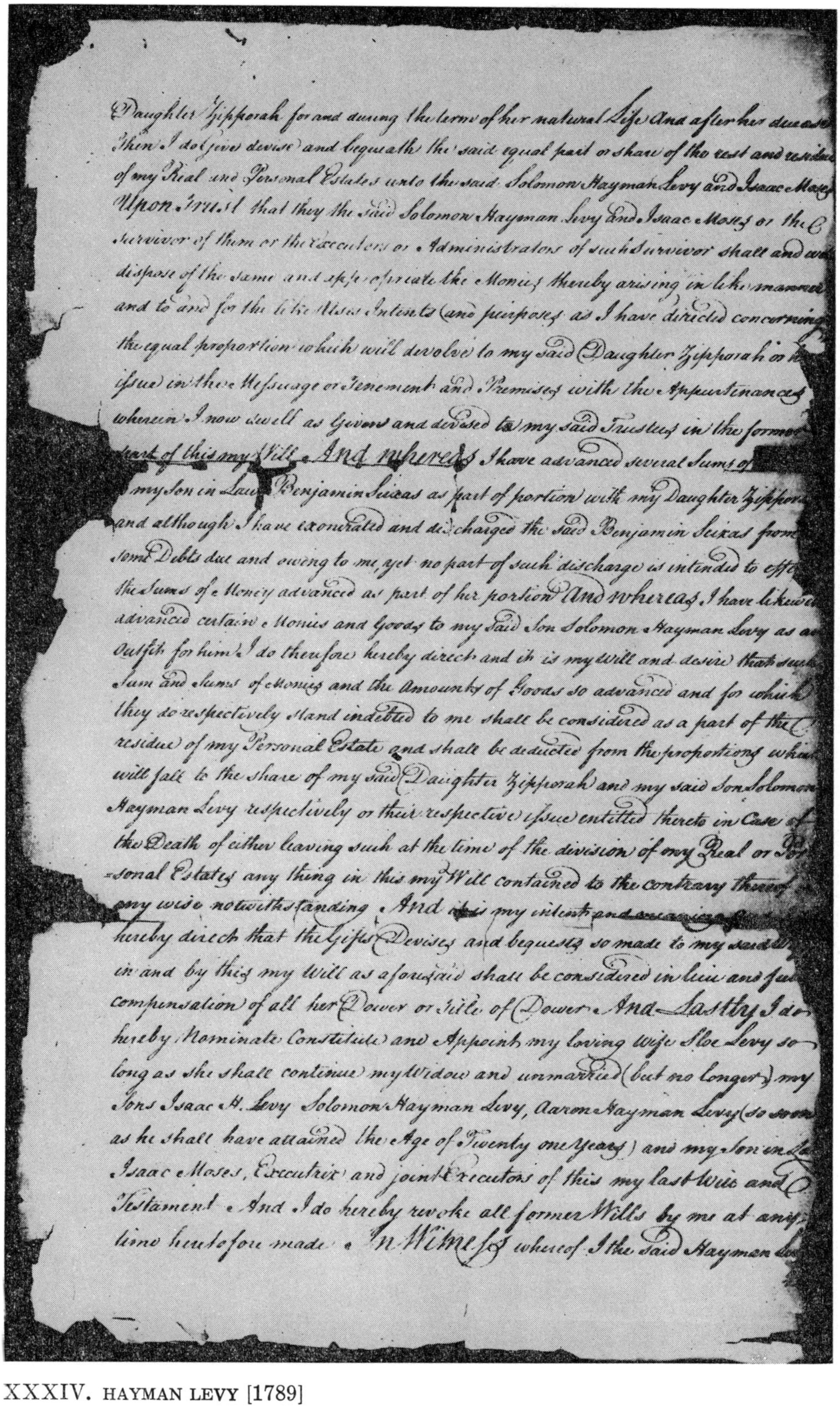

Daughter Zipporah for and during the term of her natural Life And after her decease Then I do give devise and bequeath the said equal part or share of the rest and residue of my Real and Personal Estates unto the said Solomon Hayman Levy and Isaac Moses Upon Trust that they the said Solomon Hayman Levy and Isaac Moses or the survivor of them or the Executors or Administrators of such Survivor shall and will dispose of the same and appropriate the Monies thereby arising in like manner and to and for the like Uses Intents and purposes as I have directed concerning the equal proportion which will devolve to my said Daughter Zipporah or her issue in the Messuage or Tenement and Premises with the Appurtenances wherein I now dwell as Given and devised to my said Trustees in the former part of this my Will And whereas I have advanced several Sums of [illegible] my Son in Law Benjamin Seixas as part of portion with my Daughter Zipporah and although I have exonerated and discharged the said Benjamin Seixas from some Debts due and owing to me, yet no part of such discharge is intended to affect the Sums of Monies advanced as part of her portion And whereas I have likewise advanced certain Monies and Goods to my said Son Solomon Hayman Levy as an Outfit for him I do therefore hereby direct and it is my Will and desire that such Sum and Sums of Monies and the Amounts of Goods so advanced and for which they do respectively stand indebted to me shall be considered as a part of the residue of my Personal Estate and shall be deducted from the proportions which will fall to the share of my said Daughter Zipporah and my said Son Solomon Hayman Levy respectively or their respective issue entitled thereto in Case of the Death of either leaving such at the time of the division of my Real or Per-sonal Estates any thing in this my Will contained to the contrary thereof in any wise notwithstanding And it is my intent and meaning [illegible] hereby direct that the Gifts Devises and bequests so made to my said [illegible] in and by this my Will as aforesaid shall be considered in lieu and full compensation of all her Dower or Title of Dower And Lastly I do hereby Nominate Constitute and Appoint my loving Wife Sloe Levy so long as she shall continue my Widow and unmarried (but no longer) my Sons Isaac H. Levy Solomon Hayman Levy, Aaron Hayman Levy (so soon as he shall have attained the Age of Twenty one Years) and my Son in Law Isaac Moses, Executrix and joint Executors of this my last Will and Testament And I do hereby revoke all former Wills by me at any time heretofore made In Witness whereof I the said Hayman Levy

XXXIV. HAYMAN LEVY [1789]

have to this my said Last Will and Testament contained in Six sides of Paper
to the first five sides thereof set my Hand and to the last Side thereof Set my
Hand and Seal the day of In the Year One thousand seven
hundred and eighty nine and teenth of the Independence of the United
States.

Signed Sealed Published and declared
the said Hayman Levy the Testator as and
for his last Will and Testament in the presence
of us, who at his request, in his presence, and
the presence of each other, have subscribed
names as Witnesses to the same.
the word "[illegible]" being first interlined in the twenty fifth
line of the [illegible] side.

XXXIV. HAYMAN LEVY [1789]

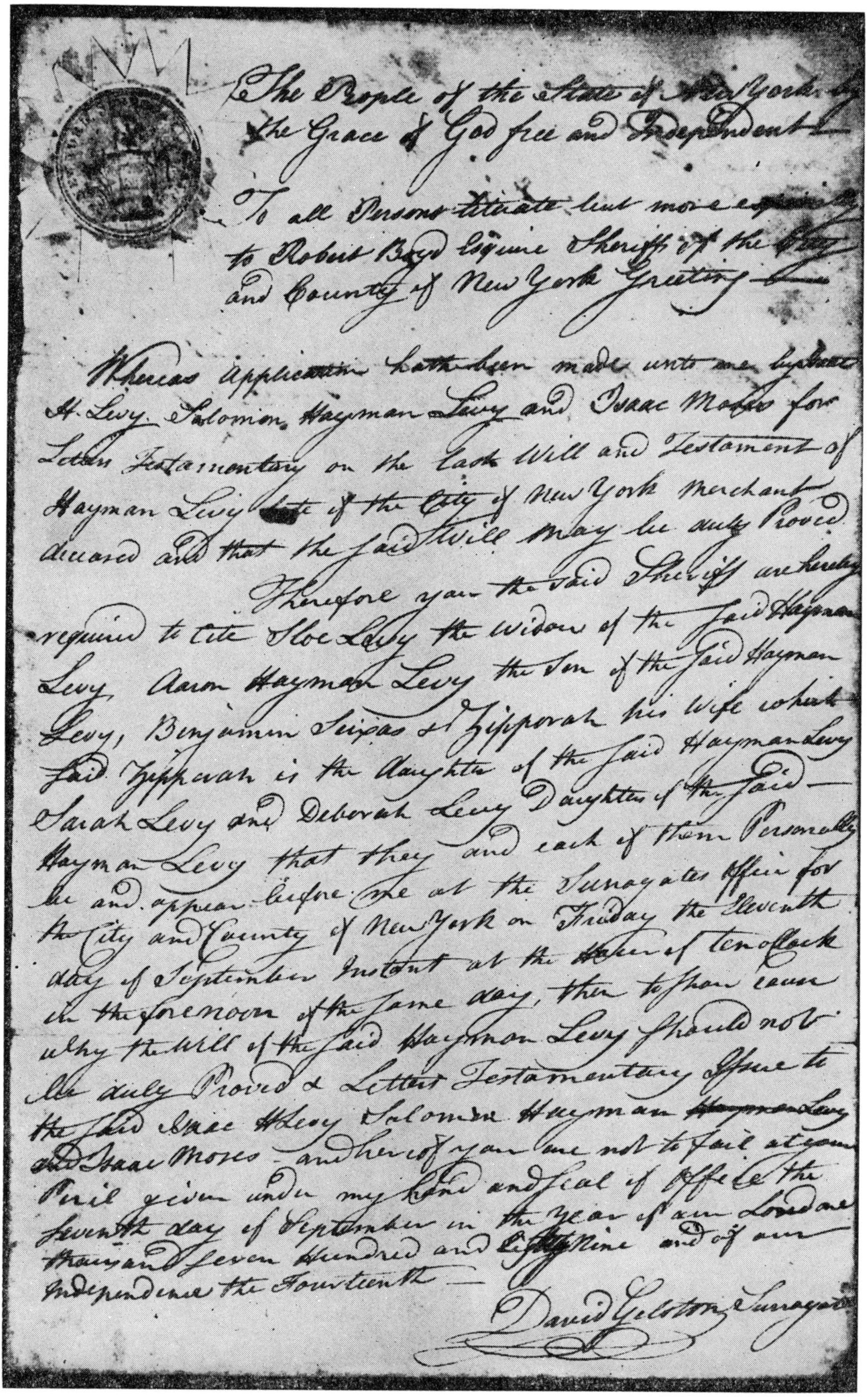
The People of the State of New York by the Grace of God free and Independent

To all Persons [illegible] but more especially to Robert Boyd Esquire Sheriff of the City and County of New York Greeting

Whereas application hath been made unto me by Isaac H. Levy, Solomon Hayman Levy and Isaac Moses for Letters Testamentary on the Last Will and Testament of Hayman Levy late of the City of New York Merchant deceased and that the said Will may be duly Proved. Therefore you the said Sheriff are hereby required to cite Sloe Levy the widow of the said Hayman Levy, Aaron Hayman Levy the son of the said Hayman Levy, Benjamin Seixas & Zipporah his wife which said Zipporah is the daughter of the said Hayman Levy, Sarah Levy and Deborah Levy Daughters of the said Hayman Levy that they and each of them Personally be and appear before me at the Surrogates Office for the City and County of New York on Friday the Eleventh day of September Instant at the Hour of ten oClock in the forenoon of the same day, then to shew cause why the Will of the said Hayman Levy should not be duly Proved & Letters Testamentary Issue to the said Isaac H Levy Solomon Hayman ~~Hayman Levy~~ and Isaac Moses — and hereof you are not to fail at your Peril given under my hand and Seal of Office the seventh day of September in the Year of our Lord one thousand Seven Hundred and ~~Fifty~~ Eighty Nine and of our Independence the Fourteenth —

David Gelston Surrogate

XXXIV. HAYMAN LEVY [1789] (For transcript of this page, see Appendix I, p. 214.)

XXXV

JOSEPH ISRAEL LEVY[1]

[1789]

In the Name of God Amen I JOSEPH ISRAEL LEVY of Leman Street Goodmans Field in the parish of St. Marys White Chapel of London in the County of Middlesix being in Bodily health and of sound and disposing Mind and Memory and Considering the Perils and other Uncertainties of this transitory Life do for the avoiding Controversies after my decease make publish and declare this my last will and testament in manner following that is to say First I recommend my soul to the Almighty God who gave it me, my Body to the Earth as it shall please God to order and as to and Concerning my Bodily Estate and Effects I give and bequeath and dispose thereof as follows to say first towards the paying of my debts and it is my Will that my Body after my death shall Lay forty Eight hours before it is put in the Earth and it is my will also that a plain decent Tombe Shall be erected and built over my Grave I give and bequeath and dispose thereof unto the Portuguese Synagogue one hundred pounds Lawful money of Great Britain fifty pounds to the Jews College at Jerusalem twenty five pounds to be distributed among the Poor on the day of my Burial. I also Give and bequeath unto RACHEL COHEN MEDECO and unto SARAH COHEN MEDECO each of them the sum of twenty pounds Sterling I also give and bequeath unto my brother SAMUEL ISRAEL and unto my Brother BENJAMIN JACOBS and to my Sister ABIGAIL JACOBS and to my Sister RACHEL ISRAEL each and every one of them separately one shilling English money I give and bequeath unto my dear and Loving Daughter SARAH ISRAEL LEVY the nine houses appertaining and belonging unto me on a leasehold which are situate in Colbrook Square in Hoxton Town in the parish of St. Leonards Shoreditch in the County of Middlesex

[1] Albany Will Liber 1, pp. 215–218, Clerk's Office of the Court of Appeals, Albany, New York. Joseph Israel Levy appears to be the same Levy as in Will no. 33. Both have brothers named Samuel Israel, both give money to the Jews College of Jerusalem and to the poor which are unusual bequests. On the other hand, the wills differ in the omission of certain names, particularly with respect to wife and daughter. In the first will a wife's name is not mentioned and a daughter Abigail is referred to. In this will a daughter named Sarah is mentioned. It is possible, however, considering that the earlier will was drawn in 1772 and this one in 1785, a span of thirteen years, that the first child could have died prior to the making of the second will and Sarah have been born during this period. The first will was probated in New York on April 28, 1786 and this one in London on September, 1785 and in New York November 12, 1789. The New York officials may not have been aware of the existence of this will, so upon proof of Levy's death granted probate in 1786. Presented with evidence of a second will, the only one proved in London, the Court granted another probate. For material regarding Levy and some of those mentioned in his will, see Will no. XXXIII, *supra*, pp. 161–164. There is, however, little known of the testator and his relatives.

It is my will also that if it should please the almighty God to take my daughter before she arives to age that the said nine Houses Above mentioned shall belong to my wife POLLY ISRAEL LEVY. I give and bequeath unto FANNY MYERS of Elizabeth Square in the parish of St Botolphs Algate London Widow the sum of five pounds Sterling I also give and bequeath unto HARRY MYERS the sum of five pounds Sterling and the Residue and Remainder of all my Personal and worldly Estate I give bequeath and dispose of to my Loving wife POLLY ISRAEL LEVY, to say Stocks houses Household Furniture plate wearing Apparel Money debts due to me and all and every thing that shall appertain belong to or be due unto me on the day of my death all such I give and bequeath unto my Loving Wife POLLY ISRAEL LEVY and its my Will also that if it please God to take from this world my wife POLLY ISRAEL LEVY then all and every thing to her bequeathed shall appertain and belong to her Dear and Loving Daughter SARAH ISRAEL LEVY and I do by this appoint and Constitute my wife POLLY ISRAEL LEVY within mentioned and Mr. ISAAC MORAN of George Street Minories in the parish of St Botolph Algate London in the County of Middlesex Executors to this my last Will and Testament and I do hereby Revoke and disannul and make Void any will or wills by me heretofore made ratifying this to be my last will and Testament *In Witness* whereof I have hereunto set my hand and seal dated in London this Eleventh day of August in the year of our Lord one thousand seven hundred and Eighty Five JOSEPH ISRAEL LEVY [LS] Signed Sealed Published and Declared by the within named JOSEPH ISRAEL LEVY the Testator in the presence of us who have hereunto Subscribed our Names in the presence of each other SAMUEL BAKER, JOS SEG[?], S. LAZARUS *The People of the State of New York* by the Grace of God Free and Independent to NICHOLAS LOW[2] of the City of New York Merchant Attorney of POLLY ISRAEL LEVY of Leman Street Goodmans field in the Parish of St Marys White Chaple in the County of Middlesex and in the Kingdom of Great Britain widow and Relict of JOSEPH ISRAEL LEVY Late of the same place Gentleman deceased *Send Greeting Whereas* the said JOSEPH ISRAEL LEVY did in his life time make his last will and Testament in writing bearing date the Elevanth day of August in the year of our Lord one thousand seven hundred and Eighty five and thereby appointed the said POLLY ISRAEL LEVY and ISAAC MORAN Executors of his said will and soon after died *And Whereas* afterwards on the ninth day of September in the year of our Lord one thousand seven hundred and Eighty five at London before the Worshipful GEORGE HARIS Doctor of Laws Surrogate of the wright worshipful PETER CALVERT Doctor of Laws Masterkeeper or Commissary of the Pregative Court of Canterbury Lawfully Constituted the said will was proved and administration

[2] Nicholas Low had considerable property in New York including land on Gouverneur Cherry, Houston, and Bleecker streets. MCC, vol. II, p. 434; vol. III, p. 598; vol. VII, p. 342; vol. XII, p. 495.

of all and singular the Goods Chattels and Credits of the said deceased were Granted unto the said POLLY ISRAEL LEVY one of the Executors aforesaid as appears unto us by the a Certifycate thereof bearing date 9th day of September 1785 Signed by HENRY STEVENS, GEO GOSKING, JAMES TOWNLEY, Deputy Registers and we desiring that the Goods Chattels and Credits of the said deceased may be well and faithfully administered Applied and disposed of according to the true Intent and meaning of his said Will (a Copy whereof is hereunto annexed) do Grant unto you the said NICHOLAS LOW full power to Collect Levy Recover and Receive all and singular the Goods Chattels and Credits of the said deceased and the same to administer and dispose of According to the Tenor and Effect of said will and as the law directs you being first duly sworn to fulfil the will of the said deceased and to pay his debts and Legacies as far forth as his Goods Chattels and Credits will thereto extend and the law bind you and also to make or cause to be made a true and perfect inventory of all and singular the Goods, Chattels and Credits of the said deceased which have or shall Come to your hands possession or knowledge or into the hands or possession of any other person or persons in trust for you and to Exhibit the same into the Registry of the Court of Probates of this State on or before the Twelfth day of May next Ensuing and also to Render a just and true account thereof when thereunto Lawfully Required and we do by these presents ordain depute Constitute and appoint you the said NICHOLAS LOW Administrator of all and singular the Goods Chattels and Credits of the said deceased together with his will annexed *In Testimony* whereof we have Caused the seal of our Court of Probates to be hereunto affixed *Witness* PETER OGILVIE[3] Judge of our said Court at the City of New York the Twelfth day of November in the year of our Lord one thousand seven hundred and Eighty Nine and in the Fourteenth year of our Independence.

WM OGILVIE CLKE

[3] Peter Ogilvie was appointed Judge of the Court of Probate on April 6, 1787. *Civil List*, p. 224.

XXXVI

MOSES GOMEZ[1]

[1790]

In the Name of God Amen. I MOSES GOMEZ of the City of New York Merchant Being of a sound disposing mind and Memory and understanding Blessed be God for the same Yet reflecting on the uncertainty of life, I have thought proper to settle my temporal affairs by this my last will and testament in manner and form following (that is to say) I recommend my immortal Soul to the mercy of the Great God of Israel my Creator and my body I commit to the earth to be decently interred And after all my just deabts be paid and funeral Charges, I do settle and dispose of the rest of my Estate in manner and form following (that is to say) In Primis I give and bequeath unto my beloved Esteemed and Worthy Wiffe ESTHER GOMEZ[2] All my Estate boath real[3] and personal during her widowhood she reserving in her hands one half of all my rents and Incomes for my dear and beloved son ISAAC GOMEZ, JUNIOR[4] for his Edu-

[1] Will Liber 40, p. 353; *NYHSC*, vol. XIV (1906), pp. 171–172. Moses Gomez (May 29, 1728–April 12, 1789), son of Daniel Gomez and grandson of Simja de Torres, was a merchant who resided at 203 Water Street. At Daniel's death, Moses was granted letters of administration on Oct. 21, 1784, Albany Letters of Administration, HDC. He was active in the affairs of the Jewish community and was elected *parnas* three times in 1767, 1772, and 1776. *PAJHS*, vol. XVII (1909), p. 198; *ibid.*, vol. XXI (1913), p. 211; *ibid.*, vol. XXVII (1920), p. 253; *Directory, 1786*, p. 31. For example of litigation, see *Gomez v. Nesbitt and Connolly* (1785), MCP, file 1785, Sept. 12, 1785. In this case Gomez brought a £300 damage suit for rent for a house and lot he owned in the East Ward. There was a contemporary Moses Gomez, grocer, of 56 Nassau Street. *Directory, 1787*, p. 16.

[2] Esther Gomez (1739–1822) was the daughter of Isaac Gomez. She married Moses, her first cousin, on May 14, 1755. See *supra*, Will of Isaac Gomez, p. 130, note 4; *Portraits*, pp. 413–414; *PAJHS*, vol. XVII (1909), p. 198; *ibid.*, XXVII (1920), p. 281.

[3] Some of this property included land in Montgomery Ward fronting on Beekman Street and, probably lots nos. 736–754, west of Great George Street. The Beekman Street property was sold by Esther Gomez, Isaac Gomez, Jr. and Abigail, his wife, to Thomas Burling in 1794 for £1,000. Conveyance Liber 50, cp. 140–142. The Great George Street property was sold by Isaac and his wife to his mother for £700 in 1797. Conveyance Liber 54, cp. 183–184. See also a reference to a water lot between Wall Street and the Old Slip. MCC, vol. II, p. 140.

[4] Isaac Gomez, Jr. (1768–1831) was the only surviving son of Moses at the latter's death. He married Abigail, daughter of Aaron Lopez, Newport trader. Isaac, who wrote poetry and prose including a book for his children entitled *Selections of a Father in Prose and Verse*, was active in communal affairs. *Portraits*, p. 413; *Dictionary*, p. 45; *PAJHS*, vol. XXVII (1920), pp. 58 *et passim*; Elvira N. Solis, "Notes on Isaac Gomez and Lewis Gomez from an Old Family Record," *PAJHS*, vol. XI (1903), p. 139. In 1800, Isaac Gomez was requested under penalty of fine to fill in the cellar of his house at 142 Pearl Street. MCC, vol. II, p. 639. In 1813, he petitioned successfully for the passage of an ordinance to prevent the "sale of Jews meat in public markets," but it was repealed at the request of Sampson Simson and the Congregation. *Ibid.*, vol. VII, pp. 358 and 364. In 1814, he became insolvent. Insolvent Debtors' Papers, 1814, New York County Clerk's Office, copy in American Jewish Historical Society Library. In 1818 he petitioned without success to be appointed weighmaster. MCC, vol. X, p. 95.

cation Cloathing and reasonable use till he becomes of the age of one and twenty years when that happens then I leve it at the discretion of my said Wiffe ESTHER GOMEZ to give him what part of my Estate she thinks proper if she does not marry, if she does marry then I give my said son when he arrives at the age of one and twenty years all my Estate boath real and personal excepting my house in Water Street,[5] my Plate Jewels, Household furniture Horse & Shase with my Stable Provided the man she marrys before the Ceremony of such marriage is performed do give unto my said Son ISAAC GOMEZ, JUNIOR able and sufficient security for double the value of every and all such plate Jewels etc. to be to him to him delivered after the decease of my said Wiffe ESTHER GOMEZ and after the decease of my said Wiffe to go to my said son ISAAC GOMEZ, JUNIOR he paying to my said Wiffe ESTHER GOMEZ one third part of all my rents during her life time. And as to the Charitys to be giveing out of my Estate I order that the value of five pounds be giveing to our Synagogue in this City as a *Legado* to say *Escava* for me according to our Custom and *Lastly* I do nominate and appoint my said wiffe ESTHER GOMEZ and my son ISAAC GOMEZ, JUNIOR to be sole Executors of this my last will and testament hereby revokeing and annulling all former and other wills and dispositions of my Estate at any time heretofore made and declaring that these presents only to be and Continae my last will and testament.

In testimony whereof I do hereunto set my hand and seal this Twenty second day of August one thousand seven hundred and Eighty-six.

MOSES GOMEZ L.S.

Signed Sealed Published and declared by the said MOSES GOMEZ as and for his last will and testament in the presence of us who subscribe our names at the request of the Testator.

ANTHONY GRIFFITHS[6] JOSEPH GRIFFITHS[7] ABRAHAM LARZELERE[8]

City and County of New York SS

Be it remembered that on the seventh day of April in the year one thousand seven hundred and Ninety personally came and appeared before DAVID GELSTON Surrogate of the said County JOSEPH GRIFFITHS and ABRAHAM LARZELERE of the said City and being duly sworn on their oaths declared that they saw MOSES GOMEZ sign and seal an Instrument in writing purporting to be the will of the said MOSES GOMEZ bearing date

[5] Probably a reference to 203 Water Street

[6] Anthony Griffiths was a merchant of 12 South Street. *Directory, 1787*, p. 16.

[7] Joseph Griffiths was the proprietor of a ship chandlery store on Front Street. *Directory, 1789*, p. 38.

[8] Possibly Abraham Lazilier, Jr., a blacksmith appointed a fireman in 1801. MCC, vol. II, p. 702.

the twenty second of August one thousand and seven hundred and Eighty six (the preceeding whereof is a true Copy) and heard him publish and declare the same as and for his last will and testament that at the time thereof he the said MOSES GOMEZ was of sound disposing mind and memory to the best of the knowledge and belief of them the deponents And that their names subscribed as Witnesses to the said will are of their own proper hands writing which they respectively subscribed as Witnesses to the said will in the Testators presence and that they the deponents saw ANTHONY GRIFFITHS the other witness to the said will subscribe his name as a witness thereto in the presence of the Testator.

DAVID GELSTON

The People of the State of New York by the Grace of God Free and Independent, To all to whom these presents shall come or may concern Send Greeting. Know ye that at the City and County of New York on the day of the date hereof before DAVID GELSTON Esquire Surrogate of our said County the last will and testament of MOSES GOMEZ deceased (a Copy whereof is hereunto annexed) was proved and is approved and allowed of by us and the said deceased having whilst he lived and at the time of his death Goods Chattels or Credits within this State by means whereof the proving and registering the said will and the granting administration of all and singular the said Goods, Chattels and Credits and also the auditing allowing and final discharging the account thereof doth belong unto us the administration of all and singular the Goods Chattels and Credits of the said deceased and any way concerning his will is granted unto ISAAC GOMEZ, JUNIOR one of the Executors in the said will named he being first duly sworn well and faithfully to administer the same and to make and exhibit a true and perfect Inventory of all and singular the said Goods Chattels and Credits and also to render a just and true account thereof when thereunto required In testimony whereof we have caused the seal of office of our said Surrogate to be hereunto affixed. Witness DAVID GELSTON Esquire Surrogate of the said County at the City of New York the seventh day of April in the year of our Lord one thousand seven hundred and Ninety and of our Independence the Fourteenth.

DAVID GELSTON

XXXVII

ESTHER BENZAKEN[1]

[1790]

In the Name of the God of Israel, Amen. I ESTER BENZAKEN of the City of New York, being Infirm of Body & Sound of mind and knowing the certainty of humane Life — do make & ordain this to be my last Will & Testament, vizt.

Item

My Body I commit to the earth Decently to be buried — And after the Expenses of said interment I do leave & bequeath the following Legacys which are to be paid & delivered by my Executor & Executrix hereafter named after paying all Just Demands against me.

Item

To my Eldest Son ISAAC[2] I leave & bequeath unto him his Heirs or assigns all the wearing apparil that were belonging & wore by my Husband ELEAZER BENZAKEN[3] — To the only use & benefit of my said Son ISAAC.

Item

To my affectionate & beloved Son ABRAHAM[4] I leave & bequeath for his only use & benefit to him his Heirs & assigns forever Six Silver Tea Spoons as a token of his Dutifull Conduct towards me.

[1] Original Will unnumbered, HDC; Will Liber 40, p. 382; *NYHSC*, vol. XIV (1906), p. 176. The will was proved July 1, 1790. Esther Benzaken, who resided on Barclay Street in 1789, was a comparatively unknown figure. *Directory, 1789*, p. 12. She does figure in a number of court cases during 1788 and 1789, as for example, *Templeton and Stewart v. Esther Benzaken, adm. of Eleazer* (1789), MCP, file 1789, March 24, 1789 (Keese's Rules).

[2] Isaac Benzaken lived from 1764 to 1799. *Dictionary*, p. 12. He too was involved in a number of court cases, e. g. *Benzaken v. Parks* (1793), file 1793, November 26, 1793. This was a case of slander.

[3] Eleazer Benzaken died about 1787. He married Esther in Philadelphia before 1763. In 1770, he twice lost an election for the congregational office of *shoḥet*. Letters of administration were granted to his wife on July 11, 1787. *Dictionary*, p. 12; *PAJHS*, vol. XXI (1913), pp. 106 and 108, see also pp. 148–149; *NYHSC*, vol. XIV (1906), p. 352. Other children of the testatrix who died before this will was written were Joseph (1763–1779), Jacob (1770–1771), Jacob (1772–1773), and Princeada (1774–1775). Her daughter Simha mentioned in the will was born January 15, 1769. Register of Congregation Shearith Israel, pp. 20, 33a, 40a, 41a, 43a, 45a and 45.

[4] Abraham Benzaken, circumcised on March 8, 1776, later became a tailor at 14 Broadway. "Miscellaneous Items Relating to Jews in New York," *PAJHS*, vol. XXVII (1920), p. 13; *Directory, 1790*, p. 13.

Item

I do leave & bequeath all my Estate real & personal both in Law & Equity whatsoever & wheresoever unto my Dutiful & beloved Daughters SYMEY & RACHAEL to be Equaly Divided on their acquireing the same (Except a Silver Bell & Correl I leave as a token of Remembrance unto my Eldest Daughter SYMEY and as token of my further Love & affection I give unto my yongest Daughter RACHAEL a Silver Stone pin Together with an Equal Division of my property aforesaid for the only use & benefit of my Daughters aforesaid to them & to their Heirs & assigns forever.

Item

I do will & ordain my Trusty & beloved Son ABRAHAM Executor & my Trusty beloved Daughter SYMEY Executrix of this my last will & Testament.

In Testimony hereof I hereunto Set my hand & Seal in New York June the 8th 1790 & of the Jewish year & month Sivan 26th 5550.

her
ESTER X BENZAKEN
mark

[seal]

Read, published & Declared
to be last will & Testament
in the presence of us

s/ BENJ. JUDAH[5]
s/ JOS. JONAS[6]
s/ HERCULES WENDOVER[7]

[5] Probably Benjamin S. Judah (1760–1831), a prominent New York and Philadelphia merchant who resided at 22 Dock Street, New York in 1786 and four years later was located at "19 Corner of Duke Street and Old Slip." He was elected *parnas* in 1813 and 1814. *Directory, 1786*, p. 34, *ibid., 1790*, p. 55; *Portraits*, pp. 43–44 and 74; *Dictionary*, pp. 78–79; *PAJHS*, vol. XXI (1913), pp. 142 and 212.

[6] Possibly Joshua Jonas who was in Philadelphia in 1786 and in Charleston between 1783 and 1800. *Dictionary*, p. 76.

[7] Hercules Wendover, a cartman, was admitted as freeman on July 13, 1785. *Burghers*, p. 273.

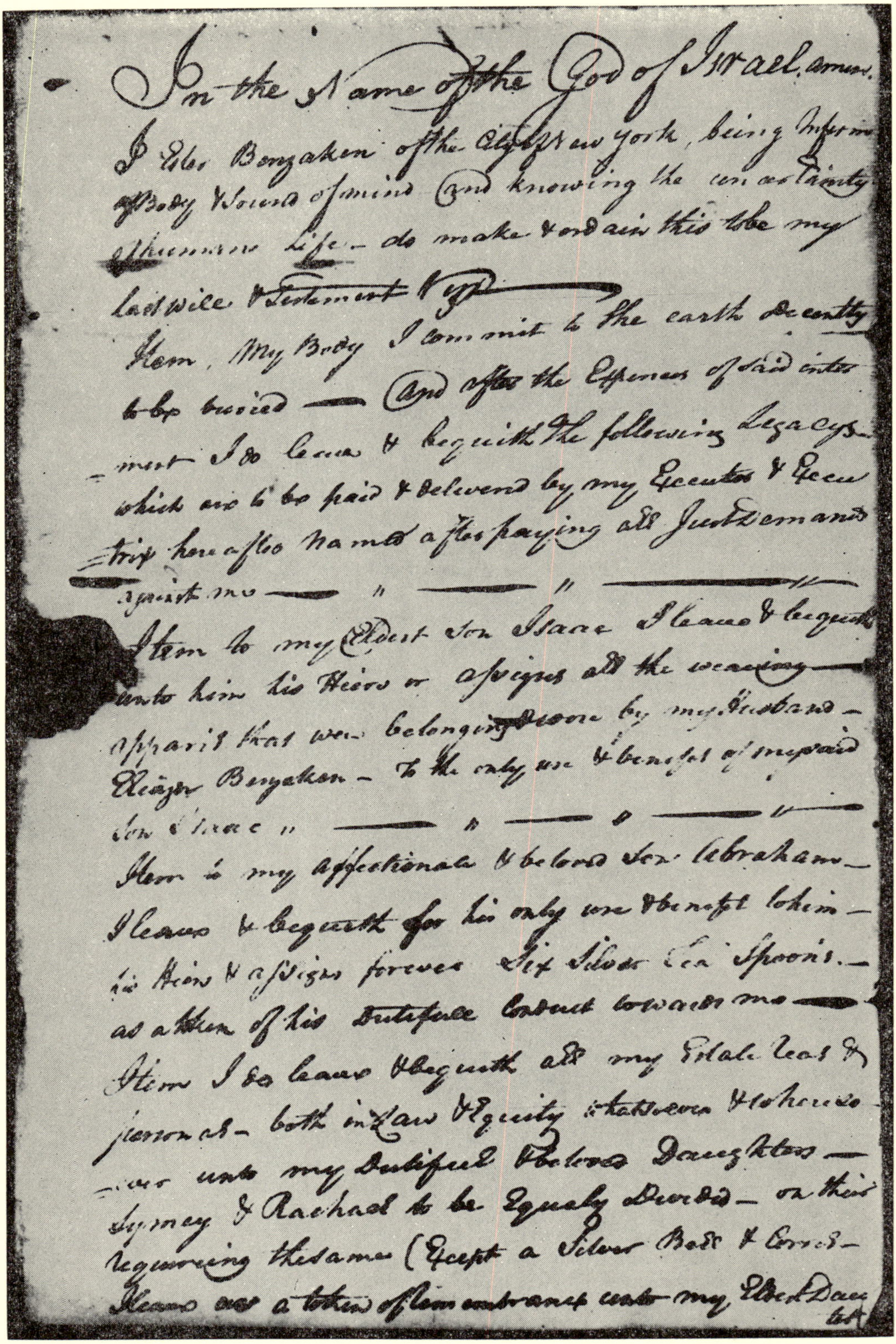
In the Name of the God of Israel, amen.
I Ester Benzaken of the City of New York, being Infirm
of Body & Sound of mind and knowing the uncertainty
of humane Life — do make & ordain this to be my
last will & Testament
Item, My Body I commit to the earth decently
to be buried — And after the Expences of said inter-
-ment I do leave & bequith the following Legacys
which are to be paid & delivered by my Executors & Execu-
-trix hereafter named after paying all Just demands
against me — " — " —
Item to my Eldest son Isaac I leave & bequeath
unto him his Heirs or assignes all the wearing
apparil that were belonging & wore by my Husband
Eleazer Benzaken — to the only use & benefit of my said
son Isaac " — " — " —
Item to my affectionate & beloved son Abraham —
I leave & bequeath for his only use & benefit to him
his Heirs & assigns forever Six Silver Tea Spoons —
as a token of his dutifull conduct towards me —
Item I do leave & bequeath all my Estate real &
personal — both in Law & Equity whatsoever & wheresoever
unto my Dutifull & beloved Daughters —
Sipory & Rachael to be Equaly divided — on their
requiring the same (Except a Silver Box & Cross —
I leave as a token of Remembrance unto my Eldest Daughter

XXXVII. ESTHER BENZAKEN [1790]

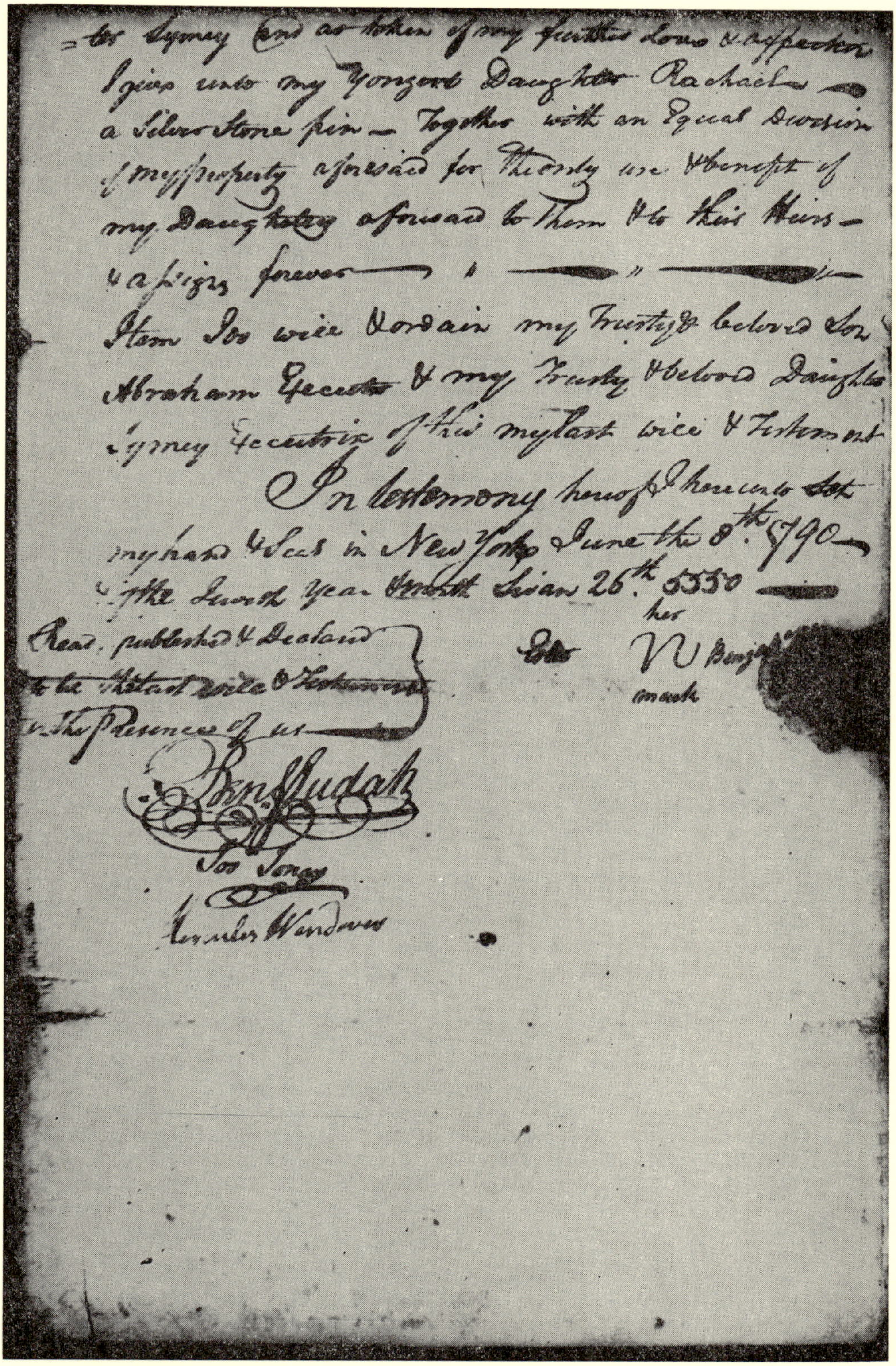

-ter Sipey and as token of my further love & affection
I give unto my Youngest Daughter Rachael
a Silver Stone pin — together with an Equal division
of my property aforesaid for the only use & benefit of
my Daughters aforesaid to them & to their Heirs —
& assigns forever
Item I do will & ordain my trusty & beloved Son
Abraham Executor & my trusty & beloved Daughter
Sipey Executrix of this my last will & Testament
In testimony hereof I hereunto set
my hand & Seal in New York June the 8th 1790
& of the Jewish Year Month Nisan 26th 5550

Ester her V mark Benzaken

Read, published & Declared
to be the last will & Testament
in the Presence of us

Benj. Judah
Joe Jones
Cornelius Wendover

XXXVII. ESTHER BENZAKEN [1790]

XXXVIII

MOSES LEVY[1]

[1792]

By Virtue of the Power Granted to the Town Council of the Town of New Port in the County of New Port and State of Rhode Island Etc. for the probate of Wills and Granting forth Letters of Administration upon Intestates Estates within said Township *To All People* to whom these presents shall Come Greeting Be it Known and manifest that on the second day of July AD 1792 in Council was Exhibited the last Will and Testament of MOSES LEVY late of said Newport Merchant (deceased) which was proved and approved according to Law and HIAM LEVY,[2] MOSES SEIXAS,[3] SIMEON LEVY[4] the Executors named in the said Will appeared also in Council and having fulfilled the will of the Testator preparatory thereto Received their Executorship and having given bond according to Law Therefore Letters Testamentary is hereby Granted the said HIAM LEVY, MOSES SEIXAS, and SIMEON LEVY upon said deceased Estate they having received their appointment By order of Council I have given forth this Letter Testamentary under my hand and Council Seal of New Port aforesaid this third day of July one thousand seven hundred and ninety two and sixteenth of Independence.

PELEG BARKER, JUNR. Coun. Clk.

[1] Albany Will Liber 1, pp. 359–365. Moses Levy (1704–June 18, 1792) was the son of Isaac Levy, but which Isaac Levy has not been ascertained. He was not either of the Isaac Levys whose wills have been reproduced. This Moses has erroneously been referred to as the son of Moses Levy (see Will) of New York but the former's tombstone makes it clear that he was not. *PAJHS*, vol. XXVII (1920), p. 192. The testator was a long time resident and merchant of Rhode Island. In 1759, he petitioned the New York congregation for assistance to build a synagogue in Newport. In June of the same year, he along with others received a deed for the land on which the synagogue was to be constructed. *Ibid.*, pp. 179–180 and 184–185. Levy was *parnas* to the Newport congregation in 1775. Jacob R. Marcus, *op. cit.*, p. 101. For business affairs, see Petitions re taxes and custom house, and his service as arbitrator in *ibid.*, pp. 211–212, 214 and 407. He left almost all of his property to the children of his brother Benjamin.

[2] Hiam Levy (1729–1795), son of Benjamin (1692–1787) and Judith Levy (1702–1786), married Grace Mears (1742–1817) on July 26, 1768 in Newport. *PAJHS*, vol. IV (1896), p. 213; *ibid.*, XXVII (1920), p. 348; *ibid.*, vol. XXXIII (1934), p. 203.

[3] Moses Seixas (1744–1809), son of Isaac M. Seixas and Rachel Levy (see *supra*, Will of Isaac Levy, p. 159, note 5), married Jochabed Levy (1746–1828), daughter of Benjamin Levy and niece of the testator on October 3, 1770. *PAJHS*, vol. IV (1896), pp. 201 and 203; *ibid.*, vol. XXVII (1920), p. 346. He was the first cashier of the Bank of Rhode Island and Grand Master of the Masonic Lodge and in 1790 wrote letters concerning George Washington's addressing the Jewish communities of New York and Rhode Island. *Ibid.*, pp. 210 and 218–221.

[4] Simeon Levy (1748–1825), also son of Benjamin and Judith Levy, married Hester Levy. *PAJHS*, vol. IV (1896), p. 213; *PAJHS*, vol. XXXIII (1934), p. 210. He may have been the Simeon Levy who was a teacher of Hebrew in Shearith Israel from 1792 to 1816. *Ibid.*, vol. XXVII (1920), pp. 51, 95 and 397.

State of Rhode Island and Newport July 14th 1792 the aforegoing is Copied from Council Book No. 2 since the Evacuation of the British forces and Compared by

PELEG BARKER, JUNR. Coun. Clk.

I MOSES LEVY of New Port in the County of Newport and State of Rhode Island Etc. Merchant being advanced in years but of sound Mind and memory do make and publish this my last Will and Testament as follows to wit first my will is that my debts and funeral Expences be paid as soon after my decease as the same Can be Conveniently done and within Twelve Months next after my decease that the Executor or Executors who shall become qualified to Execute this my will as is herein After Ordered Cause to be erected over my Grave[5] and that of my late niece BILHA LEVY[6] decent Tomb Stones with suitable inscriptions thereon and also suitable stones at the Graves of my late Brother BENJAMIN LEVY and his wife[7] I give and bequeath unto MOSES LEVY[8] the son of my nephew HIAM LEVY four hundred spanish milled Dollars I give and bequeath unto MAGARET MCMAHONE the bed bedding and bed stead she now Occupies in my Dwelling house and thirty spanish Milled Dollars and unto her Daughter ANN MACMAHONE Ten Dollars I do hereby Release and discharge all such ballances as shall at the time of my decease be due and unpaid of Monies by me heretofore advanced towards building the Synagogue in Newport on Condition that there Shall be a solemn prayer said for me in the said Synagogue yearly and every Year on the evening or day of Kipue or attonement and Whereas I have already Granted and Conveyed unto MOSES SEIXAS in trust and for the use and behoof of my Nephew HIAM LEVY his wife and Children[9] the house and lot of land heretofore occupied by the said HIAM and situated in Newport[10] Aforesaid and it being now my intention to distribute the Remainder of my Estate Real and personal among my kinsmen HIAM LEVY, MOSES SEIXAS, and SIMEON LEVY and being at the same time desirous that the same shall be peaceably enjoyed by them and of preventing any disputes arising among my said Kinsmen After my decease Relative to any Accounts or demands which they may now have against each other my will and meaning there-

[5] The tombstone located in the Newport *Bet Ḥaim* was placed next to that of Bilah, Judith, and Benjamin Levy. *Ibid.*, p. 192.

[6] Bilah Levy (1742-1781), daughter of Benjamin and Judith, died as noted on her tombstone as a "modest virgin." *Ibid.*

[7] Benjamin Levy was remembered on his tombstone as an "honored old man" and his wife Judith as a "venerable virtuous woman." They were ninety-five and eighty-six respectively at the time of their death. *Ibid.*

[8] Moses Levy (b. 1792), son of Hiam Levy, married Rosetta Almund in Bristol, England. *Ibid.*, vol. IV (1896), p. 213; *ibid.*, vol. XXXIII (1934), p. 203.

[9] Hiam had three children, Moses, Judah (b. 1778), and Judith (d. 1833). *Ibid.*

[10] Possibly, this was a building on the south side of Washington Square, Newport, *Ibid.*, vol. XXVII (1920), p. 456.

fore is that the said HIAM LEVY, MOSES SEIXAS and SIMEON LEVY to entitel themselves to take any benefit from the divises and bequests herein After Contained and within Two Months Next After my decease shall make and Execute each to the other Releases of all accounts and demands which they now have against each other and in Case either of them shall Refuse or neglect to give said Releases within the Time aforesaid then my will is that all and every the Devises and bequests hereinafter Contained and made to him so Refusing or Neglecting or for his benefit shall Cease determine and be utterly Void and that then and from thenceforth I do give and devise all the Real and personal Estate herein After given and devised to him so Refusing or Neglecting unto the other two of my said Kinsmen their heirs and Assigns for ever provided they shall within two months next after my decease execute Releases of all the demands which they now have against each other and if it shall so happen that only one of my said Kinsmen shall be willing to execute Releases as is herein Required if he shall make the same known to the Town Council of the Town of Newport within two months next after my decease as aforesaid then my will is and I do then and from thenceforth give and devise all my Estate Real and Personal hereinafter named and discribed to him who shall so manifest a disposition on his part to comply with this my will to him and his Heirs for ever I give and devise unto MOSES SEIXAS and his heirs for ever my Dwelling house fronting the public parade in Newport[11] Aforesaid with the land whereon it stands and the yard and Garden Adjoining with the appurtenances I also Give and bequeath unto the said MOSES SEIXAS the pair of Looking Glasses Mahogany Chairs Tables Tea board and Irons shovel and tongs Carpet and China usually standing and belonging in my northeast Parlour in my said Dwelling house and also the Plate now in the Possession of the said MOSES SEIXAS excepting a Tankard which I give to his Daughter BILHAH SEIXAS[12] all the Residue and Remainder of my Real and Personal wheresoever the same may be found I give devise and bequeath to my said Kinsman HIAM LEVY, MOSES SEIXAS, and SIMEON LEVY & their heirs for ever Equally to be divided among them subject nevertheless to the Condition herein before prescribed and the divises and bequests aforesaid to the said MOSES SEIXAS are upon this further Condition that in Case the said SIMEON LEVY the Releases Aforesaid he shall Execute as is herein before directed then the said MOSES SEIXAS shall make and Execute to him the said SIMEON his heirs and assigns a deed in due form of law thereby Investing to the said SIMEON the fee simple of the Dwelling house in which he the said MOSES now lives and the land belonging to the same situate

[11] This house, a "simple, frame house of three stories," built before the revolution, was square in shape and had a wide hall and large rooms. It was occupied by Moses Seixas on October 23, 1792, shortly after the death of his uncle. The building eventually became the residence of Commodore Matthew Perry. *Ibid.*, pp. 214 and 456.

[12] Bilah Levy Seixas (1781–1860?) had three sisters Abigail (b. 1782), Grace (b. 1786), and Esther (b. 1790) and a brother Gershom (b. 1784).

in said Newport with the appurtenances Saving and Reserving to himself his heirs and assigns all his the said Moses Right and Interest in and unto the Spermacitae Manufacturing adjoining the said premises and the emplements and utencils belonging to the same and the lands whereon it stands as also the Right of passing and Repassing either for Man or beast and with teams Goods Wares merchandise in the Cart way leading from the said manufactory to the street and upon this further Condition that if the said Hiam and Simeon shall Execute the Releases aforesaid and within the time prescribed then and in that Case the said Moses Seixas shall in due form of Law Grant and Convey to the said Hiam and Simeon the lot of Land which the said Moses Seixas purchased of Abigail Grant and Abigail Cheesborough Grant to hold to them as tenants in Common and in fee simple and my mind and will further is that if my said Kinsmen or either of them shall decease before me or within two months next after my decease Without Executing the Releases aforesaid and if either the Children or the Executors or administrators of him or them who shall so decease, shall perform the Condition to the said devises and bequests annexed that then and in that Case the Children of either of my said Kinsmen shall be entitled to all the Real and Personal Estate devised to their parents so deceased and I do hereby give and devise the same to the Children of my Kinsman who shall so decease to them and their heirs and to be equally devided among them. I hereby nominate and appoint Hiam Levy, Moses Seixas, and Simeon Levy to be Executors of this my Will upon their executing Releases to each other as is hereinbefore directed and in Case either of them shall Refuse or Neglect so to do within the time prescribed then I appoint the other two of my said Kinsmen my Executors they Executing Releases to each other as aforesaid and if one only of my said Kinsmen shall intitle himself to the devises and legacies herein Contained given to my said Kinsmen on the Condition aforesaid then I appoint him sole Executor of this my Will and I do humbly Request that agreeable hereunto Letters of Administration may be Granted and I do hereby Revoke all former Wills by me heretofore made *In Witness* whereof I the said Moses Levy have hereunto set my hand and Seal this sixth day of June in the year of the Christian Era one thousand seven hundred and Ninety two Moses Levy [LS] Signed Sealed published and declared by the above named Moses Levy as and for his last Will and Testament in the presence of us who have hereunto subscribed our names as Witnesses thereunto in the presence of each other (the words time house in the Cart way being first Interlined Jon^{A} Willson, John Anthony, Edmund I Ellery, State of Rhode Island Etc. Newport July 2d 1792 at a Town Council in their proper persons Come Jonathan Wilson, John Anthony, and Edmond G. Elleroy, and being duly engaged in form of law to wit upon their oath declared and saith that they were present at the time that Mosses Levy the Testator named in the annexed two sheets of paper purporting his last will Executed the same to wit upon the sixth day of June in the year of our Lord one thousand seven hundred and ninety two and that he was then of a sound and disposing mind and memory and that they saw him sign and seal the same and heard him publish and declare the same as for and to be his last will and Testament and that they signed thereto as Witnesses in the presence of the said Testator and in the presence of each other wherefore said will is proved and approved PELEG BARKER JUNR. Council Clerk Newport July 3rd 1792 Recorded and Compared by

P BARKER J, Co. Clk.

The People of the State of New York by the Grace of God free and Independent To all To whom these presents shall Come or may Concern *Send Greeting Know Ye* that at a Town Council of the Town of Newport in the County of New Port and State of Rhode Island for the Probate of Wills and Granting forth Letters of Administration upon Intestates Estates within said Township that on the second day of July in the year of our Lord one thousand seven hundred and ninety two the last Will and Testament of MOSES LEVY late of said New Port Merchant (deceased) in said Council was Exhibited and duly proved and by order of the said Council letters Testamentary thereon were on the third day of July then next Granted unto HIAM LEVY, MOSES SEIXAS, and SIMEON LEVY the Executors in the said will named as appears by a Certified Copy thereof and hereto annexed and the said deceased having whilst he Lived and at the time of his death Goods Chattels or Credits within this State by means whereof the Registering the said Will and the Granting Administration of all and singular the said Goods Chattels and Credits and also the auditing allowing and final discharging the account thereof unto PETER OGILVIE Esquire Judge of our Court of Probates doth belong the administration of all and singular the Goods Chattels and Credits of the said deceased and any way Concerning his Will is Granted unto SIMEON LEVY one of the Executors in the said Will Named he being first duly sworn well and faithfully to administer the same and to make and Exhibit a true and perfect Inventory of all and singular the said Goods Chattels and Credits and also to Render a just and true Account thereof when thereunto Required *In Testimony* whereof we have Caused the seal of our Court of Probates to be hereunto Affixed Witness PETER OGILVIE Esquire Judge of our said Court at the City of New York the third day of September in the Year of our Lord one thousand seven hundred and Ninety Two and in the seventeenth year of our Independence.

s/ WILLIAM OGILVIE CLK.

XXXIX

JOSEPH SIMSON[1]

[1792]

In the Name of God Amen.

I JOSEPH SIMSON Late Merchant of the City of New York but Now Resident of the Society of Whelton[2] in the Town of Norwalk being of Sound Mind and memory and Considering the Uncertainty of this frail and transitory Life, Do therefore make and Ordain this my Last Will and Testament, That is to Say I desire my body may be decently intered unto

[1] Original Will unnumbered HDC; Will Liber 41, p. 87; *NYHSC*, vol. XIV (1906), pp. 218–219. Joseph Simson (1686–November 1787), a well-known merchant, arrived in New York together with his uncle Nathan Simson in 1718. In 1722, he married Rebecca Isaacs and had two sons, Solomon and Sampson, and a daughter Sarah who married Raphael Jacobs. *PAJHS*, vol. XXV (1917), pp. 87–91. On February 1, 1743, he was made a freeman of New York City. *Burghers*, p. 146. He and his wife actively engaged in real estate transactions, particularly in Oyster Bay, Long Island. In 1726, Rebecca bought a ten-acre plot, house and gardens for £148 in that area. On March 4, 1727 and on June 8, 1730, Joseph purchased another twelve acres. For these and other transactions, see *Oyster Bay Town Records* (New York, 1929), vol. IV, pp. 260–261; vol. V, pp. 1–2, 4–6, and 8; vol. VII, pp. 150, 203. On August 15, 1737 he seems to have sold all his Oyster Bay holding of some 120 acres. *Journal*, Aug. 15, 1737. Joseph and his son-in-law Raphael Jacobs ran an advertisement on February 11, 1750 for the sale of a house, barn, and 812 acres in Rye, Westchester County. *Gazette*, Feb. 11, 1750. For other business activity, see Account Book of Elizabeth Schuyler, p. 153 *et passim*, and Peter Jay Day Book, pp. 289 and 334 *et passim*, New-York Historical Society Library. For references as owner of the brigantine *Samuel*, see NOL, CO 5/1226, entry of March 8, 1743; also see Entry Books, vol. VI, items 1409, 1243 and 1373. Simson seemed quite interested in fashion. In 1741, he began an account with William DeWitt, wigmaker. He was charged £1.16 for a "gresel boob Wigg" and at the same time his son was charged 18 shillings "To macken a brown boob Wigg Sometime in Jan. 1740." In March, 1753, Mr. Simson "begun to shave fr yr quarter 0.7.0," and at another time "yong Mr. Semson" was charged £1.6.0 "To Maken a dark brown boob wigg and puten on more harr to it." Entries of March 20, 1741, April 11, 1742, November 3, 1742, August 27, 1743, April 8, 1745 and March 2, 1753, Account Book of William DeWitt, New-York Historical Society Library. He was extensively involved in litigation, see *Hampton v. Simson* (1738), MCM, vol. 1736–1742, p. 226; *Simson v. Lockwood* (1740), MCM, vol. 1736–1742, p. 419; *Simson v. Hyatt* (1751), MCP, File 1750–1752, Sept. 2, 1751 (involving four barrels of "Traine oyle.") *Simson v. Mills* (1753), MCP, file 1753–1759, Feb. 27, 1753. His congregational activities were varied and involved. He was elected *parnas* in 1748, 1755 and 1762. As early as 1728, he contributed twelve shillings to help purchase the burial ground from the widow of Moses Levy. *PAJHS*, vol. XXI (1913), pp. 8, 10, 16, 21 and 211. The will was not probated until October 3, 1792. *NYHSC*, vol. XIV (1906), p. 219.

[2] Simson married his wife Rebecca in Wilton, Connecticut. He is probably referring to this area of Norwalk. *PAJHS*, vol. XXXIII (1934), p. 210. The Congregational Society which administered Wilton affairs was synonymous with the town. The two were not separated until 1818. Marion Ollmstead, *Wilton Parish, 1726–1800* (Wilton, 1900), pp. 15–16; *New York Times*, Jan. 21, 1961.

our burial Ground in the City of New York at the discrition of my Executors after all my Just Debts be Paid and Discharged. I Give and Bequeath unto my Son SOLOMON SIMSON[3] all my Estate both Real and Personal with Remainders and Reversions of What Nature and kind whatsoever and wheresoever to be Disposed of as he may think fitt for his benefit and for his Childrens and to be paid them when of Age at his Discretion Vizt. Unto my Grandson JOSEPH SIMSON[4] and his Heirs, I give the Lot of Land in Stone Street,[5] City of New York the House in which I formely Lived on Said Lot being burnt, unto my Grand Daughters REBEKAH,[6] JOCHABET,[7] and ELLEN,[8] I give the Mortgage of three Hundred Pounds I have on the House and Lot of Land of JOHN SEBASTIAN STEPHANY Chymist in New Duch Church Street New York,[9] to be Equally Divided between them, and I desire my Executors will give unto my other Grandson SAMSON SIMSON[10] as much more of Estate (if ther Should be Sufficient as will make him Equall with his Brother JOSEPH SIMSON) and I desire the Interest as it may Come in may be Lade out for there Education, all to be Left at the discretion of my Executors, as for my other Grand Children BENJAMIN,[11] JOSEPH,[12] and ABRAHAM JACOBS[13] with there Sister JUDITH[14] they having been brought up [and] Educated at my Expense, with other advantages they have had will fully compensate for Leaving my Estate in the manner I have ordered in this my Said Will.

[3] See *supra*, Will of *Sampson Simson*, p. 141, note 15.

[4] Joseph Simson (1779–1842), son of Solomon Simson and his wife, Sarah Mears, married his cousin Frances Mears Isaacs on June 21, 1806, *PAJHS*, vol. XXXIII (1934), p. 202; *Dictionary*, p. 161.

[5] An indenture signed February 14, 1750, between David Taylor and Joseph Simson gave the latter a lot on Stone Street bounded on the east by the house and ground of the late Rodrigo Pacheco. Photo of indenture in Oppenheim Collection, American Jewish Historical Society Library, original in New-York Historical Society Library. Simson might have built a house on the lot, which as he indicates burned down before the execution of the will.

[6] Rebecca Simson (September 19, 1769–February 22, 1854), daughter of Solomon Simson, married Abraham Mears Isaacs on June 18, 1806. *Dictionary*, p. 161; *PAJHS*, vol. XXXIII (1934), p. 202.

[7] Jochabet Simson (1771–1814) daughter of Solomon. *Ibid.*

[8] Ellen (or Helena) Simson (1773–1819), daughter of Solomon. *Ibid.*

[9] On November 12, 1759, John Stephany and his wife mortgaged this property to Sampson Simson for £300. Although the money was to be repaid in one year, it still appears to be open more than twenty years later. Liber 1, cp. 143. Apparently Joseph became the holder of the mortgage after his son's death.

[10] Sampson Simson (1780–1857), founder of Mount Sinai hospital, was probably one of the first Jewish lawyers in New York. He died unmarried. *PAJHS*, vol. XXXIII (1934), p. 202.

[11] Benjamin Jacobs, son of Raphael and Sara, Joseph's daughter, was a *shoḥet* in New York City in 1790. *Portraits*, p. 326; Will of Sampson Simson, *supra*, p. 139, note 4.

[12] See Will of Sampson Simson, *ibid.*, p. 139, note 5.

[13] See Will of Sampson Simson, *ibid.*, p. 140, note 6.

[14] See Will of Sampson Simson, *ibid.*, p. 140, note 7; *infra*, Will of Manuel Myers, p. 208, note 2.

Likewise I make and ordain my Son SOLOMON SIMSON and my Daughter SARAH SIMSON[15] to be Executor and Executrix of this my Last Will and Testament, hereby utterly Disallowing and Revoking all former Wills by me Maid In Witness Whereof I have Set my hand & Seal the 5th of November one thousand Seven Hundred and Eighty one.

Signed, Sealed, Published and Declared by the Said JOSEPH SIMSON to be his Last Will and Testament in the Presence of us the Subscribers.

s/ JOS SIMSON [seal]

s/ NATHAN HUBBELL[16]
s/ SETH ABBOTT
s/ THOS. MADDEN

[15] The Sarah Simson referred to is Sarah Mears Simson his daughter-in-law. His daughter Sara the wife of Raphael Jacobs had died in 1762. Sarah Mears, the daughter of Judah and Johevit Mears, married Solomon on October 26, 1768. *PAJHS*, vol. XXXIII (1934), p. 202.

[16] Nathan Hubbell was probably Nathaniel Hubbard of "Stampford" Esquire. See *NYHSC*, vol. XII (1904), p. 340. Seth Abbott and Thomas Madden were also probably residents of Connecticut.

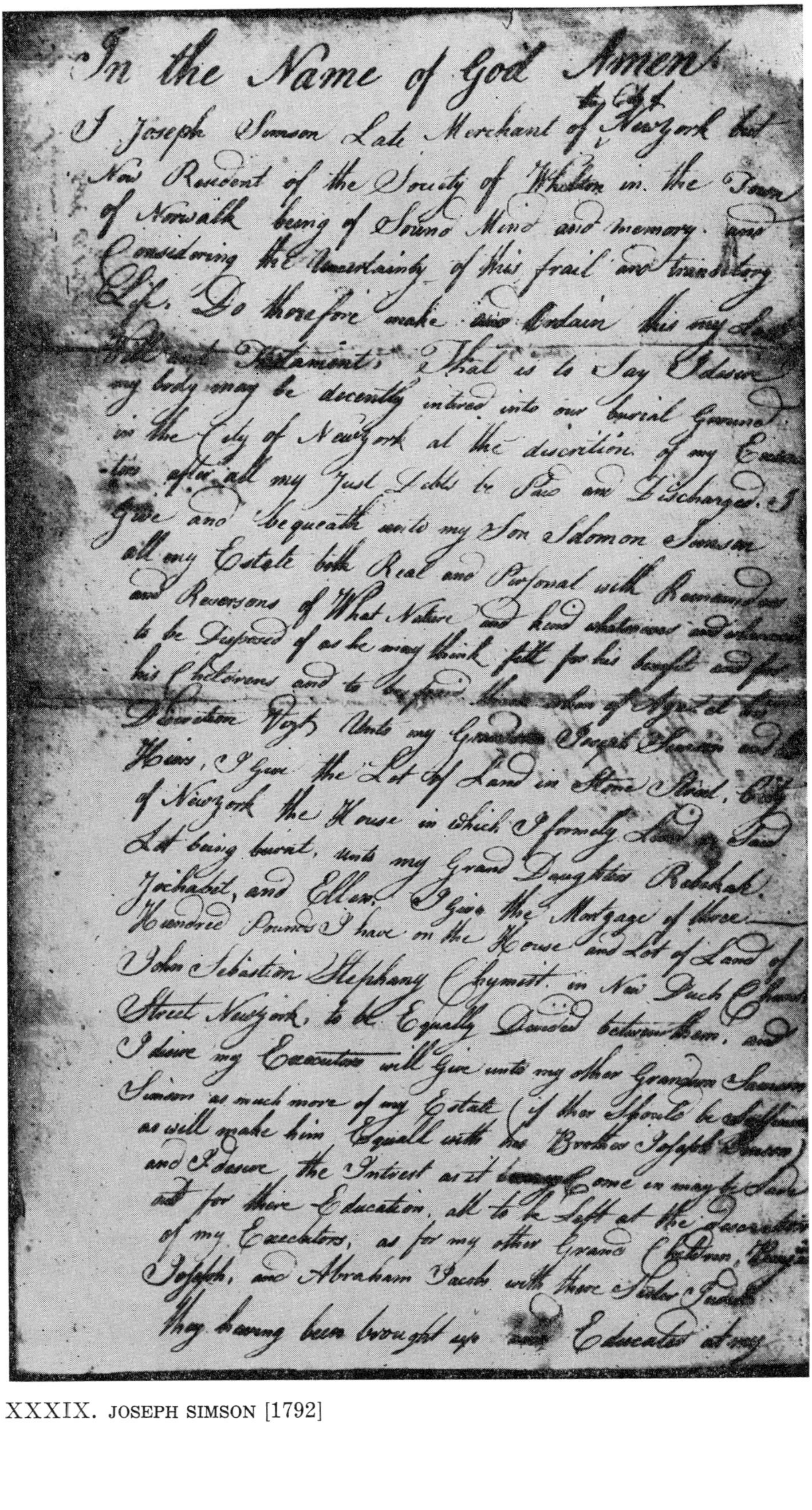
In the Name of God Amen
I Joseph Simson Late Merchant of the City of New York but
Now Resident of the Society of Wheaton in the Town
of Norwalk being of Sound Mind and memory and
Considering the Uncertainty of this frail and transitory
Life. Do therefore make and Ordain this my Last
Will and Testament. That is to Say I desire
my body may be decently intered into our burial Ground
in the City of New York at the discretion of my Execu-
tors after all my Just Debts be Paid and Discharged. I
Give and Bequeath unto my Son Solomon Simson
all my Estate both Real and Personal with Remainders
and Reversions of What Nature and kind whatsoever and otherwise
to be Disposed of as he may think fitt for his benefit and for
his Childrens and to [illegible] them [illegible] of Age at his
Discretion Vizt. Unto my Grandson Joseph Simson and his
Heirs, I Give the Lot of Land in Stone Street, City
of New York the House in which I formerly Lived on Said
Lot being burnt, unto my Grand Daughters Rebekah
Jochabed, and Ellen, I Give the Mortgage of three
Hundred Pounds I have on the House and Lot of Land of
John Sebastion Stephany Chymist in New Dutch Church
Street New York, to be Equally Divided between them, and
I desire my Executors will Give unto my other Grandson Sampson
Simson as much more of my Estate (if ther Should be Sufficient)
as will make him Equall with his Brother Joseph Simson)
and I desire the Intrest as it [illegible] Come in may be Laid
out for their Education, all to be Left at the discretion
of my Executors, as for my other Grand Children, Benjamin
Joseph, and Abraham Jacobs with there Sister Judith
they having been brought up and Educated at my

XXXIX. JOSEPH SIMSON [1792]

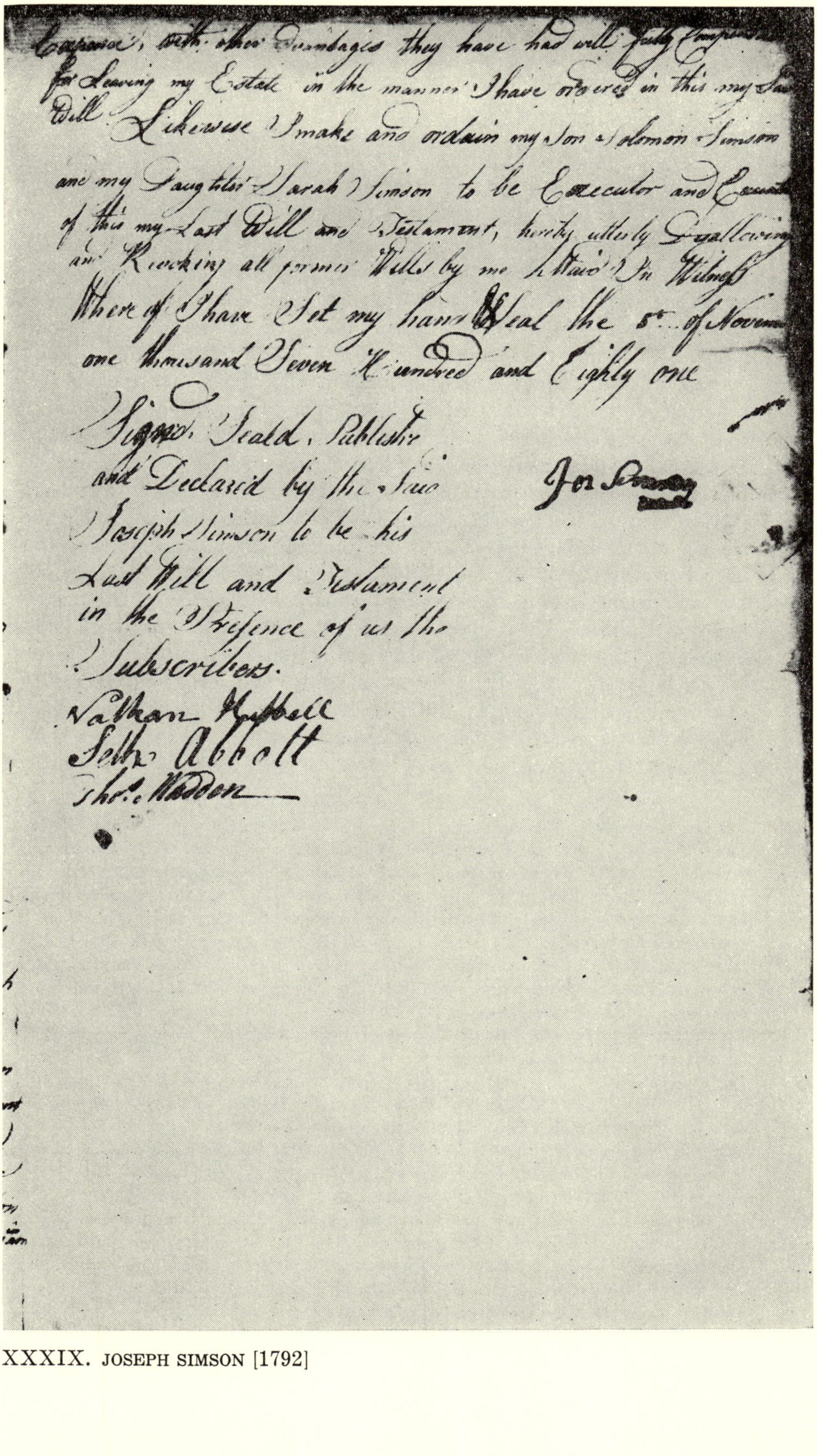

Expence; with other Advantages they have had will fully Compens
for Leaving my Estate in the manner I have ordered in this my Sai
Will Likewise I make and ordain my Son Solomon Simson
and my Daughter Sarah Simson to be Executor and Execu
of this my Last Will and Testament, hereby utterly Disallowing
and Revoking all former Wills by me Made In Witness
Whereof I have Set my hand & Seal the 5th of Novem
one thousand Seven Hundred and Eighty one

Signed Sealed Published
and Declared by the Said
Joseph Simson to be his
Last Will and Testament
in the Presence of us the
Subscribers.
Nathan Hubbell
Seth Abbott
Thos. Waddon

Jos Simson

XXXIX. JOSEPH SIMSON [1792]

XL

MICHAEL HAYS[1]

[1799]

In the Name of God, Amen. I, MICHAEL HAYS of North Castle in the County of Westchester and State of New York Yeoman, in perfect health of body and of sound mind and Memory, Thanks be given unto God, Calling unto mind the mortality of my body and knowing that it is appointed for all men once to die do make and ordain this my last will and Testament that is to say principally and first of all I give and recommend my soul into the hands of God Almighty, that gave it me, and my body to the earth to be buried in a decent manner at the Discretion of my Executors: Nothing doubting I shall receive the same again by the mighty power of God: and as touching such worldly Estate wherewith it has pleased God to bless me with in this life, I give devise and Dispose of the same in the following manner and form. first and last I give and bequeath unto DAVID HAYS[2] of Bedford Merchant my Dearly beloved brother in the same county and state above said whom I likewise Constitute make and ordain the sole Executor of this my last Will and Testament all and Singular all my Real and personal Estate of What Nature soever where it may be found all my Lands lying on Philips mannor[3] so called freely to enjoy and possess and I do utterly disallow and revoke all and each other former Testaments wills and Testaments and legacies bequeathed and Executors by me in any ways before named willed and bequeathed

[1] Westchester Will Liber B, pp. 168–169, Clerk's Office of the Surrogate's Court, White Plains, New York. Michael Hays (1753–1799), son of Jacob Hays (d. 1760) and Hetty Adolphus (d. 1783), had two brothers David (1732–1812) and Benjamin (d. 1816) and two sisters Charity (1740–1813) and Abigail. Stern, *op. cit.*, p. 75. A long-time resident of Westchester County, he built up considerable real estate holdings. In 1755, he resided in Dutchess County where he purchased some twenty acres of land for £80. Five years later living in North Castle he bought thirty acres and in 1764 he added another 33¾ acres to his holdings in the same area. In 1765, he bought an additional acre and two years later another twelve acres. In 1775 and 1776 he added still more. *PAJHS*, vol. XXVII (1920), pp. 318–320. After the Revolution, still a resident of Westchester County, he took an oath of allegiance and abjuration. *Hays v. Burling* (1784), MCP, file 1784, July 27, 1784.

[2] David Hays (1732–1812), married Esther Etting in 1764 and the couple had six children, one of whom Jacob became High Constable of New York. David, a merchant, lived mostly in Westchester in either Bedford or Mount Pleasant. Like his brother, he acquired several tracts of land in Westchester. *Portraits*, pp. 328–331; *PAJHS*, vol. XXVII (1920), pp. 318 and 320–321. See his will and inventory of his estate, *ibid.*, pp. 323–324.

[3] Philipse Manor was a huge area of southwestern Westchester County bounded by the Hudson, Bronx, Harlem and Croton rivers. The first "Territoryes" were purchased by Frederick Philipse, first Lord of the Manor, in 1672. In 1785, the Philipse lands were confiscated because of their support of the British. Though the Manor as a legal entity ceased to exist, the name continued to apply to the region for many years.

Ratifying and confirming this and no other to be my last will and Testament in witness whereof I have hereunto set my hand and seal in North Castle this second day of January one thousand seven hundred and eighty six.

MICHAEL HAYS (L.S.)

Witnesses

JOHN BEERS MERIAM BEERS, JUNIOR GILBERT HUNTER

Westchester County, ss

Be it Remembered that on the twenty seventh day of May in the year of our Lord one thousand seven hundred and ninety nine personally appeared before me PHILIP PELL[4] Surrogate of the said County of Westchester GILBERT HUNTER of York Town in the County aforesaid Farmer, and solemnly sincerely and truly declared and affirmed that he did see MICHAEL HAYS sign and seal the preceeding written Instrument purporting to be the Will of the said MICHAEL HAYS bearing date the second day of January in the year one thousand seven hundred and eighty six: and heard him publish and declare the same as and for his last will and Testament: That at the time thereof he the said MICHAEL HAYS was of sound disposing mind and memory to the best of the knowledge and belief of him the Affirmant and that JOHN BEERS MERIAM BEERS JUNIOR and the Deponent severally subscribed the said will as witnesses thereto in the Testators presence.

PHILIP PELL

[4] Philip Pell, Jr. was Surrogate of Westchester County from March 13, 1787 to October 31, 1800. *Civil List*, p. 362.

XLI

MANUEL MYERS[1]

[1799]

In the Name of God Amen, I MANUEL MYERS of the City of New York in the State of New York, Merchant being of sound disposing mind and Memory, and considering the uncertainty of this transitory life, do make, ordain and publish this my last will and Testament, in manner and form following, that is to say, first, It is my will and I do hereby order and direct that all my Just debts and funeral Charges shall be paid and discharged by my Executrix and Executor hereinafter named as soon as conveniently may be after my decease, and also that my said Executrix and Executor shall cause a Tomb Stone to be erected for me of the value of Ten pounds current money of the State of New York at least — and also that my said Executrix and Executor shall pay unto the Trustees of Sheareth Israel in the City of New York the sum of Ten pounds current money aforesaid for an *Escovau* in the Synagogue according to custom after my decease.

Item

I do do give and bequeath unto my loving wife JUDITH[2] my Mulatto Boy slave named HARRY, during the term of her natural life, and upon the decease of my said wife, I do manumit set free and release from Slavery my said slave named HARRY; but it is my will that my said wife may Manumit my said Slave HARRY at any time she shall think proper.

Item

I do give and bequeath unto my beloved Sister SARAH (otherwise Sorlah the wife of Rabbi ASHER, one of the *Bettdin* of Fürth near Nurenbergh in

[1] Original Will unnumbered, HDC; Will Liber 42, p. 605; *NYHSC*, vol. XV (1907), pp. 156–157. Manuel Myers (d. May 21, 1799), a merchant and distiller, was probably born in Furth, Germany. He was made freeman on July 3, 1759. *Burghers*, p. 193; MCP, file 1786, Petition of Joshua Isaacs. During the Revolution he spent a considerable period of time in Stamford, Connecticut avoiding the British occupation of New York City. *Portraits*, pp. 280–281. He first appears in the Minutes of the Congregation in 1761 when he was elected as assistant to the *parnas*. In 1768, he was second *parnas* and in 1769 *parnas*. Altogether he held that office ten times and died in office. *PAJHS*, vol. XXI (1913), pp. 85, 101–104 and 211. For litigation in which he was involved, see for example *Michael v. Myers* (1784), MCP, file 1784, March 23, 1784; *Myers v. Wismer, Jr.* (1786), MCP, file 1786, Feb. 11, 1786; MCP, file 1784, Petition of Manuel Myers *et al.*, dated May 11, 1784 for a license to be issued as a cartman.

[2] Judith Jacobs Myers (1758–1832) was the daughter of Raphael Jacobs and Sara Simson Jacobs. Manuel Myers married his first wife, Miriam Pinto (1730–1781) on May 31, 1759. Register of Congregation Shearith Israel, p. 45. See will of Sampson Simson for legacy of £300 left to her by her uncle (*supra*, p. 140).

Germany) and to her heirs the sum of four hundred dollars, to be paid unto my said Sister SARAH or unto her heirs in case of her death out of my personal Estate by my said Executrix and Executor within six months after my decease.

Item

I do give and bequeath unto my beloved Sister HANNAH (otherwise called HANNAKLAH, the wife of MOSES LEVY RINTZKUPF of Fürth aforesaid) and to her heirs the sum of four hundred dollars to be paid unto my said Sister HANNAH or unto her heirs in case of her death out of personal Estate by my said Executrix and Executor within Six months after my decease.

Item

I do give and bequeath unto my Nephews and Nieces named in my said will to wit my Nieces SORLAH otherwise called SARAH — HANNAKLAH otherwise called HANNAH and TETTZLAH otherwise called DOROTHY (Children of my deceased sister EDDLE) and my Nephews and Nieces MANDLE otherwise called MANUEL, YOUZEL otherwise JOSEIL, BILAH and HANNAKLAH Children of deceased Sister SHINELAH and to each of them my said Nephews and Nieces the sum of One hundred dollars to be paid to them respectively or to the heirs of such of them as may happen to die, out of my personal Estate by said Executrix and Executor within six months next after my decease.

Item

I do give and bequeath unto my said Wife JUDITH her Executors Administrators and Assigns all the rest residue and remainder of my personal Estate to have and to hold the same and every part thereof unto my said Wife JUDITH her Executors Administrators and assigns to her and their only proper use benefit and behoof forever.

Item

I do give and bequeath unto my said Wife JUDITH during the term of her natural Life the use Rents, Issues and Profits of all my lands, Tenements and Real Estate and after the decease of my said wife, I do give devise and bequeath all my said Lands Tenements and Real Estate[3] with

[3] Myers owned property on the west side of Broad Street which he purchased from John Marston on July 25, 1791. Conveyance Liber 47, cp. 262. See also Conveyance Liber 40, cp. 259-261.

the hereditaments and appurtenances thereunto belonging or the monies arising from the sale thereof unto my said Sisters SARAH and HANNAH above named and unto my beloved Nephews and Nieces herein after named that is to say my nieces SORLAH otherwise called SARAH HANNAKLAH otherwise HANNAH and TETTZLAH otherwise DOROTHY being three Children of my deceased Sister EDDLE and my Nephews and Nieces MANDLE otherwise MANUEL YOUZEL otherwise JOSEIL, BILAH and HANNAKLAH otherwise HANNAH being four Children of my deceased Sister SHINELAH and to their respective heirs and Assigns forever equally to be divided between them my said Two Sisters, Two Nephews and five Nieces above named Share and Share alike. And for the more easy and equal division of my said Lands Tenements and Real Estate in manner aforesaid, I do hereby fully, authorize and empower my Executor herein after named after the decease of my said Wife to grant Bargain sell and dispose of all my said Lands, Tenements and Real Estate for the most monies that can be had or gotten for the same, and in due form of Law to sign, seal execute and deliver good and Sufficient deeds of Conveyance for the same to the purchaser or purchasers thereof, his, her or their heirs and assigns for ever in fee simple and to divide the monies arising from the sale thereof amongst my Sisters Nephews and Nieces above named and their heirs according to the True intent and meaning of this my Will.

Item

In case any or either of my said Sisters Nephews or Nieces above named shall happen to die before a division of my real Estate is made, leaving lawfull Issue, then it is my will, that such Issue shall stand and be in the place and stead of his her or their parent so dying and shall have receive and take the part share and portion of my Estate or the money arising from the sale thereof, to which such parent if living would have been entitled by virtue of this my will. And lastly I do nominate Constitute and appoint my said wife JUDITH to be Executrix and my worthy and Esteemed friend Mr. EPHRAIM HART[4] of the said City of New York Merchant to be Executor of this my last will and Testament, hereby utterly revoking and making void all former and other wills and Testaments by me at any time heretofore made declaring these presents only to be and contain my last will and Testament. *In Witness* whereof I the said MA-

[4] Ephraim Hart (1747–1825), son of Samuel Hart, was a stockbroker and one of the original members of the New York Stock Exchange. In 1818, he was a state senator as well as canal commissioner. In 1820, he was a member of the Council of Appointment. He sold his house on 11th Street in New York City to John Jacob Astor for $10,000. He married Frances Noah. Being born in Furth, Germany, he was a *landsmann* of Myers. *Portraits*, pp. 289–290; *Civil List*, pp. 170, 239 and 249.

NUEL MYERS have hereunto set my hand and Seal the thirteenth day of **May in the year ~~of our Lord~~ one thousand seven hundred and ninety nine.**

Signed, Sealed, published and declared by the said MANUEL MYERS as and for his last will and Testament in the presence of us who have hereunto subscribed our names as Witnesses at the request of the said Testator in his presence and in the presence of each other.	s/ MANL MY seal

The words "of our Lord" on the last line being Erazed before the executing of this will.

s/ ISAAC GOMEZ JUNR[5]
s/ ELIAS NOAH[6]
s/ JOHN W. WILLIAMS

[5] This may have been Isaac Gomez, Jr. (1768–1831), son of Moses Gomez or Isaac (1767–1810), son of Mattathias Gomez. *Dictionary*, p. 45; Will of Benjamin Gomez, *supra*, p. 136, note 7.

[6] Elias Noah (1766–1824) may have been a relation of Frances Noah, Ephraim Hart's wife. *Dictionary*, p. 134.

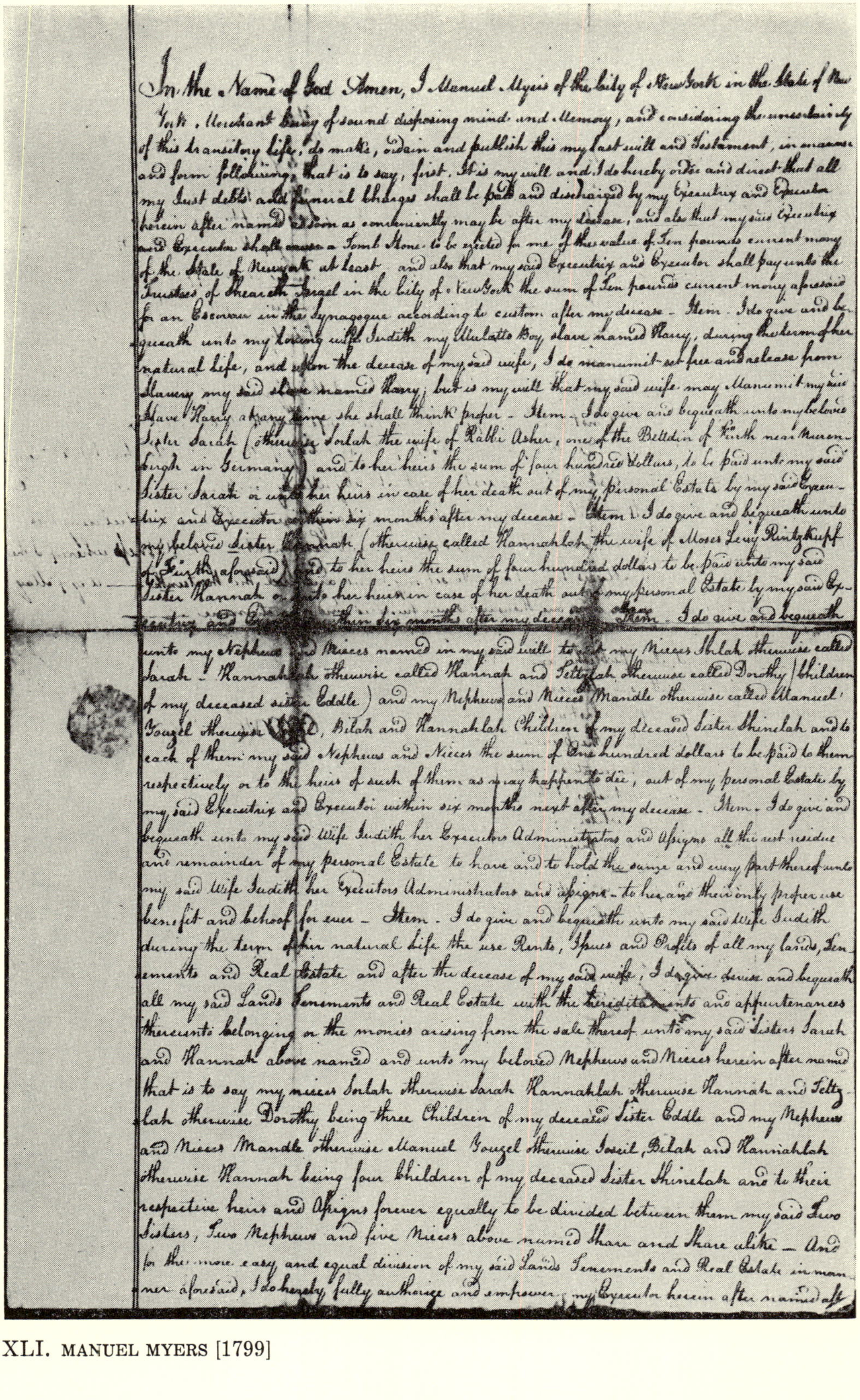
In the Name of God Amen, I Manuel Myers of the City of New York in the State of New York, Merchant being of sound disposing mind and Memory, and considering the uncertainty of this transitory life, do make, ordain and publish this my last will and Testament, in manner and form following, that is to say, first. It is my will and I do hereby order and direct that all my Just debts and funeral Charges shall be paid and discharged by my Executrix and Executor herein after named as soon as conveniently may be after my decease, and also that my said Executrix and Executor shall cause a Tomb Stone to be erected for me of the value of Ten pounds current money of the State of Newyork at least and also that my said Executrix and Executor shall pay unto the Trustees of Shearith Israel in the City of New York the sum of Ten pounds current money aforesaid for an Escavaa in the Synagogue according to custom after my decease – Item. I do give and bequeath unto my loving wife Judith my Mulatto Boy slave named Harry, during the term of her natural life, and after the decease of my said wife, I do manumit set free and release from Slavery my said slave named Harry; but is my will that my said wife may Manumit my said Slave Harry at any time she shall think proper – Item – I do give and bequeath unto my beloved Sister Sarah (otherwise Sorlah the wife of Rabbi Asher, one of the Belldin of Furth near Nurenburgh in Germany) and to her heirs the sum of four hundred Dollars, to be paid unto my said Sister Sarah or unto her heirs in case of her death out of my Personal Estate by my said Executrix and Executor within six months after my decease – Item. I do give and bequeath unto my beloved Sister Hannah (otherwise called Hannahlah the wife of Moses Levy Rintzkupf of Furth aforesaid) and to her heirs the sum of four hundred dollars to be paid unto my said Sister Hannah or unto her heirs in case of her death out of my personal Estate by my said Executrix and [illegible] within six months after my decease – Item – I do give and bequeath unto my Nephews and Nieces named in my said will to wit my Nieces Sorlah otherwise called Sarah – Hannahlah otherwise called Hannah and Settylah otherwise called Dorothy (Children of my deceased sister Eddle) and my Nephews and Nieces Mandle otherwise called Manuel Youzel otherwise [illegible], Belah and Hannahlah Children of my deceased Sister Shinelah and to each of them my said Nephews and Nieces the sum of One hundred dollars to be paid to them respectively or to the heirs of such of them as may happen to die, out of my personal Estate by my said Executrix and Executor within six months next after my decease – Item – I do give and bequeath unto my said Wife Judith her Executors Administrators and Assigns all the rest residue and remainder of my personal Estate to have and to hold the same and every part thereof unto my said Wife Judith her Executors Administrators and assigns – to her and their only proper use benefit and behoof for ever – Item. I do give and bequeath unto my said Wife Judith during the term of her natural Life the use Rents, Issues and Profits of all my lands, Tenements and Real Estate and after the decease of my said wife; I do give devise and bequeath all my said Lands Tenements and Real Estate with the hereditaments and appurtenances thereunto belonging or the monies arising from the sale thereof unto my said Sisters Sarah and Hannah above named and unto my beloved Nephews and Nieces herein after named that is to say my nieces Sorlah otherwise Sarah Hannahlah otherwise Hannah and Settylah otherwise Dorothy being three Children of my deceased Sister Eddle and my Nephews and Nieces Mandle otherwise Manuel Youzel otherwise Joseil, Belah and Hannahlah otherwise Hannah being four Children of my deceased Sister Shinelah and to their respective heirs and Assigns forever equally to be divided between them my said Two Sisters, Two Nephews and five Nieces above named Share and Share alike – And for the more easy and equal division of my said Lands Tenements and Real Estate in manner aforesaid, I do hereby fully authorize and empower my Executor herein after named aft

XLI. MANUEL MYERS [1799]

the decease of my said Wife to grant Bargain sell and dispose of all my said Lands, Tenements and Real Estate for the most monies that can be had or gotten for the same, and in due form of Law to sign, seal execute and deliver good and sufficient deeds of Conveyance for the same to the purchaser or purchasers thereof, his, her or their heirs and assigns forever in fee simple and to divide the monies arising from the sale thereof amongst my Sisters Nephews and Nieces above named and their heirs according to the true intent and meaning of this my will — Item. In case any or either of my said Sisters Nephews or Nieces above named shall happen to die before a division of my real Estate is made, leaving lawfull Issue, then it is my will, that such Issue shall stand and be in the place and stead of his her or their parent so dying — and shall have receive and take the part share and portion of my Estate or the money arising from the sale thereof, to which such parent if living would have been entitled by virtue of this my will — And lastly I do nominate Constitute and appoint my said wife Judith to be Executrix and my worthy and Esteemed friend Mr Ephraim Hart of the said City of Newyork Merchant to be Executor of this my last will and Testament, hereby utterly revoking and making void all former and other wills and Testaments by me at any time heretofore made declaring these presents only to be and contain my last will and Testament — In Witness whereof I the said Manuel Myers have hereunto set my hand and Seal the thirteenth —— day of May in the year of our Lord one thousand seven hundred and ninety nine ——

Signed, Sealed, published and declared by the said Manuel Myers as and for his last will and Testament in the presence of us who have hereunto subscribed our names as Witnesses at the request of the said Testator in his presence and in the presence of each other ——

The words "of our Lord" on the last line being Erazed before the executing of this will —

Isaac Gomez Junr

Elias Noah

John M Williams

XLI. MANUEL MYERS [1799]

APPENDIX I

SURROGATE'S ORDER, 1789*

The People of the State of New York by the Grace of God free and Independent

To all Persons literate but more especially to ROBERT BOYD Esquire Sheriff of the City and County of New York Greeting —

Whereas Application hath been made unto me by ISAAC H. LEVY SOLOMON HAYMAN LEVY and ISAAC MOSES for Letters Testamentary on the last Will and Testament of HAYMAN LEVY late of the City of New York Merchant deceased and that the said Will may be duly Proved

Therefore you the said Sheriff are hereby required to cite SLOE LEVY the widow of the said HAYMAN LEVY, AARON HAYMAN LEVY, the Son of the said HAYMAN LEVY, BENJAMIN SEIXAS & ZIPPORAH his wife which said ZIPPORAH is the daughter of the said HAYMAN LEVY, SARAH LEVY and DEBORAH LEVY, Daughters of the said HAYMAN LEVY, that they and each of them Personally be and appear before me at the Surrogates Office for the City and County of New York on Friday the Eleventh day of September Instant at the Hour of ten oClock in the forenoon of the same day, then to show cause why the Will of the said HAYMAN LEVY should not be duly Proved & Letters Testamentary Issue to the said ISAAC H. LEVY, SOLOMON HAYMAN LEVY and ISAAC MOSES and hereof you me not to fail at your Peril given under my hand and Seal of Office the Seventh day of September in the Year of our Lord one thousand seven Hundred and Eighty Nine and of our Independence the Fourteenth

DAVID GELSTON *Surrogate*

* See facsimile, p. 185.

APPENDIX II

ALPHABETICAL INDEX

	Name	Date of Probate
1.	Adolphus, Isaac [XXX]	September 13, 1774
2.	Benzaken, Esther [XXXVII]	July 1, 1790
3.	Brown, Esther [IV]	May 28, 1708
4.	Brown, Joseph [II]	November 21, 1704
5.	Bueno, Joseph De Mesquita [V]	November 1, 1708
6.	Cohen, Samuel Myers [XVI]	Date of Probate 1743
7.	De Lucena, Abraham [VIII]	September 2, 1725
8.	De Torres, Simja [XIX]	November 13, 1746
9.	Fonseca, Jacob [X]	August 9, 1729
10.	Gomez, Benjamin [XXVIII]	September 22, 1772
11.	Gomez, David [XXVI]	August 14, 1769
12.	Gomez, Isaac [XXVII]	October 1, 1770
13.	Gomez, Luis [Lewis] [XV]	May 7, 1740
14.	Gomez, Mattathias [XXXI]	January 2, 1784
15.	Gomez, Mordecai [XX]	November 12, 1750
16.	Gomez, Moses [XXXVI]	April 7, 1790
17.	Hart, Aaron [XXIV]	September 17, 1763
18.	Hayes, Judah [XXV]	August 27, 1764
19.	Hays, Michael [XL]	May 27, 1799
20.	Hyam, Uriah [XIII]	January 14, 1740
21.	Isaacs, Joshua [XVII]	August 6, 1744
22.	Isaacs, Phillip [XXI]	March 1, 1756
23.	Isaacs, Solomon [XXIII]	July 18, 1757
24.	Levy, Hayman [XXXIV]	September 28, 1789
25.	Levy, Isaac [XVIII]	September 18, 1745
26.	Levy, Isaac [XXXII]	November 6, 1785
27.	Levy, Joseph Israel [XXXIII]	April 28, 1786
28.	Levy, Joseph Israel [XXXV]	November 12, 1789
29.	Levy, Moses [IX]	December 5, 1728
30.	Levy, Moses [XXXVIII]	September 3, 1792
31.	Levy, Samuel [VII]	May 21, 1719
32.	Luis, Rachel [XII]	April 13, 1737
33.	Marques, Isaac Rodriquez [III]	March 24, 1707
34.	Michaels, Michael [XI]	March 31, 1737
35.	Moses, Michal [XIV]	March 26, 1740
36.	Myers, Manuel [XLI]	May 28, 1799
37.	Nunez, Joseph [I]	November 10, 1704
38.	Pinheiro, Isaac [VI]	April 13, 1710
39.	Seixas, Abraham Mendes [XXII]	June 25, 1756
40.	Simson, Joseph [XXXIX]	October 3, 1792
41.	Simson, Sampson [XXIX]	January 18, 1774

BIBLIOGRAPHY

PRIMARY SOURCES

PERIODICALS

London *Gentleman's Magazine.* I–LXX, 1731–1800.
New-York Gazette. 1725–1744.
New-York Gazette or Revised Weekly Post-Boy. 1747–1773.
New-York Weekly Journal. 1733–1751.

UNPUBLISHED MANUSCRIPTS

Alexander, James, Papers (18th Century). New-York Historical Society Library.
Alexander, Mary, Papers. New-York Historical Society Library.
Alexander, William, Papers (1717–1783). New-York Historical Society Library.
Bradford, William, Papers. New-York Historical Society Library.
Congregation of Shearith Israel Register (18th century). Archives of Congregation Shearith Israel.
DeWitt, William, Day Book (1739–1752). New-York Historical Society Library.
Eardeley, William A., Collection of Wills. Long Island Historical Society Library.
Etting Papers. Historical Society of Pennsylvania.
Franks, Abigail, Letters (1733–1748), Lee M. Friedman Collection. American Jewish Historical Society Library.
Gratz Papers. Historical Society of Pennsylvania.
Jay, Peter, Day Book (1724–1748). New-York Historical Society Library.
Jay, Peter, Ledger Book (1724–1768). New-York Historical Society Library.
Oath of Allegiance, dated April 27, 1741, signed by David, Daniel, and Mordecai Gomez, Samuel Myers Cohen, and twenty-five other Jews. New-York Historical Society Library.
Oppenheim Collection. American Jewish Historical Society Library.
Schuyler, Elizabeth, Account Book (1737–1769). New-York Historical Society Library.
Simson, Nathan, Letter Books. Public Record Office, London, England.
C104/13 (Microfilm copy in American Jewish Archives and American Jewish Historical Society Library.)
Trinity Vault Records (18th Century). Trinity Corporation Library.

UNPUBLISHED LEGAL AND OTHER PUBLIC DOCUMENTS

Chancery Decrees Before 1800, Office of the Clerk of the Court of Appeals, Albany, New York, now at the Historical Documents Collection, Queens College of the City University of New York, Flushing, New York.
Conveyance Libers (to 1800)
Albany, Office of the Secretary of State, Albany.

New York, New York City Register's Office, 31 Chambers Street, New York.

Philadelphia, Department of Records, City Hall, Philadelphia.

Entry Books, 1728–1766. New York State Library, Albany, New York.

Insolvent Debtors Papers (to 1800). New York County Clerk's Office, 31 Chambers Street, New York.

Inventories of Estates

Albany, 1664–1884. Office of the Clerk of the Court of Appeals, now at the Historical Documents Collection.

New York, 1665–1800. Surrogate's Court, New York County, 31 Chambers Street, New York, now at the Historical Documents Collection.

Manifest Books, 1753–1776. New York State Library.

Mayor's Court Minutes, 1674–1800. New York County Clerk's Office.

Mayor's Court Papers, 1664–1800. New York County Clerk's Office.

Minutes of Chancery, 1711–1760. New York County Clerk's Office.

Minutes of Court of General Sessions, 1684–1800. New York County Clerk's Office.

Minutes of Supreme Court of Judicature, 1691–1800. New York County Clerk's Office.

Naval Office Lists, 1714–1760. Public Record Office, London, CO5/1222–CO5/1229.

New York Assessment Lists, 1699–1734. New York City Comptroller's Office, Rhinelander Building, 238 William Street, New York (vol. 1709–1721 missing).

Wills

Albany, Originals, 1664–1800. Libers, 1664–1800. Office of the Clerk of the Court of Appeals, Albany.

New York, Originals, 1665–1800. Libers, 1665–1800. Surrogate's Court, New York County, now at Historical Documents Collection.

Philadelphia, Libers. Registry of Wills, City Hall.

PUBLISHED LEGAL AND OTHER DOCUMENTS

Abstracts of Wills, Collections of the New-York Historical Society (New York, 1893–1906), 14 vols.

Arnold, Arthur P., "Anglo-Jewish Wills and Letters of Administration," *Anglo-Jewish Notabilities* (London, 1949).

Brock, R. Alonzo, ed. "Journal of William Black, 1744." *Pennsylvania Magazine of History and Biography*, I (1877), pp. 415.

Burghers and Freemen of New York, Collections of the New-York Historical Society (New York, 1886).

Colonial Laws of New York (Albany, 1894–1896), 5 vols.

Corwin, E. T., ed. *Ecclesiastical Records of the State of New York* (Albany, 1901–1916), 7 vols.

"Gomez Ledger." *Publications of the American Jewish Historical Society*, XXVII (1920), pp. 279–317.

Hamlin, Paul M., and Baker, Charles E., eds. *Supreme Court of Judicature of the Province of New York 1691–1705* (New York, 1959).

Hutchins, Stephen C. *Civil List of New York* (Albany, 1880).
Korn, Harold, ed. "Receipt Book of Judah Hays 1759–1760." *Publications of the American Jewish Historical Society*, XXXIV (1935), pp. 117–134.
Marcus, Jacob R., ed. *American Jewry-Documents Eighteenth Century* (Cincinnati, 1959).
Minutes of the Common Council of the City of New York 1675–1776 (New York, 1905), 8 vols.
Minutes of the Common Council of the City of New York 1784–1831 (New York, 1917–1930), 21 vols.
"Minutes of Shearith Israel," *Publications of the American Jewish Historical Society*, XXI (1913), pp. 1–171.
Morris, Richard B., ed. *Select Cases of the Mayor's Court of New York City, 1674–1784* (Washington, 1935).
New York Directory and Register for each year commencing 1786–1800.
O'Callaghan, E. B., ed. *Calendar of New York Colonial Commissions, 1680–1770* (New York, 1929).
O'Callaghan, E. B., ed. *Documentary History of the State of New York* (Albany, 1849–1851), 4 vols.
O'Callaghan, E. B., and Fernow, Berthold, eds. *Documents Relative to the Colonial History of the State of New York* (Albany, 1856–1887), 15 vols.
Oyster Bay Town Records 1653–1763 (New York, 1916–1931), 7 vols.
Street, C. R., ed. *Huntington Town Records including Babylon, Long Island, New York 1653–1873* (Huntington, 1887–1889), 3 vols.
Sullivan, J., Flick, A. C., and Hamilton, M. W., eds. *Papers of William Johnson* (Albany, 1921–1953), 11 vols.

SECONDARY SOURCES

BOOKS

Elzas, Barnett A. *The Jews of South Carolina* (Philadelphia, 1905).
Emmanuel, Isaac S. *Precious Stones of Curaçao (1656–1957)* (New York, 1957).
Lamb, Martha J. and Harrison, Mrs. Burton, *History of the City of New York* (New York, 1896), 3 vols.
Lipman, Vivian D. *Three Centuries of Anglo-American Jewish History* (London, 1961).
Marcus, Jacob R. *Early American Jewry, 1649–1794* (Philadelphia, 1951), 2 vols.
Miller, John. *New York Considered and Improved* (Cleveland, 1903).
Olmstead, Marion. *Wilton Parish, 1726–1800* (Wilton, 1900).
Pool, David de Sola. *Portraits Etched in Stone* (New York, 1953).
Pool, David and Tamar de Sola. *An Old Faith in the New World* (New York, 1955).
Rosenbloom, Joseph R. *A Biographical Dictionary of Early American Jews* (Lexington, 1960).
Schiltkamp, Jacob A. *De Geschiedens van Het Notariaat in Het Octrooigebied van de West Indische Compagnie* (s'Gravenhage, 1964).
Stern, Malcolm H. *Americans of Jewish Descent* (Cincinnati, 1960).

Stokes, I. N. P. *Iconography of Manhattan Island* (New York, 1895–1928), 6 vols.

Wolf, Edwin and Whiteman, Maxwell. *The History of the Jews of Philadelphia from Colonial Times to the Age of Jackson* (Philadelphia, 1957).

ARTICLES

Publications of the American Jewish Historical Society

Friedenwald, Herbert. "Jews in the American Revolution." X (1902), pp. 163–166.

Friedman, Lee M. "Wills of Early Jewish Settlers in New York." XXIII (1915), pp. 147–161.

Friedman, Lee M. "Early Jewish Residents in Massachusetts." XXIII (1915), pp. 79–90.

Hilfman, P. A. "Notes on the History of the Jews in Surinam." XVIII (1909), pp. 179–207.

Hirsch, Iyda R. "Mears Family and Their Connections, 1696–1824." XXXIII (1934), pp. 199–210.

Huhner, Leon. "Jews of New England (Other than in Rhode Island) Prior to 1910." XI (1905), pp. 75–99.

Huhner, Leon. "Wills of Jews on File in the Surrogates at the City of New York, 1754–1760." XII (1904), pp. 165–167.

"Items Relating to the Seixas Family." XXVII (1920), pp. 350–352.

Jastrow, Jr., Morris. "Joseph Simon of Lancaster, Pennsylvania." I (1905), pp. 121–122.

Kanof, Abram. "Uriah Phillips Levy." XXXIX (1949), pp. 1–66.

Kayserling, Mayer. "The Earliest Rabbis and Jewish Writers of America." III (1895), pp. 13–20.

Kohler, Max J. "Phases of Jewish Life in New York Before 1800."
Part 1, II (1894), pp. 77–100.
Part 2, III (1895), pp. 73–86.

Kohler, Max J. "Civil Status of Jews in Colonial New York." VI (1897), pp. 81–106.

Kohler, Max J. "The Jews in Newport." VI (1897), pp. 61–80.

Miller, George J. "Early Jews in Middlesex County, New Jersey." XXXIII (1936), pp. 251–254.

Morais, Sabato. "Mickve Israel Congregation of Philadelphia." I (1905), pp. 13–24.

"Necrology of Henry S. Hendricks." XLIX (1959), pp. 56–63.

Oppenheim, Samuel. "Jews and Masonry in the United States before 1810." XIX (1910), pp. 1–94.

Oppenheim, Samuel. "Jews Who Died of Yellow Fever in the Epidemic in New York in 1798." XXV (1917), p. 123.

Phillips, N. Taylor. "The Levy and Seixas Families of Newport and New York." IV (1896), pp. 189–214.

Phillips, N. Taylor. "Notes on Genealogy of the Gomez Family in America." XVII (1909), pp. 197–199.

Phillips, Rosalie S. "A Burial Place for the Jewish Nation Forever." XVIII (1909), pp. 93–122.

Pool, David de Sola. "Notes on American Jewish History." XXII (1914), pp. 167–175.

Solis, Elvira N. "Some References to Early Jewish Cemeteries in New York City." VIII (1900), pp. 135–140.

Solis, Elvira N. "Note on Isaac Gomez and Lewis Morris Gomez from an Old Family Record." XI (1903), pp. 139–144.

Solis-Cohen, Solomon. "Notes Concerning David Hays and Esther Etting, His Wife, and Michael Hays and Reuben Etting, Their Brothers, Patriots of the Revolution." II (1894), pp. 63–72.

OTHER PUBLICATIONS

Hyamson, Albert M. "Dictionary of Anglo-American Jewish Biography," *Anglo-American Jewish Notabilities* (London, 1949), pp. 1–128.

Osterweis, Rollin G. "The House of Ralph Isaacs, Jr." *The Connecticut Antiquarian,* VII (1955), pp. 18–25.

Scott, Kenneth. "A 'Dust' at Yale and a 'Blessing' for President Clap," *The Connecticut Historical Society Bulletin,* XXIII (1958), pp. 46–49.

Scott, Kenneth. "Early Original New York Wills," *National Genealogical Society Quarterly,* LXI (1963), pp. 90–99.

INDEX